Also from Michael Lewis

Altering Fate: Why the Past Does Not Predict the Future
Michael Lewis

Handbook of Emotions, Third Edition
Michael Lewis, Jeannette M. Haviland-Jones,
and Lisa Feldman Barrett, Editors

Lying and Deception in Everyday Life
Michael Lewis and Carolyn Saarni, Editors

The Rise of Consciousness and the Development of Emotional Life

MICHAEL LEWIS

THE GUILFORD PRESS
New York   London

© 2014 Michael Lewis
Published by The Guilford Press
A Division of Guilford Publications, Inc.
72 Spring Street, New York, NY 10012
www.guilford.com

Printed in the United States of America

This book is printed on acid-free paper.

Last digit is print number: 9 8 7 6 5 4 3 2 1

Library of Congress Cataloging-in-Publication Data

Lewis, Michael, 1937 January 10–
  The rise of consciousness and the development of emotional life / Michael Lewis.
      pages cm
  Includes bibliographical references and index.
  ISBN 978-1-4625-1252-2 (hardback)
  1. Consciousness.   2. Emotions.   I. Title.
  BF311.L484 2014
  152.4—dc23
                                                    2013024971

For Susannah, my autumn love

About the Author

Michael Lewis, PhD, is University Distinguished Professor of Pediatrics and Psychiatry and Director of the Institute for the Study of Child Development at the Rutgers Robert Wood Johnson Medical School. He is also Professor of Psychology, Education, and Biomedical Engineering at Rutgers, The State University of New Jersey, and serves on the Executive Committee of the Cognitive Science Center.

Dr. Lewis is a Fellow of the New York Academy of Sciences, the American Psychological Association (APA), the American Association for the Advancement of Science, and the Japan Society for the Promotion of Science, and is currently in the top 1.5% of scientists referenced in the Social Science Index. He is a recipient of the Urie Bronfenbrenner Award for Lifetime Contribution to Developmental Psychology in the Service of Science and Society from the APA, the Hedi Levenback Pioneer Award from the New York Zero-to-Three Network, and the Distinguished Scientific Contributions to Child Development Award from the Society for Research in Child Development.

Dr. Lewis has written over 450 journal articles and book chapters and 35 books, including *Social Cognition and the Acquisition of Self, Children's Emotions and Moods: Developmental Theory and Measurement, Shame: The Exposed Self,* and *Altering Fate: Why the Past Does Not Predict the Future.* He is also coeditor of the *Handbook of Emotions.*

Preface

This is a book about the development of emotional life. For 50 years, the nature of development has been of central concern to me. In a 1967 article, "The Meaning of a Response, or Why Researchers in Infant Behavior Should Be Oriental Metaphysicians," I tried to show that a single infant behavior can be seen in the service of different processes and that the same process can lead to different behaviors as the infant develops. For example, a newborn's imitation is in the service of contagion, while a 24-month-old's imitation is in the service of the desire to be like the other. Likewise, crying in a 5-month-old can be in the service of attempting to obtain a lost object, while crying in an 18-month-old can be in the service of asking for comfort.

Development is a puzzle. In *Altering Fate: Why the Past Does Not Predict the Future*,[1] I tried to show that our ideas about the continuity of our lives, something we all believe in, has more to do with our need for identity than with the literal facts of our lives. The need we have for identity includes the idea of continuity, both in time and space: this "me" today is the same me as yesterday and will be the same me tomorrow. Me eating dinner, me writing this book, and me kissing my wife are all the same me in spite of the overwhelming evidence that this me—my personality—is not the same me in all circumstances. Although we all know this reality from the lives we live, it is a hard idea to accept.

Even more puzzling is the expectation that what our infants and children are like now, and how we treat them now, will somehow determine what they will become in the future. The idea of a smooth trajectory from now until then fills our theories and gives rise to untold numbers of papers, books, and advice on how to produce a more perfect adult.

Kierkegaard's idea of existential contingency tells us that fear is produced because the past does not provide meaning for the future; it is the present that provides meaning to the past.[2] If we cannot predict the future from the past because of accidents and chance encounters, then how to live our lives becomes a problem. It seems to me that given the human condition—the ability to be in the now, and at the same time to be in the past and in the future—an alternative to prediction is necessary. That alternative is to treat the present in the best possible way. That is, what the present demands is to create a good story about the now, a story making the best of this now. Indeed, I would argue that the ability to make a good story of the now is not only the mark of mental health, but the way to live a good life in spite of our inability to predict the future. Given the problem of prediction of what a good life in the future might be, I am reminded that the early Greek philosophers grappled with the same problem of what a good life should be. In their inquiry, what they did not solve, and what I have spent much of my life trying to understand, is the problem of what a good life is, since a good life in September may not be a good life in December.

Without the ability to predict, we need to ask what might be the good story of now to help resolve Kierkegaard's quandary. This is not an easy question. In part, the good story has to focus on the positive rather than on the negative features of the now. The good story needs to connect the now with history, either modifying the now or altering the past. The good story involves the courage to take action toward a future while knowing that we can only point ourselves in a direction because even though the unknown future induces fear, when it becomes now, we will again be able to make a good story of it.

This human capacity to be in the past and in the future while being in the present can occur because of our rather unique ability that can have many names but here I will call "consciousness." Consciousness is our self-referential ability, the ability to think about ourselves. It allows for the projection of our lives both backward and forward, and enables us to make choices, to evaluate our behavior, and to make plans for the future. It is this ability that gives meaning to our emotional lives, to be able to say to ourselves and to others that "I am happy" or "sad," "ashamed" or "proud." Consciousness is our ability to have and to recognize feelings about ourselves.

Human emotional development is not well studied, which seems to me to be somewhat peculiar. Although we all have emotions and we see them in others, we are stumped by the simple questions of what emotions are and how they develop. From our first-person perspective we know when we are sad or happy and have a good idea about other people's emotions. But what emotions are remains unclear and this is part of what I wish to answer.

This first-person perspective exists and, because of it, we have some innate capacity to know about the internal lives of others, and what they are feeling, thinking, planning, and desiring. Yet what these things we call emotions are is not so easy to explain when we try to define them. This is not a problem only for people living their lives, but even for those of us who are committed to studying emotion. Carroll Izard, a pioneer in the study of emotion, highlighted the problem when he recently surveyed a group of well-known research scientists to define what emotions are and found as many answers as the people he asked. When we discuss the subject that will be central to this book, the development of emotional life, the definitions become even harder. Is my 1-year-old granddaughter, Vivian's, fear of the stranger the same thing as my fear that the IRS will audit my tax return? Is my 4-month-old grandson, Maron's, fear of heights the same thing as his fear of strangers? While these questions remain unanswered, there are some questions we do have answers for.

> Nineteen-month-old Vivian, when she goes to her pediatrician's office, clings to her mother and shows a wary face since she seems to remember that the last time she was at the office she received her well-baby shots and howled in pain.

We can say of Vivian's wary face and her clinging in the context of the doctor's office that she feels fearful, and we base our belief on observing her *behavior in context*. While we all most likely would believe this is so, our belief about our child's emotional life, based on our understanding of the behavior-in-context, is, in part at least, based on how we ourselves would feel—what emotion we would have—in a similar circumstance. Whether or not the baby has the same feeling as ours, by our behaving as if she does, we will make her feel the way we do through our own behaviors, ideas, and beliefs. The process is something like wishing it were so, and behaving as if it is so, does make it so! Because of this, I can say that the development of emotional life requires an understanding of our biology as well as the transmission of our culture, beliefs, values, and ideas. In any model of development all these features need to be understood.

This is the intellectual journey that I wish to take you on in this book about emotional development. Surprisingly, there are few such books. In part, this is due to the dominance of the mother–infant relationship in developmental theory. The prevalent view of emotional development is that mothers and their infants together form a cauldron in which emotions are formed and individual differences established. So, for example, insecure attachments lead to emotional mismatches that, in turn, lead to nonoptimal emotional development. This limited view will not do. Research on emotional development suggests that there is more. This book will try to aid in the understanding of emotional development. It is from Darwin rather than from Freud or Bowlby that I will take my lead in considering the nature of emotional life, including bodily action patterns and evolutionary adaptive principles as they relate to the development of emotions and feelings and their role in everyday life.

The theories of Freud and Bowlby are based on the child's needs: for Freud, the child's drives, and for Bowlby, the child's attachment—the secure base from which the child explores the world. Both theories involve ideas, or mental processes: Freud's involve both conscious and unconscious ones and Bowlby's involve a mental representation of the mother–child relationship. They both share the common belief that personality development occurs as an interaction between the child's needs and the rules of the culture as expressed through the particular parenting received.

For both Freud and Bowlby, emotions are the material basis for the interaction between child and parent. Implicit in both theories is the idea that moods, the enduring feature of emotions, develop in children through their social interactions. Yet neither Freud nor Bowlby are interested in directly understanding what an emotion might be: a physiological state, a set of behaviors including expressions, an idea, or all three. Nor were they much interested in understanding typical or normal development; rather, as clinicians, their focus was on how psychopathology developed. They only generally described the role of emotions in this process: an unsafe environment produced anxiety or fear, the familiar caregiver inspired joy, and her loss brought sadness. For both theorists, individual differences in children reflected individual differences in parenting; while they gave lip service to the possibility of individual differences in biology, they believed that the essential causes of pathology were to be found chiefly in parenting failure.

Freud's and Bowlby's theories emphasize the mother–child relationship to the exclusion of others, despite the evidence of a rich social life involving others besides the mother, including the father, siblings, and peers. This monotropic view, the dominant role of the mother as the chief socializing/ attachment object, runs from Freud through the object relation theories of Klein, Horney, Sullivan, and Winnicott and then through the attachment theory of Bowlby and Ainsworth.[3]

Freud's view of attachment differed from Bowlby's with respect to his therapeutic ideas. Whereas Freud's theory was deterministic, Freud also did believe that environmental social intervention by the analyst could alter the client's earlier history and could, therefore, alter the effects of the past on the future. Although Bowlby's attachment theory always held out the possibility that the patient's mental representation of the past could change, nevertheless it was believed that the model of the patient's attachment relationship to the mother would always play a role in the future. Like an inoculation, a secure attachment would protect the child, while an insecure attachment would likely doom the child. Although Alan Sroufe and colleagues have changed their views on this subject as a consequence of their longitudinal research, Sroufe's 1983 statement still reflects the majority view of those practitioners who still adhere to the attachment tradition and the idea of early models: "Even when children change rather markedly, the shadows of the earlier adaptation remain, and in times of stress, the prototype itself may be clear."[4]

My purpose here is not to question whether Freud's and Bowlby's approaches constitute systems that can properly be called theories of emotional development, but rather to use their insights as well as Darwin's to create a theory of the development of emotional life.

* * *

In graduate school, I started to study clinical psychology, but also became interested in doing research. I first studied a simple problem, the idea that some rewards were more valuable than others; that is, a reward could serve as a better reinforcer depending on the organism's evaluation of its value. Working with Richard Solomon, my professor, on a study of rats, I observed that if I made one rat work harder than another rat for one reward—in this case the reward was Rice Krispies—the rat that worked harder valued it more. It turned out that the Protestant work ethic was alive and well, even in rats. The same problem, this time using young children as subjects, served as my doctoral dissertation. In other studies I used the verbal reinforcement "Uh Hum," a sort of confirmation of what the speaker was saying. If I said "Uh Hum" after leaving a child in a room alone for 10 minutes, my "Uh Hum" was more valuable to her than if I left the child alone in a room for only 3 minutes. These early studies showed me that meaning and value were located in the past experiences of the organism rather than in the reinforcers themselves. Somehow there was a self there, although I certainly did not understand that yet.

In my first job after graduate school as a research scientist at the Fels Institute in Yellow Springs, Ohio, I studied infants' attentional processes with Jerome Kagan. Here, William James's views of attention immediately impressed themselves on us. James had discussed two types of attention: a passive attention, which imposed itself on the person and commanded their interest (such as a loud and sudden noise), and an associative attention, which attracts the person's interest because of its meaning to that person, such as seeing the face of a friend.[5] I found that again the infant's past, including memories and reinforcement history, determined how the child would act. This is not the place to continue my personal story, except to say that differences in attention led me to study maternal behavior toward the infant and how it affected attentional processes, which resulted in my learning about the reciprocal interactions between the infant and its social world and the idea that the infant was as actively influencing the mother as she was actively influencing him. While observing the behavior of the infant within its social world, it seemed that while his cognitive development played an important role in his attention, the context of the social behavior was emotional.

This early work led me to believe that I might be studying interlocking themes, an idea that reminded me of a conversation I had about creativity with Howard Gruber, the author of an award-winning book on Charles Darwin.[6] He observed that creative people usually had a central or major theme of their work. For the most part, they were unaware of the theme and did not necessarily see their work characterized in this way, but if they were fortunate, he said, their curiosity and research led them there. The emergence of the theme allowed for the highest form of creativity. Darwin's emergent theme of evolution and random unplanned change was a case history illustrating Gruber's idea. Gruber's idea had great appeal for me. It inspired me to search for the central theme around the work that I have done.

I think that I have found my central theme in the ideas of development and of identity, the role of agency, and the emergence of consciousness that gives rise to an active self, a self that creates the material of its life and the thoughts, feelings, and emotions of its social engagement. This conscious self can think of its past, act in the present, and plan for the future. It can change the past to fit the present or the present to fit the past. It can plan and yet hope. Our mental capacity, evolutionary history, and bodily actions reflect the emotional heritage of our past, but it is our consciousness, the idea of ourselves, that allows us to transform our biological underpinnings and to construct a culture. And it is culture that produces plans, values, goals, and desires, and that, with our ability to speak to ourselves and others, gives rise to the social connections and feelings that we possess. This is not only an evolutionary change through eons of time, but is also a developmental change in the lifetime of the human child. Our biology allows for the creation of a conscious self, while our experiences in our culture give meaning to our consciousness. This is the theme I hope to show takes place in emotional development and that alters emotions from their original biological bodily actions into our use of ideas.

Therefore, this book is about the biological–cultural connection in the development of emotional life. In the early years, human emotional life can be seen as a set of sensations and bodily action patterns, which through adaptive processes in our evolutionary history are connected to unique contexts. These processes give rise to sadness, fear, disgust, anger, happiness, and joy, which I call the early emotions.

Of central importance to the development of emotional life is the emergence of consciousness. With the rise of consciousness, somewhere in the middle of the second year of life, the human child can now connect his consciousness to these sensations and body action patterns-in-context. This consciousness gives rise to feelings. Importantly, the development of consciousness not only gives rise to feelings with respect to the early action patterns, but also gives rise to new sensations and action patterns through the creation of new contexts. With the development of consciousness, the child is able to think about himself and to compare himself to others, or to his own standards, rules, and goals, thus providing a set of contexts that could not exist prior to consciousness. These new contexts, which include self-representation, then serve as the elicitor of a new set of emotions, the "self-conscious emotions."

Here, too, our evolutionary history is at work. As with the earlier sensations and action patterns, consciousness not only gives rise to a new set of emotions, but also allows for the experience of them, hence prompting new feelings, or what Darwin called the "self-conscious emotions."[7] Consider that shame, a self-conscious emotion, is also a biological event in response to a particular context, a context in which the child knows that he has failed vis-à-vis his *own* standards or goals. It is the child who defines the context through the cultural set of standards and goals.

This pattern of early emotions, feelings, and self-conscious emotions is, in brief, the theory of emotional development I propose. Such a developmental analysis will allow us to move past the first 3 years of life from the literal context of the physical world defined by biological dispositions, to contexts defined by complex cognitions that involve the self and that are culturally imparted. In this model, the development of emotional life is first driven by biologically powerful connections and later by strong cultural and, therefore, learned cognitions. It is a fugue involving both biology and culture. It is this developmental process that is at the heart of this book.

* * *

I would like to thank my students and collaborators over the years for their important contributions to my thinking about these problems. They include Jeanne Brooks-Gunn, who studied self-referential behavior with me; Linda Michalson, who helped me think about how to measure emotional behavior in context—which gave rise to a measurement system and a way of looking at infant behavior; and Margaret Sullivan, who studied the early emotions as well as the self-conscious ones with me through the use of novel experimental paradigms. I thank Kristal Hawkins, Editor at The Guilford Press, whose careful reading and encouragement made this a better book. Special thanks to Stacey Napoli, who helped with both the typing and editing, as well as reference hunting over the several drafts of the manuscript.

It must be said that my children, Benjamin and Felicia, and now my grandchildren, Rana, Tamara, Vivian, and Maron, as a family have provided me a context in which I could observe the ongoing development of emotional life outside the laboratory.

The writing of this book occurred at a time that was both painful and joyful for me. My sister, Barbara, the last of my kin in my family of origin, died after a long illness; a bout of cancer, although now cured, reminded me of the brevity of life; and a failed marriage led me to the Internet to find someone with whom to share my remaining years.

With unbelievable luck, in a chance encounter, I found a wonderful woman who has become my wife. Susannah has become a source of personal renewal and has taught me that it is possible at any age to find a place of peace and love, which has enabled me to finish this book. She has also given me the desire to explore new ways of being by returning to New York City, my place of birth. Through her psychoanalytic approach, I have learned that new theories of psychoanalysis have much to offer as I tried to understand how our emotional lives come about. That said, I cannot claim that all that is written here would please her, even though she shares with me the need to better understand emotional development.

My deep appreciation goes to Patricia Whitley-Williams, Chair of the Department of Pediatrics, and Peter Amenta, Dean of the Rutgers Robert Wood Johnson Medical School, for their support, which has enabled me to write this book.

Contents

CHAPTER 1.   **Studying Emotional Development**   1

CHAPTER 2.   **Deconstructing Emotions:**   25
             Elicitors, Action Patterns, and Experiences

CHAPTER 3.   **Multiple Emotions and Moods**   46

CHAPTER 4.   **The Early Emotions**   63

CHAPTER 5.   **The Rise of Consciousness**   86

CHAPTER 6.   **The Transforming Role of Consciousness:**   109
             Self-Conscious Emotions,
             Social Relationships, and Mentalism

CHAPTER 7.   **Lying and Deception in Emotional Life**   129

CHAPTER 8.   **The Self-Conscious Emotions**   145

CHAPTER 9.   **Temperament, Emotion, and Stress**   177

CHAPTER 10. **The Socialization of Emotion** 197

CHAPTER 11. **Emotional Development Gone Awry** 227

CHAPTER 12. **The Fugue** 262

Notes 273

Author Index 326

Subject Index 336

CHAPTER 1

Studying Emotional Development

Emotions surround us every moment of our waking lives; even when we sleep we are in emotional states. We are happy, sad, confused, interested, joyous, or shamed. The minutiae of our lives are made up of these emotions. They are the subjects of our thoughts and feelings and they are the material of our interactions with others. Emotions are a natural part of what is human and their power and effectiveness derives from their evolutionary interconnection with the world. And yet, if we stop to think about it, we quickly come to realize that we know very little about the "stuff" that we call emotions. What is an emotion and a feeling and how are they different from a thought? Where do these emotions and feelings come from? How do our early lives affect them? How are people different? What is the origin of these differences?

To clarify what is to follow, I will state an explicit definition: *Emotions are thoughts about our evolutionary-derived action patterns that occur within and are molded by our social niche.* This definition includes the term "thoughts about." Here is another major theme of the theory of development to be presented. "Thoughts about" has a developmental course. The most important feature of human emotional development involves the emergence of the self and, in particular, the emergence of self-referential behavior. I will call this development of self-referential behavior "consciousness." It is what allows us to have "feelings." Thus, it is not just any thought about action patterns-in-context that is an emotion; it is thoughts about the self.

The second feature of the definition of emotion is the "action patterns-in-context." As I will try to show, the human infant, at birth and soon thereafter, exhibits highly specific actions in the world. These actions, which are

1

necessary for survival, have evolved, but—and this is an essential feature—are open to the influences of the infant's social niche.

Emotions affect our bodies, influence our will, control our memories, and shape our interactions with others. Yet, despite their centrality to our very being, little study and thought about their development exists. Emotions, especially in Western society, are viewed as suspect, and perhaps even as irrational.[1] But what is irrational about the love of a child for his parent, the child's fear of an approaching stranger, and the child's shame over failure? In order to get past this bias, we need to look at the development of this "stuff" called emotions.

Emotions are real stuff; they exist in our actions and in our units of language.[2] We think about thinking and we think about emotions. But what is it that we mean when we use the term "emotion"? Perhaps an example from an older child's statement, "I am happy," would help. While an infant does not yet have language, perhaps this example in an older child who possesses language will capture the definition of emotion that was just offered. The child first means that she is in a state of happiness, and second that she has knowledge that it is she who is in this state. Such a definition of emotion was made popular at the turn of the century by William James. This dual meaning of emotion fits both with bodily sensations, or what I will call "action patterns," and with ideas about our selves. Our emotions are created out of how we think: we are proud when we are able to help someone by giving him money and we are disgusted and outraged by the random killings of innocent civilians in ethnic strife. Besides the action patterns emotions require elaborate thinking and memory.

For the purpose of this book we need to consider several commonly used words, such as *emotion, experience, consciousness,* and *feelings.* In a strict sense, I will use the word *emotions* to mean thoughts about our action patterns-in-context. I will use the word *feelings* to indicate our thoughts about ourselves. "Feelings," "thoughts about ourselves," and "experiences" are all terms having the same meaning; they are my experience of me or, as I have come to believe, what is essentially what we mean by consciousness. The task in studying emotion is not only to find ways to observe these action patterns-in-context and to measure them, but of equal importance, to study the child's experience of them. Darwin, in his classic book *The Expression of the Emotions in Man and Animals,*[3] suggested that emotions were action patterns, having external signs as well as internal states that could be found in expressions in the face, voice, and posture of humans and beasts. Certainly, in everyday life we seem to believe that facial expressions and internal states are likely to go together. When someone cries at a funeral, we tend to assume that he or she is sad. Yet, we humans are more complex than animals and are capable of masking our behavior; for example, we sometimes laugh at a joke we do not really think is funny because we do not want to hurt the joke teller's feelings. Deception in terms of facial expression is as real a feature of emotional life as facial expressions reflecting what we are really experiencing. While internal changes may exist, the history of the study of emotion over the last 100 years reveals that we have not been able to measure them very well.[4] This lack of measurement has led to the belief that there are no internal changes and that all there is are thoughts. Such a belief holds that the discrete emotions are nothing more than different ways of thinking about things. Emotion only as thought relegates emotion to second-class status by making it an epiphenomenon of thought. This is tempting for our Western minds, where Descartes holds sway. To paraphrase him, feelings are the waste product of thought—feelings are base things, they are like the sweat of our mental lives. We will argue against these strong forms that suggest that emotions are action patterns or that they are only thoughts; rather, emotions involve both.

In the theory of emotional development to be presented later, I argue that Darwin's action patterns are shared by many animals including humans. However, biological properties interact with human consciousness in specific cultures. Consider the example we call "sadness." Sad behavior over loss seems likely to be either innate or readily learned. However, one child may have more sadness than another as a function of her temperament and environmental differences in the amount of loss that occurred, and these will affect and produce individual differences between children.

The problem of the nature of emotion also makes the study of development that much harder. For example, do children have the same emotions as adults? Does Maron's sadness over his mother leaving him at the baby-sitter's represent the same sadness that Maron's mother feels when she leaves him? When we address the question of whether human adults have the same action patterns and thoughts that children do, we are immediately met by the same question in an adult. For example, when I say I am fearful of a hornet stinging me while I sit on my porch, do I mean that I have the same feeling as when I say I am fearful that there is someone following me down a dark street? Is fear in one situation the same as fear in another? These questions lead to the belief that my experiences of myself and my action patterns are only loosely related and that they may be different things. We will assume that our experiences, our thoughts about our action patterns-in-context, are not the same as the action patterns themselves. Thus, my experience of my fear is likely to differ as a function of the causes that elicit it.

Emotional life is made up of a set of three features. The first is *emotional elicitors,* literal events in the world and later in the infant's development of his thoughts or ideas. In the discussion throughout the book I will use the term "ideas" for thoughts. The second feature is the *action patterns* including expressions that have evolved and that are located somewhere in the body. The third is the *ability of the child to experience her action patterns,* the ability to think of herself. By dividing the term "emotion" into these features, my belief in the development of emotional life becomes more clear. Consider the following case:

> I am driving down the highway at 60 miles an hour when suddenly my left front tire blows out. For the next 45 seconds, my attention is directed toward bringing the car to a safe stop at the side of the road. I am attending to many things at once, including the movement of the steering wheel, the feel and sound of the tire, and the noise of the cars going past me—all of which capture and maintain my attention. Having successfully reached the side of the road, brought the car to a safe stop, and turned off the ignition, I finally start to attend to myself and notice that I am shaking. At this moment, with my attention turned to me, I experience what I label as fear since it fits my knowledge about action patterns-in-context. Earlier, while trying to regain control of my car, I was likely to be showing the action pattern of fear if I had had electrodes attached to me that could probe those parts of the body likely to be markers of fear. However, at the time of the blowout, it was not to my adaptive advantage to pay attention to myself, for my attention was needed elsewhere to safely bring the car to a stop. While I was likely showing a specific action pattern, fear, and may have shown a fear face, I certainly was not experiencing myself as fearful until that car was safely brought to rest.

This example raises a number of issues that will lead to strong disagreement unless we can come to terms with the problems to follow.

WHAT KIND OF A THING ARE EMOTIONS?

To begin with, there is probably no advantage in using the common term "emotion" to cover what we may mean since the term has a surfeit of meanings. Arguments are bound to ensue when we do not carefully articulate what we are referring to. The debate that occurred between Robert Zajonc and Richard Lazarus, two eminent emotion theorists, in the 1980s might not have taken place had they understood that while one was referring to action patterns, the other was referring to cognitive evaluation.

As in *Children's Emotions and Moods* and in Nico Frijda's classification system, as well as in Chapter 2, we will try to deconstruct the term emotion into several of its component parts such as elicitors, action patterns including expressions, and self-experience.[5] These types of deconstruction may allow our studies and conversations to go beyond the single term emotion, and may provide the type of clarity necessary for research to progress.

Thus, "action patterns" are innate responses based on our evolutionary past that are adaptive behaviors designed for action in response to specific environmental events; these events are called "elicitors." However, because innate responses are inherently plastic, they are affected by individual differences in children's temperaments, their concurrent environmental conditions, and the cultural rules that we call "socialization." Because of this inherent flexibility, the difficulties in finding a close association between an elicitor and an action pattern should not be taken to negate the assumption that there are such innate responses. In addition to this inherent flexibility two other difficulties exist that make the association even more difficult to observe. These difficulties will be discussed in more detail in Chapter 2. Just to mention them now, the first has to do with the nature of the elicitor itself. For the most part the elicitors used in research to date tend to be multiple. For example, holding down an infant's arms and restraining him is made up of multiple elicitors including sudden movement toward the child, physical contact, smiling, and unexplained action that is not in keeping with the preceding events. Since multiple elicitors are involved, the association between them and a single action pattern would be hard to observe. One solution to this problem is to very carefully select the elicitor to be used. We will see that in my work, I use a single specific elicitor, the blockage of a learned response to a desired goal, to study anger, since from Darwin on it has been argued that such a blockage should elicit anger, which is just what we observed in infants as young as 2 months old.[6] When careful choices of elicitors are made, we are more likely to find a greater association between them and specific action patterns.

However, another issue that is likely to prevent our ability to examine innate response is the real possibility that multiple emotions, even to a specific elicitor, are more likely the rule than single emotions. At least our adult sense suggests that at the funeral of a friend we may likely experience both sadness and fear, or at the wedding of a daughter both joy and sadness. The nature of emotional life may be made up of a fugue, with the flow of emotions and thoughts entwined so that multiple emotions rather than *an* emotion may be what our lives are made up of. It is only when we try to study them in the laboratory that we break the flow apart.

If we reject the idea of an innate response to a specific context, we are left with the unanswered question of how action patterns including facial and bodily expressions as well as physiological responses are organized. The idea that these complex coherences are socialized, that is, they are learned, is difficult to imagine, and there is no direct evidential support that they are acquired. It is only the fact there is difficulty in finding specificity between facial expression and contexts that moves us toward accepting the acquired theoretical viewpoint. At the moment we need to accept the idea that action patterns such as fear, joy, and sadness are part of the human condition and that these action patterns are inherently flexible. In the manner of language acquisition, the innate structure or procedural rules for action patterns are already formed, but they are plastic so as to be open to the pressures of experiences.

THE PROBLEM OF FEELINGS

We all use the term "feeling" in describing our emotions. I can say to you that I am feeling happy, and it is because of both our common language and mentalism, that is, your knowledge that you and I share internal states such as thoughts, desires, motives, and the like, that you can find in yourself what I am feeling. In fact my feeling of happiness may make you feel happy. But what, then, does feeling happy mean? As suggested, the terms feelings, thoughts about myself, experience of me, and consciousness all speak to the process that assesses something about me.

Certainly the infant cannot utter the words "I am feeling happy," although we caregivers often say that the baby is happy. If the infant could utter the sentence "I feel happy," it seems that the access to his feelings would be dependent on his ability to know at least that the feeling is his. It is not events out there that are the feelings, they are not someone else's feelings, they are private and not known by anyone else but me unless I speak about them, although if I behave in a certain way in a particular context someone else might guess what my feelings might be. The child's ability to access either his bodily states or his thoughts about himself is dependent on his ability to be able to know about himself; first, that there is a self, a me, and second, that there is some unique combination between the self and action patterns-in-context. It is this self-referential ability that will be used to denote the term "consciousness." Consciousness is not about the aboutness of what is accessed, the content, it is the process of accessing itself.

But there is another use of the word *feeling* and for that matter the word *self-experiencing,* and it is this usage that gets us into difficulties when we discuss emotional development. Let me give you an example. A friend of mine recently laughed over the idea that some people believe that newborn infants cannot feel pain. He is not alone in his disbelief. If we prick them with a needle, don't newborns cry and haven't we found that their stress hormone, cortisol, goes up when this is done? When we say that the infant feels or experiences pain, what other meaning might we give to these words?

The common meaning of the words *feeling* or *experience* is likely to continue to give us a problem in trying to understand emotional development. The meaning of *feeling* or *experience* that I refer to is not a bodily feeling or experience, but rather an experience or feeling as in self-referential thought, something called consciousness. Let me suggest how we might think about these two different meanings of the word *feeling*. Consider that I am at the dentist's office and he wants to fill a cavity. He gives me a shot of Novocain and after a moment or two he pricks my gums and asks, "Do you *feel* this?," meaning, "Does it hurt?" My answer is that I do not *feel* it. He then begins to perform a procedure. If we had a meter that was capable of measuring pain at the pain receptors in my gum or along the neural pathway from the receptors to some central processor, it would register as pain. From a physiological perspective I have pain, but I do not *feel* pain. It does not mean that the body does not experience the pain in some way, nor does it mean that much pain will not have a powerful effect later in life. What it does mean is that I am not conscious of the pain; I do not feel it.

Perhaps another example can be found to make this point that does not involve pain, since some might say that pain is a special case. Here is an example from the research of Michael Gazzaniga. A patient with her corpus callosum severed because of her epileptic attacks is asked to haptically finger a wooden number under a blanket so that she cannot see her fingers move nor see the number, and by raising her fingers, she tells the experimenter what number she felt, a question that she can answer easily. However, when the experimenter asks her to tell out loud what the number was, she cannot tell him; "I don't know," she says. She clearly knows since she raised her fingers correctly but yet she does not know what it is that she knows. But isn't this what we mean by consciousness?[7]

Our bodies have a life of their own; they know many things that we, our consciousness, do not know. Our bodies know that when we eat too much sugar, that they need to secrete insulin. This is something known by ourselves, that is, by our bodies, but not known by our consciousnesses. We cannot readily access many things that are happening in us. In all these examples we can see that some part of us, our body, is experiencing something that enables other parts of our body to act. But we, our conscious or self-referential self, do not know of it, and therefore we cannot feel it.

My claim, therefore, is that before we can think about ourselves, before there is self-referential behavior, and therefore before consciousness, the infant may have or may be in a particular state as a consequence of a particular elicitor; however, the infant is not able to think about or experience that state as we adults do. Thus, if we restrict feeling to the body, then, of course, we can say a newborn feels pain. But if we mean that the infant can access this bodily state and know that it is her pain, then no, she does not feel pain. The infant does not have the privilege of the first person, reflected in the statement, "I am in pain." To avoid the problem with the word *feeling* I will use the terms *experience* or *consciousness* to speak not of bodily action, but of ideas about the self. I will explore this idea about different levels of self-knowledge in Chapter 5.

I AM I, I AM

I take this title from the character Sam I Am in the child's book *Green Eggs and Ham* by Dr. Seuss. The issue of consciousness plays an important role in the theory of emotional development that will be articulated here and developed more fully in Chapter 5, as well as in Chapters 8 and 10. We make much use of the development of consciousness in the theory of emotions and therefore in trying to find ways to measure it. Looking at self-referential measures, such as touching the marked nose while looking in the mirror, enables us to understand that the child knows that the image *there* in the mirror is located *here* in space, the same here in which I stand; this is also demonstrated in self-referential language such as in the use of personal pronouns like *me* and *mine,* and in pretend play in which the child reveals that he knows that something he is doing is not literal. Here I will try to both define consciousness and to argue that it has a developmental course and that it is the basis of mentalism. When we talk about consciousness we are not making reference to a consciousness that is not conscious since in effect this is what Freud tried to do. I do not see the mental processes as a struggle between the conscious and the unconscious. Rather there is only the conscious. What, then, is there that the consciousness struggles against? When I say that I am not going to eat dessert and then I do eat dessert, or when I say that I will finish painting the wall but do not do it, what is my conscious desire struggling against? It has for some time been our common belief, and a firmly embedded one at that, that there must be something "there," inside us, that is preventing us from doing that which we desire to do. This something we assume to be the unconscious, some kind of wild beast with a will of its own. It would appear that this puzzle has always been with us; the Greeks had a word for it, *akrasia,* and later it was the devil in Western belief, and now for the last century it has been called the unconscious.

However, if we stop for a moment and think about all the different things we do that we are not conscious of, from solving a problem to rote physical activity, from speaking sentences without knowing what will come next to suddenly remembering, it seems clear that there is something in there, and that something is likely to be sets of processes, habits, and the like. Some who are interested in this problem have called the thing inside "procedural rules," others have called them "action patterns," and still others have called them "instincts" and "innate releasing mechanisms." This thing or things inside us are not considered unconscious but rather not conscious. I will refer to them as *the machinery of the self* or core bodily processes and will argue that this machinery is a highly organized, complex, evolutionary-adapted set of processes that control both the internal workings of our bodies and much of our dealings with the outside world. This machinery is innate but highly plastic and capable of learning.

When we are not conscious of ourselves we are not unconscious. The interpsychic conflicts we have are between our conscious self and the machinery of our selves, machinery of which most of the time we have very little knowledge and until this last century we knew almost nothing about. In fact it is our consciousness that has allowed us to learn about this machinery, something that we are still learning about. Interestingly, we still do not know a great deal about what it is. Is it a modular system made up of many parts that are organized in some fashion, or some highly interactive system in which the activity of the whole system is what determines the outcome? Both of these possibilities find support in the research on the topic, which will be presented shortly. The point that I wish to make here and that I will try to make throughout the book is that this consciousness exists but that it is a distributive system, and once developed and used can be rewarding but at the same time highly disruptive. We do not want to think about ourselves when we are involved in a task but do want to think about ourselves to define the task or when the task is completed or when we have failed. We want to think about what we want to do, that is, to plan, but during the execution of the plan it is probably better not to think about ourselves.

So when does consciousness emerge in the human child or, for that matter, when does it emerge in the evolution of life on earth? To ask this question is to suppose that there is a way to measure consciousness. I have proposed and tried to show that there are measures that are close to consciousness, and that is self-referential behavior.

The ability to make reference to oneself is a reasonable measure of consciousness that can be measured by self-recognition in mirrors as well as in the use of personal pronouns and in pretend play. We will not go into the argument here since we will spend a considerable amount of time in Chapter 5 doing so; however, the coherence between these measures and the subsequent development of the self-conscious emotions such as shame suggest that these self-referential measures are a good approximation. Our studies suggest that consciousness develops in the human child sometime in the middle of the second year of life and that it can be seen in self-referential behaviors. The rise of consciousness has a profound effect on the development of a child's emotional life.

People have claimed that consciousness is only an idea and that for other cultures this consciousness either does not occur or that it is a collective consciousness.[8] However, such an argument has to do with the aboutness of consciousness and that is not what we are referring to. The aboutness is a cultural artifact. However, consciousness, the self-referential ability, is more likely a function of the nature of the human brain. Richard Shweder has shown that in some cultures there is a we-self aboutness.[9] However, even in we-self cultures there is no question that when a woman is menstruating, and therefore considered to be polluted, it is the woman herself who is not touchable. Even in we-self cultures the idea of a person bounded and separated from other such selves plays some role.

Having consciousness creates the challenge of maintaining our identity in the face of change. The function of the self-concept is to construct identity, that is, to maintain the cognition that all of this is me. Sometimes it means adding pieces together, sometimes it requires a separation of parts. Sometimes the elimination of one or more parts and sometime the distortion of parts or even a distortion of the composition of the whole is necessary. All of the thoughts about ourselves are designed to maintain the idea of "me." The idea of me consists of at least two features: unity, that is, I am one person and continuity, that is, I am the same person over time and that what happens now will have consequences for me in the future.

Consciousness transforms the human infant since it is the first of the emerging ideas and as such allows for and aids in the transformation of the child's action patterns or procedural rules into mentalistic thoughts, about herself, and through that to thought about others, and finally into thought that connects the past, the present, and the future. Consciousness is, as we will try to show, the most powerful of human features, the ability to be both in the present and at the same time somewhere else.

THE SAME IS NOT THE SAME

I wrote a paper on the complexity of the developmental process over 45 years ago in which it was argued that the study of infant development requires that one be an Eastern metaphysician: to study development requires that we deal with the meaning of a behavior. This is a serious problem since the equivalence of behaviors at different ages causes all sorts of difficulties. We often observe that a very young infant can perform some action that when performed at an older age would be considered to represent a complex mental state. The example of the newborn imitating the behavior of another, in particular, a tongue protrusion, on the surface seems no different than a 2-year-old imitating another child's play with a toy. We could claim that there is no difference between the two types of imitating and thus give to the newborn mental states, or alternatively we could say—which is more likely the case—that the same behavior can be used in the service of different processes.

The history of the study of infant behavior over the last 50 years has gone from the early belief in the incompetent infant who could not see well, learn easily, or remember (what William James called a "bundle of confusion") to a present belief of an infant who now is supposed to be capable of doing almost anything, and because of this is considered to be more like a scientist in a crib. The number of competencies that now has been demonstrated is quite amazing, which seems to me to reflect the innate action patterns of which the very young are capable. While some have recognized that these competencies are not predicated on mental states, others, especially those interested in the infant's interaction with its social world, have attributed unrealistic abilities that include such claims as the infant knows its mother and has the concept of itself as a "good" or a "bad" infant.[10] I will not dwell on all of the attributes that the 3-month-old infant is given since they will be covered later, but what we need to do is to make sure that we understand that the same behavior can be produced by many different processes. Without this understanding we are readily forced into the conclusion that there is no development at all since the infant can do everything at the beginning of life or soon after. In the study of emotional development we need to understand that the early action patterns are not the result of mental states whereas later in development these same action patterns can be the result of mental processes. A sad face in the 4-month-old can be due to a literal elicitor such as the cessation of an interaction either with people or while operating on an object, while a sad face at 24 months can be due to a thought about the cessation of an interaction not yet begun.

More specifically, as I discuss in Chapter 3, the earlier action patterns are elicited by the literal world, and therefore are mostly biological or innate in origin. However, they are influenced both by the temperament of the child and by the nature of the social experience the infant is subjected to. The later action patterns are elicited mostly by ideas that are a function of the maturation of consciousness as well as development of the ideas about the self and the action of the self in the world, all of which are imparted to the child by the social nexus in which he is raised.

INDIVIDUAL DIFFERENCES
WHERE NO TWO ARE ALIKE

Lucky is the student of psychology who does not have to contend with the problem of variance around a mean value. This variance represents what we in effect mean by individual differences. Even with these individual differences it is possible to talk about a process or a relationship between sets of events as general rules, which implies that the process holds for all children. While such a state of affairs might exist, the variance-around-a-mean tendency is not possible to ignore when we study human development, especially if the problem is emotional development. While there are some general facts about what babies do, for example, sit up before they crawl, or crawl before they walk, even these simple motor rules show large individual differences and these differences are the rule. Children differ for at least two reasons. To understand the development of emotional life requires that we consider these reasons, which we will be done in Chapters 9 and 10. The two reasons have to do with what I call biological or temperament, which affects the innate action patterns so that something that might elicit joy for one infant might elicit fear in another, and socialization or individual difference of the child's interactions with her social and nonsocial worlds. The diversity of the infant's social and object worlds are so different because they are a function of the forces acting on the immediate family with differences both within and between them. This is related to group membership, cultural factors, and historical factors. These are usually grouped together under the general topic of socialization. Socialization can imply a process involving action on a passive child by others who surround him. What is referred to is a broader idea than the child being acted on. In our studies, everything indicates that the child both is acted on and is acting on. The child helps to create his own world. All of this is going on within the context of the values of the family. It is the family and its circumstances that determine to a large degree the kinds of elicitors the child will be exposed to, and therefore the kind, frequency, and intensity of the action patterns that will be produced. Even climate will have an effect on the child, to say nothing of the type of dwelling the infant lives in and the temperature during the day and night. When we include the number of people in the immediate group, the ages of the other children in the family, and so on, all these are going to impact to produce individual differences.

One of the least studied aspects of emotional life is geography. This seems like a strange statement to make, but an observation made years ago about the relation between emotional expression and geography has been confirmed by recent studies.[11] The finding is that as one moves either north or south away from the equator, emotional expression decreases. In the northern hemisphere, southerners are more emotionally expressive than are northerners. This is true across countries as well as within countries; so, for example, northern Italians are less expressive than southern Italians. This is also true in Japan, with the northerners less expressive than the southerners, in China, and even in India. It may have something to do with the heat;

perhaps warmer temperatures somehow encourage more facial movement. Clearly temperature may play a role. Exactly how this may work is not clear, although I believe that temperature, family living density, and emotional contagion may be responsible for this.[12] If living density increases in cold weather with people staying closer to keep warm, then northern people should have greater living density than southern people. If it is also true that emotional expression has a strong contagion element, then people living in cold climates who live close together to avoid emotional contagion decrease their expressive behavior. On the other hand, those who are warmer do not need to live closely, and therefore do not need to inhibit their emotional expression. The point is that individual differences are considerable and that in studying emotional development, this fact needs to be kept in mind.

Now these two factors, temperament and socialization, will have a profound impact on individual differences. Since they are interactive, they produce large numbers of possible permutations. The factors impact on the infant's early emotions and they impact on the self-conscious emotions. That we can find any general pattern is amazing since these individual differences make the mean value nonrepresentative of any one child. To say, for example, that the response to holding an infant's arm down is an anger action pattern is to forget that for almost 10% of the infants, sadness, not anger, is the response, and for others it is a combination of them both, or even no reaction at all.

The possibilities that flow from the interaction of so many varied social events as they interact with temperament differences are so large that between individuals there are at best only weak coherences. Individual differences in fear of a stranger are not correlated with fear of falling off a visual cliff; the threshold to respond to pain is not correlated with the ability to dampen a response once pain occurs. Physiological responses such as heart rate or cortisol release are only weakly correlated with behavior. Individual differences swamp our findings. However, rather than despair at this outcome, we need to remember that while innate connections exist, these connections are innately plastic. How to proceed having this point of view is not easy, but perhaps it suggests that a nomothetic, rather than a mean data approach is called for.

MAMMALS, GREAT APES, AND HUMANS

There is both a phylogenetic and an ontogenetic perspective with respect to emotional development, in particular consciousness, something that I will discuss in Chapter 5. Darwin certainly tried to connect the expressions of man with the expressions of beasts but had considerable difficulty in doing so. The reasons are complicated but they are likely to center around his lack of information in regard to human cognition. Because Darwin did not have access to theories of cognitive development, in particular, attribution theories about the self, he was unable to separate out the various self-conscious emotions. Since the various self-conscious emotions require different ideas about the self, such as responsibility for a success or failure, or about differences in self-focus, such as task orientation versus performance orientation, as well as about the standards, rules, and goals of the group in which the child is embedded, Darwin had difficulty differentiating between shame, embarrassment, guilt, and shyness.

Certainly Darwin cannot be faulted for his limited understanding of children's and adults' cognitive capacities. In fact, he shared some of the prejudices of his day, including comparing children with retardation to monkeys. Given what we know now, it is possible to try and phylogenetically connect the emotional development of humans and other mammals. Toward this end here is what I see as a possible phylogenetic sequence.

1. To begin, Darwin was correct in pointing out that all mammals, including the great apes and humans, share the same early action patterns to the extent that their particular niche allows. Facial, vocal, and bodily aspects of these early action patterns are shared by us all.

2. The rise of consciousness separates all other mammals from the great apes and humans, which are likely alone to possess this capacity, perhaps with the exception of some of the sea mammals. Because of the development of consciousness, the early self-conscious emotions, those that we will call the "self-conscious exposed emotions," embarrassment, empathy, and envy, are likely to some extent shared by the great apes and humans.

3. However, the self-conscious evaluative emotions, those like shame, pride, and guilt, require culture for the rules, standards, and values as well as for other self-cognitions. Because only humans possess these cognitions, it is only humans that possess these action patterns. What this analysis suggests is as we move from the early to the later action patterns we leave behind first the other mammals besides the primates and then finally we separate the great apes from humans as we reach the most cognitively produced emotions. It is interesting in this regard to remember that another term for these self-conscious evaluative emotions is the "moral emotions." It is these that we humans alone demonstrate. It is only humans who seem to possess a moral code that controls a good deal of our

actions toward one another and that also gives rise to religious and spiritual beliefs.

SELF-DECEPTION, PRETENDING, AND LYING

As soon as consciousness emerges in the development of the child, the literal world as a control on action gives way to cognitions or ideas that can take a variety of forms. One of the forms is that we can think about the unreal besides the real. We call it pretense, where the known real is suspended for make-believe. The 2-year-old child begins to be capable of manipulating the literal world at will. The ability of the human child to pretend, that is, to negate the real, we call play. Another form of play is the ability to deceive others and ourselves. Each of these forms, pretend play, self-deception, and other deception, is the property of a conscious mind; they are discussed in detail in Chapters 7 and 8. But more, they are the bases of the creative aspect of humans. It is these abilities that appear early and that later become the art forms that only humans are capable of making. That we can think what we wish, that we are not bound by the limits of the literal world, and that we have larger brains than the other mammals allow us to create the cultural artifacts that surround us and that come to influence us. These cultural artifacts multiply and in doing so create even more cultural artifacts. So besides the moral sense that we come to have, we also have the ability to create art forms, which no other creatures on the planet are likely to possess. But perhaps more, with consciousness we are able to dream and to hope, which allows us to be in the here-and-now, yet not to be. Pretense and deception are not only essential for the creation of the high culture of art, music, theater, dance, and comedy, but for use in our interpersonal commerce. While these emergent capacities in the growing child bring pleasure, they also create the means for misunderstanding. How much simpler would the lives of humans be if each of us were bound by a sign system where pretense, deception, and play would give way to unambiguous signs that would inform each other of specific motives and desires.

I mention these issues now because they are most likely to cause controversy with what is proposed in the chapters to follow. Given my commitment to the idea of development, I will try to engage both biology and socialization into the theory of emotional development, holding to the view that human life, and with it emotional life, is largely made up of innate evolutionary-derived action patterns—procedural rules and the like— which are by their nature plastic; this plasticity is in large part due to the caregiving world of the child, to her temperament, and to the emergence of consciousness. Before doing so, let me state again that for the purpose of this book, emotional life is made up of innate action patterns and our experience of them as they interact in our social worlds.

TOWARD A THEORY
OF EMOTIONAL DEVELOPMENT

One evening in a hotel room, before I was to deliver a lecture on infants' fear of strangers, I came across a copy of the Bible. The section in Genesis, which has to do with the violation of God's requests to Adam and Eve, seemed to me to contain the ideas of a theory of emotional development that I was trying to articulate in my lecture the next day. The King James version of the creation myth says,

> And the Lord God planted a garden in Eden . . . and caused to grow out of the ground every tree . . . and the tree of life in the midst of the garden and the tree of knowledge of good and evil. . . . God commanded the man saying that "Every tree in the garden now thou mayest freely eat but of the tree of knowledge of good and evil thou shall not eat of it for if on the day thou eateth thereof thou shalt surely die." . . . And the serpent (to encourage evil said) "Ye shall surely not die for God doth know that on the day ye eat thereof your eyes will be open ye will be as God knowing good and evil." . . .
>
> She [Eve] took of its fruit and did eat and give also onto her husband with her and he did eat and the *eyes of both of them were open and they felt that they were naked*. And they *did hide* from the Lord God and when he called to them they did not answer. And he said to them "Why are you hiding from me?" And they answered *"Because we are naked"* and he knew therefore that they had eaten of the tree of knowledge.

This story provides a framework for the theory of emotional development that will be articulated in the chapters to follow. In the beginning, Genesis argues for the existence of the early action patterns such as interest, joy, happiness, and curiosity, which can be seen in Adam and Eve's behavior in the Garden of Eden. The particular action pattern talked about was curiosity, which we know is an approach emotion; that is, it leads toward action in the world. In this case it was the eating of the apple. The eating of the apple from the tree of knowledge made them wise. From our point of view, this gaining of wisdom was about themselves: "They did eat and the eyes of both of them were open and they *felt* that they were naked." The consequence of this acquisition of knowledge, the story tells us, resulted in a new set of emotions, in particular, the self-conscious emotion of shame. They knew they were naked and were ashamed. This story suggests a progression: Early emotions lead to knowledge, what we call cognitions, in particular cognitions about the self, which in turn lead to the self-conscious emotion of shame. This creation story matches the developmental theory that we will follow.

We will take the work of Charles Darwin and a biological evolutionary position as our point of reference in order to focus on the issue of development. Even so, we need to emphasize that emotional life is embedded in the child's social and cognitive development and that this embeddedness gives to the basic biological form its content and meaning. This broad view is similar to that of our understanding of language in which the biological form, embedded in a social context of a particular language, becomes that language. Therefore, part of the central theme of this book is the belief that socialization and maturation are equally important in determining development and leading to individual differences in emotional life.

In humans, the earliest development of emotional life resembles what we see in other animals, the common action patterns-in-context between animals and us. Later, emotional development is dependent on the emergence of consciousness. These I call the self-conscious emotions. Thus, to begin with, emotions are tied to a behavior–environment connection. Darwin described this connection well when he suggested that emotions in man and animals are action patterns that are tied to particular situations because these action patterns proved to be adaptive, and therefore were likely to survive. For example, anger is an action pattern designed to overcome a blocked goal, sadness an action pattern associated with loss, and fear an action pattern associated with both movement away from and interest toward. For the most part these action patterns are common across species, differing as a function of the different physical features and environmental niches each species possesses and inhabits. These action patterns have been called by several different names; for example, in the cognitive development literature they have been called "procedural rules." I have chosen the term "action patterns" because it is broad enough to encompass emotional, social, and cognitive behaviors.

In the second and third year of life these action patterns interact with the emergent consciousness, consciousness here being taken to mean the idea of "me." It is a mental state best captured by the phrase "I am happy" or in its most mature form "I know, you know, that I love you." While the emergence of consciousness has a biological basis, it does not concern the nature of the child's aboutness. Rather, it is the idea that the human child and then the adult has the capacity to consider its aboutness. Once consciousness appears in the human child there emerges as a consequence a transformation, in part of which a new set of emotions, those that involve the self-in-action, emerge. Unlike the earlier emotions, these self-conscious emotions are elicited by cognitions that involve the self and are less elicited by the literal world; thus, "I am proud" because I achieved a sought-after goal by my own efforts. These new emotions are based on ideas and like the earlier emotions exist because of their adaptive significance.

Our emotional lives are first characterized by the existence of these early action patterns, then by the emergence of consciousness, which in turn gives rise to the self-conscious action patterns. Both the early and later action patterns are innate responses tied both to the literal world and to the world of ideas. Even so they are readily affected by environments. These environmental influences are what constitute the familial and cultural rules that surround the child from birth, and perhaps even from before birth.

We can use the action pattern of disgust as an example of this development since it captures well what is proposed. Bitter and sour tastes elicit in the very young infant a disgust-like face: the infant displays an open mouth and a nose with a wrinkled-like expression as he rejects the food in his mouth. This is an innate response, part of the adaptive system designed to prevent the taking in of potentially dangerous substances. This disgust action pattern is later combined in some fashion with ideas about standards, values, and rules. These ideas are learned through the child's interaction with his social world including parents, siblings, and peers. Ideas like the action pattern are related to the earlier general withdrawal pattern seen at birth. In this way the action pattern of disgust becomes available for use as part of our idea system and thus becomes moral disgust, the elicitor of which now has to do with failure vis-à-vis standards. For disgust to become connected to ideas requires the rise of consciousness.

Figure 1.1 shows in schematic form the theory proposed. As can be seen, emotional development over the first 3 years of life is divided into the early emotions, the rise of consciousness, the early or exposed self-conscious emotions, and, finally, the evaluative self-conscious emotions.

Following Katharine Bridges,[13] as well as others, we believe that the child at birth shows at least a three-part emotional life. First, the infant exhibits a general distress marked by crying and irritability. Second, the infant displays pleasure marked by smiling. Third, the infant displays attention to and interest in the environment from the beginning of life, without either the positive or negative action patterns. Certainly by age 3 months, if not before, joyful expression emerges, infants start to smile, and they show excitement/happiness when confronted with familiar events, such as faces both human and animal. Also by 3 months, sadness emerges, especially in connection with the withdrawal of positive events, like when their mothers stop interacting with them. Disgust also appears in a spitting out and getting rid of unpleasant-tasting and -smelling objects placed in the mouth. Children by 3 months are already showing action patterns of interest, joy, sadness, and disgust, and exhibiting these facial expressions to appropriate events.

Although anger has been reported to emerge between 4 and 6 months,[14]

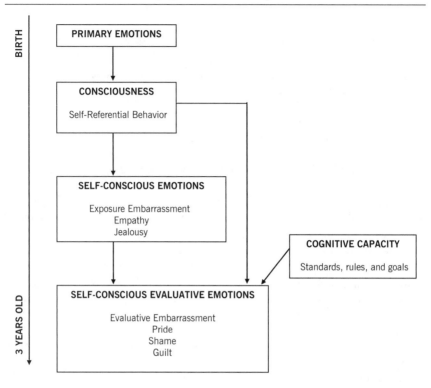

BIRTH

3 YEARS OLD

PRIMARY EMOTIONS

CONSCIOUSNESS

Self-Referential Behavior

SELF-CONSCIOUS EMOTIONS

Exposure Embarrassment
Empathy
Jealousy

COGNITIVE CAPACITY

Standards, rules, and goals

SELF-CONSCIOUS EVALUATIVE EMOTIONS

Evaluative Embarrassment
Pride
Shame
Guilt

FIGURE 1.1. The theoretical model. Adapted from Lewis, M. (1992). *Shame: The exposed self* (p. 87). New York: Free Press. Copyright 1992 by Michael Lewis. Adapted by permission of the author.

we believe that it appears even earlier. As our studies have shown, anger is a particularly interesting emotion, since, from Darwin on, it has been associated with a desire to overcome an obstacle.[15] Fearfulness seems to emerge a bit later, since fearfulness requires further cognitive development. Rudolf Schaffer[16] has shown that in order for children to show fearfulness, they need to compare the event that causes fearfulness with some other event. For example, in fear of a stranger an infant has to compare the face of the stranger to its internal representation or memory of faces it has seen before. Children's ability to show fearfulness, therefore, does not seem to emerge until this comparison ability emerges. Children begin to show this behavior at about 7 to 8 months, although it has been reported by some to occur even earlier, especially in children who seem to be precocious. Surprise also appears in the first 6 months of life. Children show surprise when there are violations of expected events.[17] Surprise can also be seen as a response to discovery, as in "Aha!" experiences.

In the first 8 or 9 months of life, children's emotional behavior reflects the emergence of the six early emotions or as Darwin called them, action patterns. These action patterns evolved because of their adaptive significance, as they are associated with particular classes of elicitors. They are not learned, although they are affected by the environment in which the child is raised. Moreover, there is no reason to assume that mentalism is necessary for their appearance.

Sometime in the second half of the second year of life, the emergence of consciousness, the mental representation of "me"—seen in self-referential behavior—occurs. When it does, it gives rise to the *self-conscious exposed emotions*, which include embarrassment, empathy, and jealousy. While I will report on the studies of development of these emotions later, I will mention briefly that we have shown that the emergence of embarrassment takes place only after self-recognition or consciousness occurs.

Two points are to be noticed about this class of new emotions. First, observation of these emotions requires not only measuring a facial expression, but measuring bodily and vocal behavior as well. Whereas the earlier emotions can be observed readily in specific facial configurations, these new emotions require measurement of bodily behavior. Embarrassment, for example, is best measured by such signs as smiling, nervous bodily touching, and short duration head and gaze aversion. The second point is that although these emotions require self-referential behavior, they require few other cognitive abilities. The emergence of these self-conscious emotions is related uniquely to the mental representation of the self and the utilization of that representation in regard to others.

A second cognitive ability occurs sometime between 2 and 3 years of age. This ability is characterized by the child's capacity to evaluate his behavior against a standard, rule, or goal, as in the case of parental or teacher sanction or praise, or it can exist internally, as in the case of the child's own understanding of others' standards. This new cognitive capacity allows the child to evaluate her own behavior and gives rise to still another set of emotions, which I have called *self-conscious evaluative emotions*. They include pride, shame, and guilt, among others. These emotions require that a child have a mental representation of herself and be capable of comparing her behavior against standards, rules, and goals of the culture in which she is embedded. If the child fails vis-à-vis the standard, she is likely to feel shame, guilt, or regret; if she succeeds, she is likely to feel pride. It is important to note that these new classes of emotions are quite different from the early emotions; pride and shame are quite different from happiness and sadness. So while we feel happy about winning money in a lottery, we would not feel pride because we would not view the winning of the lottery as having anything to do with our own behavior. The same is true for failure; sadness is not the same as guilt or shame. These complex evaluative emotions make their appearance between 2½ and 3 years of age.

Thus, by 3 years of age, the emotional life of the child has become highly differentiated. From the original tripartite set of emotions, the 3-year-old has come to possess an elaborate and complex emotional array. Although the emotional life of the child will continue to be elaborated and will expand, the basic structures necessary for this expansion have already been formed. New experiences and more elaborate cognitive capacities all serve to enhance and elaborate the child's emotional life. However, by 3 years of age, the child already shows those emotions that Darwin characterized as unique to our species—the emotions of self-consciousness. With these emotions now acquired, a large part of the major developmental activity has been achieved.

A CHAPTER OUTLINE

This book is arranged as follows in order to present the theory of emotional development as outlined.

In Chapter 2, *Deconstructing Emotions*, we take up the question "What are emotions?" and try to show that by talking about the events that elicit emotions, emotions as action patterns and self-experiences, we are better able to look at issues in development. We argue that the elicitors are, in early life, made up mostly of the literal events in the world, which from an evolutionary adaptive perspective are linked to unique action patterns. Later, the elicitors become ideas; thus, emotional development moves from literal events to cognitions. Action patterns also have an evolutionary adaptive connection, although they are highly adaptive to the current life of the child. Self-experiences or consciousness may also have an adaptive significance since they are part of the growth of mentalism.

Chapter 3, *Multiple Emotions and Moods*, continues the discussion of the nature of emotional life, offering the idea that single emotions may not be the rule; rather multiple emotions are as likely to occur to any single elicitor. That we can experience both sadness and happiness in response to the same event suggests that the idea of one emotion rather than a set of emotions needs reconsideration. Moreover, in talking about an emotion, we need to make some distinction between a transient emotion and one having a longer duration. The latter are called "moods." Indeed, it is the array of different moods that are often used to characterize a child's personality.

Chapter 4, *The Early Emotions*, starts us on the construction of the theory of development as we try to demonstrate that the early action patterns of approach and withdrawal differentiate themselves. The early emotions or action patterns of joy, anger, and interest derive from the primary approach pattern, while disgust and sadness emerge from the primary withdrawal pattern. Interestingly, fear appears to be some combination of the approach and withdrawal patterns. What is important to note is that these primary approach and withdrawal patterns by 6 to 8 months have differentiated themselves into these early emotions, each linked in part to specific elicitors, the consequence of their adaptive significance.

Chapter 5, *The Rise of Consciousness*, is perhaps the most important one for our theory of development for it is here, in the middle of the second year of life, where mentalism, the child's earliest ideas about herself, emerges. While it is likely to be a gradual process, its emergence appears to be a consequence of the maturation of specific regions of the human brain. This idea of "me" is differentiated from the machinery of the self, biological features that until the emergence of consciousness are more likely to control our actions through such processes as procedural rules as discussed by Josef Perner.[18] Our work on self-referential behavior such as mirror self-recognition, use of personal pronouns, and pretend play has been used as measures of this emergent capacity from which the later self-conscious emotions emerge.

The role of consciousness is not limited to the development of emotional life. As we try to show in Chapter 6, *The Transforming Role of Consciousness*, consciousness underlies the development of our social and cognitive lives. As Joyce Carol Oates recently wrote, "It is our human capacity for being in one place, while having the mental capacity to imagine another place, as we have the mental capacity to recall the past, learn from, and calculate the future; that is our specific exceptional talent."[19] The emergence of this capacity of consciousness gives rise to a new set of emotions that begin to appear simultaneously with self-referential behavior. First is the emergence of the self-conscious emotions, which require the least additional cognitive capacity. Thus, embarrassment, empathy, and envy make their appearance around 2 years. Keep in mind that the earliest type of embarrassment, as Darwin wrote, is caused by our attention to others attending to us, and that empathy involves placing ourselves in the role of the other, which means that these abilities require self-representation, or what we have called consciousness.

Chapter 7, *Lying and Deception in Emotional Life*, brings us back to the issue of mentalism and the role of consciousness. Moreover, it also attempts to show that lying and deception changes the child's experiences of her own action patterns. Lying and deception is possible to oneself since it is an emergent property of consciousness. Self-deception allows us to manipulate and change or alter our self-experiences, thus allowing us to create a flow of emotions, changing, for example, shame to guilt or joy to sadness.

Chapter 8, *The Self-Conscious Emotions,* discusses the growth of other cognitive abilities by age 3, such as standards, rules, and goals, and the idea of ownership, leading to the final set of the self-conscious emotions. Thus, shame, guilt, pride, and embarrassment are seen at this time. With the onset of these moral emotions, the human child has in 3 years moved from an undifferentiated emotional life to one that is adult-like and complex, although much more development will occur. The emergence of these self-conscious emotions is differentiated from the earlier ones. Most important, the elicitors of these complex emotions are no longer the features of the literal world; rather, they are self-referential cognitions, and as such are highly influenced by culture.

Chapter 9, *Temperament, Emotion, and Stress,* makes the case that, while the effects of socialization are most important, individual differences in temperament have an equal role. While the influence of the social world, in particular the mother, is considerable, I think that this role is overstated. Until relatively recently, it was the mother and her mothering that was held responsible for such diverse differences as autism, homosexuality, and colic; indeed it is still believed to play some important role in attention deficit disorder (ADD).[20] It is now recognized that some individual differences in emotional behavior may be more likely a consequence of temperament than of socialization.

In order to explore the role of socialization in emotional life, Chapter 10, *The Socialization of Emotion,* discusses the role of the social world in affecting both the young infant's action patterns and the self-conscious emotions. Clearly, environments that favor events connected to specific action patterns have to play an important role. Thus, a social world full of events of loss or uncertainty will promote the action patterns of sadness and fear. Facilitating one action pattern over another has to have profound effects. It is likewise true for the more complex self-conscious emotions: since the eliciting events for these are ideas, they are socialized not only by the children's mother, but by the child's entire social world, including father, siblings, and peers. As we will try to show, the standards a child holds, the self-attributions he possesses, including attributions about responsibility, are part of the role of the social world. Thus the role of the social environment of the child increases with development.

Chapter 11, *Emotional Development Gone Awry,* provides a discussion of less typical development, first of the early emotions, and then of the self-conscious ones. Based on data on children with Down syndrome, children with autism spectrum disorder, and children with other pathologies, it explores how the typical process as described in the early chapters goes awry. Because the ideas that are the elicitors of the self-conscious emotions are most affected by socialization factors, children who are abused and neglected provide a special case for seeing how really poor parenting can and does affect children's emotional development.

Chapter 12, *The Fugue*, serves as a summary of the theory of emotional development and suggests the direction of where we might go to further its study.

Make no mistake, while I have tried to be comprehensive in outlining a theory of emotional development in these 12 chapters, there is much more that needs to be said. More important, as one of the few attempts to build a comprehensive theory of emotional development using the data now available, I consider it only the beginning of our search.

CHAPTER 2

Deconstructing Emotions

Elicitors, Action Patterns, and Experiences

In order to understand emotional development we need to continue to ask, What are emotions? I have already suggested that our language usage often leads to confusion and disagreement about this issue. We need a better definition of the term "emotion" if we are to understand development. This will be provided here, arguing that the thing we call an emotion is a combination of innate action patterns, the elicitors that produce them, and our self-experience.

While our everyday experience confirms the existence of emotions, and while people can generally identify different kinds of emotion, a survey of the literature continues to reveal that attempts to define emotion frequently devolve into elaborate systems of taxonomy in which the classification of different emotions becomes the primary task. So, for example, we can talk about negative and positive emotions, or moral emotions. The question then turns from what an emotion is to how many there are, which emotions are fundamental, and what relations exist among the specific emotions and between emotions, cognitions, and social behavior. The lack of agreement about what constitutes an emotion continues to hinder its study; indeed, this lack of definition has made the study of the phenomena both difficult and suspect. Some years ago, in an issue of *Emotion Review*, 18 authors had been asked by Carroll Izard to describe emotions and how to study them. They provided eighteen different answers, some of which suggested that there are no such things as emotions. Almost 80 years ago, for example, Duffy[1] argued that it is essentially meaningless to try to study emotion at all because emotion "has no distinguished characteristics," and that emotional behaviors are not different in kind from other behaviors, since all behaviors follow the same principles. Some contemporary theorists hold similar views.

The problem of definition is always present in science. It affects our operational definition of variables as well as our measurement of the phenomena under study. Indeed, the diverse definitions of the term "IQ" as either a set of skills or a single competence have plagued us for nearly a century.[2] In the study of thinking psychologists have come to appreciate the distinction between *competence,* some underlying structure or ability, and *performance,* some measurable manifestation of that competence. In the definition of emotion that will be proposed, this distinction is maintained by separating emotion into its various components such as emotional elicitors, emotional action patterns including expressions, and emotional experiences.

When we speak of emotion we mean to talk about a complex set of behaviors that occur around an equally complex set of situations and cognitions. Examples of what these may be and how they can be measured will occupy our efforts. Perhaps we can approach this difficulty through a specific example, the emotion of fear. In the book *The Origins of Fear,*[3] I enumerated five different types of elicitors that can produce fear in an infant or young child. In the examples to follow, although we are talking about the elicitors of fear, the case studies depicted can pertain to all emotions, since these fear examples explore the elicitor–response connection and how we come to measure, in part, emotions. In these examples, what we will see is that the child exhibits a unique yet specific set of behaviors in specific situations from which we adults infer a specific emotion. However, one important aspect of the fear emotion is the child's experience of her fear action patterns-in-context. The ability to experience, that is, the child's mental representation of her fear, depends on her developmental level. Our observations in the very young allow us to say that a specific action pattern to a specific situation has occurred. The observation, whether by the scientist or by the caregiver, is the basis for our attribution about the child's emotional life, and it is these attributions that are likely in turn to play an important role in the child's development.

> *Example 1.* A 1-month-old infant is lying in a crib looking at the mobile above it. Suddenly a loud bang sounds behind the crib. Someone has dropped a pile of dishes. The infant startles, and if we could measure them, she would show blood pressure and heart rate increases as she throws out her limbs and starts to cry.

In this example, the infant reacts to an intense, sudden, and unexpected change in the level of energy reaching her sensory system. Without question, stimulus events characterized by these three elements—intensity, suddenness, and unexpectedness—seem capable of eliciting responses we label as fear. This is true not only for young infants, but for children and adults as well. Thus, it is reasonable to recognize a class of events that are automatically associated with a fear response. It should not be surprising that the human nervous system has evolved to respond to some stimuli as noxious. Fear may be part of the response to a noxious event, that aspect that protects organisms by enabling them to avoid similar situations in the future. The innate, biological wiring of specific classes of responses to specific stimulus events may not involve much, if any, cognitive activity, except insofar as the perception of the event is a cognitive activity itself. The classic studies by Susan Mineka, in which chimp babies with only minimum exposure can be shown to have more fearful-like behavior to snakes than to flowers, are examples of such a kind of unlearned response or a predisposition to rapidly learn.[4]

> *Example 2.* An 8-month-old infant girl is sitting in her mother's bedroom. Her mother is dressing for the evening and is putting on a new long-haired wig. As she puts it on and turns, the infant stares at her intensely for a moment and suddenly begins to cry.

In this example, a discrepancy seems to result in a particular set of emotional responses. The infant has formed a schema, or representation, of her mother, and this representation involves the integration of the stimulus properties of her. The schema is highly complex and because the child has already reached some of the cognitive milestones toward object and person permanence, an important and radical change in the mother representation produces an emotional response, in this example, fear. With another infant, however, this unexpected change might elicit interest and smiling behavior; as we will see, the infant's response to the mother in a wig is likely dependent on the infant's temperament. The child tries to make sense of this alteration in a familiar stimulus array and if it cannot easily assimilate this transformation or accommodate the old representation to this new event, as Hebb has held, fearful behavior may be the result.[5] The connection between cognition and an emotional response in some cases may be prewired, and the inability to assimilate an event may automatically produce fearfulness. In other cases, the connection between the cognition and the set of emotional behaviors may be learned, and the inability to assimilate an event is perceived by the child as loss of control. Loss of control itself may be associated with fearfulness.

> *Example 3.* An 18-month-old child is pedaling slowly with his mother at his side through the park. A stranger walks over to the little boy,

says hello to the mother, and asks the child if he likes the bottle he is sucking. The mother smiles and returns the greeting, while the child freezes, stops pedaling, turns to the mother, frowns, and starts to whine.

This phenomenon has most commonly been called "stranger fear" or "stranger anxiety." The child is afraid of new people but shows positive behavior to familiar people. The development of this fear response, sometimes called "wariness," usually occurs after the first 8 months of life. Before this age children generally exhibit positive behavior to all people. Thus, at an earlier age, this stranger, who now elicits this fear response, may have evoked affiliative behavior such as smiling. Stranger fear has been considered by some to be a maturationally determined, biologically derived response, the function of which is to limit the number of people to whom the infant can become attached.[6] Also, it has been considered a manifestation of the child's cognitive ability to compare various events in his world and has been associated with memory development. For example, the toddler in this case has to compare the stranger to all the representations of others he knows, and then conclude that there is no match. Moreover, the unique feature of stranger fear has been considered within the attachment literature since if the child shows fearful behavior to the stranger, but not to the mother, it represents the onset of the child's attachment relationship.[7]

> *Example 4.* A 4-year-old child sits with her mother in the pediatrician's office. It is their turn to see the doctor. As they enter the examining room, the child stares at the doctor and her white coat, screams, turns away, clutches her mother's leg, and says, "I am afraid, no injection, it hurts!"

This example is a case of learned fear to novel elicitors. Having received a series of inoculations over the past 2 years, in the context of the doctor's office, the child is capable of remembering the past events, and behaves with fear-like behavior. The doctor and the white coat are associated with an inoculation and pain. The child therefore responds with a fear emotion to the anticipated pain. Later the child may remember and associate pain simply with the words "going to the doctor," or the child may not remember or associate the event until an event triggers the memory, such as being in the doctor's office or seeing the doctor's face or white coat. Moreover, by 4 years of age the child has a self-representation and therefore experiences her fearfulness behavior in context. She knows she is afraid, as marked by her reflection on herself and her use of the personal pronoun "I."

FEATURES OF EMOTION

These examples of fear-like responses to different events at different ages raise many questions pertaining to learned and unlearned elicitors of sets of behaviors, mostly those visible to others but also those like stress hormone or heart rate increases, not visible to others but which take place as part of the infant's or child's response. It also addresses the cognitive changes in the child as a function of age, and in particular the older child's self-referential behavior as she experiences her behavior-in-context.

This brief introduction makes it clear that any attempt to define the term "emotion" will not be easy, nor will any attempt at looking at the various components that make up the person–context behaviors. Nevertheless, I shall take up the challenges since much if not all to follow, and certainly my model of emotional development, is dependent on my efforts to do so. While these components have been addressed before, they need to be repeated since they play an important role in what is to follow. Nico Frijda,[8] for example, has used terms like the stimulus, psychological manifestations, and experience in addressing a working definition of emotion. He states that emotions consist of features of behavior, psychological changes, and "the evaluative, subject-related experiences as evoked by external or mental events" (p. 41). As we will see, these features are similar to what I propose here and have proposed before in earlier work.[9]

In what follows three components and their development are considered: elicitors, emotional action patterns including facial and bodily behaviors as well as physiological responses, and experiences.

EMOTION ELICITORS

In order for an emotional response to occur, an elicitor must affect an organism's behavior. The elicitor may be either an external or an internal stimulus. External stimuli may be nonsocial, such as loud noises or a hot stove, or may be social, such as seeing the face of a familiar person.[10] Internal elicitors may range from changes in blood sugar level to mental activity, such as making a self-attribution. Since it is obviously much harder to identify and manipulate an internal elicitor than an external one, most of the research done on emotion elicitors, at least with young children, has dealt with external stimuli. One of the major problems in defining emotional elicitors is that not all events that produce action patterns can be characterized as emotional elicitors. For instance, a blast of arctic air may cause a drop in body temperature and elicit shivering, but one is reluctant to classify these bodily changes as an emotional event, although some have thought of them as affects and the terms "affect" and "emotion" have at times been used interchangeably. The definition of an emotion elicitor tends to be somewhat circular, inasmuch as an elicitor is defined in terms of the consequence it produces. Since feeling cold is not considered an emotion, the blast of arctic air is not regarded as an emotional elicitor.

The developmental issues associated with elicitors are many. First, there are classes of elicitors with little developmental history. A hot stove when touched causes pain throughout life. The sight of food, once it is associated with relief of hunger, almost always serves as a positive elicitor—but only if the person is hungry and not sated after eating a big meal. Even for automatic elicitors such as a hot stove, the life events of the organism may be such as to inhibit or restrict the elicitor from operating in its natural way. Consider the Melzack and Wall studies of dogs raised so as to be unable to respond appropriately when they touched a hot plate. That is, the elicitor, if it could be measured, remains consistent in its effect but other aspects necessary for the organism to realize its effect may interfere. Exactly how or where in the emotional process this interference occurs is not known. Or the effect of the elicitor may be modified by the deactivation of the action pattern. For example, the pain action pattern can be deactivated by competing stimuli, such as loud music played into the patient's ears during dental surgery, or by drugs that inhibit receptor functioning or block information from reaching the spinal cord or brain.[11] Finally, an elicitor may be rendered ineffective through failure on the part of the organism to experience the action pattern. The failure to experience the action pattern might be the result of a reinterpretation of the action pattern through competitive learning—for example, in anorexia, food and eating are associated with negative outcomes—or of some unknown motivation that prohibits the experiencing of a particular elicited response.

The model connecting elicitors to action patterns has many examples, from those that appear almost hiccup-like to those that are learned. Consider what happens when we hold an infant up by its hands from a supine position and let her drop. The infant exhibits an automatic action pattern of hands and arms flailing out and in, almost like she is trying to hold on to something. We say the falling sensation (an elicitor) produces a Moro reflex (an action pattern). This flailing is biologically connected, having the function of helping the infant to hold onto something when falling. When I talk about the early emotions, the elicitors of the action patterns will be described in some detail. However, even these elicitors, which may have some one-to-one correspondence with specific action patterns, can be conditioned to other elicitors so that elicitors may be acquired through an associative learning process that was not present until learning took place. Moreover, ideas can be the elicitors of complex action patterns such as shame or pride. These ideas and attributions about the self can serve as elicitors once the child is capable of cognition necessary for these ideas. These mental elicitors not only serve as elicitors to new action patterns such as shame or pride, but influence the action patterns originally elicited by the literal physical events in the world.

This approach is based on the assumption that emotional behavior has an evolutionary history and is linked to specific biological programs. In the case of facial expressions, in particular, but in all aspects of the action patterns as well, evolutionary adaptive processes resulted in the connection of these specific elicitors to specific action patterns. This view has been espoused by Izard, who has asserted that "emotional expressions are innate and emerge ontogenetically as they become adaptive in the life of the infant and particularly in infant–caregiver communication." Moreover, studies show that certain emotions are associated with similar facial expressions across widely different cultures, a finding that "provide[s] a sound basis for inferring that the fundamental emotions are sub-served by innate neural programs." For Izard, there is also a strong link between the action patterns to an elicitor and to the experiences of the child: "It is reasonable to infer that the link between facial expression, neurochemical processes and emotions, and certain actions or action tendencies is the inner emotion experience and its motivational properties."[12] Izard views emotion as an isomorphic relationship among elicitors, action patterns including expressions, and experience. While I agree that there may be a strong connection between elicitors and behaviors, the "inner emotion experience" is not so connected initially but develops over time.

The alternative view that does not necessarily postulate a tightly knit connection is one that can be called an "arousal attributional model." In this model there are no tightly knit connections between elicitors and behaviors, but rather the idea of general arousal to an elicitor and the interpretation and attribution of this arousal utilizing information learned and interpretation about context, social expectations, and cognitive capabilities.[13] Such a view has a long history in the study of emotion, with such contemporary supporters as Andrew Ortony and Joseph Campos, and the early work of Stanley Schachter.[14] It may also be related to socialization of specific scripts that inform members of the group about what behaviors are appropriate for what situations. Of course such theoretical approaches require that sufficient cognitive capacity be present early in life for the infant to exhibit specific behaviors-in-context.[15]

In my model the idea of action patterns connected to natural elicitors that mostly dominate the infant's behavior at the beginning of life, change so that later in development the child's ideas become the elicitors of action patterns. The argument will rest on the assumption that things like fear, love, and anger (as action patterns) are not learned. What is learned has to do with the stimuli that elicit them, how they are expressed, what they are called, and how they are experienced.

As we have seen in the above examples, the structure that supports the elicitor–action pattern connection undergoes change. Within the class of early elicitors there are some that appear strongly biologically connected to an action pattern—although socialization factors may strengthen or weaken them—as well as elicitors that are connected to an action pattern through learned associations. For example, infants' wariness of strangers may have an underlying biological program. However, over time, stranger fear declines because the biological structure supporting the elicitor–action pattern connection has broken down as a function of learning. Learned associations between elicitors and responses also may be subject to developmental change because new abilities come on line or old ones are extinguished. For instance, the elicitor may change with cognitive development.[16]

Another difficulty in tracing the developmental course of elicitors is that a single elicitor may represent a category or class of elicitors. Take as an example fear. It is possible that some elicitors of fear, like a snake or a spider, will likely always produce a response because it has a specific prewired context. However, learned fear may be elicited by a class of events that are uncertain and sudden. The specific events of the class of uncertainty may change even though uncertainty itself always remains an elicitor. Likewise, the class of elicitors for sadness may be that of loss and the class of elicitors for anger may be blockage of a desired goal. The specific features that are involved in uncertainty, loss, and goal blockage are likely to change with age and with development, and most certainly with cognitive development. This problem of looking at specific elicitors occurs because even the most biological elicitor–action pattern connections are subject to developmental change.

There is a developmental sequence related to the elicitor–action pattern association. Very young infants' elicitor–action pattern connections are for the most part unlearned and part of the early adaptive response system that promotes action-in-the-world. However, as the infant gets older, the elicitors become more related to learned associations, and by age 2 years the elicitors become, in large part, ideas. To summarize, the developmental process in terms of elicitors is a changing one, one that starts out in a more hiccup-like fashion where specific elicitors in the child's environment produce specific action patterns. Over time these action patterns are recruited to other elicitors through learning. Finally ideas become the elicitors.

Tracing this developmental course is not easy. The development of other cognitive processes—categorization, classification, reasoning, and the like—is also likely to influence which elicitors produce what action patterns; for example, failure in a task in children prior to 24 months of age produces sadness, while failure at a task after 24 months is likely to produce shame or guilt, as well as sadness. The same elicitor produces different action patterns, depending upon children's cognitive capacity. Before children can evaluate their actions against some standard, the success at achieving a goal results in happiness. Once children are capable of this *evaluation of self* the emotion as a consequence of the success is likely to be pride as well as happiness. Such findings as these alert us to several problems concerning emotional elicitors, including (1) specific elicitors may have an automatic biological adaptive connection to specific action patterns, whereas others are connected more through learned associations; (2) individuals may differ in the extent to which the same elicitor produces different emotions; and (3) the relation between emotional elicitors and emotional outcomes changes as a function of the meaning system of a particular individual.

One final issue in regard to the elicitor–action pattern has to do with the existence of what have been called "emotional receptors." Briefly, emotional receptors provide a way to connect the elicitor to a unique action pattern. Emotional receptors may be relatively specific loci or pathways in the central nervous system (CNS) that mediate between the elicitor and the particular action pattern, or a more general arousal and the cognitions about it. Information about infant emotional receptors is rare, so that any discussion of their development is speculative.

Specific receptors—likely select cells or neurostructures located in the CNS or in the autonomic nervous system (ANS)—are thought to be innate, which require a highly specific stimulus. When these receptors are activated by a particular elicitor, instinctive behavioral patterns are released that presumably increase the organism's chance of survival.[17] For instance, the quality of "babyishness" is considered a releaser of the action pattern of approach in adults, children, and even other babies.[18] It has been speculated that the schema of the human face constitutes an innate releaser of the smiling response in babies, and John Bowlby hypothesized that smiling behavior increases the chance of infant survival since it makes the infant more appealing to the mother.[19]

Electroencephalogram (EEG) and brain imaging studies have not located specific brain centers for the different emotions, only hemispheric differences, with the left hemisphere associated with approach action patterns and the right with withdrawal action patterns. Although the amygdala has been shown to play a critical role in emotional behavior, its activity interacts in complex ways with other areas of the brain, particularly structures of the limbic system and hippocampal regions. Theories of specific cells for perception come from the work of David Hubel and Torsten Wiesel,[20] who identified specific cells in the visual cortex of the cat that are activated only when a bar of light is presented at a certain angle. Different cells respond to different angles. Other cells respond only to movements through the visual field and movement only in a single direction. Some cells are so highly specialized that they are activated only by a line in a particular orientation and of a specific length and width. Other cells in the visual cortex respond to patterns such as curves and animals. In monkeys, some cells are so finely attuned that they respond only to specific shapes and objects.[21]

Silvan Tomkins has suggested the idea of affect receptors and speculated on the role they might play. "These organized sets of responses are triggered at subcortical centers where specific programs for each distinct affect are stored."[22] Little attention has been paid to development issues pertaining to specific receptors. In general, these receptors are thought to be in place at birth and to be biologically determined and genetic in origin. Speaking about the program of these receptors and the consequence of their elicitation, Tomkins states that these programs are "innately endowed and have been genetically inherited" (p. 243). Thus there may be little reason to postulate a developmental course in the maturation of specific receptors. If Tomkins is correct, they exist at birth and are influenced by neither development nor culture.

Why do we need a concept of receptor at all or of specific receptors? The reason seems pretty simple, especially in the case of innate responses. Assume there are some elicitors of fear, such as loss of support. The loss of support should induce a triggering of a receptor, with specific loci, the consequence being a whole series of connected behavioral and physiological responses including ANS and CNS behaviors—for example, the elicitation of the Moro reflex, with concomitant changes in heart rate, increased stress response, and adrenal–pituitary system release of cortisol. These responses would constitute the action pattern, something to be discussed shortly. The action pattern itself is the consequence perhaps of specific loci. On the other hand, there may be no specific loci for the set of reactions to a specific elicitor. While certainly not a central feature of my consideration of the development of emotional life, the development of receptors has some interest, especially given the research in a variety of domains that suggests that specific receptor activity is associated with specific events. Although there is little information on the topic, much of the research on emotion is predicated on the notion of specific brain regions that are related to specific responses.

ACTION PATTERNS IN HUMANS AND ANIMALS

While some researchers have considered emotional expressions apart from other emotional responses, here we will include emotional expression within the larger set of responses and use Darwin's phrase "action patterns." *Action patterns* are particular constellations of changes in the body including facial configurations, body movements, and changes in the ANS and CNS as well as in the hormone systems. Let us look at this set of responses while separately keeping in mind that their coordination is rather loose.

Expressions

From Darwin on, facial expressions are the one aspect of action patterns that have received the most attention. As we shall see, however, emotional action patterns include much more than facial patterns. In particular, the later, more complex self-conscious action patterns include bodily movement as well as facial expression. Thus shame is accompanied by body collapse while pride is accompanied by body expansion.

Emotional expressions are those potentially observable surface changes in face, voice, body, and activity level that make up part of an action pattern. Elaborate coding systems have been designed to measure the facial muscular changes in children and adults. The measuring systems were derived initially from Darwin's observations. Tomkins elaborated on these expressions, and both Izard and Paul Ekman devised facial coding systems that look at and examine muscle groups in the face that define specific emotions.[23] According to Ekman and Wallace Friesen, there are more than 10,000 possible combinations of facial muscle movements. The evolutionary history of facial neuromusculature suggests that facial expressions are a phylogenetic development, with human beings having more neuromusculature than any other mammal, including the great apes. The coding systems for both Ekman and Izard attend to those areas of the face that seem to reflect the most differentiated action patterns; these appear around the eyes, including degree of eye openness and eyebrow movement, and mouth.

Other manifestations of an action pattern are bodily movement. People studying body posture consider it under the rubric of nonverbal communication, while those studying facial expressions consider it under the rubric of emotion. The two groups publish their findings in different journals. This absence of any integration between the study of face and body movements is a problem both for understanding emotional action patterns and for studying their development. There is no question that bodily posture and facial expression inform the observer about the specific action pattern. For example, sitting upright and leaning forward in a chair when someone is speaking is associated with interest and attention, whereas slouching and turning away may indicate boredom. Some bodily postures convey sexual interest. For example, Birdwhistell suggests that, when courting, adults often throw the pelvis out to display more of the lower parts of the body.[24] Unfortunately, little work has been done in terms of body posture as a measure of emotional expression as it relates to other features of an action pattern, especially in children.[25] It is likely that for humans as well as for animals there are elaborate bodily displays or action patterns in need of greater clarification. As we shall see, from a developmental perspective, facial expressions are the usually measured action patterns in the young child, whereas expressions of posture and body movement as well as facial expression are measured in older children.

Vocalizations are also an aspect of emotional expression, and are certainly part of an action pattern. Klaus Scherer has developed techniques for analyzing the frequency patterns of infants' vocal behavior, finding, for example, that average pitch frequency can be used to determine anxiety or tension level.[26] Vocal expressions are extremely powerful and may have the capacity to elicit similar emotional action patterns in others, that is, they are contagious.[27] For example, movies seem to be much funnier when seen in the company of others who laugh out loud than when seen with a silent audience. For another example, people express more sadness and cry when others around them are crying. Because of their potential contagious nature, vocalizations may be the target of early socialization efforts in terms of eliminating them from the infant's behavioral repertoire. Although not well understood, vocal displays of the action patterns are considered inappropriate in many cultures, certainly in upper-middle-class American culture. People are not supposed to laugh too loudly when happy, to cry too intensely when sad or frustrated, to growl when angry, or to groan in pain. It is clear that we socialize verbal behavior. Think of what we say when we comfort a child with the words "It's okay, don't cry" or when we socialize an older child with the words "Don't cry, only babies cry." No wonder that in our studies of crying, we find a significant decrease in crying over the first 2 years.

Locomotion and body posture are other modes of expression. Running or moving away and moving toward an object or person are locomotive responses associated with the withdrawal and approach action patterns. Indeed, infant movement away from an unfamiliar toy or person, independent of facial expression, is often used to reference fear.[28] Following and holding a caregiver also reflects an attachment to the adult.

Although there is some data on emotional expressions in each of these four different modalities (facial, postural, vocal, and locomotive), the relation among the four has received almost no attention. It seems reasonable to assume that facial sobering, crying, and running away form a cohesive pattern of responses that reflect an action pattern associated with fear. On the other hand, a particular modality may be used to express an action pattern as a function of specific rules of socialization or a response hierarchy in which one modality takes precedence over another. It may be the case, for example, that the least intense action patterns are expressed first in facial, then in bodily, then in vocal behaviors. Such a hierarchy might be determined either by a set of biological imperatives or by a set of socialization rules. In the absence of any data on this problem, the relation among these different expressive modalities can only remain speculative. However, it is reasonable to propose that the more intense the action pattern, the greater the number of different modalities that would be used to express it.

The use of one or more channels to express a particular action pattern may be determined by a complex set of processes. Of particular interest is the effect on an expression when another is inhibited. Inhibition in a particular channel can be experimentally produced, for example, by preventing a child from moving about. Such conditions of inhibition may modify or alter the use of the uninhibited channels. For example, we have found that infants between 8 and 15 months, when prevented from running away from an approaching stranger because they are restrained in a highchair, will express their action pattern more intensely through facial neuromuscular changes. Interestingly, if children of similar age are allowed to roam freely, their facial expressions are significantly less active. The expression of locomoting away is sufficient to indicate distress, and thus facial expressions are needed less. Moreover, our research with Japanese and American babies reveals just such a process. When we observed facial expression and cortisol stress reactivity to inoculation in Japanese and American babies, we found that the Japanese infants showed far less facial reactivity, but higher levels of stress hormone than did the American babies.[29] Such a finding suggests that when facial expression is minimized for whatever reason, the other features of the action pattern may be more intense. Stephen Suomi found a similar negative association between increased stress hormones and decreased expression in his studies of monkeys. Thus the inhibition of one expression may lead individuals to express their action patterns in other ways.[30]

Emotional expressions also serve an important communication function; however, how people respond to expressions varies as a function of both their own values and cultural rules. Dacher Keltner and colleagues have addressed the importance of the communicative functions in that they provide information to others of individuals' emotional states, their intentions, and their relational status. Facial expressions can even serve as signals that elicit prepared responses in others.[31] This communicative function has two aspects. The information function serves to tell others what the child may be feeling, which in turn allows the adult to act accordingly. The development of knowledge about emotional expressions exists but it is mostly about the discrimination of different facial expressions in young children. As we will see, by 3 years of age children are quite good at knowing what facial expression is likely to occur in a particular context. Once consciousness emerges, the child can use emotional expressions to mislead the other as well. Feigning disappointment or anger, for example, can be used to manipulate others. Such deceptions serve a wide set of social needs. For example, the toddler can scream when his parents attempt to go out as a means of controlling their behavior. In fact, once the parents leave, most children quickly become calm and playful.

Moreover, deceptive expressions can be used to convey mock emotion; the exaggerated expression can have just the opposite intention. The Japanese are quite good at expressing mock emotions. For example, if your radio is too loud and is annoying your neighbor, a Japanese individual might say, "Oh what a lovely tone your radio has" or "I really enjoyed hearing that program." Because of the communicative value of expressions, it is important to remember that people's knowledge of the meaning of the expression, situations, and what cultural rules are appropriate for expressions, as well as the ability to control and manipulate internally one's own behavior, must play a significant role in emotional development. The topic of lying and deception, which I speak about later in Chapter 7, becomes important when studying emotional development.

In our discussion of the different aspects of expression, we need to consider two important questions. From a developmental perspective, how do the different expressive features of face, gestures, activity, and vocal behavior get organized? While Linda Camras has suggested the facial neuromusculature gets organized through a dynamic systems process, there is an even broader question, namely, how do all the expressive features of face, voice, and body movement get organized?[32] Perhaps, as she suggests, a dynamic system approach can handle this issue, but that remains to be seen. What are the governing rules that connect and disconnect emotional expressions of facial signs, body gestures, and vocal behaviors? Clearly the organizational principles for either question seem to need both learning and a biological perspective, like that of specific action patterns as suggested by Darwin. The dynamic system approach, with the idea of an attractor, seems similar to a biological-programmed action pattern since both are innate, and therefore it remains to be seen whether an attractor is a useful idea.

Theories about the development of emotional expressions depend on whether emotional expressions are seen as part of the innate adaptive action patterns that evolved to be connected to particular elicitors. Even more central to the issue of the development of emotional expression is the particular system used to measure expressions. Most of the information about emotional development derives from studies of facial expression.[33] Because the measurement systems for coding expressions other than facial ones are scarce, little is known about the development of other modalities of expression. In the study of facial expression, one problem that arises has to do with the nature of the elicitor. Since emotional expressions are the consequence of some elicitor, either learned, unlearned, or a combination of both, we need to know what situations are likely to make a child sad in order to study sad expressions. Since emotion elicitors have a developmental course, for no other reason than because of the growth of cognition, the study of the development of expressions is more complicated than it would seem at first. For example, the failure to observe an expression in response to a particular elicitor does not constitute grounds for concluding that the expression is not present at that age since it might appear under other elicitors. In the case of sadness, the selection of the elicitor has consequences since it seems that making an infant or young child very sad may raise a moral issue.

The meaning of the set of expressions is another issue. Investigators assume that particular faces reflect the emotion they expect to find. For example, in the stranger approach situation, we examine the expressions produced with the belief that they are part of the fear action pattern. In fact, it is uncertain whether infants in this situation are fearful, wary, or attentive, or if all strangers elicit fear. Since wary and attentive faces, as measured by current systems, have much in common, the context and its meaning is often used to interpret the particular face. The circularity is clear. We want to measure the fear response so we create situations that we think should lead to fear, and we measure the expressions produced as indicating fear.

The developmental course of the set of emotional expressions is relatively uncharted. Nevertheless, parents have no difficulty in responding to questions designed to examine their beliefs about when and where their children express emotions. Generally, parents tend to agree about when they think their children first show a particular emotion. It remains to be determined whether the parental responses are congruent or whether their answers reflect the belief system of their society. What little evidence is available on this question suggests that parents' belief systems trump what they actually observe in context, some of which will be discussed later when I talk about socialization and emotions gone awry in Chapter 11. Parents in cultures that place a strong emphasis on particular emotions may perceive these emotions emerging earlier than parents in other cultures. Thus, in one study, most American parents saw anger expressions in their babies within the first 3 months of life, whereas Japanese parents saw less anger overall and saw it emerging somewhat later.[34]

The development of emotional expression can be considered in terms of the ability both to produce various expressions and to recognize or discriminate among expressions. Although there is a considerable literature on infants' ability to discriminate facial expressions as well as their differential preference for certain facial expressions, only limited work has been done on the nature of the discrimination aspect of those features. An important theoretical issue is therefore raised. For the most part, investigators have concluded on the basis of such discrimination and preference data that infants are capable of facial expression differentiation. In fact, the data may not reflect the ability to discriminate emotions but a preference for a highly specific aspect of the face that has a different salience.[35] For example, is the discrimination of a sad versus a happy face based on differences in the hedonic qualities of the face or in teeth exposure, since the smiling face usually has more teeth showing?

There are those who see these expressions as having specific elicitors, although we recognize that even prototypical elicitors do not always produce specific facial patterns. This fact is likely to cause us to reject the idea that faces, body movements, and vocal behaviors may have a biological connection to specific elicitors. Clearly, the data do not support the strong view that specific elicitors are *always* hard-wired through evolutionary adaptive processes to specific action patterns. This belief has led to the counter idea, that there are no specific action patterns. However, as already suggested, we may not have a good sense of the nature of elicitors. J. J. Gibson, a perceptual–cognitive psychologist, wrote a wonderful paper on the nature of the stimuli (elicitor in our terms), arguing that psychologists spend too much time looking at responses rather than the nature of the stimulus. This conclusion is particularly relevant here since it may be that we have not looked carefully enough at the eliciting stimulus.[36]

Individual differences in the elicitation of expressions as a function of temperament also has not received the attention it deserves in relation to studying stimulus events that are related to action patterns. To reject the idea of an elicitor–action pattern as biologically connected leaves us with the idea that these expressions of face, body, and voice are learned and that their organization is learned. This alternative is hard to imagine.

In our discussion of the development of emotional life, an action pattern is viewed as a particular constellation of changes in the ANS, the CNS, and hormone system that accompanies emotional expressions and bodily behavior. These action patterns can and often do occur without the child's perception of these changes. For example, we find that 2-month-old infants who are frustrated by the blockage of a goal show an action pattern of approach. For the approach action pattern the infant shows an angry facial expression, increase in arm pull to reinstate the reward, increase in heart rate, and no increase in stress hormone. However, some few infants show a withdrawal action pattern; there is a sad face, little pulling, some increase in heart rate, and a large increase in stress hormone. These different action patterns to the same elicitor are likely due to differences in temperament and in socialization, although when older the child's own appraisal may produce individual differences as well.

Specific action patterns of the ANS, CNS, and hormonal system have received little support. It has been both a historical reality and a present result to find among these measures any coherence to such action patterns we call fear, happiness, sadness, and anger. Both the William James and Carl Lange and the Walter Cannon and Philip Bard theories of emotion stress somatic change, either muscular or neurophysiological, and the conscious feelings of these changes. These theories propose that emotion is an activating or energizing system, part of a drive-like system that led to the study of physiological manifestations.[37] In the 1950s, the work of John Lacey et al. most notably concluded that there was little synchrony between measures of the ANS such as heart rate, galvanic skin response (GSR), and respiration, and that without synchrony it was difficult to see a relation between the ANS and specific emotions.[38] This lack of association between specific emotions and physiology, more recently measured by brain activity, does not show any better association. Only hemisphere differences between such emotions as fear and sadness versus joy and anger, and little else, have been found.[39] The study of emotion has not provided us with data to support a strong association between expressions and physiological change. This seems to be true for infants and young children as well as adults.

In a recent review of the research with infants on facial expressions and the ANS, CNS, and hormonal system, we found that in the studies to date there is little relation between these systems; the overall correlation between expression and physiology was about .30. Nevertheless, as already reported, we have shown some association between specific facial expression, body activity, and the ANS and hormonal systems. To find such associations, however, required us to select our elicitors carefully. Even so, the synchrony between expressions and physiological responses was found to be moderate. Our work over many studies looking at the ANS and hormonal systems has found only modest support for the specific elicitor–action pattern association.[40]

Given the belief in the relationship between specific action patterns and specific elicitors, at least in the early part of life, why did we find only a weak association? This may well be due to our measurement procedure. Improved measurement techniques, however, may never result in a high association between features that make up expected action patterns and the elicitors of them. The need of children may be that both synchrony and asynchrony are structural properties of their biological systems. Both may be essential for efficient functioning since it is necessary for the organism both to act and to inhibit action. Synchrony between physiological systems and expressions may be needed to produce action. Having all response systems acting together in concert would seem to provide a most powerful response. Nevertheless, it might not be efficient for inhibiting the action pattern once elicited. If all response systems are activated and highly synchronous when activated, there are few ways that the organism can inhibit the actions; there are no aspects of the response system when highly synchronous that are left to help inhibit ongoing behavior. Thus, it may be the case that a critical feature of any organism's behavior is its ability both to activate and to inhibit ongoing behavior.[41] *I would propose that the asynchrony between the ANS, cortisol reactivity, brain, and behavioral systems function in order to inhibit as well as to activate behavior.* This suggests that in highly arousing conditions action patterns are activated faster and take longer to terminate, with the termination being affected by the general inhibitory activity responses, a kind of fatigue. For everyday situations, and certainly for laboratory situations, where ethics limit our ability to create highly arousing stimuli, lower or little-organized action activating patterns are needed. Much of the results in the literature in infancy make sense in light of this need for action and inhibition. Frightened infants left alone without their mothers and approached by a stranger in a strange situation are in high state of arousal, and as Campos et al.'s results suggest, facial expression, motoric activity, and heart rate are more likely to show a higher coherence than when the infant's mother is physically close, which produces a less arousing condition than when she is not close.[42]

Although there are little data to support individual child differences, it does not seem unreasonable to imagine individual difference in action pattern synchrony. Some organisms, as a function of some combination of temperament, nervous system efficiency, or even socialization, may show more covariation than others. Almost 100 years ago, Edmund Prideaux found individual differences in synchrony. Adults who showed large and frequent GSR also showed less overt emotional behavior than adults who showed less GSR. Similar findings have been reported by others.[43] This lack of synchrony has been used by some to categorize individuals into internalizers and externalizers, those who express emotion internally, as in GSR, and those who express emotion externally, as in facial changes.[44]

Our studies, as well as the studies of others, have shown that specific elicitor–action patterns, having unique sets of behaviors including facial, bodily, and vocal changes, exist, although the association is weak for some connections. There may be many reasons for these findings including measurement error, individual differences including temperament, and socialization factors, all of which decrease the association between specific events and the child's action pattern.

Nevertheless, I hold to the view that there are biologically organized action patterns, that they are evolutionarily derived and therefore adaptive, and that they provide the engine for the infant and young child's response to a set of elicitors in the physical world. Discovering these coherent patterns is not easy given that they are influenced by many factors including temporal discontinuity between responses, temperamental and cognitive differences in children, and variations in the socialization practices of the child's caregivers and family.

EMOTIONAL EXPERIENCES

The discussion of experience brings us back to our consideration of consciousness. William James defined emotions as the experiencing of the body: "the bodily changes [that] follow directly the perception of the exciting fact and our feeling of the same changes and as they occur."[45] Following James, for some theorists, the emotional experience rather than any bodily change is what we mean by an emotion. The question then, is What is an experience? As I tried to make clear in Chapter 1, one of the most complicated concerns centers around experience. To repeat, experience can be at multiple levels, including the body experiencing the level of sugar in the system and adjusting the secretion of insulin. In any complex system like a body, one part has to experience something in another part in order to regulate bodily functioning. These experiences are not mental representations, they are not open to our awareness. At another level, experience can mean a mental act or mentalism having a representation of me. Such a mental representation is what I mean by consciousness. The difficulty of distinguishing between these two levels of experience is made even more so when we use the term "feeling," since feeling, like experience, can be considered to have two different levels. For the sake of the theory of development, I hold to the belief that the bodily experience or feeling is present at birth and is likely to exist across the animal kingdom. It is the second level of experience or feeling that may be unique to humans and that has a developmental course. It is this second level of experience that finds common ground with attribution and evaluative theories since the cognitions involved with these are complex and require time for their development.

In order to have an emotion, a precipitating event or elicitor ("exciting fact") must occur and cause a bodily change, or an action pattern, and this pattern has to be experienced. Thus, emotion is not defined only as the precipitating event, nor as the bodily change associated with that event, but as both, as well as the experiencing of that bodily change. Although the nature of the bodily change has been questioned, proponents of James's theory have maintained that the conscious feeling of bodily change is as central to the concept of emotion as is the bodily change itself. This experience or feeling of James has become, at least for some—for example, Richard Lazarus—an evaluative process that determines what emotion we will have. This evaluation may involve contextual cues and past experiences, and is likely to have large individual differences.[46]

The experience or feeling of the person, defined as a feeling by James, is a cognitive evaluation that I believe develops over the first years of the child's life. Emotional experience is, therefore, not an automatic bodily response connected in a one-to-one relation to an action pattern, although Izard, for one, has thought so.[47] Rather, emotional experiences, more than any other component of emotional life, are the most cognitive and learned aspect of what we think of as emotions. Cultural and individual differences are apt to be the most apparent here.

The development of emotional experience is one of the least studied aspects of emotion and emotional development, perhaps because the idea of experience is a difficult concept in the study of development. When I speak of experience, reference is made to a specific mental activity, one that I have called "consciousness." While I have touched on the development of self-referential behavior and self-attribution, here and in Chapter 1, it will be discussed in more detail in Chapter 5.

Since there is no reason to assume that emotional experience necessarily has a one-to-one relation with an action pattern-in-context, the development of experience may occur long after the emergence of these action patterns that we see at the beginning of life. What this means is that while newborns may show an action pattern called sadness when interactions with their mothers suddenly stop, it does not necessarily follow that they have an experience of that sadness.

The topic of emotional experience is quite complex, requiring us to distinguish between the organism's possession of some fundamental cognitive ability—including the ability to perceive and discriminate, recall, associate, and compare at a minimum—and emotional experiences that require a particular cognitive ability, which is a self-representation. Until an organism is capable of a mental representation of itself, something that occurs between 15 and 24 months of age in the normally developing child, the second aspect of experience is not possible. In Chapter 5, I make the argument that emotional experience is a maturational process dependent on the development of particular areas of the brain. Although it likely develops slowly, we can observe it by the end of the second year of life. Besides maturation of specific brain regions, the emergence of an "I" who can experience particular elicitors and action patterns is dependent on children's interaction with their social world. The expressions in context are what adults use to interpret their children's emotions, which with brain maturation give content to the child's experience. Thus the very act of interpretation and evaluation by the social environment provides the rules by which children learn to evaluate and interpret their own action patterns once they become capable of cognitively representing themselves.

* * *

Having separated the term "emotion" into its components, we need to put it back together again, for indeed these features of emotion occur altogether in an organism and are connected intimately one to another. This reconstruction will occupy much of what is to follow in the subsequent chapters. The term "emotion" is a fuzzy concept which is nonetheless familiar to all members of our species. When I say or think that "I am happy," I am referring to a complex set of loosely connected events. These include an elicitor or context, which is adaptively connected, but culturally influenced, to a set of action patterns that consist of external manifestations called expressions, as well as a set of physiological responses. Because humans have consciousness, that is, a representation of themselves, they are capable of interpreting these elicitors and action patterns as a function of cultural exposure through the caregiving environment. Since there is emotional development, we need to keep in mind that elicitors, which in the beginning of life are literal physical events, later become ideas. Thus the thrust of the developmental model to be presented is that action patterns originally produced by specific elicitors in the physical world become, with time, elicited by ideas, by human constructions.

CHAPTER 3

Multiple Emotions and Moods

Having dissected what it might mean when we say an "emotion" into at least the three elements of elicitor, action pattern, and experience, two further questions need to be considered. Until now we have been talking as if we can study a single emotion, implying that our emotional life is made up of a series of single emotions. The idea of single emotions has received some attention; however, in the study of development not much interest in this problem has been shown. Is there a series of single emotions, one like joy and one like sadness, or is it our idea about our emotional lives and our use of language? For example, when the father of the bride says that he is both sad and happy when his daughter gets married, he is acknowledging that two different emotions, even opposite emotions, can be elicited by a single event. Our emotional lives may be made up of multiple emotions at any one time. In this chapter, this problem will be addressed in the section called "I Can Be Sad and Happy at the Same Time." A child's response to the approach of a stranger can elicit both interest and wariness at the same time. This reaction has important implications for development since it raises the question of what does "at the same time" mean? This issue addresses the important question of whether there are such things as a single emotion or is it likely to be a function of our language use. James Russell has been a leader in trying to understand this quandary from a developmental perspective.[1]

The second question addressed here is about the difference between transient and enduring action patterns. I use the term "action pattern" instead of the term "emotion" since we have no measure of the child's experience. Most studies of development examine the infant and young child's response to a single elicitor, such as the taste of something sour or the approach of a stranger. But the study of individual differences in emotional development, whether the subject is developmental psychopathology or differences in personality, has relied on the report or the observation of enduring action patterns. These enduring patterns are also called "moods," and as such have been related to the idea of personality.[2] Enduring action patterns or moods refer to children's characteristics or enduring likely patterns of behavior. How these characteristics are related to transient responses to particular elicitors is not understood. Moreover, the terms "temperament" and "moods" are confusing since temperament has been defined by some as enduring moods. What we have then is some overlap between the idea of a personality, having a particular mood, and temperament. This distinction can be illustrated by the transient sad response of a child to an ice cream cone falling on the ground versus enduring sadness in a depressed child.

In *Emotions and Moods*, Linda Michalson and I discussed how we used multiple eliciting situations to measure the likelihood of a particular set of enduring action patterns. We used repeated transient responses to repeated classes of elicitors and summed the responses across days to allow us to create a measure of a child's enduring action pattern to that particular class of elicitors. By using such an observational approach it was possible to classify one child, relative to another, as appearing to show more of a particular emotion and therefore exhibiting a mood. Looking across different moods we were able to measure a child's profile. Let us consider sadness as a mood. By measuring the child's behavior to multiple situations of potential sadness in a daycare environment (e.g., the mother leaving her child, the child's response to a broken toy) we were able to capture the differences in children's overall sadness behavior. Our measurement of sad responses allowed us to estimate how sad a child appears to be. Looking across different situations thought to produce such responses as happiness or anger, we created a profile of enduring emotional responses for each emotion for each child. This profile of moods looked surprisingly like a personality description. We found these profiles of enduring moods to be most similar to what is obtained by having the teacher or mother of the child fill out a questionnaire that when summed across items also generates a personality profile. The Child Behavior Checklist, a widely used profile of the child's potential psychopathology, does just this.[3]

In this chapter we will examine multiple transient responses to a particular elicitor and multiple examples of an elicitor in order to obtain the likelihood of eliciting the same action pattern over and over again.

I CAN BE SAD AND HAPPY AT THE SAME TIME

In the preceeding chapter we discussed the structure of emotion as having an action pattern to an elicitor, which consists of facial expressions, bodily activity, and physiological responses, as well as experience. In that discussion we considered *an* action pattern as a basic unit of emotional life. However, we have already raised the question of whether we have specific action patterns or whether we have multiple action patterns to a specific elicitor. Given that experiences are also part of what we have called emotion, is it the case that we have a specific experience to a specific action pattern-in-context, or might we have multiple experiences?

The developmental model found in this book suggests only a weak connection between an action pattern and a mental experience of it. This weak connection between the two is readily influenced by socialization factors and the infant's temperament. Specifically, the relation between action patterns-in-context and the toddler's mental experiences of them follows this developmental course: prior to the infant's development of a mental self-representation, an elicitor, for example, a blocked goal, is likely to produce the specific action pattern-in-context, in this case anger. Once a mental self-representation appears—something we call consciousness—children experience their anger. Socialization practices, including language usage, give rise to specific experiences, language, and representations, including facial recognition. For example, the specific action pattern of anger to a blocked goal once the child has the capacity to experience it, can through the socialization practices of the parents be labeled anger and therefore experienced as anger.

Here the case of the difference in Japanese and American socialization practices around the anger action pattern should be noted. That Japanese mothers report less anger in their children than American mothers report suggests that the Japanese mothers' socialization practices will result in the Japanese child's experiencing less anger than the American child around the same elicitor. Indeed, if one witnesses the behavior of Japanese in the Tokyo subway system and then asks riders about their experience during the crush of rush hour, one finds that few Japanese label their experience as "anger." Of course socialization practices, including language, can produce mental experiences of multiple emotions that are at odds with the action pattern exhibited.

Part of the problem in studying development is that the elicitors used in studies are usually complex and therefore are likely to produce multiple action patterns, either in series or all at once. Under such conditions, socialization practices can give rise to a predominant experience, or to multiple experiences in a sequential pattern, or to a mixture of experiences at the same time.

The question of the relation between an action pattern and an experience as influenced by socialization, including language and temperament, raises the related question of whether there are multiple action patterns to many elicitors and if we experience them as a singular one in a connected series as a function of language, learning, or labeling. James Russell has grappled with these questions for some time, as has Izard.[4] In an attempt to answer these questions, Russell and his colleague, Sherri Widen, have proposed that emotions (or at least experiences of them) occur around two possibilities:

> One possibility is that children begin with an innate, or at least prepared, set of discrete mental categories for at least those emotions with corresponding facial expressions. . . . With a prepared understanding of the link between emotion [experience] and facial expressions, a child can build a script of that emotion by adding information about the causes, consequences, label, and so on, as that information is acquired. In other words, the early recognition of facial expressions in terms of discrete emotions has been assumed to be the basis—the bedrock—of young children's understanding of emotion and to provide the foundation on which later learning about emotion is built.[5]

They also suggest an alternate explanation, which involves the socialization of experiences: "Children initially understand emotions in very broad mental categories and over the course of development differentiate these categories into narrower, more adult-like ones. . . . Initially, children begin with two categories based on a single pleasure versus displeasure dimension. What cues are initially tied to these categories is an empirical question."[6] This view suggests that experiences may have some limitation and are tied to broad categories of action patterns, such as approach and withdrawal. These undifferentiated action patterns have associated with them two undifferentiated experiences, which through socialization are differentiated.

Russell and Widen address this question by looking at script knowledge and preschoolers' categorization through the study of knowledge as a way to observe mental states or experience.[7] The problem in studying experience developmentally is that experience needs to be language-based and therefore can only be studied at age 3 or so, far after experiences as mental states about "me" develop.

I suspect that the development of language and that language itself tend to restrict our idea of whether there are specific experiences. In the same manner, does our language about emotions work this way? We have words for each separate action pattern and emotion, and thus we may think about them and perceive them in others in a particular way. The question becomes, Are the emotional words real scientific units or just units of words that we learn and that may differ by culture? For those who believe in single units biologically linked with specific behavior, our experiences of them must be based on cultural learning. The action patterns and our experiences are both real, with the former more based on biological forces, while the latter is more based on culture.

Following Russell's suggestion, we can explore whether multiple emotional expressions are prompted by an elicitor in both children and adults. To do so we presented young children with pictures of specific situations as elicitors and we asked them to choose from a set of facial expressions which they thought the children in the situations were likely to have. In one study we presented schematic drawings of specific situations without faces, like a girl's birthday party, and asked children, some as young as 2½ years, to look at a set of facial expressions from which they could choose the facial expressions the birthday girl might have. The facial expressions included happy, sad, angry, disgusted, and fearful. When asked what face would go with the birthday party, the young children chose happy first, but since we gave them the opportunity to pick more than one facial expressions, they did. Surprisingly, these second choices included sad faces and fearful faces. When asked about being lost in a store, the children chose sad faces, but also angry faces. In another study, we asked adolescents about what emotions go with different situations: "What do you think people feel when they are (1) at the wedding of a friend, (2) their own wedding, (3) at the wedding of their children? What do you think people feel (4) at their graduation ceremony and what do you think parents feel (5) at their children's graduation ceremony?" Finally, we asked, "What do you think people feel at a friend's funeral and what do you think people feel at their parent's funeral?" The results of these studies reveal the kinds of experience that are elicited when subjects are presented with different elicitors. First, it is clear that young children, like adolescents and adults, have knowledge about what emotional faces are appropriate in what situations. None, for example, said that happiness is the emotion experienced when being lost in a store or at the death of a friend. For young children, those ages 2 to 5 years, there appears to be less disagreement as to the experiences the other child might have, as a function both of their labeling behavior and of their knowledge of what faces go with what situations.[8] What is clear is that both Lewis and Michalson and Widen and Russell found that 2-year-olds seem to have knowledge about the experiences of happy and sad.

Another result is that young children, when given the opportunity, will identify multiple-emotion facial expressions in each of these situations. Most all adolescents, for example, in response to the question about the graduation of a friend, gave us as the first emotional term, happy, while the second emotional term varied from excited, to proud, to jealous, to relieved, and even to cynical. In answer to the question, "What would you feel when *you* graduate from school," fewer than half the adolescents gave happiness as their first response; many others gave fear or sadness. While it appeared that happiness was the one most likely emotion experienced when graduating from school, it was not the only emotion expressed since most of the adolescents chose more than one facial expression for this situation. They seem to believe that more than one emotion is likely to be experienced to any particular elicitor. To extrapolate from these limited findings, it appears that people understand that specific situations are likely to elicit multiple emotions. Indeed, it is likely that multiple emotional responses to any situation may be more the rule than the exception.

Take for another example the wedding of one's child, which is likely to elicit the experiences of happiness and sadness. This response raises several questions: Are two separate emotions elicited by this situation? Or is this situation in reality a multiple elicitor—of success and of loss? Perhaps any situation produces multiple elicitors. Another possibility is that we do not have language that would capture these two experiences at the same time. We just do not know the answer to all these questions. However, I do want to pursue the language question.

Because we only have the emotional words *happy* and *sad,* they are likely to be experienced as separate. If we had a term for the combined experience of happy and sad, for example, if we used the term "hady," and we had learned that "hady" occurs at weddings, then if we were required to report on the emotions elicited, we would be likely to say "hady" rather than happy and sad. If this is so, then can we say that happy and sad are separate experiences or is our experience only dependent on language? Does the absence of a language that could describe both experiences at the same time limit our ability to think of them as mixtures? The absence, at least in the English language, of unique labels for mixed experiences leaves the question unanswered. Perhaps an analogous case in the color lexicon may be of help.[9] The English lexicon includes terms for mixtures of simpler colors, for example, aqua, a mixture of blue and green, and purple, a mixture of red and blue. The terms "aqua" and "purple" convey meaning in themselves apart from the colors that comprise them. In analogous fashion, language can be adapted to include terms that convey mixed emotions.

Mixed emotional terms can readily be found. For example, "abhimen" is an Indian term for the experience of prideful loving anger, and "liget" is the word for a mixture of grief and anger for the Ilongot people.[10] However, it is clear that in the English language there are a multitude of emotional mixture words in usage, some of which are quite familiar—for example, melancholy is a mixture of sadness and grief. Like the names for the mixtures of color, of which there are many—Crayola has 128 different colors in its largest box—one's knowledge of them has to be learned and so they are therefore differentially known. How many people can describe the color burgundy and therefore know its components of brown and red?

It is likely that multiple action patterns as a result of an elicitor exist in infancy and early childhood. Certainly the approach of a stranger can elicit both interest and wariness action patterns in infants as young as 8 months. Moreover, at very early ages elicitors like a sour taste, the approach of a stranger or an unusual robot, or constraining the child's arm movements produce multiple emotional facial expressions.[11] Multiple emotional faces are given by children as young as 2 to 3 years when they are allowed the choice of multiple faces to assign to a heroine in a story, and multiple emotions to a spoken script can be seen in adolescents and adults. However, often in studies the first emotional expression elicited is the only one scored since if we believe a certain single emotion will be connected to an elicitor, it is only the presence or absence of that emotion that will be scored. See, for example, the studies of Michalson and Lewis and Widen and Russell. In addition, while the facial coding systems that now exist for studying infants' facial expressions do allow for mixtures of action patterns—for example, it is possible to record the eye opening and the mouth muscle movement that are not concordant with a "given" emotion expression—most studies only report on the facial expressions that are concordant with a known facial expression, such as sad or joyful. Margaret Sullivan and I, looking at infants' responses to specific elicitors, found that at least 30–40% of the facial expressions elicited contained mixed facial neuromusculative activity; the percentage was even higher relative to specific emotional expressions.

Given these data, I think it safe to conclude that the problem of the stimulus, as J. J. Gibson wrote,[12] remains. Most of the elicitors (stimuli) that we use to study infants are too complex to get at both unique action patterns. Moreover, once the development of mentalism occurs, the child's idea about the elicitor (which is unknown) is more likely the elicitor and these ideas are apt with increasing maturation to be complex and to vary by both socialization and temperament.

A Study of Disgust

The issue of multiple emotions aroused by an elicitor is beginning to receive more attention in the study of adult emotional life. To look at this issue in more detail we will discuss what we have found using the emotion of disgust. Based on Darwin's work, we consider the elicitation of disgust as an example of an action pattern related to food rejection and characterized by raised nose, open mouth, and sometimes tongue protrusion. This view of disgust as a single action pattern rests on the belief that disgust is biologically fixed with distinct characteristics. The behavioral, physiological, and expressive characteristics were originally viewed as a distancing/rejection response to food-related stimuli, such as rotting foods or odors. However, we now know that there are many elicitors that evoke disgust, including insects, invertebrates, other animals, body products, poor hygiene, mutilation, sex, and death. Moreover, we have learned that disgust can be elicited by people considered foreign or "socially deviant" (e.g., Muslims, for Westerners) and to acts of racism or human rights violations.[13] While a wide range of elicitors may produce disgust, the question is, Is disgust the only emotion elicited?

To study this problem Jason Gold and I asked undergraduates to view 20 color pictures representing four different types of disgust elicitors and to rate the amount of disgust, fear, anger, sadness, and happiness they felt when seeing each picture. The four categories of disgust elicitors were *Bugs*, which included images of insects, spiders, cockroaches, and invertebrates such as worms; *Mutilation,* which consisted of pictures of human or animal injuries such as a severed hand, a half-severed jaw, or a deformed mouth; *Dirt,* which was made up of images of garbage and debris; and *Body Products,* which included images of human and animal feces, vomit, and mucus.

We found that for *Bug* pictures, disgust was the dominant response; however, fear was the next most elicited response. For pictures of *Mutilations,* disgust again was the most elicited response; however, sadness, fear, and anger were also elicited. For *Dirt* pictures, disgust was most mentioned, while anger and sadness were next. For pictures of *Body Products,* disgust was the predominant response while few others were mentioned. Thus for the *Body Products* category, it appears that disgust was singularly elicited.

Since our interest was in disgust experiences, we expected disgust to be the dominant emotion reported. However, we found complex multiple emotions and the pattern of these multiple emotions differed by the type of elicitors. What are of particular interest are the multiple emotions experienced. *Bugs* evoked both disgust and fear and this combination seems to play a central role in the human fear of small animals, like spiders and, at its extreme expression, phobic responses.[14] That insect pictures evoke multiple emotions of disgust and fear has implications for the treatment of phobias since this finding may be helpful in understanding avoidant behaviors as well as their association with maladaptive thoughts and beliefs. Pictures of *Dirt,* on the other hand, elicited disgust and anger. Disgust and anger at a perceived fouling of the environment is often evident in racist propaganda. For example, Nazi propaganda portrayed Jews as rats and referred to them as vermin. During the Rwandan genocide Hutu leaders referred to the Tutsis as "invenzi," or "the cockroaches that need to be crushed."[15] In specific contexts, the mixture of disgust and anger or disgust and fear may limit empathy and support prejudice, racism, and direct aggression.

The greatest mixture of emotions was found in response to the *Mutilation* pictures, where both sadness and fear along with disgust were evoked. Bodily mutilation may be a complex elicitor, prompting disgust at body mutilation, sadness out of empathic pain for the other, and fear for one's own safety. We both pity the leper and fear him; we have a desire to be compassionate toward the ill or injured as well as to isolate ourselves from them. Bodily mutilation may elicit different cognitions since the mutilations are due to accidents, which makes it different from those elicitors that appear more natural. If so, bodily mutilations may be a multiple elicitor.

Pictures of *Body Products* only elicited disgust. Disgust by itself is likely to lead to high avoidant behavior, which serves to protect us from disease. In the case of psychopathology, individuals with obsessive–compulsive disorder may misperceive their vulnerability to infection or contamination, which results in pathological behaviors, such as intense washing rituals. It is interesting to note that the study of multiple emotional responses to a class of stimuli bears some relation to characterological as well as to cultural types of behavior. As disgust has been linked to psychopathologies such as specific phobias, obsessive–compulsive disorders, sexual dysfunction, and eating disorders, understanding the full range of emotions that accompany disgust also has implications for understanding many different clinical disorders.[16] Moreover, the multiple emotions associated with types of disgust stimuli can clarify inconsistent and contradictory results in studies attempting to identify the neurological correlates of disgust. For example, several studies find brain activation in response to disgust in the anterior insula region, while others do not. The use of different types of disgust stimuli and the different and multiple emotions they may elicit may explain this lack of consistency.

Our results show that multiple emotions are elicited by disgust pictures and situations such that even these elicitors, which easily produce disgust ratings, also produce multiple emotions. Such findings suggest that elicitors are likely to produce multiple emotional experiences as well as action patterns rather than just one. This should be the case for all types of elicitors. That this is the case can be seen in the work of John Cacioppo and Jeffrey Larsen, who have shown that for adults, multiple experiences can be produced when asking them what emotions they would experience in response to particular events. In one study, Larsen and colleagues asked adults about what emotions they might feel when they graduated from college and found that multiple emotions, even opposite emotions such as happy and sad, were offered, a finding similar to our own.[17]

One of the issues raised by these findings is related to our earlier question about when there are two different action patterns or experiences, do they follow in some order one after the other, or are they experienced at the same time? This distinction is important for many reasons. For one, James Russell's conception of emotional life argues against the elicitation of opposite emotions such as happy and sad.[18] For another, sequential elicitation of multiple emotions still allows us to consider that there is such a thing as a single emotion. This is so even if we could show vacillation between them.

A variety of methods have been used to try and separate out whether the multiple emotions elicited are sequential or simultaneous, including having people press buttons for each of a set of emotions. If they pressed them at once, then it could be argued that they were occurring simultaneously. This research and more recent work by Larsen and colleagues suggest simultaneous emotions can be elicited.[19]

While these studies indicate that in adults, these verbal responses suggest simultaneous emotions to an elicitor, problems still exist. Of most concern is the problem of language, in that both *happy* and *sad* were words used in the study. Thus the adults had two separate basic units to address. Second, since they were thinking of the two emotions, their thoughts had to be sequential since they had no word for a combined emotion. Such concerns do not allow us to answer the question in a satisfactory manner. As I suggested earlier, the best way to address this is to use a term that combines happy and sad, such as "hady," and then train people to use three buttons to press, one for sad, one for happy, and one for hady. If after training hady was used more than sad or happy, when appropriate we might have a better idea as to the nature of multiple emotional elicitations.

The production of multiple and mixed emotional facial expressions to an elicitor has been used by Linda Camras among others to argue against the idea perpetuated by Darwin that through evolutionary adaptive processes there develops an association between an elicitor and a particular action pattern.[20] As I have already stated, there are several difficulties with the association between elicitor and action pattern. To begin with, the nature of an elicitor is not always so simple. Thus, the wedding of a daughter may not be an elicitor but a collection of them. In the same way the restriction of the infant's hands by its mother or an unfamiliar adult in order to elicit anger has to involve a complex elicitor including physical touch, social exchange, unexpected behavior, and an unusual blank facial expression of the adult. In this case it would be difficult to say that there was *an* elicitor, and thus multiple or mixed action patterns are likely to occur to the multiple elicitors. In order to really test the elicitor–action pattern association as proposed by Darwin, a highly specific elicitor needs to be presented. In fact, as we will see, when we make an elicitor highly specific, a highly specific action pattern results. We shall talk about such studies later but mention now only that the elicitor of a blocked prelearned response to a goal is, as Darwin suggested, an elicitor of the action pattern we call anger.

It also needs to be kept in mind that an elicitor can produce multiple action patterns that are hierarchically arranged. Thus, as in the example of disgust stimuli, disgust may be the primary action pattern elicited, but others too may be produced as a function of the exact nature of the disgust elicitor. Finally, to these issues we need to add the fact of individual child temperament differences that may affect the nature of the set of action patterns produced by an elicitor. Given these factors, it is too early to reject the idea of an adaptive association between elicitor and action pattern. What the findings do inform us of at this point is that an easily elicited single action pattern is too simple an idea, and that any theory of emotional development needs to take into account the idea of multiple emotional responses to any elicitor as well as the real possibility that an elicitor is likely, if we are not careful, to be an elicitor of more than one action pattern.

EMOTIONS AS MOODS

In any discussion of the idea of the enduring quality of an emotion we need to address several issues: (1) how long a discrete action pattern lasts; (2) the effect of another, or even the same, action pattern on the following action pattern; (3) the manner in which an enduring action pattern may set the background for other action patterns—for example, the role of a traumatic event and its effect on subsequent patterns, or as a setup to produce more of the same action pattern; and (4) temperament as an enduring action pattern and how the set of enduring action patterns fits with our idea of what a personality is.

The enduring features of an emotion can be described from several points of view. Keeping in mind that emotions are made up of elicitors, action patterns, and experiences, each one of these elements can be enduring. While most focus has been on the duration of an action pattern, duration of ideas about the self and others, including events, can also vary. If we examine the duration of emotion, for example, sadness over an ice cream cone falling to the ground, we see it can be of short duration in both the duration of the action pattern and/or the experience of the child, especially if another cone is provided. However, this emotion, both its experience and its action pattern, could be of a longer duration depending on the child's desire to eat the cone, or could be of longer duration if another sad eliciting event occurred prior to the cone falling. So, for example, if the child was given the cone because earlier she had scraped her knee, the sadness emotion to the cone falling would likely be longer and perhaps even more intense. Such an observation should alert us to the realization that even transient elicitors, their action pattern responses, and experiences are part of the continuous flow of our emotional lives, with previous events affecting later ones. The study of transient events distorts this flow. Although this distortion occurs in the observation of children's emotional life, it would be most difficult to measure it as a continuous series of elicitors, responses, and experiences. Certainly, almost all of the studies of emotional development and emotional responses are more like snapshot photographs than motion pictures or, as I have suggested, a fugue (see Chapter 12), especially when other mental activities, such as experiences, in addition to action patterns are considered.[21]

   The problem of a continuous flow of elicitors, action patterns, and self-cognitions creates difficulties in studying them because an elicitor can lead to an action pattern and to an experience, both of which can serve as an elicitor of the same or a different action pattern and experience. Then exactly what precedes what? The breaking of this fugue is arbitrary and has led some to claim that mental acts produce emotional action patterns, while others claim that action patterns lead to mental acts.[22] What is important for our purpose is to keep in mind that in any study of a transient event, the preceding events may strongly influence the observation itself.

   Let me give you an example of the influence of earlier emotions on later ones. Gail Wasserman and I studied a group of mothers and their 1-year-old children.[23] The children were divided into two groups to counterbalance the presentation of two events in order to observe the effect of an earlier elicitor on a subsequent one. For the first group of 1-year-olds, the first elicitor was the mothers' interaction with their babies in a play situation for 15 minutes, and the second elicitor was the termination of their interaction and the mother remaining passive and unresponsive for the next 15 minutes. For the second group of children the elicitors were reversed; first, the passive experience and second the interactive one. The results supported the idea that earlier elicitors can affect the action patterns of later ones. For example, the infants touched their mothers more in the noninteractive condition if it occurred after the interaction one, which was also the case for the infant's proximity seeking. While there are few studies of this type, it is reasonable to think that a stressor after an earlier stressor will have a greater effect than the same stressor without the earlier one. This is why Mary Ainsworth's attachment paradigm uses two stressors, in this case the mother leaving the child alone in a strange room.[24]

   Exactly what sequences facilitate, inhibit, or alter subsequent experiences is unclear since there has been relatively little work on this topic. I would predict that if a child experiences a sad event after having experienced a previous sad event, sadness will endure longer and be more intense. Thus, if the child's dog dies after his best friend goes on vacation, the sadness experienced over these sequentially occurring events is likely to produce a different quality or intensity of sadness than if there were only one event. Many examples of the combined effects of sequential elicitors and action patterns can be imagined; a sad elicitor followed by another sad one is likely to result in a longer action pattern and certainly a longer or stronger experience than an isolated occurrence of the sad elicitor. Repeated elicitation of an excitement action pattern is also likely to lead to an unpleasurable action pattern; continuous tickling may at first lead to laughter and glee, and then later lead to upset and crying. On the other hand, an elicitor leading to an amusing experience that occurs after an elicitor leading to a frightening experience may not be amusing or might be more so. We just do not know. In all the examples that we could produce—the elicitor, the action pattern, and the experience—the experience may be prolonged, enhanced, or altered by the events preceding it. These examples underscore the interdependence of emotions as well as the flow of emotional life. If we consider that the emotional life of the infant, child, and adult is a complex fugue of elicitors, action patterns, and experiences as a function also of socialization and temperament, we must appreciate that there is never a "base" period where nothing is happening. Instead we are likely to move from one experience to another, and this being the case we need to begin to study the ongoing contextual features in which emotions take place.[25]

EMOTIONS AND PERSONALITY

When we talk about a person's personality that involves emotions we are talking about something like a mood; for example, "he is a sad person" implies that he shows us sad behaviors and/or that he reports that he feels sad. These sad behaviors and feelings are not transient actions but have a long duration or occur frequently. *Personality* is usually defined as enduring behaviors or experiences over time and over different events. In some sense, then, action patterns and experiences that are enduring are similar to at least some aspects of personality.[26]

This observation fits with our understanding that personality profiles are in fact made up of emotions that are enduring. Exactly how enduring these emotions are and what causes their long duration, therefore resulting in a personality characteristic, is not clear. So, for example, the loss of an ice cream cone can cause a short duration of sadness, while the death of a pet can cause a longer duration of sadness; thus, besides a connection to past events, the enduring feature can in large part be made up of how a person experiences the elicitor and/or action pattern. We even know that a single elicitor is capable of producing an enduring sadness, as well as a series of sad elicitors can. The case of a single elicitor of sadness producing an enduring characteristic is captured by the idea of a traumatic event. Characteristic sadness, then, might produce a background wherein other transient sadness might be more likely to occur. Thus, a traumatic event can act both to produce the enduring emotion and to increase the likelihood of further ones.

This idea sounds familiar to us since it is the basis of theories of developmental psychopathology for both Freud and Bowlby.[27] In Bowlby's analysis of Darwin's emotional life, for example, he emphasizes the idea that Darwin's later physical illness was a consequence of the depression, an enduring sadness, which was the result of the death of his mother when he was 8 years old. This produced a background characteristic that affected each stressful moment (elicitors) during his life and resulted in somatic complaints. The interaction of the child's temperament with the occurrence of traumatic events is given only brief attention by Bowlby, but as I have indicated there are only a few studies that examine the interaction of temperament with attachment. The recent work by Suomi with monkeys, in which specific genetic factors are shown to interact with different rearing conditions, is an example of the research that is needed.[28] Later in this chapter, the topic of temperament as enduring emotions is addressed; a more complete discussion of temperament will be found in Chapter 9. A produced enduring emotion need not be permanent. While an enduring emotion may act on subsequent life events, the enduring emotion could be either sustained or altered. The underlying belief in all different types of psychotherapy rests on the assumption that enduring emotional patterns can be altered through psychotherapy.

We have not discussed the role of temperament, an enduring feature of personality, in the context of enduring emotions. The role of temperament in emotional development is a somewhat confusing issue since for some researchers temperament is a set of specific behaviors, while for others temperament interacts with elicitors to produce behaviors. Temperament as described by some is defined as emotional dispositions, while for others it is a property of some underlying process such as reactivity or inhibition; in either case temperament is regarded as unlearned.[29] However temperament is described, it is believed that temperament differences affect emotional patterns. For example, in studying individual differences in embarrassment behavior we have found that a child with a difficult temperament, measured either by maternal report or by observation, is associated with greater amounts of embarrassment.[30]

INDIVIDUAL DIFFERENCES
IN EMOTIONAL BEHAVIOR:
A MEASURE OF PERSONALITY

My discussion of enduring emotions has touched upon the nature of personality. Here I wish to end my discussion by arguing that it is possible to characterize adults as well as young children by their enduring emotional behaviors. Thus we can say that "Rana is a happy child who is not fearful" as a way of speaking about her personality but also about her enduring emotions. Carol Magai and Jeanette Haviland utilized this idea in their descriptions of three well-known psychotherapists.[31] Years ago my colleague Linda Michalson and I developed an observation system for use in a nursery school setting whereby we could rate the children along five enduring emotions: fearful, angry, happy, sociable, and competent—although one might not think of competence as an emotion. We created an observational system based upon our idea that by specifying specific behavior in response to specific elicitors that we called "situations," we could observe and rate the children's emotional action patterns over many situations and thus generate an enduring emotional profile.

By creating sets of elicitors in a daycare setting believed to elicit a particular action pattern, we thought to measure individual child differences in that particular emotional pattern. What we did for the laboratory study of individual differences in embarrassment can serve as an example of this approach. For these studies, we created four or five different eliciting conditions that we determined beforehand elicited embarrassment. Infants were said to be easily embarrassed if they showed embarrassment for three out of the four conditions. In the same fashion we could say that an infant was fearful if he showed many fear-like action patterns to a set of fear elicitors occurring in a daycare setting.

For example, our observational items (elicitors) included behavior on arrival of the infant at the daycare center, behavior during free play, behavior in groups and in peer interactions, behavior in caregiver–child interactions, behavior in interactions with toys, behavior in interactions with strangers, and behavior in departure from the daycare center. An observer watched one child each day, arriving at the daycare center before the child and staying until after the child left. The observer checked off on the scale which behaviors the child expressed as each elicitor occurred. Thus, each elicitor of the happiness scale was observed as was the child's behavior to it. In this manner, it was possible for the observer to calculate an overall elicitor happiness score for each child. This was done for each emotion, with each child having a mean score for each enduring action pattern.[32] The results of this observation system generated profiles for each child. In order to verify the validity of the profile of the child, what we called their personality profile, teachers of the child were asked to describe the child's personality to us independent of their performance on the scale. Let us look at several examples.

> Sanya is a 16-month-old girl who had been in the daycare program for 2 months. She suffers from being a neglected child, sent by the court to the daycare center. Her emotional profile showed that she is relatively high in sadness; high in fear, competence, and anger moods; and low in happiness and sociability.

The teacher's description taken from her notes reads:

> *When left alone to play, Sanya initiates her own activities. She persists in her play, and when she tries to reach something too high for her, she stands on a box or moves a chair (in imitation of another child) to reach it.*

Such behavior suggests a competence in object play, which is reflected in Sanya's competence mood score. A score of 112 on the Bayley Scales of

Mental Development shows this child to be performing at an above-average level of cognitive capacity.

In talking about Sanya's behavior toward caregivers, mother, and peers, the teacher wrote:

She has fear of strangers and hesitates or freezes when she sees a stranger looking at her, attempting to pick her up, or directing any attention to her, as in starting a conversation. . . . She does not appear to be attached to the caregivers, and while accepting what they give her, she is likely to move away from them as soon as she can. Her behavior toward peers appears to be distant, cold, and aggressive. She often plays by herself and vocalizes very little to other children. When they approach her or when she engages them in play, she is often physically aggressive. It is necessary to separate her from her peers on many occasions. She seems easily frustrated and is easily angered.

Her sadness is reflected in comments about her often playing alone, crying or fretting easily, and seldom going to a caregiver for help. Sanya shows many of the more traditional signs of neglect. One way in which the scores might be used for this child would be to assess the effects of daycare intervention on the child's enduring emotional behavior made by making ratings on the scales before and after the daycare experience.

Here is an example of another child.

Mark has spent the last 4 of his 11 months in a daycare setting. Mark's mother is a single parent. Her parents, leaders in the local church, threw her out of her home for becoming pregnant. Mark's mother is quite punitive and harsh, although she does not appear abusing or neglectful. On the contrary, she is highly demanding, and Mark comes to daycare well dressed and clean. The demands that Mark's mother places on him appear excessive for his developmental level. Mark's profile is indicative of an enduring sadness (depression), showing, relative to the other children, low emotional behavior across almost all the situations. In particular, his lowest score is on happiness and this low score, as well as his low scores on fear and anger behaviors, suggests that the child is depressed and may be overwhelmed by parental demands and regulations. Mark's sociability score (the highest of his scores) indicates that he may have unfulfilled needs in this area. Specifically, he seems particularly attached to one caregiver, Pauline, who has been his caregiver all along.

The teacher notes:

Mark seems to be having problems with caregivers. He usually refuses to go with anyone but Pauline. He often needs affection and one-to-one attention from Pauline. His depression may be manifested by sleeping difficulties. He usually has trouble taking a nap and needs to be rocked and held before falling asleep.

The teacher further noted that Mark infrequently engages peers and needs assistance in playing with objects because of his short attention span. His relatively low affiliation score probably reflects his inability to engage adults other than the caregiver and his mother, as well as his low peer interaction. His low happiness score and the flat nature of the profile suggest a general depression, which may also be reflected in his low anger score. The teacher wrote, "When Mark is attacked by other children, he rarely fights back and usually allows them to take the toy he is playing with." Mark appears to be a child seriously affected by harsh and punitive childrearing practices. His response to such experiences is a low and relatively flat affective mood. Mark's profile appears as a prime example of a depressed infant.

Michalson and I developed the scales by looking at emotional behaviors to particular contexts. By grouping contexts to create classes of elicitors for fear, sadness, happiness, anger, affiliation, and competence, we were able to create a profile of enduring emotional behavior. Since action patterns for a particular emotion were elicited over multiple events and days, it was possible to go beyond the idea of a transient emotion to a measurement of amount of times an emotional behavior appeared for a given set of elicitors.[33] What we hoped to achieve was a measure of a set of enduring emotions. This set surprisingly seems to measure something very similar to what we usually refer to as personality. These scales have been used by Susan Denham in a study of children's daycare behavior and more recently in a study in Rome by Rosa Ferri on over 450 infants from 12 to 48 months old. In both studies the situations and the behaviors observed proved useful in producing profiles of the children's personalities. The scale profiles of the five emotions explored over 25 years ago appear to be valid today. This technique should be used by anyone who wishes to assess young children's emotional behavior, as well as to measure their cognitive and sensory abilities. The need to translate our laboratory work on emotions and emotional development to the "bedside" is obvious. The use of enduring behavioral patterns observed in a multitude of specific situations appears to generate what looks like personality profiles. This study, reported in detail by Lewis and Michalson, would seem to support our idea that specific behaviors elicited in specific situations can be used in everyday situations as well as laboratory studies to look at personality as well as study the elicitor–action pattern association over age.[34]

CHAPTER 4

The Early Emotions

The emergence of the early action patterns and individual differences in infants' behavior has been central to theories about the nature of emotions and their development. The demonstration that within the first year of life infants show emotional behaviors such as joy, interest, fear, sadness, anger, and disgust suggests that however we come to understand the developmental process, it occurs quickly. It is not until the middle and end of the second year that we see another burst of emotional behavior as the set of the self-conscious emotions emerges.

In this chapter I discuss further the issues surrounding the context-specific action patterns. Action patterns-in-context are used to trace this development since it is a major premise of the theory that the mental experiences of emotions, as I have defined them, do not appear until the middle of the second year of life. How we understand these action pattern context interactions gives rise to the development of the early phase of emotional life.

THE ACTION PATTERN–CONTEXT ASSOCIATION

Taking Darwin's description of the early emotions and how they bear a similarity to those of nonhuman animals as a starting point, I state again the belief that these early action patterns evolved because of their adaptive significance, that is, for their usefulness in organizing and motivating the infants' actions in the world as a function of specific contexts. Because they are readily affected by social niche and by temperament, individual differences in these action patterns exist and are easily observed.

As Izard so clearly stated, these context–action pattern connections are the motivational force that allows the infant to make adaptive responses to its social and nonsocial world.[1] These action patterns, occurring in specific

63

contexts, are also communicational acts that inform the social world surrounding the infant. The communication information is perceived within a
cultural framework and is thus defined by the culture of the caregivers. Perhaps what is needed to begin the study of the early emotions is an example
to help guide the discussion.

> Eight-month-old Vivian looks at a stranger who moves toward her.
> As her grandfather leans over to touch her, Vivian starts to cry, leans
> toward her mother and away from the stranger, and protests the close
> proximity.

Seeing this occurrence, we would have no difficulty in saying that Vivian
is showing fear of the stranger and that it marks an important milestone in
her cognitive as well as her emotional development. How is it that almost
any adult in our culture when seeing this sequence would say that the child
was frightened by the stranger or, for short, shows "stranger fear"? Two
features of this scene inform our belief: first is the facial, vocal, and bodily
movement of Vivian, and second is the context of the scene, which is the
movement of the child toward her mother. That is, we are informed by the
child's behavior, or the visible portion of the action pattern, in this particular context.

Let us explore this example more closely, by just looking at Vivian's
behavior. Her facial expression of wariness, that is, her specific movement
of select facial muscles; her cessation of ongoing activity; her vocal behavior—all seem coordinated. Moreover, if we had measured Vivian's nonvis-
ible physiological responses we would have seen heart rate and stress hormone increases as well as activation of the right hemisphere of her brain.
For our purposes these somewhat correlated behaviors are what I have
called an action pattern elicited by situations of uncertainty or situations
previously associated with pain.

When considering the complexity of the set of observed behaviors, we
have to ask the obvious question, namely, Are these behaviors and their
organization learned, and if so how? Or if they are not learned, how do
they come about, both as individual sets such as the expressions on the
muscles of the face, bodily activity such as moving toward or away, or vocal
behavior, and as physiological changes? As we can readily see, the occurrence of unique sets of behaviors and their organization are quite complex.

Quite simply, there is no ready answer to the question of how these sets
of behaviors get organized, although we will consider at least the two major
choices that are available: these are either unlearned sets of action patterns
or learned sets. If these patterns or sets are learned, we need to think about
how the environment favors particular patterns of the muscle movement
of the face, body, vocal, and psychological behaviors that make up these

different action patterns; that is, for example, how does a fear face with unique neuromusculature tone come to be organized, and how does this fear face become related to behavioral, vocal behaviors, and physiological responses?

ARE THEY LEARNED?

Some theorists, Linda Camras, for example, have argued that these sets or patterns of behavior must be learned since these particular action patterns in specific contexts are not clearly seen early in life.[2] Because they are not seen to begin with, they therefore must be learned. However, there is little direct evidence that shows how the different facial musculature patterns are shaped by the environment, let alone evidence of how these patterns are tied to other behaviors such as bodily activity, vocalization, and physiology. While some studies suggest that parents differentially engage in coordinating their facial patterns with their young infants,[3] there is little data to explain the complex coordination that occurs in the first 6 months of life. While there are suggested ideas, including principles of complexity or the theory of mirror neurons that might be able to account for select facial neuromusculature, there are no direct data yet to support this learning argument.

One possible explanation has to do with mirror neurons. While even the existence of mirror neurons is questioned, it might be the case that the infant's observation of the facial patterns of the caregiver is in some matching fashion capable of producing the infant's unique facial patterns.[4] Since imitation has been shown to occur soon after birth for some simple mouth and hand movements, one also might argue that infants match the facial patterns of the adults around them. For over 40 years intersensory integration, that is, the organization of various sensory–motor coordinations, has been shown to exist in the young infant. For example, Harry McGurk and I showed that displacement of the mother's voice from her face causes 4-week-old infants discomfort, demonstrating their competence in organizing face–voice synchrony.[5] Moreover, the young infant's ability to process visual information about another's movement and to be able to match that movement to one's own body suggests that very young infants have the capacity to organize their own body movements according to those that they see in others. These examples suggest learning through imitation and the possible role of mirror neurons; however, there is no clear brain region that has been identified as a locus for these cells, nor any real demonstration of their effect.

Complexity theory is another possibility worth considering. Infant facial expressions may be organized, as described for all complex systems, where random behaviors become elaborated and connected around attractors described as a kind of limitation of possibilities. Specific attractors could organize the facial neuromusculature. Given Paul Ekman's claim that there are approximately 10,000 possible facial patterns, theories about complexity and their attractors can be one way to reduce these many possible faces to the few ones we see. What, then, are the attractors that allow for some organization? Since attractors by definition are a type of limitation that exists in nature, the question becomes whether attractors as forces of limitation are any different from what some have called "evolved adaptive action patterns," which themselves exist as biological limits. Given that both biological-type and complexity-type theories describe limitations, the nature of the limitation may not provide much of a solution to our possible cause.

However, in all these cases the infant would need not only to observe the caregiver's facial patterns, but to observe them in particular contexts, a task that is too difficult for the young infant. Moreover, adding behavioral action and vocal behavior only makes the infant's observational task that much more difficult. While learning could account for such organization and for the association between these behaviors by context, there is another possibility that, starting with Darwin, others have considered and that is consistent with the theory proposed here.

INNATE BUT FLEXIBLE

Darwin proposed two important ideas: emotions are action patterns of the face, body, and physiology, and these action patterns are adaptive responses to particular contexts. This Darwinian view, for infants and children, was further developed by Carroll Izard. Izard's theory is called "differential emotions theory," or DET.[6] This theory proposes that specificity exists between situations and emotional responses or action patterns, and that such specificity is present from a very early age. The amount of specificity, however, is somewhat limited.

The lack of support for specificity seems to occur for many reasons, as discussed in Chapter 2. First, studies that fail to show specificity have any number of limitations, including the measurement of general facial patterns rather than the elaborate facial coding systems that are now available; the failure to look at multiple facial expressions in multiple situations; and finally, the fact that the mother–infant interaction is often used as the general context in which specific contexts are created. Second, subject variability of action patterns within specific contexts exists, as a function both of early socialization and of temperament.[7] Third, as already mentioned, the relation between specific action patterns and specific contexts or elicitors needs to consider the many problems that exist. In order to make any progress on this problem, we need to determine whether there is only one action pattern that is elicited by any specific context since when given the opportunity, children and adults report the elicitation of multiple emotions for any specific context.

The difficulty of finding clear specific action patterns that match specific elicitors rests with the problem of defining specific contexts. The two contexts used to measure fearfulness are the approach of a stranger and movement across what is perceived as a visual cliff. In the stranger approach studies, the stranger slowly approaches the infant and touches the infant's hand while maintaining a neutral, silent face and not talking. In the visual cliff studies, the infant is made to crawl across what appears to be a change in the depth of the surface. While a fear facial pattern is not seen, what is observed is a wary expression as well as physical movement that is used to reflect fear, moving away from the stranger in one case, and not crossing over what is seen as a cliff in the other. The finding of the relative lack of a fear face continues to this day.[8] Why is the fear face lacking in these experimental conditions, even though other aspects of the fear action pattern are present, such as bodily movement and heart rate changes? Perhaps these two experimental elicitors of fear in fact elicit two different action patterns, one of fear and one of interest, as expressed both on the face and in the bodily actions and physiology.

The same problem exists when we look at angry expressions. Arm restraint is often used as the elicitor since it is believed that restraining the infant's arms will cause frustration and therefore anger. Consider the procedure in this paradigm. Sometimes the mother, but most often the experimenter working with the child, suddenly moves so as to place her hands on the arms of the infant and prevent children from moving their arms for 30 seconds or so.

Although this context is assumed to elicit an angry face, we do not see it often. Again, the nature of the elicitor may hold the answer as to why the angry facial action pattern is not seen. Infants may not understand why the person is holding their arms and why the person is in such close physical proximity. Emotions other than anger, such as sadness, interest, and surprise, may be elicited in this context. Thus, facial expressions specificity must remain unclear since multiple action patterns besides anger are likely to be elicited by arm restraint. Given this fact in most studies of infant and young children's facial expressions using either Izard's or Ekman's facial coding systems, it is not surprising that a large number of the movements of the facial neuromusculature are not scorable, suggesting that multiple action patterns may be produced wherein the eyes and eyebrow muscles reflect a different emotion than does the lower face or mouth. As has been already pointed out in our work, a large number of facial movements are scored as mixed emotions. More to the point about the nature of the elicitor is our work on anger as a response to a learned, blocked goal. In this paradigm, anger faces as well as bodily activity and physiological responses are clearly seen, which is not surprising given Darwin's belief that anger is the action pattern elicited by a blocked goal.

STUDYING CONTEXT
AND ACTION PATTERN SPECIFICITY

The problem in studying the elicitor–action pattern specificity can be solved by looking more carefully at the nature of the elicitor, which my colleagues and I have been investigating. Based on the Darwinian viewpoint suggesting that anger is an action pattern with the function of overcoming a blocked goal, my colleagues and I have devised an elicitor specific to a blocked goal. By creating a context in which the infant shows that she has learned a motor action to produce a reward, we can observe what happens when the motor action no longer produces the reward. In particular, we created a simple instrumental learning paradigm in which the infant learns to pull a string in order to get a picture to appear on the screen. Infants as young as 2 months of age who are developing typically can learn within 3 to 5 minutes to pull the string to produce a visual reward. Moreover, by setting a criterion of learning as an increase in arm pulling over a base period when no picture appears, we could ensure that the infant had learned the response leading to the desired goal.

After the infant learns this response, we sever the connection between arm pull and reward such that the arm pulls no longer result in the desired goal, thus setting up a specific context of goal blockage that will lead to an action pattern that should include an angry face. Moreover, since the child is in an infant seat we could carefully measure facial expression, arm pull behaviors, and physiological responses including heart rate, heart rate variability, and stress hormone reaction. The findings from our large number of studies of this learning paradigm support the idea that the problem of the nature of the elicitor can be solved, and when it is solved, there is a high specificity of the action pattern to a particular context. As early as 2 months, but also across the first year of life, infants show an action pattern that involves a complex set of behaviors. To begin with, the blockage of the goal results in increases in arm pulls, as if to get the machine to deliver the desired outcome. In addition, there is an increase in the facial expression of anger, and at the same time a decrease in smiling/joy which was seen when the infant learned the association between pulling the string and the picture outcome. Heart rate increases while heart rate variability decreases and, most interestingly, there is no increase in stress hormone as a function of the blockage.[9]

This action pattern is specific to when the goal is blocked. Interestingly, there is also an action pattern associated with the infant's learning control, that is, learning to pull the string to get the reward. This action pattern is one of increased joy and interest on the face, heart rate changes, and an increase in arm pulling. We might wish to call it pleasure in learning and control, and it is unrelated to the action pattern we called anger when, after learning, the goal is blocked.[10] This suggests that these two different action patterns are related to two different contexts.

Even in these highly regulated contextual situations, there are large individual differences that result in different action patterns. These individual differences raise the probability that, even for very specific contexts, individual infants may differ in their action patterns. These differences may be a function of temperament; thus for one child the blocked goal may lead to a desire to overcome the barrier while for another child the blocked goal may lead to withdrawal from the task. This possibility will be returned to shortly. It might also be the case that past experiences, even in early life, may affect the action pattern–context specificity. This too will be considered.

INDIVIDUAL DIFFERENCES IN ACTION PATTERNS

The learning/blocked goal paradigm I have described leads to the specific action pattern called anger-approach for most, but not all infants. In fact, about 10% to 15% of the infants we have studied show a very different action pattern. When the goal is blocked, these children show sadness on their faces, they stop pulling to try to get the reward to occur, and they exhibit little change in their heart rate and heart rate variability. What they do show is a significant increase in their cortisol stress response. We have called this action pattern "sadness-withdrawal." Thus, two different action patterns occur in response to the same context as a function of some individual difference.

We have thought of these individual differences seen so early in life as a temperament-like quality in the infants studied. It seems to me that these individual differences are differences in will, a term made popular by William James, but now in disuse. In our studies of these individual differences and their developmental course, we have found that the anger-approach and sad-withdrawal action patterns to a blocked goal persist over age, however their form changes. These differences can be seen in toddlers and in 2- to 3-year-olds' behavior when confronted with tasks that require persistence. The angry-approach expression of the infant is associated with the 2-year-old persisting significantly longer on difficult tasks than the sad-withdrawal children, who tend at 2 years to give up when confronted with a barrier to a goal. Thus, these individual different action patterns to the same context are likely to reflect some characteristics unique to the child.[11] However, the more general point is that any specific action pattern to a specific context will not be the same for all children (or adults) unless we consider that action pattern–context specificity, in part as determined by temperament-like individual differences in addition to the other factors already mentioned like multiple action pattern responses.

While we have focused on temperament as an individual difference in the specificity of action patterns to context, specificity may be influenced by past experiences that exist even in young infants. Although there is little data on this topic, we have no difficulty in recognizing that specificity is readily altered by cultural rules, beliefs, and parenting practices. So, for example, crying when sad is normative in children, but such crying by boys in the United States is altered by their parents' belief and admonition that "boys don't cry." The question is, Does socialization affect specificity early? In the present example of the response to a blocked goal, it might be the case that an infant whose mother is highly responsive to the child's cries will build an expectation in the infant about the efficacy of his behavior and thus, when confronted with a barrier to a goal, the child will persist and show an angry-approach action pattern. Although our data do not support such a hypothesis, socialization differences might provide an answer to individual differences in action pattern–context specificity. Socialization may affect specific action patterns, whether that socialization is thought of in terms of the child within the family or of the child/family within the larger culture. While we will take up the role of socialization later, here we will only mention that our work on infants' reaction to physical pain, as in well-baby inoculation, reveals differences between American and Japanese 2-month-olds, with American infants showing greater vocal and body reactivity to pain than Japanese infants.[12]

Diverse behaviors that make up an action pattern do seem to get organized. Moreover, action pattern to elicitor specificity can be demonstrated, especially when care is taken in specifying the nature of the elicitor. However, the infant's embeddedness in his family, as well as his embeddedness in different cultures that give different meanings to behaviors in context, to say nothing of individual differences in temperament, are all bound to affect this specificity. Nevertheless, we accept the basic idea that these action patterns-in-context are part of the evolved and adaptive biological organization of the child. In the approach to follow, we shall try to articulate a view that supports Darwin's and Izard's action patterns idea but is anchored in a developmental-maturational process, including individual differences based on both temperament effects and different patterns of socialization.

THE DEVELOPMENT
OF EARLY EMOTIONAL BEHAVIOR

Earlier we discussed the emotional components of elicitors, action patterns, and experiences. When we study the development of the early emotions we have limited information available to us, only that of expressions and other components of action patterns as well as the context in which they occur. We do not have the luxury of asking the infant about her experience. The most useful way of studying early emotional development is to observe emotional expressions and other aspects of behavior in context.[13] This strategy is the same one we use to understand the emotional life of older children and adults, except for the fact that with these subjects we can ask them questions such as "What emotions do you experience?" The scientist operates no differently than the rest of us do in everyday life. While we have already indicated that the formal study of development is no easy task, there is no question that even in everyday life we make mistakes about people's emotions. A good example of this problem is the gender difference observed when an adult receives a gift. While men are likely to smile and appear happy, women sometimes look sad and even cry when receiving a gift. When asked why she is sad, the woman is likely to say, "I am not sad, I am happy," to which the man may reply, "Then why are you crying?" since for him crying is an expression of sadness.

The problem is made even more complex when we consider lying and deception in Chapter 7. There is no question that our ability to lie, which is related to the development of self-awareness, separates expression from context and makes understanding emotional life difficult even when we have both behavior and context to help. In studying infants and young children what is mostly available are facial and bodily action expressions in context.

THE FIRST EMOTIONS

Many attempts have been made to plot the relatively undifferentiated facial expressions and behavior seen at the very beginning of the life of the infant and the highly complex and differentiated facial expressions and behavior seen by the third year of life. Whatever the process, it occurs quickly! To try to capture this differentiation, Bridges suggested a pattern of differentiation that I will elaborate on, taking into account that by 2 months of age context-specific action patterns can be seen. In all the diverse theories of development of emotions at the start of life at least three patterns appear: an attentive one, a sleeping one, and an upset one.[14]

However, rethinking the findings on the early emergence of action patterns-in-context, it seems that a somewhat different scheme can account for data better than this old one. This scheme relies on the idea that at the very beginning of life there are two primary action patterns, which we here call the approach and the withdrawal patterns. In the 1950s Theodore Schneirla, like many before him—including Darwin, Walter B. Cannon, John B. Watson, and Floyd H. Allport, to name but a few—was intrigued by the concept of a biphasic behavioral pattern. As Schneirla wrote, "The aspect of towardness or awayness is common in animal behavior" and these "are applicable to all motivated behaviors in animals."[15]

Darwin also believed in this dichotomy in emotional life. He wrote that emotions can be classified as exciting or depressing, which we take to mean that he was referring to approach and withdrawal, especially given his examples:

> When all the organs of the body and mind . . . those of voluntary and involuntary movement of perception, sensation, thought, etc.—perform their functions more energetically and rapidly than usual, a man or animal may be said to be excited [approach] or under an opposite state, to be depressed [withdrawal].

Darwin went on to describe anger and joy as well as sadness in these terms:

> Anger and joy are from the first exciting emotions as they naturally lead, more specifically the former, to energetic movements which react on the heart and thus again on the brain. A physician once remarked to me as a proof of the exciting nature of anger, that a man when excessively jaded will sometimes invent imaginary offences and put himself into a passion unconsciously for the sake of reinvigorating himself; and since hearing this remark I have occasionally recognized its full truth.

In other words, anger habitually leads to action. Darwin also thought that sadness has a withdrawal characteristic.

> As soon as the sufferer is fully conscious that nothing can be done, despair or deep sorrow takes the place of frantic grief. The sufferer sits motionless, or gently rocks to and fro; the circulation becomes languid; respiration is almost forgotten, and deep sighs are drawn. As associated habit no longer prompts the sufferer to action, he is urged by his friends to voluntary exertion, and not to give way to silent, emotionless grief.[16]

If it is indeed the case that the basic pattern is one of approach and withdrawal, we might use this as our starting point in the early undifferentiated action patterns of the newborn. Figure 4.1 presents the scheme utilizing these two behavioral action patterns, and although there are some

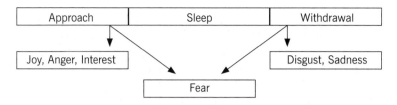

FIGURE 4.1. Development of the differentiated early action patterns.

data on differential brain hemisphere differences to support such a scheme, it is presented here for heuristic reasons.[17]

To begin with, infants show general approach behavior, an engagement with the social and object environment. This engagement or approach mode soon differentiates into three of the primary action patterns: joy, anger, and interest. We include interest as an emotional behavior, although some might not. The joy action pattern is related to contexts involving social stimuli such as faces and voices, and also to contexts of control or mastery on objects as well as people. The anger action pattern is related to the overcoming of a blocked goal. The interest action pattern is related to attending to novel and familiar events, both social and nonsocial; it is mostly controlled by context change, although there may be some innate elicitors.

The basic withdrawal action pattern is designed to remove the infant from active engagement with the world. The two primary emotions that are derived from this pattern are disgust and sadness. Disgust is an action pattern adapted to remove from the mouth noxious tastes and smells and thus acts to disengage the infants' appetitive behavior. Sadness is an action pattern evoked by the loss of both people and objects.

In these cases the withdrawal pattern removes the infant from active engagement and turns action into inaction. At the beginning it is associated with sleep, which is also a mechanism for disengagement with the outside world. The literature on early sleep patterns suggests that the newborn spends a high percentage of time sleeping, and of experiencing rapid-eye-movement (REM) sleep, which rapidly decreases over the first 3 months. This disengagement from the outside world appears to be necessary for the development of normal brain function as well as for the reinstatement of information obtained from the approach action patterns. The approach and withdrawal patterns seem to work in some synchronous fashion.

We have left fear, one of the early action patterns, for last. Although one might believe that fear too is a withdrawal action pattern, it seems to me that it is a consequence of a combined approach and withdrawal pattern. Fear is a response to either an unfamiliar context or to some prewired-like mechanism, similar to what ethnologists describe as innate releasing mechanisms (IRMs). While the work of Susan Mineka reveals that some animals, like snakes or spiders, may not innately elicit fearful behavior in children, they appear to be prewired in some way and therefore need minimum experience to turn the animals into feared creatures.[18]

However, if unfamiliar or innate stimuli only elicited fear, with withdrawal tendencies, there would be no trouble classifying them as part of the withdrawal pattern. However, consider that if unfamiliarity only elicited fear, how could the child learn about new things? If there was no movement toward, nothing new could be added to the child's repertoire. Clearly, the child has both to withdraw for safety, and to approach, as in interest, to learn and profit from novelty. Indeed, that is just what we see when we examine children's behavior, both toward the visual cliff as well as to the approach of a stranger. In both cases the infant shows what has been called "wariness," which may be part of the interest action pattern, while also showing a cessation of activity and movement away. In fact if the infant is allowed to crawl on the floor with her mother present, when the stranger approaches, the child will move away from the unfamiliar person, go toward her mother, and hide behind her, all of which fits into a fear-like action pattern, while *at the same time* looking out at the stranger. This behavior combines the approach with the withdrawal patterns of action.

As can be readily seen, this view of the emergence of the primary emotions grows out of the two basic action modes of approach and withdrawal. At the beginning of life, these two modes are undifferentiated but quickly develop as maturation takes place, into the action pattern-context-specific patterns that we see by 2 to 3 months. While not enough data are available, there is some reason to believe that these two basic action modes are connected to hemisphere differences in the brain, as well as to the ANS, in particular heart rate changes, and through these changes to changes in the vagus nerves that increase information by acting on the perceptual/cognitive system of the child.[19]

Thus, while the description here is somewhat similar to Bridges's earlier scheme, it places the emergence and differentiation of these primary emotions within the more general framework of general approach–withdrawal action modes that rapidly develop into the Darwinian idea of differential action patterns associated with specific contexts.

With this in mind the model of emotional development can be seen in its complete form. While our discussion of the various problems associated with studying these early action patterns has been considered, it is to their early development that we now turn our attention. There is considerable information available, mostly around facial expression-in-context, although some bodily activity is also available, to demonstrate that they emerge in the first 6 months of life, especially if the context for their elicitation is taken into account.[20]

These six primary facial patterns appear in the early months of life when we look at context specificity. While these six emotions are mentioned by most researchers, others have considered other emotions in this early grouping, including some of what I have called self-conscious emotions. When discussing the self-conscious emotions, I will demonstrate why these emotions are likely not to be present in the early months of life, mostly because considerable cognitive capacities are necessary for their elicitation, cognitions that are not available to the infant in the first year of life.

Interest

Whether we consider interest an emotion or a cognitive action pattern depends on our perspective. If we call interest "attention," then it is quite clear that from the very beginning of life infants show this emotion. In the early 1960s Jerome Kagan and I, as well as others, demonstrated that infants could attend to external stimuli including visual, auditory, and tactile events. Attention was measured by receptor orientation, including eye gaze and turning toward the source of the stimulus, as well as by physiological responses including heart rate and respiration rate changes. There is little doubt that from the beginning of life infants show interest in the world around them. The details of the studies have been discussed elsewhere, and the reader is referred to them for further information in regard to this emotional action pattern.[21]

Fear

The interest in infant fear originally centered around the attempt to understand the infant's early social life. Capitalizing on animal data on imprinting, Bowlby, as well as others, argued that infants' fear response to a stranger reflects the child's attachment to his mother. Since fear develops in order to terminate the child's indiscriminate approach to all other people, it reflects the child's imprinting on the familiar. Thus fear has an adaptive function, protection of the child from strangers who might do him harm.

A second area of interest in fear had as it source an interest in the child's perceptual–cognitive development and used the fear response as a measure of the child's cognitive ability. For example, Eleanor Gibson's visual cliff experiment used fear as a measure of the child's ability to distinguish spatial depth.[22] In this experiment the infant, prior to walking but able to crawl, is placed on a platform that creates an illusion in which one half of the platform seems to drop off by several feet. The fear response was reported to show that the infant had gained the perceptible–cognitive ability through interaction with its physical world, and thus recognized the potential of falling. The approach of a stranger and the visual cliff are still used to elicit a fear response. Although these two experiments sometimes reveal the facial action pattern of fear as measured by any of the facial coding systems, what is seen mostly is bodily hesitation and movement at times away, in addition to an attentive face, sometimes called "wariness."

Earlier, I suggested that fear has both a withdrawal and an approach component. It is clear that stimuli that elicit fear can also elicit approach behavior. For example, incongruity or discrepancy is thought to elicit fear, but can also elicit smiling and laughter. While most theories, especially those using fear as a marker of the child becoming imprinted or attached to its mother, view fear as a consequence of discrepancy, discrepancy itself is not a sufficient cause for fear. In a series of studies we have been able to show that the specific context in which the discrepancy appears determines to a considerable extent whether there is a fear-like or a joy-like response.[23] Over 40 years ago Alan Sroufe showed that many events that can potentially produce laughter, such as gently tossing the baby in the air or playing peek-a-boo with the infant, can also produce fear and upset.[24] Fear also appears in contexts where there are sudden changes in the physical features of the environment or when experiencing pain.

Individual differences in temperament may also play an important role in what elicitors produce fear behavior. Perhaps the simplest example of this is observing individual differences in infants when they are tossed in the air: one infant laughs and smiles at this unusual stimulation, while the other is frightened and may even cry. Context and temperament are deeply involved in the fear response. *As a working hypothesis, I suspect that difficult temperaments are likely to increase the withdrawal component of fear, while easy temperaments are likely to increase the approach component.*

From a developmental perspective there is a connection between maturing cognitive processes and the contexts that elicit fear. While there was a strong belief that fear required cognitive capacities, which do not emerge until after the first half of the first year of life,[25] there are now data to support the idea that simple associations with pain can cause fear. Thus Izard has reported fear faces in infants being inoculated, and we have shown that a fear face is part of what Pavlov and Simonov have called a "defensive reflex," the response to the sudden onset of something unexpected.[26]

While fear may appear early, cognitive factors need play a more important role in the second half of the first year of life. What is clear is that such cognitive capacities as memory and the ability to make comparisons underlie fearfulness. Moreover, Therese Decarie suggests that object permanence may be another important cognitive factor. If this theory is correct, it may explain some of the individual differences in the timing of the onset of fear. For example, Gordon Bronson has shown stranger fear in 3-month-old infants, and we have reported that gifted children are likely to show stranger fear prior to 6 months.[27] If cognitive capacities emerge earlier in some infants than in others, the children with precocious cognitive development are likely to show fear responses earlier. However, we need to keep in mind that cognitive maturation also must interact with children's temperament.

However we consider the emergence and development of fear, the discrepancy factor continues to be implicated in studying the difference between familiar and unfamiliar people, with unfamiliar people sometimes eliciting fear-like responses certainly after 3 months. Even here, though, there are some interesting contextual factors in responses to strangers. In a series of studies, we have examined whether the nature of the unfamiliar person might play a role in infant and toddler fearfulness. We had male and female young children and male and female adults, all strangers, approach infants ages 7 to 19 months in a stranger-approach situation. Infants show wariness at the approach of the unfamiliar adult but joy and attention at the approach of the unfamiliar child.[28] This phenomenon can be seen in public places like airports where stranger infants and toddlers will approach each other but avoid or move away from stranger adults. Such findings as these support our view that unfamiliarity and discrepancy are an insufficient explanation as elicitors producing the fear response since the unfamiliar adult is more like the mother—less discrepant—than the strange child. These findings suggest that either past experiences or biological factors like IRMs play some role in determining the early fear action pattern. Many different experimental paradigms have been used to elicit fear in young children besides stranger approach and the visual cliff, including loud and sudden noises and robot toys moving toward the child. To some degree all appear to elicit mostly a wary response. Even so, large individual differences are shown. One might assume that a fearful child would show high fear to any one of these different elicitors, and at the extreme ends of the spectrum of fearfulness that may be the case, yet the results of several studies reveal only weak consistency in children's fear across different elicitors.[29]

In studying fear we have not escaped the problems of multiple response system evocation. When one response system is engaged, another may not be displayed. Fear research is a perfect example of this problem. In our laboratory, a stranger can approach an infant while the 1-year-old is in a highchair or approach when she is on the floor, in both cases near her mother. When the stranger approaches the child in the highchair, the child's response consists of changes in facial expression, turning away, and movement backward in the chair. When she is on the floor, the stranger evokes less negative expression but quick movements away. When she is near the mother, she is likely to look at, rather than avoid the gaze of, the stranger. The physical response limitation of the highchair relative to the floor appears responsible for the different displays of fear. What these data suggest is that fear-like responses in infants can be seen by 6 months when measured by interest, movement cessation or movement away, and sometimes a fear expression.

Anger

When asked, most parents report that their infants show anger. They report that this can be seen in the infant when being fed: the infant turns his head away and raises his hands to push the spoon away. Research seems to support our everyday observations. Part of our problem is in the reporting. As already mentioned, American mothers report more anger in their infants than do Japanese mothers. Such a finding either means that (1) American babies actually show more anger responses than do Japanese babies or that (2) American mothers are more likely to see more angry behavior than Japanese mothers because of their varying interpretations of the child's behavior. Parental reports of anger, perhaps just like most of the other early action patterns, have multiple meanings, including embedded cultural meanings. For example, anger as an attempt to overcome a blocked goal is often confused with aggression or hate and linked to acting-out or violent behaviors.

Nevertheless, we have argued that infants' anger is, in general, and for adults some of the time, an approach emotion. As we have already noted, its evolutionary adaptive significance is in its motivating property of action toward overcoming a barrier. While angry faces have been seen when 8-month-olds' hands are held and constrained, anger is seen earlier in life when an infant's learned response to a goal is blocked.[30] When 2-month-olds learn to pull a string to turn on an interesting picture, they show an angry face when pulling no longer produces the picture. Moreover, there is individual difference consistency over time. Infants who show more anger behavior at 2 months do so at 4 and at 6 months in the same context. Moreover, early individual differences in the amount of anger expressed are related to the 2-year-old child's persistence in overcoming a difficult problem.[31] This early form of angry behavior functions as an adaptive action pattern in overcoming barriers. The parental interpretation of these angry faces and action patterns varies as a function of parental personality, socialization rules, and culture, and they are likely to subsequently turn this early action pattern into a variety of emotional outcomes. For example, if a parent views the infant's attempt to continue or persevere at a task she does not wish the infant to do, the parent's anger at the infant's behavior may turn the infant's anger to overcome a barrier into anger as aggression or even rage. The difference between anger and rage was discussed when I talked about the self-consciousness emotions, for I see rage as the consequence of shame and this is quite different than the anger action pattern.[32]

Joy

Joy has been studied primarily in terms of a smiling face, with much of the research conducted in the early 1960s and 1970s. Smiling is present from the beginning days of life and is likely state-dependent during the neonatal period; that is, a smile occurs almost reflexively and does not seem to be related to any specific contexts. Smiling even appears during sleep in the newborn. However, smiling behavior as a response to social objects including other infants, children, adults, and animals with human-like faces appears between 6 and 8 weeks and is more likely to occur in these contexts than others; however, gentle tactile stimulation also appears to elicit enjoyment behavior in 8-week-olds.[33] Expressions of enjoyment in very early life are closely tied to the physical quality of stimulation, which can be auditory, tactile, or visual. However, enjoyment of social events and stimulation increase dramatically by 4 months of age, with social smiling peaking between 12 and 14 weeks of age in home-reared infants in Western culture. Infants at this age seem to enjoy people and will smile readily at most children and adults who interact pleasantly with them. After 16 weeks, however, most infants can discriminate between faces. Then familiarity and the behavioral style of the interactive partner become important factors in smiling behavior, suggesting that smiling and enjoyment are now being influenced by the infant's growing cognitive development. By age 12 months infants vary in their social smiling, reflecting not only temperament differences but possible differences in their quality of enjoyment within social situations.[34]

While smiling is present early, laughter appears somewhat later. Blurton-Jones characterizes laughter or a play face as a wide-open mouth expression with sounds adults associate with laughter.[35] The play face seems to make its appearance by 4 or 5 months in normally developing infants and occurs at first to vigorous auditory and tactile stimulation, seen in the infant's response to tickling. After 7 months, visual stimulation becomes more effective in eliciting this laughter expression. By 12 months incongruency and novelty, especially if it involves the infant's own participation, elicit laughter and the play face—for example, in such games as peek-a-boo.

Finally, what we know about atypical development may aid our understanding of joy. Studies of infants with Down syndrome show that while social smiling peaks at the same mental age, that is, 4 to 5 months, as it does for typically developing infants, the intensity of enjoyment appears to be less. Moreover, infants with Down syndrome are not able to sustain social enjoyment in spontaneous interactions to the same degree as infants without the syndrome and they may also be less likely to initiate smiling.[36]

Of particular interest in the development of joy is the work on blind infants. Visual input for the first 3 months does not appear to be necessary for smiling to occur since blind children produce recognizable spontaneous smiling.[37] However, after this period children who are blind show different patterns of smiling, suggesting that the early smile may be of a different kind than the later smile.

While smiling and enjoyment have been studied for the most part in the context of social interactions, there has been considerable neglect in studying enjoyment (with or without a smiling face) in contexts that are not social. In particular, there is relatively little study of infants' responses to mastery. This is somewhat surprising but in keeping with the overestimation of the theoretical linking of emotional development with social contexts and social development. There is every reason to assume that in the development of enjoyment, the organism's interaction with its physical world, a necessity for survival, requires enjoyment.[38] The overestimation of the child's emotional expressions as only signals to others has led to the study of the role of emotions as motives. As such, enjoyment around action on objects (as well as people) is an important action pattern necessary for exploring, learning, and remembering and has a significant adaptive function as the child interacts with his physical world.

Work in our laboratory around learning as well as in responses to goal blockage demonstrates that when infants as young as 2 months are provided the opportunity, through pulling a string to cause a picture to appear, enjoyment occurs. In other words, enjoyment is associated with learning that their action causes something to happen. Moreover, we have also demonstrated that when 4-month-old infants learn the contingency between their arm pull and an outcome, those who show more enjoyment (smile more) are more likely to remember that their arm pull caused something to happen.[39]

While these studies are quite clear in showing that smiling and enjoyment can be seen in both social interaction and object mastery contexts, more study is necessary to explore the mastery aspect of enjoyment. It will be necessary also to explore how smiling behavior in social interactions may differ from smiling mastery in the object world. Given that there is some evidence that there are different kinds of smiles (at least in adults), we may be able to make some distinctions within the emotion of joy/enjoyment depending on the particular context.

Although the topic will be considered in more detail when I address lying and deception in Chapter 7, I need to mention now the Duchenne smile. Paul Ekman coined the term "Duchenne smile" (named after a French neurologist) to refer to a smile that engages both the mouth and the eye muscles. He considers the Duchenne smile to be a true expression of joy. A smile that only involves the mouth and not the eyes is considered to be a pretend or false expression of joy. Given the importance of smiling behavior in social commerce, the ability to distinguish between false smiles and true smiles becomes important for the detection of deception. More important, it points out the problem of the reliance solely on facial expression to represent the action pattern of joy.

Sadness

Sadness is often associated with loss but can occur for other reasons as well. Sadness typifies the withdrawal aspect of the original modes of approach and withdrawal patterns. Its adaptive significance is unclear, but its association with crying behavior suggests that it serves as a powerful signal to the caregiver of the child's discomfort. The action pattern when it includes crying is complex as it both causes a cessation or reduction of action and at the same time the cry feature constitutes an active response for others to help.

Perhaps crying, while being a component of sadness at the beginning of life, is an action pattern designed as a powerful signal calling for care. It seems that at least in the early weeks of life, crying (usually interpreted as sadness) is not elicited by loss but by discomfort. Loss requires sufficient cognitions such as a sense of object permanence in order to remember that there existed something or somebody that is now lost.

While crying is the most visible aspect of the emotion of sadness, it is important to remember that some of the other features as described by Darwin may lead us to a better understanding of the adaptive significance of the action pattern. Recall that Darwin suggested the cessation of activity, repetitive motions such as gentle rocking, "languid circulation," and decreases in respiration, as well as particular facial expressions, as other aspects of sadness. While crying is often used to mark sadness, adults who cry for joy or even when angry are examples that suggest that crying alone is an insufficient marker of sadness.

Perhaps an example of sadness without crying is the cessation of action and movement, as demonstrated in the work of Suomi with monkeys, who has shown that when a monkey mother leaves her baby, the baby shows a decrease in its activity as well as an increase in its cortisol stress response. He argues that this reduction of motor activity is adaptive for the infant for two reasons. First, the cessation of activity decreases metabolism and thus the need for food, necessary since its mother's absence means the infant is not being fed. Second, decreased activity decreases noise, and thus limits the possibility of discovery by a predator that without the protection of its mother endangers the baby.[40]

Our problem with studying the early emergence of sadness rests on the use of the crying response to signal the action pattern. So, for example, in studies of crying, a behavior seen at the very beginning of life, different types of cries can be used by caregivers to differentiate the different types of discomfort—for example, cries of pain have a different pattern than cries of hunger.[41] However, we need to remember that it is possible to differentiate a sad face from a crying face. The sad face has brows that are raised and angular with narrowing of the eyes. The mouth is drawn down, often with the lower lips protruding and covers the upper lip in a pouting-like expression. Most important, crying does not have to occur.[42]

The study of sadness is like that of the other action patterns: it is often explored in the mother–infant interaction, and in particular in what has been called the *en face* experimental paradigm. In this paradigm, mother and infant sit across from each other and engage in social and affective exchanges. When signaled, the mother, without warning, suddenly drops her head and stops engaging the child. Among the many possible responses of the child, some infants show sadness. The sadness shown by the infant is thought to reflect the infant's loss of its mother. Since the behaviors are studied in 3-month-olds, the infant's response of sadness appears to reflect the loss of its mother and therefore is considered to be part of the ongoing establishment of an attachment between the infant and its mother.[43]

Another way to look at sadness is through the learning and goal blockage paradigm that I have previously discussed. While most infants respond to the loss of the picture with arm pulling and an angry action pattern, at least 10% of them show a sadness action pattern at the loss. Sad facial expression, cessation of activity, and little change in heart rate fit the action pattern as described by Darwin. While we see the sad response as nonadaptive in this situation, it is clear that the elicitor of this action pattern is the loss either of control or of the picture presented as a consequence of the pulling. However, in another study, for one group we did not terminate the pictures' appearance as the blockage, but only terminated the control of their appearance in an attempt to examine whether it was the loss of control or loss of the picture. To study this, the group that lost control saw the pictures at the same level as the other group, but their arm pull did not control the picture onset. Sadness was still observed, indicating that sadness was produced by the loss of control.[44]

It should be noted that the sadness action pattern is seen in response to the loss of control of objects as well as to the loss of control of people. These findings strongly suggest, and reinforce the idea, that individual differences related to temperament may play an important role in the action pattern displayed. They also point to the problem already mentioned, namely, that the same context may elicit multiple action patterns. Later in life the same context but with different interpretations as to the meaning of the elicitor may do the same thing. Our learning paradigm studies show that the action pattern of sadness can occur in both social and nonsocial contexts. However, we must keep in mind that the crying response, most often used to indicate sadness, is not seen in the nonsocial context; we do not use crying as part of our definition of a sad action pattern. Rather, we see crying behavior as a general response to any sort of discomfort, including pain, the physical discomfort of a soiled diaper, or ever hunger and gas. Crying may elicit sadness and concern on the part of the caregiver but caution should be used in labeling it as a marker of sadness.

Disgust

Of all of the early emotions, disgust appears to be the one that is most immediate and likely to require the least cognitive capacity. It is an adaptive response designed for dispelling from the mouth objects that do not taste or smell good. The disgust action pattern is immediately obvious: it consists of opening the mouth and raising the nose, which causes the upper lip to rise. The tongue can protrude from the mouth but does not do so in all cases. The disgust action pattern has much in common with the contempt or shame patterns and can in infancy be mistaken for them. Certainly the disgust action pattern can be seen in various forms throughout life and has an interesting developmental course.[45]

Even newborns show this action pattern: their responses to bitter and sour tastes are distinct from their responses to water and sweet solutions.[46] Quinine and other bitter tastes are potent and rapid elicitors of disgust. The developmental course of the disgust action pattern has been little studied, mostly because the action pattern is so clear in the newborn period and therefore a developmental pattern is not likely to be seen. Moreover, disgust seems to be part of the withdrawal pattern and needs little cognition. Support for this conclusion comes from Steiner's extensive studies of disgust and enjoyment taste reactions in a variety of infants with disabilities.[47] The disgust expression was recognizable in all populations studied despite their considerable variation in cognitive and motor control. Because of this finding Steiner argued that disgust expressions across a wide range of cognitive and motor dysfunctions are controlled by the brain stem and therefore need little cognitive ability. While there are large individual differences in the stimuli that elicit disgust, no work on individual differences early in life have been reported. In our studies of individual differences in 4-month-olds' responses to lemon applied to their tongues, we observed large individual differences, although no consistent individual differences over time were noted.

Perhaps the most interesting aspect of disgust expressions, and the one about which little is known, is how the subtle variations in responsiveness observed even in newborns are related to individual differences in nervous system functioning or other factors, such as temperament. Another question of interest is, When does this expression begin to occur in response to non-taste stimuli, and to representation? The presumption is that disgust occurs later to new elicitors and to representations rather than to actual tastes or smells. Nontaste stimuli that might be sufficient to produce a disgust response in infants have not yet been reported, but can be imagined since disgust signals stimulus rejection or withdrawal. Although data are lacking, too rapid or too sudden occurrence of a stimulus might elicit disgust expressions if the stimulus overwhelms the infant's ability to process it. We have observed this response on some occasions in the learning paradigm. Sometimes an infant pulls the string so rapidly that the stimulus appears within a second of its previous appearance and *before* the infant's reaction to the first appearance has subsided. When this occurs, we have seen nose wrinkling or asymmetrical mouth and lip movements in response, suggesting a kind of recoil reaction to the overwhelming, too rapid reoccurrence of the elicitor. Such observations suggest that prior to 6 months of age components of disgust may occur in response to visual and auditory stimulation, setting the stage for their later function in social situations. Nevertheless, the forms of disgust observed in this case do not involve the intense, gaping reactions observed in response to bitter tastes.

Clearly the disgust action pattern is a withdrawal response, with the infant rejecting the unacceptable taste and/or smell. Because of the significance for adults of the disgust emotional expression, the child's disgust response is often seen as rejection of what the parents are doing, such as feeding the child. The child's disgust therefore often elicits a strong negative feeling in the caregiver since it may be interpreted as rejection of her. As we have seen, disgust in one person often elicits shame and anger in another. For example, John Gottman has argued that the disgust expression in one marital partner is often the elicitor of anger and depression in the other.[48]

Because the disgust action pattern is easily observed at the beginning of life and continues across the lifespan, we can use it as a prototype of a more general developmental pattern. Following some of Paul Rozin's ideas, we can say that (1) early action patterns have strong biological roots, the consequences of evolved adaptive responses to specific features in the social world; (2) while early action patterns are at first elicited by the literal world, they can at later ages be elicited by ideas; (3) once consciousness appears these early action patterns are related to ideas about me, others, things, and events in the world; and (4) disgust as part of a general withdrawal pattern may be the precursor for the more complex emotions seen later.

Clearly, disgust facial patterns are observed very early, and therefore little learning is needed for the development of disgust. To begin with, it is clear that tastes and smells are the literal elicitors of disgust. However, with development, disgust can be elicited by ideas (e.g., moral disgust), or by seeing mauled bodies or bodily discharges. With the development of new cognitive capacities as well as the effects of socialization, the biologically based action pattern of disgust can be used for the rejection of bad ideas and images. It is also used to describe rejecting interpersonal interactions such as "You are disgusting."

Perhaps this is the fate of all of the early action patterns? I suspect that this may be so. What we need to understand is how these early adaptive action patterns interact with the maturing cognitive and social capacities as well as the knowledge the child gains to produce new patterns and new elicitors. For me, the biological underpinnings of these early action patterns reflect their motivational power, which with maturity produces actions patterns associated with thoughts and ideas.

CHAPTER 5

The Rise of Consciousness

I have used the term "consciousness" in the title of this chapter, although I have been cautioned about using such a term given the difficulty there is in defining its meaning. Perhaps I should use the term "self-referential behavior," for this is how we measure the term referred to in the title. Ned Block, a philosopher, in an article entitled "On a Confusion about a Function of Consciousness" wrote, "The concept of consciousness is a hybrid or better, a mongrel concept: the word 'consciousness' connotes a number of different concepts and denotes a number of different phenomena." He goes on to say, "We reason about 'consciousness' using some premises that apply to one of the phenomena that fall under 'consciousness,' other premises that apply to other 'consciousnesses' and we end up with trouble."[1]

In Chapter 1 we tried to examine this problem about the concept and pointed out that when we use terms other than consciousness, such as the term "feeling," we run into the same problem. John Searle, another philosopher with a different perspective on the meaning of the term consciousness considers that "the central feature of consciousness is that for any conscious state there is something that it feels like to be in that state."[2] Notice, however, the use of "feels like" since we already have tried in Chapter 1 to consider what "feeling" may mean, deciding that feeling can be a synonym with what is meant by consciousness in one sense of its meaning, but not in another.

We have already used a variety of terms to capture consciousness, including feeling, self, experience, and a mental state having the idea of me. The use of all these terms has to be confusing but they were introduced and discussed since in the study of development each of them has been used by others. More important, their use by others is often quite different from my usage when talking about emotional development. To try to avoid some of the problems with the term consciousness, I have used the term *experience* to highlight one feature of emotion. When talking about experience we need to distinguish bodily experiences, procedural rules, and the machinery of the body from experiences that involve a mental state, this idea of me.[3]

For now, in my discussion of the experiential aspects of an emotion the term consciousness will be used but with hesitation. My research on this problem focuses on the measurement of self-referential behavior, so at least there can be some experimental basis for this discussion, even though the terms may be problematic.

Before we go further, we need to recognize that the topic of consciousness is embedded in the mind–body dilemma. While we have seen that action patterns to specific events exist—which have a materialistic basis—and that, as will be shown, self-referential behavior has specific brain maturational concomitants, consciousness is a feature of our minds, and we have no way yet of understanding how materialistic events become ideas.

With this in mind, let me start with a simple story that occurred to me one night, for what better way for me to try to explain the role of consciousness in our emotional lives than to speak in the first person, for perhaps each one of us knows about our own consciousness if not another's.

MY STORY[4]

As I sit here in my study looking out at the city, the sunrise over the tall building in front of me is blocked. The taste of my coffee in my mouth lingers as I think about the book I am writing. I have no trouble recognizing myself. I know where I am and why I am here. I can see and feel my arm and hand move as I write if I choose to. When I answer my wife's call, my voice sounds like me. Sitting here, I can think about myself. I can wonder whether we will go out for dinner tonight. I wonder about my appearance. Do I need to shave my face? Is it warm enough outside not to wear a jacket? As I get up to leave the room, I pass a mirror; there I see myself, the reflected surface of my being. "Yes, that is me," I say, fixing my hair.

I know a great deal about me. One of the things I know is how I look; for example, my beard is white. I look familiar to myself, even though I have changed considerably with age. Pictures taken of me 50 years ago look only a little like me now. Nevertheless, I know when I look at myself in the mirror I will see an image that I recognize as me.

I know many people might argue that the concept of myself is merely an idea. I would agree, but note that it is a particularly powerful idea, an idea from which I cannot part. It is one around which a good portion of the network of many of my ideas center. This is not to say that what I know about myself is all I know. In fact, this idea of myself is only one part of my self; there are many other parts of my self that I do not know.[5] The parts of my self that I do not know include the activities of my body, the joints moving, the blood surging, the action potentials of my muscle movements as well as the calcium exchange along the axons. There are many other things that are part of me I know nothing about; I have no knowledge of a large number of my motives or organized, coherent thoughts and ideas that control large segments of my life. I have no knowledge of how my thoughts occur. Nevertheless, I know that I think and have complex emotional-like behavior even without this knowledge. My body can organize early emotions or action patterns, including facial changes, psychological behavioral patterns, and even physiological actions.

Although it might be true that I could explicitly know more of some parts of my unknown self if I chose to, it is nonetheless the case that what is known and acted on by my self is greater than what I can state I know. Because of these facts I imagine myself to be a biological machine that is an evolutionarily fit complex of processes: doing, feeling, thinking, planning, and learning. One aspect of this machine is the *idea of me*. This is what I think of as consciousness, something that knows itself and knows it does not know all of itself! This self of mine, then, is greater than the me, the me being only a small portion of myself. The difference between my self and me can be understood from an epistemological point of view. The idea that *I know* is not the same as the idea that *I know I know*. The explicit aspect of the self that I refer to is that which knows it knows, what we shall call consciousness, and I will use the development of self-referential behavior to measure it.

We can say that for me as an adult human, both of these two aspects of self exist. One aspect of the self, the machinery of the body, does not have associated with it mental processes, although it might cause mental processes to occur. The other aspect is the idea of me, a mental state I will call consciousness. While the machinery of my self can learn and have memories, and while it is likely to function even in my sleep, the idea of me or consciousness is transient; that is to say I can become conscious of me but I do not have to, much like Ernst Hilgard's idea of divided attention.[6] From a developmental perspective, the machinery of self exists at birth and continues to exist through the lifetime, while the mental state of the idea of me develops over the first 2 years and then continues throughout life.

CONSCIOUSNESS AND EMOTIONAL LIFE

The central and perhaps defining feature of a child's emotional life is the emergence of consciousness. The early action patterns—complex organized behaviors to specific contexts—rest initially on the machinery of self, but with the rise of consciousness, they undergo a profound change, the change, for example, from a fear action pattern in response to the approach of a stranger, to an idea about my self expressed in language as "I am afraid of the doctor." Moreover, the rise of the idea of me allows for new action patterns that I have called the self-conscious emotions. Shame can occur only if we have consciousness, which allows us to evaluate our actions, thus allowing us to be both an object and the subject of our thoughts.

Thus in talking about consciousness and its emergence in the human child, we need to consider the change from the machinery of the self to the idea of me. Consciousness has to be about something, in particular about the self, the me. This aboutness has specific features such as gender or age, but it is not these features that draw our attention in this chapter. It is the development of *aboutness* itself. The specific features of me are likely cultural artifacts.

My definition of what I mean by consciousness and how to measure it seems explicit enough; however, the misunderstanding about the development of consciousness is widespread, with some asserting that consciousness appears early in the infant's life.[7] Why should this belief about consciousness existing from the beginning of life be so strong? To answer this question, I think we need to look in part at the very human capacity of anthropomorphization. David Hume wrote that "there is a universal tendency among mankind to conceive all beings like themselves."[8] Even earlier, the Greek philosopher Xenophames argued that gods and other supernatural agents tend to bear a considerable physical and psychological resemblance to those who believe in them and noted that if lions had gods they would look like lions. These attributions include more than physical resemblance—God envisioned as an old man with a white beard—but psychological attributes as well, including human-like intentions and emotions such as anger and sadness, but especially shame and pride, which are attributed to newborn babies, animals, and even plants. Even children ascribe human-like intentions to nonhuman stimuli.[9] This capacity to attribute adult human-like emotions to animals such as dogs and cats is echoed by adult's attributions about infants, which include infants' emotions of shame, pride, and trust.

Perhaps some recent research with dogs will shed some light on our adult capacity to anthropomorphize our pets' behavior. In two recent papers, psychologists Julie Hecht and Alexandra Horowitz found evidence that dogs were likely to display guilt-like behavior after they had been scolded, whether or not they had actually been guilty of some prohibited action. Dogs who had not misbehaved and were scolded showed more guilt-like behaviors than dogs who had been scolded and had actually misbehaved. More recently, Adrian Ward and Daniel Wegner found that people attribute minds to robots and even corpses that are targets of harm. That parents and some scientists attribute minds to very young infants should not be surprising.[10]

When talking about human infants, Edward Tronick and Marjorie Beeghly, in an interesting article on the mother–infant interaction, stated that "developing a failed reparatory history with a specific person leads to an implicit knowing by infants [3 to 4 months old] that we can't repair mismatches. This sense of failure may lead to an insecure attachment relationship with that person and may undermine infants' trust in others." They add, "Infants with a positive affective core may be more likely to explore and consequently more likely to discover new meanings about themselves in the world."[11] The degree of selfhood Tronick and Beeghly attribute to these young infants and their use of the mentalistic terms "meaning," "trust," and "repair" reflect the kind of difficulty we face when we try to use adult terms for 3-month-old infants' mental lives.

The argument that infants, from the earliest point in life, possess a mental life that allows them to discover new meanings about themselves fails to allow for any development. The view as expressed throughout this book is that a developmental approach is necessary in order to understand emotional life as well as the factors that lead to failures in emotional development. Because infants show complex actions to events in their worlds early, we need to explore the meaning of these actions by looking for a moment at the specific issue of intention since the actions of the infant bring to mind the idea of actions as intentions. This may allow us the opportunity to understand how complex actions can take place with a minimum of mental capacity.

In trying to understand very early infant action patterns, including such phenomena as a newborn or 2-month-old being able to learn—for example, to pull a string to get a reward—we are confronted with the infant's intention. In the same way, the infant smiling to a conspecific—part of the action pattern associated with joy—seems to be an intention.[12] Thus, in any discussion of an infant's action we come upon the idea of intention since for the most part the adult's social world is likely to assume an intention, as when we say "My baby understands that when she pulled the string the picture appeared."

After considering this problem, I have decided to use the broadest definition of intention by saying that intentions are any actions that have goals. Action patterns, such as smiling to a face-like stimulus or pulling a string to get a picture to appear on a screen, are examples that we have discussed. However, there are different kinds of intentions. To capture this difference I have divided actions into *intentions* and *intentionality*.[13] Thus, while intentions are actions that have a goal, intentionality involves actions due to the use of mental representations of goals. My argument claims that earlier emotional behaviors are bodily action patterns, which are intentions, while it is only later in development, with the rise of self-representation, that intentions become intentionality. In humans, these different kinds of actions are supported by different degrees of mental processes, in the young infant to a small degree, and in 2-year-olds and older children, to a greater degree.[14] For our discussion of the development of emotional life, once consciousness develops, these earlier intentions remain but now intentionality is added to them.

Piaget offered a blueprint of the development of causality and intention in the opening years of life[15] where in the earliest stages of development children's actions are simply biologically given action patterns, much as we have described in earlier chapters.[16] After a time, these action patterns produce (still without intentionality) outcomes. Thus, A accidentally causes B (an effect), and B, in turn, produces A. Piaget characterizes this chain of events as simple circular action pattern. The simple representation is the association that A and B are mutually connected. Nevertheless, it is B, an environmental event (an effect in the world) that causes A (the action) to occur. I think it is safe to conclude that, for Piaget, the child starts the developmental process without intentionality even though there may be bodily intentions. This is part of the distinction between action patterns with or without mental acts that we make.

However, we need to make certain that we distinguish between action patterns and mental acts.[17] Since the issue of consciousness and intentionality does lead to difficulties, let me state explicitly that all goal-directed systems have intentions. At the earliest age, the action patterns we have discussed before are intentions; that is, they have evolutionary adaptive patterns of action that lead to a goal. For example, disgust is an action pattern having a goal of eliminating from the mouth unpleasant smells and tastes, while anger is an action pattern designed to overcome a blocked goal. These action patterns have goals and are therefore intentions. However, as Piaget has made clear, it is not until there is mental representation, what I call consciousness, that we can say that the child has intentionality.

THE SELF SYSTEM

I believe that once we develop into adulthood, the machine of my body and my consciousness both exist. What might their combination be referred to? Without doubt these features of body and consciousness make reference to the self system. Since the term "self" has a long history in the discussion of consciousness, let us consider it before going on. Because the term "self" is often used with a variety of meanings, we need to consider four questions about the self that, when answered, will make clearer what consciousness refers to in the theory as presented.

What Is a Self?

There are at least two aspects of the self. In one, the self has knowledge about itself, which I call consciousness. However, innate action patterns have no such knowledge, neither for the infant nor for nonhuman life. T-cells are capable of intention since they go after foreign proteins and kill them, and they also are capable of self- versus non-self-recognition. Nevertheless, these cells do not have knowledge *about* themselves. Infants soon after birth engage in what some have called nonverbal communication, others have called social reflexive behavior, and still others have called intersubjectivity. Do these infants also have knowledge about themselves? If infants have knowledge about themselves—a claim made by many—then what develops? The problem can be solved by considering that the term self is inadequate to the task. A self is made up of too many features.[18] For example, all living creatures have self-regulating and self-organizing capabilities, and all creatures that have social lives have the ability to interact with regard to other conspecifics; human and nonhuman animals share these features.

What we might not share with most other creatures is our ability to reflect on ourselves, as well as being embedded in a culture that provides the content or aboutness of that reflection. We also are not likely to share with other living creatures the ability to understand recursive propositions involving the self expressed in knowledge such as "I know that you know that I know how to chop wood."[19]

This problem of different aspects of a self inhibits our progress, namely, that even the most basic machine aspects of self are often discussed in ways that assume that they exhibit the mental representation of me. Our language and our quest for meaning are likely to confuse us. Consider again newborn imitation. We call the tongue protrusion of a newborn to the tongue protrusion of an adult imitation. We also call it imitation when the 6-year-old wants to wear the same colored shirt as does her friend Rana. Piaget, who also observed early imitation, tried to distinguish between this early kind of imitation, which he considered reflexive behavior, and later imitation that has mental representations. He argued, as I have, that the same behavior may serve very different processes, and different behaviors can serve the same process. The developmental literature is full of such examples of the same behavior served by different processes.[20]

Another problem already discussed is that humans have the capacity as well as the need to attribute humanness to animate and even inanimate things. This anthropomorphizing has to be considered when we talk about infants and other animals and the origins of consciousness. Given our adult knowledge of situations and the emotions these situations invoke in us, we readily attribute these emotions to the infant. As this knowledge is in part culturally given, different cultures should produce different parental beliefs in regard to their infants' emotions. For example, as has already been mentioned, cultural differences in parental beliefs about infant anger differ.

Although we have the tendency for meaning seeking and anthropomorphizing, nonetheless these tendencies are an important feature in the human child's emotional development. I would propose that the meaning the parents give to behavior affects the meaning the child learns. If I find more anger in my child than another parent finds in his child, my child is likely to be more angry later in life because my attributions are conveyed to the child in many ways, including the verbal labeling of the infant's behavior.[21] What we attribute to a child is, in large part, what the child will learn and includes such cultural aspects as emotional labels and expressive interactions, as well as rules, goals, and standards.

I tried to define what I considered a self to be. Consciousness or the mental representation of me is but one aspect of our selves. This mental state is flexible in that it can be evoked or not. Indeed, it is adaptive sometime to have consciousness and sometime not to have consciousness. It is not useful for me to think about me when I am trying to bring my car swiftly to a stop on a highway after a tire blowout. My attention is drawn to the tasks of bringing my car to a safe stop. It is only after stopping by the side of the road that I can focus on myself. To do so earlier is nonadaptive.

How Do We Measure a Self?

Of course, measurement must follow from theory. If the aspect of self that we wish to observe is related to early action patterns, then we can study such behavior as pulling a string or exhibiting disgust to sour tastes. If we are interested in mental representations, then we can study self-recognition in mirrors. It seems to be a mistake to confuse measurement of one feature of self with another, and to make the claim that one measure reflects all aspects. Personal pronoun use, pretend play, or self-directed mirror behavior are all methods that should inform us about the consciousness aspect of self.

Are There Cultural and Historical Differences in the Idea of Self, or Experience and Consciousness?

We make the distinction of a bodily experience, such as my body's monitoring my blood sugar level and its subsequent production of insulin, versus experience as a mental act or consciousness. When we talk about consciousness, we mean a mental representation of me. However, we can also mean the "aboutness" of that representation. It is my belief that these two aspects of consciousness have in the first case a universal quality linked to the biology of brain maturation, while in the second case it is culturally derived and therefore may differ across cultures. Some universal features of a self include self–other discrimination, self-regulating, and self–other interactions, which can be observed in the very young infant, and later the ability to recognize oneself in mirrors. All of these features seem to be found across cultures and throughout historical time. These acts of self-referential behavior are not cultural artifacts but a part of the biology of humanness.[22] If, as some believe, the maturation of the left temporal lobe is necessary for a mental representation of "me," then the development that occurs in this brain area in the middle of the second year of life is likely to also exist across cultures. Other expressions of self-referential behavior, however, may be quite different depending on cultural specifics. The "terrible 2's," experienced in U.S. culture as part of the emergence of the toddler's will independent of the parent's wishes, may not be so marked in cultures less interested in individual autonomy and more interested in a we–self culture.[23]

William James suggested over 100 years ago that it is wise to separate features of structure from features of content. The problem of cross-cultural differences is likely to be best approached by arguing that some structures—for example, the ability to reflect on ourselves—are pancultural, but that most of the content of these structures is culturally determined. There is no reason to assume that a structural feature of the self, the emergence of consciousness, is much affected by cultural or by caregiving techniques. Unless they suffer severely bad treatment, children are likely to develop this structural feature. What is affected, however, is the content of what children come to view themselves as. Poor or abusive care is likely to result in negative and even pathological content about the self; however, it should not affect the emergence of consciousness or the mental capacity of self-representation. Likewise the content of our consciousness may differ, such as the Western idea of a single self standing alone and in opposition to other such selves, the I-self, as opposed to the we-self found in Japanese and Indian cultures.

What Does a Self Do?

This question has to do with why we need the construct of self as having both features of bodily machinery and consciousness. For example, instead of the term "self-regulation," we could simply use the term "system regulation." Self-regulation implies something unique about the self. For each of the features of self that we articulate, we can ask the same question: What would the child be like if she did not have self features? It is obvious that for the earliest features of self their absence would result in such maladaptive behavior that the child could not survive. Thus, failures of self–other differentiation or self–other interaction results in disorders that we think of as autism or some type of serious retardation. More important for this discussion is, what would happen if consciousness or the mental representation of me did not emerge? What are the differences between children who have consciousness and those who are developmentally less advanced?

In the case of a conscious organism, we could expect the conscious child to show, in addition to a variety of capabilities, such as empathy and embarrassment, and later shame, guilt, and pride, self-referential behaviors such as self-recognition, personal pronoun usage, and pretend play. Prior to the emergence of consciousness, the emotional capacities of empathy or embarrassment are not present, while the basic emotions, like fear and anger, are present. In one study my colleagues and I have shown that prior to self-referential behavior, infants show anger and fear but not embarrassment. It is only after self-referential behavior develops that the toddler shows embarrassment.[24] Darwin too believed that embarrassment exists only after we have an aware self, a "me" or consciousness, an "I" that can be the object of others' attention. He wrote, "It is not the simple act of reflecting on our own appearance (a mental representation of me) but the thinking what others think of us, which excites a blush."[25] Humans and nonhumans share many features of self; one feature that we do not share is the mental representation of me and its cognitive elaboration through cultural learning. It is this that makes us different from other creatures.

Even in our everyday lives we are confronted with explaining what a self is and how it is related to consciousness. It would seem to me that many of our motor actions, although they are initially planned, are later carried out by machine processes of our body that include, by definition, self-regulation and self–other differentiation. The same, of course, is true of the processes involved in thinking. A consciousness is necessary for us to formulate, at least sometimes, what it is that we wish to think about. But the representation of me does not appear to be involved in the processes that actually conduct the task of thinking. Consider this example: I give a person the problem of adding a 7 to the sum of 7's that precede it ($7 + 7 = 14 + 7 = 21 + 7 = 28$, etc.). It is clear that as a person carries out this task, he cannot reflect on himself doing the arithmetic. One aspect of the self, consciousness, understands the problem setup and has the intentionality to solve it, while the machine self actually accomplishes the task.

Self as a System

A self can be considered to be a system containing both biological and mental aspects.[26] As a system, it shares certain common features with other living systems.[27]

1. All living systems self-regulate. By this we mean that within any living system there is need for communication between parts of that system. This can include a system as small as a cell, a plant, or an animal, or even a more complex organism like a newborn child. As I sit here writing, my systems are regulating my temperature, producing shivering as the room cools, or regulating my blood sugar level. Self-regulation is a property of living matter. Self-regulation makes no assumptions about a mental state of me, though it could.[28]

2. Some minimal differentiation between the self and other is a necessary condition for any system to act. Whether this differentiation is a product of history or part of the process of action, including perceiving, is unknown. What appears to be so is that any organism cannot act without at some level being able to distinguish between self and other. The ability to distinguish self from other is part of the core processes of all living systems.

3. A unique aspect of the adult human self system is that it alone contains a mental representation of the system. By "mental representation" I mean the capacity of the self to know it knows or to remember it remembers. It also means that the self system has the capacity to know that there are things it does not know about itself. Not until recently did we know about our amygdala's reaction when we are fearful, something that we did not know 25 years ago. We know about our amygdala but presumably our amygdala does not know about us. It is this knowledge that is referred to when I say consciousness.

These features of a self system can be helpful in understanding the development of emotions[29] and have a developmental perspective. However, in a human adult all these features of a self system are at work. Wanting to write requires a "me wanting." The very act of writing these words, although planned and therefore involving consciousness, is carried out for the most part by the machinery of my body. This may strike one as odd since how could it be that I can write—a motor act—complicated phrases and thoughts almost effortlessly without giving attention to the processes that give rise to them? I certainly know, as I sit here writing—notice the self-reflection—that I had a plan to write and I had an outline that I made to help me formulate my thoughts. It is clear that I have intentionality and desires, and presumably the ability to carry out the task of thinking and writing, yet the acts themselves seem to emerge almost effortlessly. Indeed, as Daniel Wegner has shown, if we focus our attention on these actions we find that doing so can interrupt the very act that we are performing.[30] We can also see this in the failure of not being able to carry out a desire as in akrasia, where intentionality to do X does not lead to X or may lead to Y

instead. The idea of failed intentions suggests that one way to understand the self is to assume the idea of multiple aspects of the self, only one being consciousness. Thus, akrasia and self-deception force us to view the self as a complex system, perhaps a modular system with features not in complete communication with each other—this is not a particularly new idea about what a self might be.[31]

This notion of a self system is most important for the theory of emotional development. A revealing illustration of the system at work can be found in Karl Pribram's description of a patient in whom the medial part of the temporal lobe had been bilaterally removed. Here we see the different features of the self at work and also see the conflict between them.

> I once had the opportunity to examine some patients in whom the medial part of the temporal lobe—including the amygdala—had been removed bilaterally. These patients, just as their monkey counterparts, typically ate considerably more than normal and gained up to a hundred pounds in weight. At least I could ask the subject how it felt to be so hungry. But much to my surprise, the expected answer was not forthcoming. One patient who gained more than 100 pounds in the several years since surgery was examined at lunchtime. "Was she hungry?" She answered, "No." "Would you like a piece of rare, juicy steak?" "No." "Would she like a piece of chocolate candy?" She answered, "Um-hum," but when no candy was offered she did not pursue the matter. A few minutes later when the examination was completed, the doors to the common room were opened, and she saw the other patients already seated at a table eating lunch. She rushed to the table, pushed the others aside, and began to stuff food into her mouth with both hands. She was immediately recalled to the examining room, and questions about food were repeated. The same negative answers were obtained again, even after they were pointedly contrasted with her recent behavior at the table. Somehow the lesion had impaired the patient's feelings of hunger and satiety, and this impairment was accompanied by excessive eating![32]

Given the definition of consciousness as self-reflection, we can answer the question posed earlier: Is all information that is bodily known capable of being consciously known? The answer is not always and, in fact, most often not. Bodily processes including emotional action patterns may be available to consciousness but only at times. I may be able to learn to focus on bodily experiences, such as sensing my heart rate or my blood pressure or sensing my increases in heart rate when I am frustrated; however, this ability is limited. My consciousness may never be available to some of the machinery of my system. Thus, there may be built into the self the basis of conflict, a natural one between the machinery of the system and the self-reflected aspects of the system. Such conflicts, from a developmental point of view, must await the rise of consciousness.

MEASURING THE DEVELOPMENT
OF CONSCIOUSNESS

Measurement follows from the constructs we make; therefore, if we are interested in the development of consciousness, then we need to measure it rather than action patterns or the machine of the system. Since early imitation, intersensory integration, and coordination between infant and mother all are likely to reflect action patterns, they are not adequate measures of consciousness. In studying adults we rely on language to examine self-experience. We ask, for example, what emotions are you experiencing? Without adequate language, the infant or toddler cannot inform us in this way. One alternative is to require the child to do certain tasks and see whether and at what age he can do them. If the child understands the task given, it is possible to demonstrate that the child has the idea, even though he does not have language to express it. Thus, for example, in the work on deception and in the research on a theory of mind, it has been possible to show that the young child can deceive and also place himself in the role of another.[33]

Unfortunately, even these studies require that children understand language, although they do not necessarily have to produce it. Thus, for example, in the deception studies, children have to understand the experimenters' instructions, and therefore cannot be much younger than 3 years old. By this age, it seems clear that children have gained consciousness. The question, then, is whether consciousness emerges earlier, and if so, how it might be measured. We could still focus on language and argue that consciousness can be measured by whether children have acquired their names—after all, we are what we are called. The risk of accepting this as proof is that the child may have been taught to use his name by associating it with a visual array, a photograph of himself, without consciousness being present.[34]

Another language measure, a bit less suspect, is that of personal pronoun usage. Because parents do not use the label "me" or "mine" when referring to the child, the use of these terms by the child is likely to be a reasonable measure of consciousness. This appears even more the case when we observe children's use of personal pronouns and how they behave when using them. One can observe a toddler saying "mine" as she pulls the object away from another child and toward herself. Because moving the object toward oneself does not move the object as far away from the other as possible, the placement of the object next to the body, together with the use of the terms "me" or "mine," appears to reference consciousness and ownership. Children begin to use personal pronouns including "me" and "mine" by the middle of the second year of life, which can provide a linguistic demonstration of the emerging mental state of me.[35] It is a measure of self-referential behavior. This reminds me of a wonderful piece written by Edward St. Aubyn, which addresses the fact that personal pronoun use is more than a simple learning of words. Talking about a toddler and his mother, he writes:

> She lifted him up and sat him on her lap, rocking him gently. Whenever he was hurt he reverted to calling himself "you," although he had discovered the proper use of the first person singular six months ago. Until then, he had referred to himself as "you" on the perfectly logical grounds that everyone else did. He also referred to others as "I," on the perfectly logical grounds that that was how they referred to themselves. Then one week "you want it" turned into "I want it." Everything he did at the moment—the fascination with danger, the assertion of ownership, the ritual contradiction, the desire to do things for himself—was about this explosive transition from being "you" to being "I," from seeing himself through his parents' eyes to looking through his own.[36]

Another self-referential behavior that can be used to measure consciousness is self-recognition. Over many years, I have been studying infants' and young children's self-recognition in mirrors and have developed a measurement technique now widely used. The procedure is simple. Unknown to the child, his nose is marked with rouge. The child is then placed in front of a mirror, where it is possible to observe whether the child, looking in the mirror, touches his marked nose or whether he touches the image in the mirror. Smiling at the mirror, however, is not a good measure alone of self-referential behavior because we have found that infants even as young as 2 months, when placed in front of mirrors, will show interest, smile, coo, and try to attract the attention of the child in the mirror, although they do not behave as if they recognize that it is they themselves they see. In fact, they show the same behavior to still pictures or videos of other babies. Babies enjoy seeing other babies. At older ages, when locomotion appears, on occasion, infants have been observed going behind the mirror to see whether they can find the child behind the mirror. In addition, they often touch the mirror as if they are trying to touch the other, but do not touch their own noses. Somewhere around 15 to 18 months of age, they begin to appear to know that the images are themselves because they touch their noses or comment about the color on their noses when looking in the mirror. By 24 months typically developing children show this ability. Consciousness is captured by the children's use of this self-referential behavior. The touching of their noses when they look in the mirror seems to reveal that they know that it is "me" there.[37]

Measuring other aspects of self-referential behavior is possible, including pretend play. From a variety of theoretical perspectives, it is apparent that pretense is an early manifestation of one's mental state. Alan Leslie, for one, has argued that pretense as a measure of self-representation is a necessary precursor of a theory of mind.[38] Pretense involves double knowledge or dual representation of the literal and the pretend situation. The dissociable relation between the two allows the child to distinguish between appearance and reality. Research by Piaget and subsequent investigators reveals two kinds of pretense with a developmental history. The first type, which emerges early, is a pretense in which the child herself is the object of the pretend play. For example, Tamara will talk on a toy phone or drink from an empty cup. This first type of pretense recognizes little mental ability as children about 1 year of age can engage in this type as well. Also children with autism engage in this type. The second type of pretense involves the use of another person or social object like a doll or stuffed animal as part of the pretense. In this instance Tamara uses the other "person" as the object of the pretense. Tamara has the doll talking on the phone or drinking from the empty cup. We have called this form of pretense *pretense with other*. The capacity for pretense with others is a measure of self-referential behavior and also the beginnings of a theory of mind, as the child knows that what she is doing is not real. The mental state of me seen in pretense with others distinguishes children's consciousness from abilities likely to reflect action patterns related to the machinery of self.[39]

The relationship between the three measures of self-reflective behavior, personal pronoun usage, mirror recognition, and pretend play with others appears to be developmentally related, and occurs around the middle of the second year of life. In our studies, my colleagues and I have found that while they emerge at about the same time, mirror self-recognition seems to emerge a bit earlier than the others.[40] There are many studies linking these self-referential behaviors to other abilities that indicate more broadly the emergence of consciousness. For example, we have found self-recognition related to children's self-conscious emotions,[41] while others have found it related to altruism,[42] empathy,[43] autobiographical memories,[44] and imitation.[45] While it is likely that the development of self-referential behaviors is not an all-or-nothing process—see Kurt Fischer's idea about this gradual development[46]—the use of self-referential behaviors indicates that no infants show self-recognition prior to 15 months. Given that a mental age of 15 to 18 months is necessary for its emergence and that children with autism show an absence or delay, it is likely that maturational processes play an important role in its development.[47] Moreover, there appears to be a phylogenetic as well as an ontogenetic feature to self-recognition. Monkeys do not show self-recognition, while the great apes, chimpanzees, orangutans, gorillas, and humans do.[48] These findings provide strong support for a major role of maturational brain processes that may underlie self-referential behavior and consciousness.

Brain Maturation Related to Self-Consciousness

Over the last 75 years, the development of consciousness has been linked to social interaction, but there is relatively little data to support this view. The ontogenetic as well as the phlyogenetic findings lead to my belief that maturation of the human child's brain has much to do with the onset of consciousness. I want to be clear that what we are talking about is not the ways a toddler thinks about himself, but the fact that brain maturation affects the child's ability to be able to think about himself: consciousness as a process, not its aboutness. It is mostly the social interactive world that is responsible for the content of the aboutness. This process of thinking about the self is associated with brain maturation and activity. In adults, the left superior temporal gyrus and the left medial frontal gyrus are activated when they engage in a theory-of-mind task as opposed to when they just read sentences. Activation of the left superior temporal area, the left inferior parietal area, and the left and right occipital regions occurs when adults judge whether adjectives are relevant to themselves.[49] In a study of brain activation in children at hearing one's own name, Dennis Carmody and I have found activation in the middle and superior temporal region as well as in the left middle frontal region. In general, then, there is agreement that self-representational behaviors activate regions near the temporal–parietal junction, although there are data suggesting activation of the medial frontal cortex as well.[50]

From a developmental perspective, we would need to study the relation between the emergence of this self-representational ability and changes in brain function. Obtaining functional magnetic resonance imaging (fMRI) or positron emission tomography (PET) scans in very young children has been shown to be difficult, and there are few, if any, published fMRI studies of children between 15 and 30 months of age, which is the critical age range for the development of self-representational behaviors.[51]

However, there are other ways to study brain development. One way is to measure the relative amounts of gray and white matter in different brain regions. Magnetic resonance imaging (MRI) can show brain maturation. Changes in these MRI features are informative in determining the developmental changes in white and gray matter for normal and clinical cases, and computational analysis of MRI images allows us to detect individual changes in white matter. Quantitative measures include volumetric analyses of gray and white matter, development of white matter relative to gray matter, and the more recent diffusion tensor imaging (DTI) techniques to assess white matter connectivity. Given these techniques, it is possible to measure individual differences in development by region and to relate these individual regional differences in development to individual differences in children's self-representation.[52]

To investigate this problem, Carmody and I have studied infants from 15 to 30 months of age and related their development in brain regions with their scores on self-referential behavior. The findings from this study indicate that the degree of brain development in the left temporal region, independent of age, is related to the emergence of children's self-representation. This holds true for a total self-representation score made up of the performance on mirror recognition, personal pronouns usage, and pretend play, as well as for each of these measures separately. Our results are consistent with other findings that implicate the temporal region in its role in self-representational behavior. These are the same brain regions that have been found to be activated in adults during several types of self-representational behaviors, such as when subjects judge whether adjectives are relevant to themselves, as well as when subjects hear their own name.[53]

In support of these findings, Carmody and I have found differences in brain maturation obtained for children with autism spectrum disorder (ASD) as compared to children developing typically. Children with ASD have significantly higher levels of mylenation in both the left and the right frontal regions relative to the typically developing children. However, the reverse was true for the left temporal region where children with ASD had lower than normal mylenation in the left lobe. In a recent study, we found for children with ASD a significant association between volume size and self-referential behavior, in particular in the left temporal pole, the left temporal cortex, and the left medial prefrontal cortex—the areas predicted by Frith and Frith.[54]

Consciousness and the Social World

There are two competing views about the development of consciousness. The first involves brain maturation, which is the view that I think makes the most sense given the data we have. The second view, which is more widespread and the most referenced, involves social learning, social interactions, and how poor parenting affects the development of self-referential behavior. While this second view may account for the development of consciousness, there does not exist much specific research on early social interaction and subsequent differences in consciousness, at least as measured by self-referential behavior.[55] Nevertheless, the idea that consciousness is produced by the infant's interactions with its social world has a long history. To make sense of it we need to remember that in the discussion of consciousness, the term "self" is most often used. William James, in *The Principles of Psychology*, considered the problem of self, and mentioned its duality:

> Whatever I may be thinking of, I am always, at the same time more or less aware of myself, of my personal existence. At the same time, it is I who am aware, so that the total self or me, being as it were duplex, partly known and partly knower, partly object and partly subject, must have two aspects discriminated in it, of which, for shortness, we may call one the "me" and the other the "I."[56]

James went on to distinguish a hierarchy of selves, with a "bodily me" at the bottom and a "spiritual me" at the top, and various social selves in between. He envisioned a developmental trajectory, from the earliest physical or bodily experiences of the self to the later spiritual or nonmaterial experiences. James's duality of self can be noted in the philosophical literature from Descartes to Wittgenstein. However, James's duality and Wittgenstein's were relational in nature, not split into a dichotomy as was Descartes's duality.[57] Nevertheless, Descartes considered two classes of experience, with pain as an example of one, grief of the other. The first, pain, comes to us through our senses, or what we might refer to as James's "bodily me." Grief, in contrast, does not arise from immediate sense impressions but from ideas.[58]

James's thinking about the self and self-development branched in two directions, one cognitive and the other social. Within a cognitive framework, James Mark Baldwin described the development of the self in terms of its relationship to others, whereas Piaget viewed this development in terms of evolving mathematical/logical constructions, as the child moved from egocentrism to decentering. Although Piaget's discussion focuses on ages beyond the period of interest for our study of the emergence of consciousness, his views are still intriguing. If we ignore the fact that he is discussing children between the ages of 2 and 6, his formulation agrees with that of others about 2-year-olds. Piaget writes:

> That the child being ignorant of his own ego, takes his own point of view as absolute, and fails to establish between himself and the external world of things, that reciprocity, which alone would ensure objectivity. . . . Whenever relationships dependent upon the ego are concerned—they are at the crux of the matter—the child fails to grasp the logic of relations for lack of having established reciprocity, first between himself and other people, and between himself and things.[59]

According to Piaget, once children have reached a symbolic level of fuctioning, early reflection occurs at around age 2. This decentering is the capacity of the child to take the perspective of another. This permits viewing herself as others might view her, thereby indicating movement toward self-reflection or consciousness.

At about the same time as James, Charles Cooley, a sociologist, struggled with similar problems concerning the self and its origins. Writing about the social nature of human beings and social organization, Cooley posited a reflected or "looking glass" self. The self is reflected through the other; thus, other people are the "looking glass" for oneself. In addition, Cooley stressed the relational idea that the self and society form a common whole, with neither existing in the absence of the other. Cooley believed that infants are not conscious, do not have an "I," nor are they aware of society or other people. Infants experience a simple stream of impressions, impressions that gradually become discriminated as the young child differentiates itself, or "I," from the society, or "we," a view that I have suggested as well. However, Cooley saw the emerging "I" as a function of the child's social commerce.

George Herbert Mead also drew a distinction between the machinery of the system and consciousness, using James's "I" and "me." The "I" is the systems self, while the "me" is the consciousness self-reflecting on the "I." Mead assumed that the movement from the early systems self to the conscious self takes place within a social nexus and is made possible only through social learning. Mead saw taking the perspective of another as the way the child was able to develop consciousness, and like Cooley he argued the relational position that knowledge about the self and others developed simultaneously, with both forms of knowledge dependent on social interaction. Heavily influenced by Darwin, he felt that the human infant is active rather than passive, selectively responding to stimuli rather than indiscriminately responding to all events. Hence, Mead believed that the infant actively constructs the self—here he is referring to the mental representative self, or consciousness. He stated:

> Self has a character which is different from that of the physiological organism proper, the self is something which has a development; it is not initially there at birth, but arises in the process of social experience and activity. That is, it develops in the given individual as a result of his relations to that process as a whole and to other individuals within that process.[60]

The similarity between Mead's and Cooley's ideas and mine is considerable: we share a belief in the duality of self and the development of the conscious self, but they differ from me and my view on the role of the child's social interaction in the promotion of the conscious self.

The psychoanalytic literature is too broad to go into detail about it here. Nevertheless, the Freudian view about ego development and the system of drives matches, to some extent, and parallels the problems of the self and consciousness as we have considered it. It is reasonable to say that the drives or id operate much like what we have been calling action patterns, while the ego and superego operate much like what we have been calling consciousness. Because the id is a basic drive system, it needed to develop over time, and as such part of the ego system served this role. Thus, the preconscious and the unconscious were made up of both the id and the ego, while the conscious mental representation was made up of the ego and the superego. However, more important for the discussion of development of the self in interaction with the social world is the work of Melanie Klein, Margaret Mahler, and Donald Winnicott.

The challenge confronting the object relation theorists had to do with whether or not to consider the infant as having a self, unique from that of his mother, that is, consciousness from the beginning, or whether this self emerged from the mother–infant relationship. Winnicott's contribution to the object relations work addressed the nature of the child's dependency or, more specifically, whether from early life one could think of the infant as having a mental life—as did Melanie Klein, who viewed the infant as a distinct psychological entity from the beginning. As Winnicott wrote, "It is not possible to describe an infant without describing the mother whom the infant has not yet become able to separate from a self."[61]

Mahler also believed that the developmental process is such that the infant has to separate himself from the mother and this separation takes time for both of them. The child, to begin with, is undifferentiated and becomes more differentiated as a function of good mothering. Mahler and her colleagues articulate a self system that develops in a sequence. She describes the development of the self as a struggle between separateness and relatedness, and calls this the separation/individuation process. Of special interest for us is Mahler's description of the child in the last half of the second year of life. She posits an increased awareness of self. In addition, she feels that both empathy and understanding of what it means to be separate and autonomous emerge between ages 18 and 24 months. The child's "love affair" with the world is modified as she learns about frustrations and limitations. In the third year, individuality is consolidated, separations from the mother become easier to bear, and the ability to take another's role becomes more pronounced. The child has developed a self that is separate from, but also related to, others.[62] Daniel Stern also tried to deal with this issue in terms of the infant's developmental sequence. However, he believed in a faster development. He saw the process as part of forming an attachment, which then allows for selfhood to emerge; thus it is seen in the first year of life. However appealing this idea may be, there is not much support for the relation between attachment and the process of consciousness.[63]

Although it is unclear whether Winnicott, Mead, or Cooley saw biological processes at work in the process of the development of consciousness, they certainly argued for the child's involvement with his social world as the basic mechanism of development. The child cannot develop a sense of the self, or consciousness, alone. For example, Mead uses the example of a boy running down a road. The boy has a rudimentary awareness of his body, what I have called the machinery of the self, but this does not constitute consciousness. For Mead, the child's developmental task is to detach his awareness from within himself and to assume an outside point of view. That is, the child needs to gain a vantage point external to himself and then look back at himself. This ability to look back at oneself implies taking the role of another, as if the boy enters the head of the other and observes himself through the other's way of characterizing him. For Mead, the way others characterize one's self leads to consciousness. This view is shared by others. For example, Bannister and Agnew note: "The ways in which we elaborate our construing of self must be essentially those ways in which we elaborate our construing of others, for we have not a concept of self but a bipolar construct of self—not self or self-other."[64] Maurice Merleau-Ponty wrote: "If I am a consciousness turned toward things, I can meet in things the actions of another and find in them a meaning because they are themes of possible activity for my own body."[65] Social knowledge and social action are dependent on the role of the knower's consciousness. Like Soloman Asch, Fritz Heider reflects this as a central theme when he states: "Social perceptions in general can best be described as a process between the center of one person and the center of another person, from life space to life space. . . . A, through psychological processes in himself, perceives psychological processes in B."[66]

More recently Shelley Duval and Robert Wicklund, while arguing for the role of the social world in this process, have suggested that at least three conditions need to be met if the child is to develop consciousness: (1) there must be an entity who has a different point of view than the child, (2) the two different points of view must concern the same object, and (3) the child must be aware of these two different opinions simultaneously. They base their position on their belief that consciousness becomes differentiated from the action patterns of the self through this process. To begin with, the infant acts, perceives, and thinks, but does not turn her attention on herself. The turning of attention on the self requires a conflict between the child's action and the actions of others. This conflict enables the child to objectify her actions, thoughts, and feelings, and thus she achieves consciousness.[67] It is most likely to occur in the social world. However, it is more than possible that it also occurs in the physical world. It is the simultaneity of differing action–outcome pairings that is important. It is conflictual situations, ones in which there are varying possible outcomes, which are likely to be the most effective in generating the development of consciousness.

Interestingly, this analysis bears a similarity to the psychoanalytic view of the emergence of secondary thought processes. The inability of the id to achieve its purpose in the world creates ego mechanisms. Thus, wishing for something to eat causes lawful planning in the world only to the degree that the environment is in some conflict with the id's desires. John Watson and Gyorgy Gergely suggested a similar process of conflict. For them the contingency between the infant's action and the outcomes in the world can be perceived by the infant; if they are imperfect the infant is able to construct mental representations including a self-representation. It is the imperfect contingency between the infant's action in its world that gives rise to consciousness.[68]

The general view is that caregivers, through their interactions with their infants, will have an impact on the child's self-development. Poor caregiving, then, should result in the disruption of the process of acquiring consciousness. This view is held by almost all social theorists. Although such a view is appealing, and on its face reasonable, closer examination does not reveal much empirical support for it. There is no evidence that poor caregiving results in failure to develop consciousness. While poor parenting has been shown to be associated with how children think of themselves, for example, whether they see themselves as good or bad, or leads to reduced capacity for empathy, there is no support for the idea that poor parenting leads to difficulty in developing consciousness. It may, however, lead to a different content of consciousness, that is, differences in aboutness.

* * *

We have tried to argue that a self is made up of many features, one of which is the action patterns, the adaptive evolutionary associations between innate and coordinated sets of behaviors and specific and literal features of the world. We have also called these action patterns the machinery of the self. The adults in any particular culture name these action patterns, using such terms as fear or joy. Moreover, they respond with a variety of behaviors as a consequence of their belief systems.

Sometime in the second year of life we see the emergence of self-referential behavior, which appears to mark the onset of consciousness. The onset of a mental state, the idea of me, marks a major event in the child's emotional development. The question remains as to what gives rise to this milestone. A wide variety of theories—from a psychoanalytic to a learning theory view—suggests that the interactions of the infant with its social world, in particular with its caregivers, is responsible. Although these theories are reasonable, they have little research to support them. This is because there is a considerable lack of clarity between the emergence of the capacity to self-reflect and the content of that self-reflection.

While the social world must play a role in the content or aboutness of consciousness, I believe that the brain maturational processes, in particular the maturation of the left temporal regions of the brain, are associated with the ability to self-reflect, or consciousness. Still to be determined, however, is whether actions in the social world affect brain maturation. More studies will be needed to answer this question.

The self is made up of consciousness as well as other bodily functioning. These two features need to be considered. In a recent review of a book on Baruch Spinoza, Avishai Margalit states that for Spinoza an explanation of a girl blushing would consist of a body description: extra adrenaline leads to an increase in sympathetic nervous system functioning, which in turn widens her blood vessels. However, a parallel explanation, psychological in nature, is also possible for Spinoza and might be that the thought that she was being looked at made her feel flushed. Thus, for him, these are both reasonable explanations that unfortunately are not readily reconciled.[69]

However we decide to explain it, what is clear is that the emergence of consciousness plays a central role in the child's emotional life in addition to its social and cognitive development. The ability to measure the onset of this mentalism provides a framework for a discussion of the consequence of consciousness, a topic for the next chapter.

CHAPTER 6

The Transforming Role of Consciousness

Self-Conscious Emotions, Social Relationships, and Mentalism

It's our human capacity for being in one place, while having the mental capacity to imagine another place as we have the mental capacity to recall the past, learn from, and calculate the future; that is our species' exceptional talent. All of civilization—tradition, art, law, and domesticity—are the consequence of never being exclusively here, now but having the conscious ability to be there, then.

—JOYCE CAROL OATES[1]

The role of consciousness in human life is profound, as Oates's words inform us. While other creatures, most notably the great apes, show self-referential behaviors, their lack of other cognitive capacities, most importantly language, and their lack of culture, means that our species is likely unique. Consciousness affects our emotional lives by giving rise to the self-conscious emotions such as pride and shame; affects our social lives by changing innate interactions into relationships; and affects our cognitive lives by the creation of mentalism and with it access to the minds of others of our species. Because consciousness is essential to human development, the rise of consciousness has a profound transforming role on the human condition and on emotional life. While we have no direct measure of consciousness, I will use our data on self-referential behavior as an indirect measure of it.

Before discussing the transforming role of consciousness, I would like to review the ideas expressed in the model of emotional development so far presented. The early action patterns linked to specific contexts evolved through adaptive processes as part of the innate machinery of the self system. This innate system centers around the axis of approach and withdrawal action patterns and becomes differentiated around more specific contexts. The emotional system, to begin with, can be said to contain specific action patterns, including facial and body movement and internal physiological changes, that the social world calls specific emotions such as joy and sadness, here referred to as the early emotions. Thus, when we say that the infant is fearful, the common understanding is that the child shows specific facial patterns and bodily movements around a specific context thought by the infant's social world to produce fear. The infant through the first year and a half or so does not have a mental representation of herself. This view is consistent with that of others, as discussed in the last chapter.

The elaborate machinery of the self, already present at birth, allows for action and does so not only for actions related to emotional life but also for the infant's social and mental life. Although the transforming role of consciousness will address emotional and social life, its role in mental life is also profound—although this topic will not be considered in detail here. When considering the development of cognitive life, we can think of the early action patterns as procedural rules.[2] These procedural rules account for the infant's ability to respond with actions related to others' desires and intentions. These early infant action patterns are not based on mentalism but on procedural rules that are part of the biological capacities of the infant. Although the development of consciousness likely takes place over time, by about 18 months or so consciousness allows the toddler to start examining both his own and others' actions and, with the advent of language, gives words to these earlier self actions as well as to the behaviors of others. So if I know that I know or remember that I remember, I can find in others as well as myself these hidden mental states.

Recognition of the complexity of the self system allows us to consider many diverse problems having to do with action patterns or procedural rules as well as with consciousness and how the two systems might interact. That they interact seems obvious since conscious action can become procedural and procedural action can become conscious. Consider the following example: We all have had the rather common experience of driving our cars and suddenly arriving at a destination, like our office, without remembering exactly how we got there. We remember starting out on the journey and we remember that we planned to go to our office. We remember some things, like leaving our garage and getting onto the highway. We do not remember getting off the road or making a series of turns to arrive at our office parking lot. The well-rehearsed route of travel, with its complex turns, the stopping at traffic lights, and the shifting of gears has occurred without prolonged consciousness, although consciousness was involved when we made the plan to go to the office and may reoccur during the journey when some unexpected event happens. Here, as in skiing and other complex motor plans, an activity once learned does not require consciousness, so my attention is directed toward some thought other than driving or following a specific route. Even when thinking about something else I was able to complete complex motor plans that enabled me both to drive the car and to find my way to the office. To quote from Oates, our species has an "exceptional talent, never being exclusively there."

My second example involves crossing a busy intersection of five different avenues in the Chinese capital of Beijing. In this case, imagine that I am trying to get across this intersection facing cars moving in all directions. As I cross, for the next 30 seconds my attention is drawn to the cars around me while I pay attention to the cars behind me as well as in front of me. During this crossing I do not necessarily feel frightened. In fact, I do not feel anything since I am focused not on myself, but on the sounds and sights of the cars. It is only after I have safely reached the other side of the road that I feel fear. As this example shows, we humans have the ability to focus or not focus our attention on ourselves. During the crossing of the intersection I might have had internal bodily events associated with the action pattern of fear; however, I did not experience fear until I directed my attention toward what had just happened.

Two important conclusions about adults can be made from these types of examples:

1. We adults have the capacity to divert our attention inward toward ourselves or outward toward specific tasks. Earlier we called this "attention inward" consciousness and the "attention outward" the machinery of the system.
2. Even without directing our attention toward ourselves, our built-in action patterns are capable of performing highly complex and demanding tasks. Solutions to mental problems often "come to us" as we go about other activities.

Throughout this book, we have tried to distinguish between an emotional experience and an emotional action pattern. Like James, I accept the idea that what we commonly call an emotion consists both of changes in our own physiological state and our experiences of these changes. In the case of the tire blowout discussed earlier, we do not know whether we were having an action pattern of fear before bringing the car to a stop. Unfortunately, the term "consciousness" is used to talk about attention directed inward toward the self as well as outward toward the world. Pierre Janet and later Ernest Hilgard, for example, talked about the divided consciousness while others following Freud have talked about the conscious, the unconscious, and the preconscious. More recently, work on the modularity of brain function has shown that areas of the brain are quite capable of carrying out complex tasks or learning complex problems without other areas having knowledge of these actions. Michael Gazzaniga, for example, has shown that patients with their corpus callosum ablated—usually to reduce epileptic attacks—are capable of haptically having knowledge in their right hands while being unable to report (to know) what that knowledge is.[3] The work of Lawrence Weiskrantz on blindsightedness is another example of knowledge about where a visual object is located even though the vision cortex is damaged. His work is similar to Joseph LeDoux's work with animals that has demonstrated that both perceptual processes and complex learning can take place in the amygdala and hippocampus without cortical involvement or without knowledge of that learning.[4]

Such findings lend support to the idea of modularity of brain function— that is, for the involvement of some brain areas without the involvement of others—as well as the idea that complex mental operations can take place without the subject's own knowledge of or attention to these operations, that is, without consciousness. These relatively new findings on brain function fit with our own well-known experiences of sudden insight or the spontaneous solution of complex mental problems, as well as the set of commonly experienced phenomena that require intrapsychic differentiation and even conflict. I list in no apparent order some of these well-known phenomena: hypnotism, perceptual defense, self-deception, active forgetting, acts of loss of will, or apraxia, and multiple personality. These processes, although they have received some attention, have not been given the focus they need. Hilgard, for one, has called the underlying processes involved in all of them "disassociation," a term once in favor but now rarely used. Freud argued for an active process of repression rather than a splitting off of consciousness, a concept favored by Jean Martin Charcot and Pierre Janet.[5]

The ability to direct attention both toward ourselves and toward the outer world at the same time is an adaptive strategy rare in the animal kingdom. The adaptive significance of a divided consciousness is that it allows us to check on our own internal responses in addition to our behavior in the world, which we call self-focus, and, quite separately, to act-in-the-world, which is an outer focus. It is obvious from animal or even cell observations that it is possible to behave in a highly complex fashion in the world as a function of evolutionary-determined internally generated plans and programs. This action-in-the-world does not require us to pay attention to ourselves. Paying attention to ourselves allows us to modify action-in-the-world by thinking about our actions rather than by the use of trial and error. Thus, on the one hand, when we want to cross a busy street, it is probably adaptive not to be thinking about how well we are doing at the task but rather to be coordinating our action in context. On the other hand, if we have almost had an accident, then thinking about ourselves and our fear at being almost injured allows us to modify our plans for the future.

From a developmental perspective, what we observe in the infant's early behavior in the world is the machinery of the system. We can start to observe consciousness as a function of brain maturation, as well as the infant's actions with the social and physical world, in the middle of the second year of life. We have discussed measures of the emerging consciousness: mirror recognition, personal pronoun use, and pretend play behavior. By using these measures of self-referential behavior we and others have collected extensive data that demonstrate that consciousness, which may be developing slowly, can be seen in the middle of the second year of life, starting as early as 15 months and shown by most typically developing children no later than 24 months. This chapter will try to show what happens to the infant's emotional life when consciousness becomes present, first by describing the role of consciousness in the child's social and cognitive life, and then by focusing on the effects of consciousness on emotional life.

THE INFLUENCE OF CONSCIOUSNESS
ON DEVELOPMENT: A GENERAL MODEL

The problem in studying infants' development or, for that matter, children's behavior at any age, is that our studies usually divide the child's cognitive, social, and emotional life into separate domains. Lost in this epistemological division is the idea of the organism itself. There has been little attempt to unify these separate domains. Thus, while I shall separate out the role of consciousness in cognitive, social, and emotional development, it should be understood that these domains are connected with each other through the child's developing mental state of herself. The organization of development follows from the assumption that social, emotional, and cognitive knowledge are features of the same unified development system that is fundamental to the individual's consciousness. Individuals develop social, emotional, and cognitive knowledge in interactions with each other. Moreover, as Heinz Werner argued, development should be understood as a gradual differentiation among the various domains. The change from a unified system of knowledge based on the emergence of consciousness to one that is differentiated, integrated, and specialized occurs as a function of development.[6] The metaphor used to characterize this association is a series of concentric circles each with some overlap with the others. My preference for a metaphor is more like a tree, with the trunk representing the unified and integrated system generated by consciousness, while the branches represent the separate areas of knowledge, some of which are interrelated whereas others are independent. This model allows for both the integration of knowledge from a developmental perspective and the functional independence of the end product. Thus, as a central premise, the development of consciousness provides the scaffolding for the development, integration, and separation of the various behaviors of the child.

SOCIAL COGNITION, THEORY OF MIND, AND CONSCIOUSNESS

Older work on social cognition predates and provides the logical foundation for the newer work on theory of mind. We will address both, including consciousness as the basis of their development. When we use the term "social cognition," it implies that the self has a role in knowing, something that we consider below. I want to argue that the degree that the self as knower is part of the process of knowing is the degree to which the cognition is social. So, for example, I may know about a sunset over the hills of the Catskill Mountains by watching it, or I may know about it by reading a guidebook. In both cases, I have knowledge, but in one case that knowledge is gained through the self's experience of the phenomenon itself, whereas in the other case the knowledge is gained through the self's ability to read about the phenomenon. In French, for example, the verbs *connaître* and *savoir* capture this distinction.

Another example has to do with knowledge that involves the self, and is best captured by the sentence "I know that you know that I know your name." Such sentences and their meaning cannot be independent of consciousness since the self knows something about what another self knows about herself. The meaningfulness of such a sentence is dependent upon the knowledge of myself and knowledge of another self's knowledge of myself. While some of this knowledge may be procedural to begin with, it becomes explicit with consciousness. This aspect of consciousness has been studied under the heading of a theory of mind, something that is considered below.

The Role of the Knower in Knowing[7]

The scientific method was designed to generate theory and predict events. These goals are achieved, in part, through the separation of the scientist from the phenomena she investigates. Thus, the experimenter's worldview and beliefs are replaced by a nonbiased method. This distancing of the individual from the phenomena of study through a commonly accepted method of empirical proof—reliability of measures and logic—represents a major event in the development of science as we know it. Indeed, on an individual level, intellectual abstraction serves to distance the individual from events or objects. One function of a symbol is to separate the thinker from that which the symbol has come to represent. This process of separation serves the same function for both the individual and science. It is an attempt to know through the reification of the thing to be known and assumes, in a Platonic sense, that there exists a reality or ideal independent of the knower.

One proponent of these ideas was Francis Bacon, who in the early 17th century offered the Western mind one of the first strongly empirical views of a philosophy of science. In *The Advancement of Learning,* Bacon called for more systematic experimentation and documentation: "[The physicians] rely too much on mere haphazard, uncoordinated *individual experience;* let them experiment more widely . . . and above all, let them construct an easily accessible and intelligible record of experiments and results." In the first book of his *Novum Organum,* Bacon challenged existing metaphysical views: "Man, as the minister and interpreter of nature, does and understands as much as his observations on the order of nature . . . permit him, and neither knows nor is capable of more." He argued that scientists must rid themselves of the structure established by Aristotle and must become as "little children, innocent of ism and abstractions, washed clear of prejudices and preconceptions." In a word, Bacon counseled scientists to separate themselves from that which they wished to study.[8]

Bacon's views of science and the role of the scientist were the prevailing views until the 20th century, infusing the entire scientific enterprise. However, Bacon's view, together with the view of the universe as constructed by Newton, was to be radically altered by physicists of the 20th century. It was Einstein's revolutionary insight into the nature of relativity, and Planck and Bohr's development of quantum mechanics, that profoundly altered our understanding of the relation of knower to known, not only in physics but in other scientific domains as well. Before we apply these thoughts to our own problems in consciousness and emotional development, I will offer a brief description of Newton's ideas and the emergence of modern physics.

Newton's conception of the universe as an absolute and orderly system held sway for more than 200 years. Indeed, his view was held so strongly by physicists that they could say: "In the beginning . . . God created Newton's laws of motion together with necessary masses and forces. This is all; everything beyond this follows the development of appropriate mathematical methods by means of deduction."[9] According to this view, a person could examine the workings of this orderly universe and extract general principles and laws that could further explain the observed relations. Newton's theories represent the most powerful example of the separation between the role of the knower and the known. Scientific objectivity, for Newton, rested on the belief that there is an external world "out there" as opposed to an internal world, the "I" which is "in here." Nature is "out there," and the task of the scientist is to study those phenomena "out there."

The Newtonian universe, however, was imperfect, and toward the end of the 19th and early part of the 20th century, many scientists began to question its truths. The planet Mercury refused to conform to Newton's laws. Ernst Mach and Henri Poincaré, among others, challenged Newton's notions about absolute space and time. Moreover, a radically new vision of the universe was provided by Einstein and 20th-century quantum mechanics, accompanied by a totally new view of the nature of the scientific enterprise. The new vision of the universe and science brought with it a new thinking about the connection between the knower and the known.

No longer was the notion of "absolute" to dominate our ideas of the universe. Instead, the terms "relativity" and "probability" entered our discussions. For Einstein, relativity meant that the existing laws of nature were valid only when all observers moved at rates uniformly relative to one another. Einstein described relativity in many forms, such as one in which he speaks of simultaneity as the perceived relation between two things: "So we see that we cannot attach any absolute significance to the concept of simultaneity, but that two events which, viewed from a system of coordinates, are simultaneous, can no longer be looked upon as simultaneous events when envisaged from a system which is in motion relative to that system."[10]

Einstein's view of time, speed, and space changed the view of an absolute universe. The properties of objects, time, and space were not independent but dependent and changeable according to the particular system from which they were viewed. Events became dependent on probabilities rather than absolute certainties. The impact of these ideas was profound on all of our notions of what was "absolute" and what was "real."

For example, Arthur Eddington, in talking about changing notions regarding the properties of objects, suggested that the perspective of the knower to the known was not only of interest but was a necessity for proper interpretations of the data: "When a rod is started from rest into uniform motion, nothing whatever happens to the rod. We say that it contracts; but length is not a property of the rod; it is a relation between the rod and the observer. Until the observer is specified, the length of the rod is quite indeterminate."[11]

Such statements capture a profound change in our understanding of nature. Although this new vision of the universe may have had little impact on the everyday lives of most people and their perceptions of the world of objects and people, the effect on philosophers was profound. In Eddington's statement, "Until the observer is specified, the length of the rod is quite indeterminate," the knower and the known enter into a relationship unthought of in the Newtonian period.[12]

Einstein's theory of relativity and the study of quantum mechanics changed the notion of what science is and the perceived relation of the scientist to science. No longer could one think of either scientists or knower studying a phenomenon without considering his relation to that phenomenon. The phenomenon no longer was believed to possess absolute properties, as scientists once believed.

However, in the study of subatomic particles, quantum mechanics was to go beyond merely stating probabilities. Not only was the notion of certainty shown to be incorrect, but the belief in a reality unaffected by human action was undermined. To some degree, human observation and measurement actually create the phenomenon of study. Quantum physicists began to consider questions such as "Did a particle with momentum exist before we measured its momentum?" Thus, the relation of the knower to known became one of the major questions of quantum mechanics. A statement by the theoretical physicist John Wheeler illustrates this point well:

> May the universe in some strange sense be "brought into being" by the participation of those who participate? . . . The vital act is the act of participation. "Participator" is the incontrovertible new concept given by quantum mechanics. It strikes down the term "observer" of classical theory, the man who stands safely behind the thick glass wall and watches what goes on without taking part. It can't be done, quantum mechanics says.[13]

The developments of quantum mechanics produced startling consequences. Not only was our view of the universe changed, but we found that we could no longer describe the universe with physical models. The universe was no longer reflected in ordinary sensory perceptions. It no longer allowed for the description of things but only the relation between things, a relation that was probabilistic. Furthermore, the distinction between an "out there" and an "in here," or an objective reality independent of the observer, was not feasible because it was impossible to observe without distorting. Finally, the new view of the universe destroyed our belief that we could measure absolute truth; rather, we learned we can only correlate experience.

In summary, under the influence of Bacon and Newton, the object of the scientist was to remain uninvolved with the phenomena being studied. Indeed, the entire scientific enterprise and its methods revolved around this goal. Accompanying these aims was the notion of a reality that was independent of the scientist. New developments in the study of relativity and quantum physics, however, denied us this belief. Bohr's notion on "complementarity" directly affects the knower: the common denominator of all experiences is "I." The writer Gary Zukav states that experience, then, does not mirror external reality but "our interaction with it."[14] The effect of such a conclusion on our role in knowing is profound.

The epistemological issue of the relation between the knower and the known has been widely recognized for over 50 years.[15] Consciousness involves the bidirectional interaction of the knower with objects, events, or people. Social cognition depends on just such a connection; "I cannot know another unless I have knowledge of myself." Furthermore, a child's knowledge of self and others is developed through interactions with these others; social interaction and consciousness are the basic unit out of which social cognition derives. Many of us who subscribe to an interactionist position agree that knowledge of others (and the world in general) is derived through interaction. As David Hamlyn wrote about social cognition, "To understand that a person is . . . involves understanding what sorts of relations can exist between mere things and between people and things."[16]

In the interactions of the infant with its physical and social world, these early innate action patterns seem to be quite complex and seem for some to indicate knowledge that reflects beliefs about intentions, motives, preferences, and goals. Josef Perner has called this early kind of knowledge "procedural knowledge" since the young infant's action patterns are not yet ideas. The challenge is how these innate action patterns or procedural rules become ideas. What I am trying to say is that the rise of consciousness, itself a mental state, gives rise to other mental states. If I find one object hard and the other soft by holding them, then not only do I know something about objects—in this case, hardness—but I know something about myself, how hard the object feels to me. As Merleau-Ponty stated, "If I am a consciousness turned toward things, I can meet in things the actions of another and find in them a meaning, because they are themes of possible activity for my own body."[17]

A "theory of mind," like social cognition, involves explicit knowledge of one's own and others' mental states. The origins of a theory of mind can be found in the early work of psychologists such as Carolyn Shantz and James Youniss.[18] From the broad social cognition perspective, children's perspective-taking or role-taking ability, their ability to "put themselves in the place of the other," or their "theory of mind," has been examined in various situations, including those that assess children's capacity for the expression of empathy. It has long been recognized that taking the point of view of another presupposes explicit knowledge of one's own self or consciousness.[19]

With this in mind and especially given our work on the development of consciousness, let me suggest a brief outline for the development of a theory of mind. There are at least three or four periods in its development:

(1) I know; (2) I know I know; (3) I know you know; (4) I know you know I know.

Level 1 is called knowing (or I know). This level prevails from birth onward and is likely to be driven by action patterns or procedural rules common to other mammals. It is based on adaptive evolved complex action patterns and involves little or no language. It does not have the property of a mental state, certainly not of consciousness. For example, there is now evidence using eye gaze to indicate that young infants can anticipate the intention of another by selectively looking at one consequence over another.[20] Or the action of a rat not running into a wall as well as the 2-month-olds' learning to pull a string to turn on a picture are further examples of action patterns or procedural rules.

Level 2 is I know I know. This level involves consciousness and self-referential behavior. It is based on the emerging mental state of me and allows for the capacity to reflect on one's self and to reflect on what one knows. This mental state is a meta-representation. It is a memory of a memory. Whereas a child at the first level may have a memory, it is at the second level that a memory of a memory is possible. As we have seen, this capacity emerges somewhere in the middle of the second year of life.

Level 3 is I know you know. This form of knowing takes into account the mental state that not only do I know something, but I believe others know it as well; it is the ability and basis of shared meaning. This does not imply shared attention, which belongs to Level 1. This mental representation, that you know what I know, does not need to be accurate. Adults know more than a child knows; thus, the child may not really know what the adult knows. The child is likely to make errors, which have been called "egocentric errors," that is, she assumes that what she knows is what the other knows. At this level children know, they know they know, and they also know you know. What they cannot yet do is to place themselves in opposition to what they know. This level, in combination with the earlier ones, accounts in part for the early ability to deceive. A 2½-year-old child who deceives knows that he knows and he knows that you know; thus deception is possible. It is also the reason why children are likely to make the traditional false belief error even though they have developed a mental representation of themselves.

Before going on to the fourth level, it is worth mentioning that the third level may not be distinct from the one before it in which a child knows that he knows. It is possible that the mental state of the idea of me and what I know may emerge at the same time as the mental state of what I know about what others know. In other words, it is possible that what I know about me is part of what I know about the other. If this indeed is the case, then a separate level might not be called for.

Level 4 is the adult-like level. It addresses the interactive and recursive nature of cognition. It is characterized as I know, you know, I know. At this level, not only are there two actors, as at Level 3, but each actor has a perspective. These perspectives can be different. It is when there are two perspectives that one has the ability to recognize false belief. Only when one has reached the level of knowing that "they know I know" that your knowledge about what they know can be corrected, since you can check their knowledge of what they know about you against what you know about you. That is, once a child knows that he can be the subject and also the object of the knowledge of another, the child is capable of recognizing the difference in perspectives between individuals. It is at this final level of perspective taking that mature mental representations can emerge.

As these levels of knowing are reached and mastered, there is at the same time an increase in general cognitive competence, in particular, language usage. Language ability is laid down on the general cognitive scaffolding that allows language usage to reflect increasingly the available cognitive ability. Our problem in studying children's early development is that language ability may not precede this general cognitive capacity but may follow it. Thus, children's observed social behavior and cognition may reflect a level higher than their verbal capacities. It should also be pointed out that as a general developmental principle, I believe that each level is added to the one before and it is not transformed by it. This view allows for any regression that may be a function of many factors including brain injury.

SOCIAL RELATIONSHIPS AND CONSCIOUSNESS

When I think about my relationships, by definition they involve me; moreover, when I think about relationships, one of the things that I may think about is what the other thinks of me. Recursive cognitions can become quite complex, as, for example, when I think of what others think that I think of them. In his discussion of interpersonal relationships, Solomon Asch made a similar point: "The paramount fact about human interactions is that they are happenings that are psychologically represented in each of the participants. In our relationship to an object, perceiving, thinking, and feeling take place on one side, whereas in relations between persons, these processes take place on both sides and are dependent upon one another."[21]

Knowledge about the self and other, whether they occur sequentially or at the same time, eventually become a part of the duality of knowledge. For example, Bannister and Agnew note, "The ways in which we elaborate our construing of self must be essentially those ways in which we elaborate our construing of others. For we have not a concept of self, but a bipolar construct of self–not self, or self–other."[22] The definition of social knowledge involves the relation between the knower and the known, rather than characteristics of people as objects. By utilizing the self in knowing, we can differentiate treating people as objects from treating them as people. If the self is not involved, then the people are being treated as objects; when the self is involved, people are being treated as people.

From Interactions to Relationships

The developmental issue in social relationships is quite complex, especially given the wide acceptance of attachment theory and the argument that children form relationships with their mothers by a few months of age. While it is certainly the case that the infant and his mother exhibit complex social interactions, the question about whether these interactions are the same thing as relationships needs to be addressed. Ethologists have made the distinction between interactive behavior and its meaning. Complex interactions rest on action patterns that can be observed across the animal kingdom between infants and their mothers. They require cognitive capacities such as discrimination and contingent action-to-action behavior. There does not have to be much mental elaboration except that of contingent learning. Infant–mother interactions have been discussed as a kind of dance. I believe that relationships require something more than learning the dance. For example, Robert Hinde articulated six dimensions of interactions that take place. These are (1) goal structures, (2) diversity of interactions, (3) degree of reciprocity, (4) meshing of interactions, (5) frequency, and (6) patterning and multidimensional qualities of interactions. For him, these are six features of social interactions that are likely to be supported by innate action patterns, part of the machinery of the system, at least on the part of the infant.[23] Hinde has suggested that there are two additional features besides these six that define relationships rather than interactions. These features are (7) cognitive factors, or those mental processes that allow members of an interaction to think of the other member as well as of herself, and (8) something that Hinde calls "penetration," which I would interpret as something having to do with ego boundaries, which also has to do with the existence of consciousness of the two participants in the relationship.

If interactions alone are insufficient to describe a higher-level human relationship, then a rather asymmetrical pattern exists between the very young infant and its mother; this pattern is likely to be supported by innate action patterns or procedural rules in the case of the infant, and by consciousness in the case of the mother. Because of this unequal pattern, the interactions between the infant and his mother needs to be distinguished from the interaction between two adults. Such a view was suggested by Harry Stack Sullivan, who believed that relationships are by necessity the negotiation of at least two selves. Mentalism is vital for a relationship since without two selves, as Martin Buber stated, one has only an I–it, not an I–thou, and thus no true relationship. Robert Emde has also made reference to the "we" feature of relationships; in support of the time table of consciousness, he points to the second half of the second year of life for its appearance.[24]

Our model of mature human relationships requires that we consider different levels in the development of a relationship, rather than seeing it exist in adult form from the first. Because of this disparity we need to take care not to use mentalistic terms for the infant's behavior, as if the child *knows* its mother. Uniquely mature human relationships may arise from interactions only after the development of the child's consciousness and with it the ability to represent its self and the other. From this point of view, the achievement of adult human relationships for the child has a developmental progression. This progression involves, first, bidirectional interactions that may utilize complex machinery of the self and that may be similar at least in part to those shown by all social creatures; and second, cognitive structures or mental states, in particular, consciousness, and with it such skills as empathy and the ability to place the self in the role of the other. The interactions of 1-year-olds do not contain these cognitive structures, and therefore may not be classified as a relationship. By age 2 years most children have acquired consciousness and the beginning of such skills as empathy.[25] Their interactions are now more like those of adults. Margaret Mahler's concept of individuation becomes relevant here, for, as she has pointed out, only when the child is able to individuate can it be said that she can have a mature relationship.[26]

Such an analysis raises the question of the nature of the child's social interactions prior to the emergence of consciousness. For me, interactions not based on mental states are complex social species–action-patterned processes, which, through adaptive processes, may be a fundamental feature of social organisms. These original interactions may be hard-wired, a natural feature of all social organisms. The nature of a relationship is dependent on many factors. These include the nature of socialization practices; mental states related to the idea of me, or consciousness; and cognitions about the interactions of self and other, that is, the meaning given to them by the selves involved.

Mary Main and colleagues consider a more cognitive view of attachment, as suggested by John Bowlby, that of a "working model."[27] By a working model, Main suggests a schema concerning the mother as a secure base. By focusing attention on the child's cognitive construction rather than on just the interactive patterns of the dyad, the theory of attachment and relationships moves toward a greater realization that an attachment relationship involves the self and the mental states involved in self and other. For example, Bowlby states, "The model of the attachment figure and the model of the self are likely to develop so as to be complementary and mutually nonconforming. Thus, an unwanted child is likely not only to feel unwanted by his parents, but to believe that he is essentially unwanted."[28] Although Bowlby confuses the model of the self and the content of the self, the idea that a child's self is necessary for the development of relationships is clear. While Bowlby also falls into a too mentalistic language when he says that the child believes that he—his self—is unwanted, even so, such a representation must involve a child capable of consciousness. As soon as we consider relationships in terms of mental states or representations, we need to return to the child's capacity for consciousness, something that, as we have noted, only occurs after the first year of life and more likely toward the middle of the second year. If this is so, then our observation of the attachment relationship at 1 year may reflect (1) action patterns of interactions based on socialization patterns that the child will subsequently use to form a working model of the relationship, and (2) the adult caregivers' relationship, which includes the adults' consciousness as well as the working model of their attachment relationship with their own parents.

To summarize, the role of consciousness in social behavior involves the movement from complex evolutionary adaptive action patterns pertaining to social interactions to the development of social relationships. This belief in the gradual development of social relationships will be disturbing to those who hold to the strong view of the impact of early attachment. Nevertheless, it does agree with what we know about the effect of early attachment differences in children. Both our own data and those of the Minnesota group show that early attachment alone does not predict subsequent adult models of attachment, nor predict psychopathology. These findings suggest that later interactions and social experiences are equally important. Such findings suggest that these early interactions can be reinterpreted later once consciousness has evolved.[29] Relationships involve not only the child's knowledge about the other, but the child's knowledge about the other's knowledge of himself. As can readily be seen, underlying this ability is consciousness. While social behavior such as empathy might be considered within this arena of social development, I shall save it for our discussion of consciousness and emotional life, which follows.

Emotional Life and Consciousness: From Action Patterns to Experience

We now consider the two effects that the role of consciousness has on the development of emotional life. First, we need to examine its effect on the early action patterns associated with specific contexts, or the early emotions. As I have already argued, these action patterns are adaptive evolutionary patterns evoked by specific contexts, which are part of the repertoire of the infant, and which enable the infant to act in its world. While the action patterns by context require some cognitive capacity, they do not require nor do they contain such mental states as the idea of me. The perceptual–cognitive capacities required for these action patterns involve memory and associations, the ability to discriminate, and the capacity to utilize complex information. For example, fearfulness of the stranger requires memory about familiar and unfamiliar faces. The anger action pattern requires the cognitive ability of means–end associations. Nevertheless, these are early action patterns that will be affected by consciousness, though exactly how remains a question to be answered.

The second effect of consciousness on emotional life has to do with how a new set of stimuli or contexts give rise to a new set of action patterns that, after Darwin, I have come to call self-conscious emotional action patterns. While the literal physical stimuli of any situation define the context to begin with and give rise to the early action patterns, the development of the mental state of the idea of me becomes the context for the emergence of a new complex set of action patterns, those that I have called the *exposed self-conscious emotions*. In addition, once new cognitions about cultural and family standards, values, and goals emerge, together with the mental state of me, they become the stimuli for the elicitation of the *self-conscious evaluative emotions*.

Thus, while the earlier action patterns are elicited by physical properties, the later action patterns are elicited by ideas—ideas about me and ideas about the standards, values, and goals of the culture. As discussed in *Shame: The Exposed Self*, it is this movement from the physical properties of the environment, located for the most part outside the child, to the child's ideas that constitute the major transition of the human child from our nonhuman animal past.

Transformation of the Early Action Patterns

I shall save much of what I want to say about the self-conscious emotions until my discussion of them in Chapter 8. What I do want to discuss now is what happens to those early action patterns—the emotions of fear, sadness, anger, interest, joy, and disgust—once the child develops consciousness; then I will briefly touch upon the role of consciousness in the self-conscious emotions.

My argument clearly implies that in the beginning year of life, the expression of the action pattern of fear is not the same thing as experiencing fear, if we use the definition of experience as a mental act. The rise of consciousness also enables the child to engage in deception or to manipulate these action patterns as she chooses. Thus, for example, the infant's action pattern of fear toward a stranger seen in the second half of the first year can be used by the child in the third year to deceive her parents into believing that she is frightened so that they do not leave her with the babysitter she does not like. This use and manipulation of early action patterns will be discussed in more detail in Chapter 7 on deception and lying.

This manipulation of the action patterns for the child's purpose can be compared to an old distinction that has been made between signs and signals. Recall that signs bear a one-to-one correspondence with what they are to represent, whereas signals do not. To translate what I am implying, the above example of fear serves our purpose. With the onset of consciousness, the action pattern of fear, representing some biological connection to a set of physical properties, a sign, becomes a signal, something to be used by the child. It is important to recognize that in development, processes are not transformed, but rather the new is added to the old. In this way, consciousness of my fearfulness is added to the old action pattern itself. Because this process underlies the transformation of all the early emotions, I return to the example of disgust, to highlight this issue of transformation.

The action pattern we call disgust has as its elicitor objects/foods that do not taste or smell good and has an evolutionary adaptive function designed to rid these noxious stimuli from the infant's mouth. We, as adults, also have this action pattern to things that do not taste or smell good, although cultural rules may alter its manifestation. However, through the learning of standards, rules, and goals, we also develop moral disgust—for example, the disgust we feel at the thought of one man's brutality against another. I would suggest that moral disgust occurs only when (1) consciousness emerges, and (2) when the child develops standards, rules, and goals.[30] One effect of consciousness, then, is that it allows for the early action patterns–context association to become something mental, ideas about me and my feelings. If, as I have suggested, the early action patterns can become ideas, it may also be true that the energy or motive power of these action patterns can be used for all kinds of ideas. Again let me return to the disgust action pattern. If a person does not like another person, it may be possible to use the biological action pattern to fuel that dislike. Thus, one can say to another whom one dislikes, "You disgust me." Disgust, the idea, is then used to show contempt, to humiliate or shame the other, that is, to spit out or withdraw from him.

While others have attempted to connect the early emotions with the later ones, the scheme that we have used with the example of disgust can apply to all the early action patterns, that is, to how the action patterns without ideas become action patterns with ideas. These connections are suggestive but we need to recognize that only further careful research will be able to confirm their association. Such early action patterns can have either withdrawal or approach transformations.

1. Disgust as a withdrawal action pattern to rid the mouth of noxious tastes and smells becomes in the case of the withdrawal pattern

moral disgust, and in the case of the approach pattern humiliation and shame to others and the self.

2. Anger, an action pattern to overcome a blocked goal, becomes on the one hand, in approach, persistence of action in the world or rage and aggression, and on the other hand, in withdrawal, guilt.

3. Happiness as an approach action pattern toward the familiar becomes joy and pride and as a withdrawal action pattern, hubris.

4. Interest as an approach action pattern becomes curiosity and creativity, and as a withdrawal action pattern self-directed attention and somatization.

5. Fear, both an approach and a withdrawal action pattern to the unfamiliar, can become a withdrawal action pattern of anxiety or an approach pattern of stimulus seeking and risk taking.

6. Sadness as a withdrawal action pattern in response to loss becomes a withdrawal pattern of shame or an approach pattern of empathy.

The Rise of the Self-Conscious Emotions

I have suggested an important distinction with respect to the self-conscious emotions. There is an earlier set which have been labeled *self-conscious exposed emotions,* and a later set which have been labeled *self-conscious evaluative emotions.* These differ by the amount of other cognitions besides consciousness that are necessary for their elicitation. While all involve the mental representation of me, the earlier ones involve relatively little other cognitive ability, while the later ones involve both consciousness and self-attributional evaluation. These attributions also have to do with me, and therefore also require self-referential ability. Because all these self-conscious emotions require the development of a mental representation of the me, they are not likely to occur at the beginning of life and should not be confused with the earlier action patterns. The suggestion that these action patterns can be seen earlier rests on a set of false assumptions on the part of adults that include mistaking disgust for contempt or shame and the general anthropomorphizing of the infant's behavior.[31]

Clearly, the two classes of self-conscious emotions, the early and later ones, have consciousness in common, but differ in the degree of cognition needed for their occurrence. Because of the later development of additional cognitions, the two classes emerge at different times. The first class, the *self-conscious exposed emotions,* emerge soon after consciousness emerges. Thus, if one toddler shows self-referential ability at 15 months and another at 21 months, then the one showing self-representation earlier will also show the *self-conscious exposed emotions* earlier. For example, exposure embarrassment, empathy, and jealousy are likely to appear earlier than shame, pride, guilt, and evaluative embarrassment, all of which require additional cognitive attributes about the self. I have shown that the first type of embarrassment can be seen around 15 to 24 months of age, or whenever the infant first shows self-referential behavior. The second class occurs between 30 and 36 months as the cognitions or attributions about the self emerge.

In order to study the relation between the rise of consciousness and early self-conscious emotions, my colleagues and I measured consciousness by self-recognition in front of a mirror, fear by the response of a stranger approaching, and embarrassment when the child is the object of another's attention. The question we asked was whether there was a difference between infants who showed self-recognition in terms of their fear or embarrassment behavior. As predicted, there was no difference in children's fear whether they showed or did not show self-recognition, that is, fear or wariness was not influenced by the presence or absence of recognition. However, as predicted, embarrassment occurred only if the child showed self-recognition. Embarrassment seems to appear when the infant knows that he is the object of another's attention. As we will see later in my discussion of the self-conscious emotions, the attention of another, not necessarily a self-evaluation, can be an elicitor of this form of embarrassment.

Little work on the relation between self-recognition and the other early self-conscious emotions has been conducted; there is none on jealousy and only a few studies on empathy. The work on empathy supports the belief that consciousness is needed for the elicitation of this early self-conscious emotion. While some have argued that empathy can be seen at very early ages, they may have neglected to distinguish between empathy and contagion. Clearly, infants as well as adults are affected by the behavior of others; the basic definition of being social is to be influenced by other conspecifics. However, influence as in contagion is not empathy. Empathy requires that one put one's self in the place of another, which requires a "me," or consciousness. Contagion, on the other hand, is like the action pattern such as yawning where the yawn of one person elicits a yawn in another. Contagion has to be taken into account when studying the relationship between consciousness and empathy. In several studies that have examined this relationship, the results suggest that adult-like empathy in the young child is dependent on the emergence of self-recognition.[32] Although more studies are needed, there does appear to be an association between self-referential behavior and empathy; however, there are little hard data on the relation between self-referential behavior and jealousy.[33]

The second class of the self-conscious emotions involves self-representation and ideas about the standards, rules, and goals of the culture, as well as additional attributions or ideas about the self. Thus, these self-conscious emotions require more elaborate cognitions and as such emerge by the third year of life. Again, while some claim that these emotions, such as shame, guilt, and pride, exist earlier, the need for elaborate ideas about the self precludes the likelihood of their existence prior to this point in development. I see little support for the idea of universal physical elicitors for these self-conscious evaluative emotions. The elicitors of these emotions are ideas, and it is these ideas about the self that serve as the elicitors. Thus, consciousness as well as other ideas, which will be described in Chapter 8, are necessary as elicitors. However, it may well be the case that particular ideas could serve as universal elicitors connecting these specific ideas to the self-conscious emotions.

The notion of particular ideas about the self as elicitors of self-conscious emotions is not a new idea. Bernard Werner, Martin Seligman, and Aaron Beck have all offered the view that particular attributions about the self serve as elicitors of emotions, a view similar to the model of their development presented here. In these attributional models, the causes of emotions are found in three major ideas about the self: locus of responsibility, stability, and controllability. The locus of responsibility is similar to our model of responsibility. It refers to whether an event is caused by the self or is external to the self. The stability dimension makes reference to whether a cause varies over time. Controllability has to do with whether the child can personally affect the outcome. Effort attributions are unstable and under personal control, whereas luck attributions are unstable and are perceived as something that the child cannot influence. Other attribution dimensions, for example, the global or specific natures of a cause or performance or task presentation, have been proposed.[34] Carol Dweck has studied children's motivational beliefs and self beliefs, and finds the idea of performance or task orientation, something akin to the idea of global or specific attributions, to be useful in explaining achievement behavior. The distinction between the attributions "how I did" and "what I did" reflects children's focus either on their own performance or on the task. As we will see, these attributions lead to global or specific judgments about the self and have implications in such situations as when the child fails or succeeds in any test of his standards, goals, or rules since global attributions can lead to shame when the child fails or to hubris when the child succeeds, while task or specific attributions to success or failure can lead to pride and guilt.

In ending this discussion about the role of consciousness along with the development of other ideas about the self, I am reminded of Darwin's discussion about the self-conscious emotions. Darwin related the self-conscious emotions to the person's thinking about what others think about them, and thus to the need for self-reflection. He believed this need for self-reflection developed around the third year of life, and that self-conscious emotions had as their "essential element being self-attention," what I have referred to as consciousness. "It is not the single act of reflecting on our own appearance, but the thinking what others think of us, which excites a blush."[35]

CHAPTER 7

Lying and Deception in Emotional Life

$\mathbf{A}$s we have seen, with the onset of consciousness children become capable of experiencing their own action patterns and are capable therefore of altering features of these action patterns, including especially their communication function such as their facial and bodily expressions. The child becomes capable of responding to specific cultural demands. So, for example, little boys in our culture are told that "boys don't cry," and therefore learn to alter their crying behavior so that they do not cry when sad. It is also true that with consciousness the child becomes capable of self-deception, that is, capable of creating her own experiences of emotions. So, if there is a cultural rule not to feel anger, the child, when left alone by her mother, may be more likely to experience sadness rather than anger. This seems to be so when we look at Japanese and American children's responses to particular situations. In one of our studies, 3- to 5-year-old children were shown pictures of faces representing fear, anger, sadness, happiness, and disgust and asked to match these faces to particular situations. In one story, a young child is shown lost in a store, while her mother is shown shopping in another aisle. American children point to the angry face as most indicative of the face the lost child would show, but also choose sad and fearful faces. The Japanese children pointed most to the sad face, and then to the anger and fear faces. Perhaps this difference occurred because in traditional Japanese culture, experiencing anger and manifesting it through a facial expression is frowned upon.[1]

In the theory of development that I have suggested, the onset of consciousness allows for both lying and deception to play an important role in emotional life and therefore in development. Lying and deception allow for both cultural and family rules to alter at least three aspects of emotional life: (1) it affects what new events constitute an elicitor; (2) it alters action patterns by disengaging expressions from other aspects of the action pattern, such as physiological responses; and (3) it alters emotional experiences through self-deception. Unfortunately, there has been almost no research on this topic, especially in children in the first 2 to 3 years of life. Even in older children and adults, the impact on emotional life of self- and other deception has received little research attention, although from a therapeutic point of view such defense mechanisms as denial, forgetting, and repression, as well as cognitive styles of coping with stress, would appear to involve its use. Moreover, self-deception is likely to play an important role in the memories we have by altering the past to make it fit with the present and to set goals for the future, all involving emotional life.

Although some have argued that animals and even cells are capable of some form of deception, I agree with Robert Mitchell's analysis and argue that human deception is quite different from the deception of other animals, as it is a higher-order form that requires to some degree an organism's capacity to consider itself, or what we have been here calling consciousness.[2] Having stated this point of view, we can now proceed more directly to the ontogenetic or developmental issues rather than spend much time discussing whether a tree frog's camouflage constitutes a deception similar to a young child's lie.

In this chapter we consider how the child comes to affect its emotional life by hiding, altering, substituting, or enhancing its emotions, from others as well as himself. Lying and deception are important processes since they affect emotional expressions and action patterns, as well as the experience the child has. It disassembles elicitors from action patterns and both from emotional experiences. It clearly raises problems in the study and measurement of emotion since the ability to deceive both others and oneself means that what we measure may be different for different families and cultures. Thus, such facial coding experts as Ekman and Izard, having argued for a strong one-to-one relation between expressions, action patterns, and experiences, suggest that facial patterns are an accurate measure of experience since these expressions have an evolutionary adaptive significance, and thus the masking of facial expressions can never be truly successful.[3] This belief allows one to say that if one observes carefully the face of the child one can tell what emotion she is experiencing.

While this may be the case some of the time, there is little reason to believe it is always so. Early in life some facial expressions in the newborn period do not likely reflect specific action patterns. So, for example, REM sleep, a smiling face, and penile erection in a newborn male do not reflect a happy or sexual dream. With the advent of consciousness by 24 months, facial expressions continue to be subjected to familial and cultural rules. Thus, while a facial expression may have a one-to-one correspondence to an action pattern or experience, it is likely not to have such a correspondence for very long. The argument of evolutionary adaptive pressures producing specific facial patterns is based on the common meaning across cultures for specific faces; however, that it always represents a high degree of correspondence to other action pattern features such as physiological responses or to emotional experiences is far from certain.

In fact, when detection of facial expression masking is studied, the findings usually support the idea of deception. In one study, nurses-in-training were shown pictures of horrible accidents and told that they had to learn to deceive those around them and not show upset or disgusted faces. In an experiment, they were then shown horrible accident scenes as well as neutral scenes and an observer had to determine from their facial patterns which kinds of pictures they were seeing. The results do not support the ability to detect deception nor the inability to hide what the nurses were really experiencing. The observer could not determine which scenes the nurses were seeing. Additional work using sophisticated and trained facial coders also revealed relatively poor detection ability. It appears that adults are good liars when masking what they are experiencing.[4]

Perhaps the evolutionary adaptive argument for deception as usually stated does not take into account the idea of consciousness, and therefore the ability to deceive. In a book on lying and deception in everyday life, I suggested that lying and all forms of deception, including self-deception, may have an evolutionary and adaptive function.[5] For example, deception to spare the feelings of another may be socially adaptive since it provides a mechanism for social cohesion. When we tell a friend that we like his tie—after he has told us how much he likes it and how he purchased it for such a good price—even though we hate it, we may be aiding our friendship. Or when we say to a group of acquaintances that our vacation was just okay rather than that it was fabulous, we may deceive in order to reduce within-group jealousy. These examples suggest that deception may have an adaptive function and may have been selected for even though at the same time facial patterns for specific events also may have been selected for. Overwhelming evidence from a variety of studies indicates that observers tend to perform at chance or a bit above chance in their judgments of truth-tellers or liars.[6] Here, the position taken is that emotional expressions bear only a loose connection to other features of action patterns and to experiences. Indeed, one aspect of the developmental process related to socialization involves the detachment of facial expressions from action patterns. Rather than consider facial expressions as signs equivalent to what they represent, facial expressions are more like symbols, that is, they hold only a loose relation to what they signify. Robert Trivers, an evolutionary biologist, has recently published an essay on deception, arguing for the adaptive significance of deception and self-deception in particular.[7] He emphasizes the usefulness of self-deception on the immune system, and uses this evidence to support his view that there are evolutionary pressures on the development of deception. This is especially so in the case of self-deception. Trivers argues that having joyful experiences and avoiding shame and embarrassment improves immune function through reducing stress-related increases in cortisol, a hormone that negatively affects the immune system.[8] The positive effects of deception can also be seen in Richard Byrne and Nadia Corp's work, which has shown that the use of deception in primates is predicted by neocortical volume: the larger the volume, the more likely the use of deception. This finding is consistent with the adaptive value of deception.[9] In our studies of lying and deception in young children, this adaptive value will be made more explicit.

THE PHENOMENOLOGICAL SELF IN DECEPTION

Examining deception in young children, even those who have developed consciousness, is difficult, so one way to understand the argument presented is from our own adult phenomenological point of view. Here are several examples that may be of use.

> *Example 1.* Sometimes I want to go for a swim, but I know the lake water is cold, which makes me hesitant to dive in. On these occasions, rather than think about the cold water, I command myself that on the count of three I will jump in. When I count to three, I jump in. It is as if I have been commanded to do so, though the commander is the same me who is uncomfortable about jumping into the cold water.

What might be going on here? Through our conscious mind we are able to self-deceive and at the same time know that we are doing so. This self-deception requires us to forget what we know about ourselves, at least for a moment in time. Clearly, for some of the time we are able to deceive ourselves into believing that someone is commanding us to do something even though we know that we are both the commander and the one who has to obey. This self-deception requires consciousness and is likely to be adaptive at least in some circumstances.

> *Example 2.* At the end of a dinner party, a guest may say how wonderful the food was even though she did not like it. She deceives for politeness as well as to promote social cohesion. The host suspects that the food was not good but having gone to so much trouble to prepare it, would like to believe that the comment is true and that the food was good.

This example involves both self-deception and protecting the feelings of others. The act of deception involves a collaboration between both parties. Thus, joint interest may allow for the inability to perceive the features that if measured or observed would tell of deception, but there is no reason to do so.

> *Example 3.* This story of deception collaboration was told to me, and took place between a colleague and his daughter. The daughter, age 5, was supposed to take her medicine and when asked by her father if she did so, answered "Yes." Her father, someone who is "good-natured" and likes to believe the best about people, did not want to believe that his child lied; thus he believed her deception. However, since he knew about our studies of deception, he looked in his daughter's waste basket and found the pill. Needless to say he was quite upset since he wanted to believe his daughter would never lie to him.

Such examples point to the important general psychological principle that we attend to what we want to. It also points to the fact that ideas are what our reality is, in large part, made up of. The literal world and our perception of it is rarely isomorphic. Reality is often in the service of our emotional life and social acts often involving other people.

> *Example 4.* Consider a young man who while driving his father's car one rainy night hits a dog quickly running across the road in front of him. His first thoughts are about what has happened: he caused the animal's death, it was his fault, and he was a terrible person for doing it. These types of thoughts are self-attributions and are the elicitors of his initial emotional experience, one of shame. However, because he did not want to feel (have the experience of) shame, he rethought the accident, changed his attributions, and decided that he was not to blame for the dog's death since the dog should not have been out on such a night.

Emotional experience substitution is another form of self-deception that also is connected to ideas, this time ideas about the self as in self-attributions. In this example the young man shows that he is capable of changing his ideas about his self-attributions and does so in the service of substituting one emotional experience for another. It also demonstrates that emotional life is a flow, not a set of snapshots.

What do these examples have in common? They share at least two major features. First, they require us to posit a consciousness, since one cannot deceive oneself or another without the idea of a "me." Second, especially in the self-deception examples, they require us to believe that the self can deceive itself. Whether we want to consider such differences as implicit consciousness versus explicit consciousness, whether we want to postulate different modules or aspects of the brain, or whether we hold to the idea of a divided consciousness—a position that both Janet years ago and Hilgard recently expounded—all these explanations need to allow for the sequencing of ideas that need not include other ideas at the same time.[10]

One final question has to do with the issue of whether knowledge of one's own deception is a necessary condition for us to call it deception, a point used to differentiate humans from other animals. The definition of the human form of deception is the requirement that the liar knows that she is deceiving or lying. Thus, it might be the case that the person indeed knows of her deception if we are willing to broaden our notion of what knowing means. What it means is that I know I am deceiving myself looking in the mirror, but not at the moment of looking. I know of the self-deception before and after the act, not during it.

THE DEVELOPMENT OF DECEPTION

There are many developmental issues around lying and deception. I now turn to these issues since lying and deception, which emerge early, affect the development of the child's emotional life.

> *Example 5.* Lucy is 25 months old. While her mother is working on a law brief at home, Lucy is playing in the backyard. Through the window, Lucy's mother witnesses the following scene: Lucy runs to get a toy at the far end of the yard. She falls on her knees and starts to cry. Immediately she looks up but seeing that no one is paying any attention she stops crying and walks to the back door. As she approaches the room her mother is in, Lucy begins to cry again.

In this example we can see that facial expressions are not always determined by the precipitating event. While Lucy's first cry is probably related to her pain, her subsequent cry has more to do with an attempt to communicate a specific message to her mother. This conclusion seems to be supported by the fact that Lucy looked around first to see if anybody was watching her after she fell. Because no one was watching her, she stopped crying. Lucy's ability to produce her facial and vocal expressions at will suggests that these behaviors are under her control and not necessarily related to an underlying action pattern such as pain.

> *Example 6.* Rana is going to her grandfather's house for the weekend. At 2½ years, Rana is a verbally precocious child who enjoys being with other people. Her grandfather encourages Rana's dramatic play. One

game they play together is "make a face." In this game Rana's grandfather asks her to make different faces. For example he asks Rana to make a sad face. Rana makes a good resemblance of a sad face, narrowing her eyes and frowning. Next her grandfather asks her to make a happy face. In an instant Rana's face starts to change, the frown disappears, her eyes crinkle, and a large smile appears. Rana's grandfather continues to request other faces including a sleepy face and an angry face. Before she becomes bored with the game she produces in each instance a face that approximates the adult expression.

This example reflects the fact that by age 2 some children can produce different facial expressions on request. Furthermore, these children have verbal labels for at least some emotions and can point to a particular face picture when asked to point out an emotion. So Rana can point correctly to one of six faces when asked to point to a happy or a sad face. Had we continued to observe Rana and her grandfather we might have heard her grandfather ask Rana what kind of face a little girl would make if she got a big chocolate ice cream cone. We would have seen her produce a happy face either as a consequence of a learned association between ice cream cones and good feelings when eating it or as a consequence of her knowledge about what other people feel in certain situations. Thus, either as a function of past associations or as a function of the knowledge of situations associated with particular emotions, or even as a function of empathy, Rana can produce facial expressions appropriate to an imagined situation. Specific events and facial expressions are mediated through cognitive processes that may be as simple as associations or as complex as empathic ability.

Keep in mind that once the child has knowledge about what emotional expressions and behaviors are appropriate for a particular context, it becomes possible for the child to produce these expressions, even when she does not experience them, that is, does not feel them. We are all familiar with examples of this type of deception. For example, when we hear about some harm that has befallen a person we do not like, it is likely that we would produce a sad-like face even though we may be secretly happy.

Example 7. Twenty-seven-month-old Tamara sits in an observation room facing forward. She has been told that there is an attractive and fun toy in a box that she can play with. However, the experimenter tells her that she has to leave the room for a minute. The experimenter tells the child "Please do not peek" as she leaves the room. Within 30 seconds after the experimenter leaves the room, Tamara peeks and turns back, facing forward. Soon after the experimenter comes into the room again and asks "Did you peek?," Tamara answers "No" with a straight face. It is not detectable that she is lying.

This example is from a set of studies that we used to observe whether children this young are capable of deception and whether their deception is detectable by an adult. While I go into more detail later, here we can note that children this age are able to deceive and the detection of the deception is not above chance level for adults observing their behavior. This finding suggests that young children's deception is no easier to detect than adults' deception. The young children's deception is already quite proficient.[11]

These examples underscore the fact that there is no necessary isomorphic relation between emotional expressions and action patterns or between facial expressions and a child's experiences by 3 years of age. What these examples demonstrate is that there is a complex interplay between elicitors and their biologically programmed neuromusculature and socialization rules that govern the meaning of elicitors, expressions, experience, and the development of consciousness. The unlearned biologically determined neuromuscular patterns constitute universal attributes, whereas the socialization rules of the family and the culture represent the environmental contribution once consciousness appears.

As usual one's worldview will determine one's theory about deception. In the strong biological view the elicitor–action pattern associations are biologically programmed as is the action pattern–experience associations. This being so, deception should always be detectable. However, others who also take a strong biological view consider lying and deception to be evolutionarily adaptive, that is, something that is selected for. Thus, a strong biological view can be argued for or against deception as adaptive. The second worldview, based on learning and acculturation, suggests that lying and deception are learned through socialization. While there may be an association between elicitors, action patterns and experiences, and consciousness, cultural demands are likely to make a major contribution to the development of deception, since I know of no culture that does not employ deception. As we develop, lying and deception both to others and to the self become more prominent and play an increasing role in emotional life.

THE RELATION OF ACTION PATTERNS
TO FACIAL EXPRESSIONS

Emotional development involves an interaction between biologically given action patterns and socialization and learning experiences. Whether these action patterns are ever just related to specific contexts is debatable. What we do know is that quite early socialization acts on these action patterns and affects them. Thus, there may never be a time in development for an isomorphic relation between elicitors, action patterns, and experiences. If there is any possibility for greater isomorphic connection, it is likely to be early in life and greater for some emotions than for others. Examples of the early asynchrony are found in the research on early infant smiling.[12] Infants' early smiles are considered endogenous because they do not occur in response to external elicitors and do not seem to be related to positive action patterns. Moreover, smiles often are observed in infants asleep and appear to be correlated with spontaneous CNS activity and REM sleep. These facial expressions appear to be related to a general excitation of the nervous system, certainly not to the emotion of joy. Therefore, this first period of life has little organization and consequently little synchrony.

The second phase is marked by a greater synchrony between expressions and action patterns. Now different patterns of facial expressions have some correspondence to specific contexts and are related to other features of the action pattern. The greater synchrony is likely achieved because children's cognitive structures have not matured sufficiently to enable them to control their expressions, although parental socialization factors, like extreme cruelty, may affect them. Moreover, prior to the emergence of consciousness, the infant may not be able to deceive since to deceive, an awareness of being able to deceive is necessary.

In the third phase of emotional development facial expressions and other features of action patterns as well as elicitors are again asynchronous. Unlike earlier asynchrony, this lack of correspondence is due to the acquisition and maturation of cognitive structures and to the cumulative effects of socialization. This third phase may appear for different emotions at different times, owing in large part to the cognitive load associated with each emotion. It may be easier for the young child to deceive around such early emotions as happiness, sadness, and fear and harder to deceive for other emotions like disgust and anger, at least in American culture. As we have already mentioned, 2- and 3-year-olds recognize and can produce some emotion expressions earlier than others. This differential ability might well be connected to their ability to deceive these expressions, which is a problem worth studying.

A TAXONOMY OF LYING AND DECEPTION

In constructing a taxonomy of lying and deception, one might use many systems for the many different kinds of lies as well as the many different ways of masking or hiding our feelings. However such a taxonomy is constituted, it will be clear that all the kinds of lies are part of social life, including that of the family, that the infant is embedded in. Lying and deception are natural features of the adult environment in which the child lives from the start. Little thought is necessary to see how deception is part of our daily lives. We lie about our feelings, we lie about what happened to us, we lie about what we want, and we lie about current events as well as about what the future will be like. Lying occurs all the time. While we have strong negative moral views about lying, we need to consider that lying and deception are part of our psychological makeup, and it is a necessary part as well. It is an integral part of our outer social lives and our inner emotional lives. Even without any biological disposition to lie, the child is embedded in a social nexus where lying and deception already exist. Thus lying and deception cannot help but be a part of the young child's emotional development. I will not discuss here the extent to which lying and deception are a part of our memory system, but I will point out that there is evidence for the importance of self-deception in memory formation and recall.[13]

THE DEVELOPMENT OF DECEPTION

It is easier to talk about the development of deception by following an outline of the motives for lying and for deceptive behavior. I assume some sort of self-deception may be involved in each of them. While the four types discussed below may not be inclusive of all types of deception, these four categories capture a good deal of what has been studied. These four include (1) lying to protect the feelings of another, (2) lying for self-protection to avoid punishment, (3) lying to the self, and (4) lying to hurt others. As each form of lying is discussed, I will present existing research on the type under discussion—it does need to be noted that there is relatively little work that focuses on children. It is not clear in which order these different types of lying emerge, but they all need the preemergence of consciousness before they can appear.

Lying to Protect the Feelings of Another

> Vivian is a 3-year-old girl who is eagerly awaiting a Christmas present from her grandmother. She's hoping for a fun toy. The day after Christmas her grandmother presents her not with a toy, but with a sweater she has knitted. Vivian rips open the package, sees the sweater, and although disappointed she smiles at her grandmother. Turning to her grandmother, Vivian says, "I'm going to wear it right now."

Like many children her age, Vivian has already learned how to manipulate her facial expression and instead of showing disappointment she smiles. She has learned the social rule pertaining to deception in the service of protecting another's feelings. Examples of this type of behavior abound. There is a name for it, "little white lies," a term I do not like. This form of deception is socially useful in that it allows us to maintain social commerce through the protection of one another's feelings, sometimes even in the face of events that could be personally painful. One can argue that the function of this type of deception, the protection of the feelings of another, is adaptive: there seems to be an evolutionary history around the desire to develop and maintain complex social interactions. Although some might argue that such deception distracts from interpersonal relationships, it does seem reasonable to assume that the maintenance of social interaction requires some deceptions of this type.

Children learn the rule about such deceptive practices from significant others, most often from their parents or older siblings. They learn to protect the feelings of others by both direct instruction and through their indirect observation of parental behavior. Directly they are told "Tell grandma that you like her present even though it is not what you wanted." This type of direct instruction often occurs around presents given to the child, food offered, or for any situation where the child can perceive that any negation will result in the other person feeling sad. Children early are also informed about deceptions indirectly. In such cases, children can observe that their parents engage in deception to save the feelings of others.

Thus, for example, Maron can hear and see his mother, Felicia, say, "My friend is coming over for tea and I really don't want to see her today." When Felicia's friend arrives, the child sees Felicia smiling and hears her say, "I am so glad you stopped by." His mother's deception is observed and noted by the child. Both directly and indirectly children resort to deception in order to spare the feelings of another; this occurs early in life.

While there are many everyday examples of this motive, studying it in young children in the laboratory has proven difficult. Carolyn Saarni[14] reasoned that if a child was promised an attractive toy but did not receive it, the child might be likely not to show his disappointment so as not to make the experimenter feel bad. Seven- to 11-year-old boys and girls were used in the experiment and the results showed both age and gender effects. Younger children, especially boys, were likely to show more disappointment, while the older children showed more positive emotions, suggesting that their ability to mask their disappointment grows. Pamela Cole, in a similar study, this time using 4- to 9-year-olds, again showed that girls were better at masking their disappointment than boys, although there were no age differences. When this study was extended to preschool girls, 3- to 4-year-olds inhibited their disappointment.[15] This type of deception seems to occur quite early. But children are also told to tell these kinds of lies. More recently, the disappointing paradigm was used, with the addition that adults encouraged children to tell a "white lie." The majority of the children, 3- to 11-year-olds, told "white lies" while younger children were less likely to lie than older ones. There were no sex differences. While girls displayed more positive emotions than boys, they did so regardless of whether they received a disappointing gift or not. Thus, the sex differences reported by others may well have to do with the higher rate of smiling for girls than boys in this type of study.

Direct socialization by parents of their children's lies was explored by looking at parents' different verbal behaviors.[16] Parents told their children not to say they disliked a prize, not to hurt the experimenter's feelings, and not to say the prize was undesirable, and they suggested how the child was to respond. The results support the idea that direct socialization of lying to protect the feelings of others is learned—those children who received elaborate instruction to lie did so and showed more positive expressions compared to those who did not receive direct instructions.[17] While the experimental data are scant, there are enough to support the view that this type of deception can be seen as early as 3 years. Girls may be better at it than boys. Parental instructions to lie to protect the feelings of another are effective. Moreover, Stein Braten has shown that to help another, part of the proto-prosocial behavior of infants can be seen very early.[18] It could be argued, then, that lying to protect the feelings of another is a social competence. If this were so, then children showing this ability might show other competences. In a study of 4-year-olds, children who were successful in masking their emotions when disappointed were the children more likely to be chosen by other children to be their play dates.[19] As will be shown, deception is often associated with other positive social and cognitive behaviors.

Lying to Avoid Punishment

The most common form of lying may have to do with the motive to avoid punishment. Deceptions around transgressions are a common occurrence. Children learn readily not to tell the truth when they have done something they were forbidden to do or have not done something they were asked to do. A 2-year-old told not to eat a cookie does so. When his mother questions him about eating the cookie he may at first admit that he has. But admitting to eating the cookie immediately evokes a negative response either in the form of parental anger or the form of actual punishment. The child quickly learns after one or two of these interactions that if he admits to an action he was told not to do, he will be punished. He tries to avoid this disapproval or punishment by lying.

Although it is possible to study what children know about deception to avoid punishment, observing what they actually do, in a laboratory setting, is likely to supply more information. In studying this type of deception in young children, it is necessary to use an experiment in which little verbal behavior is required. To do this, we developed a "do not peek" paradigm. In the experiment, the young child is brought into a room and seated in front of a table. Behind the child is another table. While the child is sitting at the first table, the experimenter unpacks an elaborate toy and places it on the second table. While doing so she tells the child not to turn around and look at the toy. Once the toy is set up, while all the time the child is being told not to look, the experimenter informs the child that she must leave the room for a few minutes. Once again the child is told not to look at the toy as the experimenter leaves. Such a situation is designed to maximize the likelihood that the child will look. The child is left alone in the room for up to 5 minutes. If she looks at the toy, the experimenter returns and asks the child "Did you peek?" Of course, children in the experiment were videotaped, but had no knowledge that they were.

This simple paradigm has been used most often in studies of children's deception ability since children as young as 2½ years can be studied. The results of the studies demonstrate that children as young as 2½ years of age are capable of deception. Looking at children from 2½ to 7 years of age we find clear developmental changes in lying. Peeking decreases with age since the child's ability to delay gratification or inhibit his behavior has been shown to get better with age. However, childhood lying, if the children transgressed, increases with age; under 25% of children 2 to 3 years of age admit to peeking and this figure drops to 0% when children are 5 years or older. There are no gender differences in lying, although girls are somewhat less likely to peek than boys. Lying does not differ between Japanese and American children as a function of age, although the Japanese children peeked less.[20]

Support for the idea that use of deception to avoid punishment may be adaptive comes from many findings.[21] Consider that this peeking task taps two skills, the ability to delay or avoid peeking, and once the child peeks, the ability to deceive. While not central to deception, the inability to delay peeking is related to several features associated with dysfunction, besides age. For example, how quickly a child peeks is related to IQ: children who peek quickly have lower IQs.[22] Children from more risky environments peek faster and children with higher neonatal risk scores also peek faster. Finally, and most relevant here, children who peek faster show poorer emotional knowledge, that is, they have lower scores on being able to name emotional faces and lower scores on their knowledge about what emotions are likely to be seen in particular contexts. Peeking speed clearly is negatively related to a child's competence.

However, when examining the relation between lying or truth telling and competence the picture changes. Children with higher IQs are more likely to lie than children with lower IQs. Of the children who peeked, truth-tellers had lower IQs by more than 10 points. Moreover, truth-tellers had lower emotional knowledge scores. Such findings have been found by others, for example, Victoria Talwar and Kang Lee found that 64% of 3- to

8-year-old children lied in this type of experiment and that lying increased with age. Moreover, children's executive functioning was higher among liars than among truth-tellers.[23]

While there are a few more studies on children's lying to protect themselves from punishment, as opposed to sparing the feelings of others, the data here are also scant. Nevertheless, the data that we do have indicate clearly that lying to self-protect is shown early, by 2 to 3 years of age, only to increase as the child gets older. Most important, lying is associated with the child's competence and likely therefore to reflect an adaptive behavior. Clearly this type of deception has to affect even young children's emotional life.

Lying as Self-Deception

The third form of deception is likely to be the hardest to study in general and in particular in a young child. Self-deception has both advantages and disadvantages. Consider the use of self-deception by a shy young man who calls a woman to ask for a date and is told that she cannot see him since she is busy for the next three weekends. He has a choice of how to interpret that information. He can conclude that she does not want to go out with him and feel humiliated and shamed at the rejection. Alternatively he can conclude that he does not want to date such a busy woman. This spares him the shame and humiliation he might have felt. In fact both mental conclusions might occur, with him only remembering that he does not want to date her. The psychic advantage of this attitude seems clear: in certain circumstances there may be little reason to lower one's self-esteem by being honest with oneself. However, self-deception can also be very costly for the individual. Self-deception may prevent one from learning from one's mistakes or in taking action—in fact, it may even block our memories. For example, while examining one's body one discovers a lump and decides that the lump has always been there, a false memory. Under such self-deception no action would likely occur. Should the lump be an indication of the beginning of a cancer, such self-deception could result in serious health consequences and even death.

There are no data to help us in understanding children's self-deception. When and how it occurs has not received the attention it deserves. While there are little data to guide us in understanding the roots of self-deception, I will offer a view that may be useful, namely, the development of pretend play. As Piaget, and more recently, Alan Leslie, have argued, pretense involves "double knowledge," or dual representations of the literal and the pretend situation. This requires that the toddler distinguishes between what is real and what is not real, and therefore she must know that her play is not real.[24] That the child knows that her action is not literal means that she knows something about herself, and is a form of self-negation, a statement of *It is not.* This complex kind of pretense is almost never seen in children with autism.[25] Pretense seems similar to some of the examples that adults use that reflects their self-deception, that is, they have knowledge about what they do but they do not want to attend to. Thus, looking in the mirror and not wanting to see the effects of aging, even though one knows that they are there, is a form of pretend.

The beginnings of pretend play can be seen early, around age 1. This type of pretense involves the infant's copying behaviors with objects that he sees others do. So, for example, the infant sees his mother using a toy phone and is encouraged to make the same action. In this type of pretense, the child is the object of its pretense.[26] This type of pretense decreases with age and is rarely seen in the second or third year of life. In its place a new and more complex pretense emerges. This second type of pretense involves the toddler's interaction with another, either a doll or a stuffed animal, his mother, or eventually another child.[27] Of interest is the fact that this pretense, the use of another, grows in frequency whereas pretense without another declines. Pretend play, especially pretense that involves another, has been shown to be a measure of self-referential behavior or consciousness, and is related to mirror self-recognition. It is the beginning of mentalism as suggested by Leslie.

Lying to Hurt Others

The fourth form of lying is lies that are used to hurt others. We lie to hurt the feelings of others, and we lie to avoid punishment. We can lie to make others feel bad by telling them negative things about themselves, such as "I hate what you are wearing." Such lies, rather than spare others' feelings—an adaptive response—are used to inflict suffering. Such lies are not adaptive and represent some form of psychopathology.

Likewise lying to protect oneself from punishment by lying about another is also maladaptive since such lies, although sparing oneself from punishment, bring punishment to the other. The young child who scribbles on the wall and blames her sibling for doing it is an example of such lies. While understandably wanting to avoid punishment, an adaptive response seems reasonable, but placing the blame on another does not. For the most part, lying that injures another has not received much attention, although pathological lying has received some.[28]

* * *

I propose that self-referential behavior allows for the development of pretense that becomes the basis of what, in adults, we call self-deception.

Its emergence in the middle of the second year of life not only provides the toddler the ability to consider himself, but provides the child with its earliest mentalism, that is, it allows the child to think about himself not in the here-and-now, but in a world of his own making. Self-deception in adults is important for emotional life. Moreover, self-deception may be needed for all forms of deception. Certainly it seems the case that in order to deceive others one needs to deceive oneself. Given that very young children are capable of deception to avoid punishment and to protect the feelings of others, self-deception may also emerge early, and its early manifestation is in pretend play.[29]

What we have learned is that lying and deception exist early in the child's life and that they appear to be dependent on the mental representation of the self, what I have been calling consciousness. Ideas about the self in regard to one's emotional action patterns, as well as the early social and cognitive action patterns, give rise to other ideas about the real but also what is not real.

The connection between the emergence of consciousness and the ability to pretend has a logical necessity. Once consciousness emerges the transformation of the early action patterns into ideas is possible. With pretense the young child is capable of using these early action patterns as a means to affect her social environment through the manipulation of these action patterns in social interactions. Just as an adult can manipulate angry behavior to achieve a goal, so too can the young child. The ability to deceive oneself increases the child's ability to deceive others about her emotion. So, for example, Anna can say, "Mommy, I'm scared," and thus can get her mother to behave in a manner Anna wishes whether or not she is really scared.

As the self-conscious emotions emerge, pretend play enables the child to manipulate these emotions. The action patterns of the child, now through pretense, can become totally flexible and like another idea used to the advantage of the child in her commerce with her social world and in her intrapsychic life. With the growth of the child's general knowledge about the standards, rules, and goals of the family and culture, she can through deception transform the early emotional action patterns into ideas that will affect the elicitation of new action patterns, the expression of them, and the experience or feeling of them (or not), in effect altering emotional life.

CHAPTER 8

The Self-Conscious Emotions

"I am so ashamed at what I said to him."

This sentence captures my view of the self-conscious emotions, and in particular shame. There are two references to my self, the reference to an experience, "I am so . . . ," and the cause of that state, "I said . . . " The emergence of consciousness is defined by this self-reflection. It is important to note that the cause of the shame is the failure of some behavior. While the sentence itself does not specify the cause for shame other than that something was said, it implies that what was said failed to meet some standard, rule, or goal that the speaker had in regard to his behavior.

With the emergence of consciousness, a person's emotional life is transformed. In addition to the early action patterns, elicited by physical properties of the literal world, the child has now acquired added ideas as elicitors of an emotion, in particular ideas about the self. It is these ideas that now become the elicitors of new emotional action patterns. Make no mistake, these new action patterns are as biologically derived as the original ones, neither the experience of it nor the action patterns associated with it are taught. What differentiates these new action patterns from the earlier ones is that these new ones are elicited by ideas, not by the literal physical world.[1] Because these self-conscious emotions require the emergence of self-reflection, they appear in the middle of the second year of life. And because some of these self-conscious emotions require the development of other ideas, such as ideas about the standards, rules, and goals of the family and culture, as well as ideas about personal responsibility, their development spans the period from the emergence of consciousness, around 15 to 24 months, to the end of the child's third year, around 30 to 36 months. We therefore can think of the child's emotional life as consisting of three periods: the period of the early emotions or at least of their action patterns, the period of the emergence of consciousness, and the period of the development of the self-conscious emotions. However, the set of self-conscious emotions itself needs to be divided between the early ones, what I call the "self-conscious exposed emotions," and the later ones, what I call the "self-conscious evaluative emotions." The major difference between these two sets of emotions centers on the development of knowledge about the standards, rules, and goals of the family and the greater culture, and the incorporation of this knowledge into the child's mental life. The exposed self-conscious emotions appear to be tied directly to the emergence of a mental representation of self and include at least embarrassment, jealousy, and empathy. The evaluative self-conscious emotions also require the mental representation of the self, but in addition to the knowledge of some of the standards, rules, and goals the child has acquired, there is a need to develop some ideas about responsibility for her actions and thoughts. These evaluative emotions include shame, guilt, pride, embarrassment, and hubris.[2] Because the overall model, the early action patterns, and the emergence of consciousness have already been discussed, here I focus on the self-conscious emotions.

THE SELF-CONSCIOUS EMOTIONS

The self-conscious emotions—in particular, shame—can help us distinguish between those who would attribute mental representation involving the self at an early age and those who see it emerge in the middle of the second year of life. While it is the case that shame can be elicited by many causes, the claim that it exists early within the first year is similar to the claim that all emotions exist in the first months of life, for example, jealousy.[3] Historically, it has been thought that the self-conscious emotions such as shame took time to develop. Freud, for one, believed that the child needed to have developed an ego and a superego in order to experience guilt and shame. Silvan Tomkins's view had as its central theme how children think of others' thoughts about them as the elicitor of shame. Children's thinking about others thinking about them needs time to develop. Darwin thought that the self-conscious emotions required a developed cognitive system in which a mental representation of "me" is needed. Darwin related the self-conscious emotions to the process of thinking about what others are thinking about oneself. He wrote about the nature of the mental states that induce blushing. For example, he noted that the self-conscious emotions "consist of shyness, shame and modesty; the essential element in all being self-attention." Notice Darwin's term "self-attention," what we have called "consciousness," or the ability to reflect on oneself. Darwin believed that many reasons can be assigned for thinking that originally self-attention directed to personal appearance, in relation to the opinion of others, was the exciting cause; the same effect being subsequently produced, through the force of association, by self-attention in relation to moral conduct. It is not the simple act of reflecting on our own appearance, but the thinking what others think of us, which excites a blush.[4]

While various theories have postulated some universal elicitor of the self-conscious emotions, such as failure at toilet training, exposure of the backside, or the interruption of an ongoing action, the idea of an automatic noncognitive elicitor of these emotions does not make much sense. Cognitive processes have to be the elicitors of these complex emotions. It is the way we think about ourselves that becomes the elicitor. There may be a one-to-one correspondence between thinking certain thoughts and the occurrence of a particular emotion; however, for these emotions, the elicitor is still a cognitive event. This does not mean that the earlier emotions, those called primary or basic, are elicited by noncognitive events. Cognitive factors play a role in the elicitation of any action pattern; however, the nature of the cognitive events is much less complex in the earlier emotions.[5]

While the emotions that appear early, such as joy, sadness, fear, and anger, have received considerable attention, the set of emotions that appear later, which are considered here, has received relatively little attention. There are likely to be many reasons for this lack of interest. One reason is that these self-conscious emotions cannot be described solely in terms of a particular set of facial movements; identification of the self-conscious emotions requires the observation of bodily actions as well as facial cues. A second reason for the neglect of the study of these later emotions is the realization that there are no clear specific elicitors of these particular emotions. While happiness can be elicited by seeing a significant other, and fear can be elicited by the approach of a stranger, there are few specific situations that will always elicit shame, pride, guilt, or embarrassment. These self-conscious emotions are likely to require classes of events that only can be identified by the individuals themselves. For these reasons, little research has been conducted on their development.

Darwin saw these later emotions as involving the self, and emerging around age 3 years, but he was not able to distinguish among the various types. His observation and concern in regards to blushing reveals his interest in appearance and consciousness. Darwin's use of blushing as an example raises particular difficulties in large part because blushing (1) usually occurs around embarrassment rather than shame or guilt, (2) not all children or adults blush, and (3) blushing usually takes place in the presence of others, while shame can be experienced alone.

THE SELF-CONSCIOUS EXPOSED EMOTIONS

The emergence of consciousness is seen in some children as early as age 15 months, but all normally developing children show self-referential behavior by age 24 months. Whatever the age when self-referential behavior can be observed is the age when the exposed self-conscious emotions appear. If self-recognition is shown by Rana at age 18 months, she will start to show these self-conscious emotions at age 18 months, and if it is shown at age 21 months by Tamara, then for her they will start to be seen at that age. They are temporally tied to the emergence of self-reflection. This association between them has been studied in terms of exposure embarrassment, discussed next. In our studies, we have found that while fearfulness is unrelated to self-recognition, embarrassment is such that children who do not show self-recognition do not show embarrassment.[6]

The work on these exposed self-conscious emotions has centered on three emotions: exposure embarrassment, jealousy/envy, and empathy. Let us start with embarrassment because it is one of the early self-conscious exposed emotions for which there is some information.

Embarrassment

Almost all theories speak of embarrassment as an unpleasant feeling having to do with some form of the discrediting of one's own image, either through the loss of self-esteem, the loss of the esteem of others, or both. However, one of the critical issues in the study of embarrassment has to do with terminology usage. The problem concerns the difference between embarrassment and shame, on the one hand, and between embarrassment and shyness, on the other. Historically, the psychoanalytic approach made little distinction between embarrassment and shame; most of the confusion in this approach has been between guilt and shame.[7] Freud writes mostly of shame and does not employ another word that might be translated as "embarrassment."[8] If shame is discussed, it is usually discussed in terms of nakedness or in terms of impulses, either sexual or exhibitional, that need to be held in check. Of more interest is the existential approach. In this approach, embarrassment is seen as an alienation of one's own body. Erving Goffman, for example, discusses the act of blushing as occurring when an individual becomes aware of her own body, which is similar to Darwin's idea about embarrassment. Unfortunately, the term "alienation" suggests some negative attribution as in being separate from one's own body; however, I think that alienation should be viewed as self-awareness or self-reflection.

The interpersonal approach to embarrassment suggests that individuals feel embarrassed when they project an image of themselves incompatible with their own view *in the presence of others.* "Embarrassment . . . reflects a failure to present oneself in the way one would have wished."[9] Such theories assume the need for three features: the presence of another person; the person becoming aware that he is the center of attention; and the person feeling that he is being judged. As we shall see this last feature is questionable, since the distinction between embarrassment and shame is not well articulated in this approach. One could argue that the same three conditions are necessary for the production of shame, although this view of embarrassment is quite common.[10]

Embarrassment is often considered to be similar to shyness, especially to the extent to which embarrassment can be viewed as having a fear component. When we think of a shy child, we tend to think of a child who is reluctant to engage in interpersonal interactions. But this factor of sociability may have less to do with evaluation and more to do with dispositional factors.[11] Jerome Kagan argues for what he calls "inhibition," which bears a striking similarity to shyness.[12] Even when embarrassment is viewed as a form of shyness, it has a negative evaluation component. For example, Phillip Zimbardo argues that people feel most shy at being the center of attention of a large group of people.[13] For him, a person being watched implies being seen in the best light. Being seen as such, in turn, implies an evaluation of the self against some kind of ideal self. Shyness also has been related to aspects of social anxiety, which also implies an evaluative component.[14]

Since Darwin described all self-conscious emotions as including the phenomenon of blushing, the use of blushing to indicate shame, embarrassment, and guilt means that blushing as a measure of any one emotion is ineffective. By utilizing a combination of the criteria suggested by others, we have come up with an overall measure of embarrassment that is useful in studying young children. This scoring system for embarrassment agrees with those of others who have attempted to find behavioral manifestation of this emotion.[15] In general, the behaviors believed to reflect embarrassment are (1) a smiling facial expression, (2) gaze aversion, and (3) movement of the hands to the body such as touching hair, clothing, face, or other body parts. These hand gestures appear to capture the category of nervous movements that previous investigators believed were characteristic of the emotion. Such body touching can accompany smiling/gaze aversion or immediately follow it. All three classes of behavior appear to be associated with embarrassment.

Embarrassment differs from shame or anxiety/fear in a number of critical ways. First, embarrassment seems to be marked by a "sheepish" grin or a "silly" smile as described by others. In both shame and fear, smiling behavior is usually absent. Moreover, the smiling in embarrassment does not appear to be a frozen type of smile; rather, it is an active engagement with the other people present. Perhaps most important in differentiating embarrassment from other emotions is the gaze behavior and bodily action. In embarrassment, people are more apt to tilt their heads and to engage in gaze-avert/look-at behavior. It is not gaze aversion with the head bowed as in an avoidance response and it is not the immobility of action as in removing one's self from the situation. Instead it is a gaze-avert, gaze-return motion toward the other person present. This on/off sequence is typical of embarrassment, whereas in shame it is more a turning away and remaining away. Finally, nervous touching of the body, including hair, clothing, and face, seems to reflect the subject's engagement in self-directive behavior, reflecting an active focus on the self. In shame or shyness, the person is likely to be immobile, and not inclined toward self-directive behavior. The use of such behavioral criteria is in keeping with the idea that embarrassment appears to be related to the self and requires another social object. The active nature of bodily action in embarrassment, unlike that seen in shame, suggests that embarrassment and shame are readily distinguishable.[16]

Since embarrassment has been related to shyness, we need a working definition for this term. Shyness for some researchers is itself not an emotion. For example, Izard and Tyson describe shyness in terms of sheepishness, bashfulness, and the feeling of uneasiness or psychological discomfort in social situations.[17] They suggest that shyness results from a vacillation between fear and interest or between avoidance and approach. They relate shyness to fear, not to self-evaluation. Individuals who are considered shy are not too much concerned with the evaluation of their performance vis-à-vis their standards, as they are with being observed. Thus, our own observations, as well as those of others, indicate that shyness is related to a constellation of factors not related to self-evaluation. Moreover, there is some reason to believe that these individual differences have a dispositional or constitutional basis.[18]

For some researchers, embarrassment is closely linked to shame.[19] While shame appears to be an intense and destructive emotion, embarrassment is less intense and does not involve the same degree of disruption of thought and action as in shame. In terms of body posture, people who are embarrassed do not assume the shame posture of body collapse. Their bodies reflect an ambivalent approach–avoidance posture. In shame situations one rarely sees gaze aversion accompanied by smiling behavior. Thus, from a behavioral point of view these two action patterns appear to be different. Phenomenologically, embarrassment is less differentiated from shame, as people often report that "embarrassment" is less intense than "shame." Situations similar to those that invoke shame are found to invoke embarrassment. Even so, the intensity and duration of the disruptive quality of shame is reduced in embarrassment. These different descriptions of behavior appear to be indicating two different types of embarrassment, because, as our studies of toddlers suggest, one type occurs earlier than the other, and different elicitors are involved.

Embarrassment as Exposure, Not as Evaluation

Embarrassment as exposure appears to be more similar to shyness than to shame, and it is the first type of embarrassment to appear. In certain situations in which the child is observed, she becomes embarrassed. This type of embarrassment is not related to negative evaluation. One of the best examples of this kind of exposure embarrassment is being complimented. The phenomenological experience of embarrassment when complimented is well known. The adult public speaker, when introduced with praise, is often embarrassed. While complimenting may elicit the social rule of modesty in adults or older children, it is not typical for infants as young as 15 to 18 months of age who are unlikely to have learned the rule of modesty, yet show embarrassment when complimented. Another example of this type of exposure embarrassment can be seen in children's reaction to their public display. When a young child observes someone looking at him, he is apt to become embarrassed, to look away, and to touch or adjust his body. When the observed person is an adult woman, she will often adjust or touch her hair. An observed man is less likely to touch his hair, but may adjust his clothes or change his body posture. Observed people look pleased or concerned, rarely sad.

To examine the development of embarrassment my colleagues and I conducted a study with 15- to 18-month-olds, about half of whom showed self-recognition. To induce exposure embarrassment during a free-play situation both the experimenter and the mother pointed to the toddler and repeated her name while pointing. Many of the toddlers who showed self-recognition demonstrated clear examples of embarrassment to this event, suggesting that being the object of another's attention can produce a kind of embarrassment that appears to be unrelated to any evaluation of behaviors. Interestingly, in an earlier study[20] children 12 to 33 months old were asked to dance to music first by their mothers in the presence of a stranger and then by the experimenter. In another situation they were also overly praised. Those who showed embarrassment also showed self-recognition, although not all children who showed self-reflection showed embarrassment when made the object of another's attention.

In order to explore this individual difference in the display of embarrassment, in another study measures of temperament as well as measures of reaction to pain caused by inoculation were obtained for infants along with measures of embarrassment to being the object of others' attention.[21] The results strongly suggest that individual ease of embarrassment once consciousness emerges is a function of temperament, with young children with difficult temperaments as measured by a variety of indexes more likely to show this type of exposure embarrassment. These findings support the idea that exposure embarrassment is not evaluatively related. The elicitor was simply being the object of another's attention. To support this idea we found that several particularly difficult temperament children, when pointed to by their mothers and the experimenter, not only showed embarrassment but they became upset and cried. They were reported by their mothers to be very shy.

Further support for exposure embarrassment can be seen in an experiment I often perform in front of large groups of people. In lecturing to audiences, I demonstrate that embarrassment can be elicited just by exposure. To demonstrate this point, I inform the audience that "I am going to *randomly* point to someone." I further inform the audience that "my pointing has no evaluative component and is not related to anything about the person since I will close my eyes before pointing." Following these words, I turn around several times and I point to someone in the room, who, of course, immediately acts embarrassed. Everyone agrees that the person chosen will be embarrassed if he is pointed at, yet, since it is random, it cannot reflect anything personal.

The final example is another observation. I have gone to the same dental hygienist to have my teeth cleaned for several years. It occurred to me that if I were a dental hygienist I would have a favorite tooth, one that gave me particular pleasure to clean, in part, maybe because it was easy to clean. With this idea in mind, I asked Barbara, the hygienist, "What is your favorite tooth?" She stopped her work, looked embarrassed, blushed, and finally said, "How did you know?" Quite by accident I had uncovered her secret. She told me she was not ashamed at having a favorite tooth, just embarrassed at being "uncovered." This example of embarrassment at being exposed or uncovered has made me realize that the exposure does not have to be about the physical presence of the self but can also extend to the secret part of the self.[22]

There are other examples of embarrassment in which an evaluation is evoked, yet it may be that simply being the object of others' attention can be the real elicitor. Take the simple act of walking into a crowded room and having people stare at your entrance. On such an occasion, one is likely to experience embarrassment and this embarrassment turns into a negative self-evaluation, such as "I hope I have worn the correct dress." I believe, however, that the experience of embarrassment may not be caused by the negative self-evaluation, but by simple public exposure. However, rather than believe that it is the exposure that produces the embarrassment, people often look for a negative evaluation. In other words, the negative evaluation follows embarrassment due to exposure as people attempt to explain why they are embarrassed. The reason is that as adults we also possess a second type of embarrassment that occurs around a standard failure.

Embarrassment as a Function of Evaluation

This type of embarrassment is related to negative self-evaluation and to shame, topics that are covered in more detail later when the self-conscious evaluative emotions are discussed. It emerges later in development than the exposure embarrassment. This second type of embarrassment emerges after the incorporation of the standards, rules, and goals of the family, which does not occur until the end of the third year. Although both types are measured in the same way, the elicitors of this type of embarrassment are quite different than those for exposure embarrassment.

Functional Significance of Early Embarrassment

To ask about the functional significance of a certain behavior runs the risk of storytelling since it is always difficult to test such ideas. Nevertheless, I believe that embarrassment emerges at the same time that children obtain consciousness. Why, then, should self-reflection have a negative component? The emergence of consciousness carries both advantages and disadvantages. This emerging capacity allows the child to reflect on herself, to use the self to make comparisons to others, and ultimately to develop evaluative behaviors, desires, and goals that will guide her actions. At the same time, this capacity to reflect on the self can be dangerous. The dangers reside in the child being entrapped in a circular-like reaction: it is possible to think about the self thinking about the self thinking about the self. Such circularity would lead the child into a hopeless cycle of thought, preventing her from acting. To prevent such circular reactions, it would seem reasonable to imagine that self-reflection should be accompanied by arousal containing a slight negative tone. If self-reflection is a little uncomfortable, engaging in it becomes costly.

Thus, it is possible to be too self-reflective. Under such conditions people also have difficulty focusing on action. From a clinical perspective, we have reason to believe that much self-consciousness is related to a variety of problems, some of which are taken up in Chapter 11 on emotions gone awry. On this issue, Csikszentmihalyi and Csikszentmihalyi's analyses of flow may be relevant. For them, flow is a state of mind that is achieved when the adult's capacity matches some environmental challenge. Under such conditions, adults stop making reference to themselves; that is, self-reflection stops. For example, when one is deeply engaged in work, one often "loses track of the time." This phenomenological experience indicates that it is possible to lose self-reflection, at least some of the time.[23] The dangers of self-reflection, as well as its advantages, suggest that embarrassment, as related to exposure to others, reflects an emotion likely to occur some of the time to inhibit self-referential behavior when it develops.

This present model proposes a sequence that starts with embarrassment related to exposure and then is captured, in yet unexplained ways, and utilized in the evaluative processes centering on standards, rules, and goals.[24] By the second half of the second year of life, children show embarrassment to exposure; by the age of 3, children show embarrassment both to exposure and to violating a standard. Both types of embarrassment are available as a consequence of the developmental process. However, because adults utilize evaluation in all of their actions, the belief that embarrassment has to be related to some self failure is widely held. People and scientists alike tend to assume that embarrassment must be associated with evaluation. Although the developmental processes give rise to both forms of embarrassment, adults are more apt to focus on embarrassment due to evaluation.[25] Such an analysis suggests that embarrassment may play an important role in the emergence of all self-conscious emotions—those of exposure and those of evaluation. It appears reasonable to suggest some broad propositions about the development of embarrassment and its relation to other self-conscious emotions:

1. Early embarrassment is the emotional component of the cognitive process of self-reflection.
2. It emerges developmentally somewhere around the middle of the second year of life.
3. Individual differences in embarrassment appear at the point of its emergence and these differences may be related to differences in temperament.
4. The early form of embarrassment is not associated with the self's negative evaluation of the self's action.
5. Embarrassment's functional significance is in its inhibiting effect on self-reflection.
6. At some time between the second and third years of life, embarrassment becomes associated with self-evaluation. This form of embarrassment is related to other negative self-conscious evaluative emotions such as shame and guilt.
7. Evaluative embarrassment is a less intense form of shame.
8. The exposure-related and evaluation-related forms of embarrassment coexist in children over 3 years of age and in adults, although they are often confused.

The other two exposed types of self-conscious emotions that have been studied are jealousy and empathy, although empathy is considered by some as both an emotion such as sympathy and as a social cognitive action.

Jealousy

Jealousy usually arises from the loss of something valuable to another, and is most often used when talking about the child as being jealous about the attention or time his mother spends with another, not with him. To be sure, jealousy and envy are often confused and used interchangeably; however, envy refers more to wanting something another possesses. In the case of the child and her mother, the child could be both jealous of the time her mother spends with her sibling and envious of the sibling for being the focus of their mother's attention. As can be seen from this example, these two ideas are not at all clear or distinct, which accounts for their mixed usage. Whether we use the term "jealousy" or "envy," implied in these emotions is a self-referent, the I of consciousness that wants something it does not have. Thus, for these emotions to emerge, consciousness is required. Other cognitive capacities may also be needed; however, jealousy over a mother's attention turned elsewhere, say to a sibling, does not require elaborate cognitions since the direction of another's attention is readily discriminable. A recently published handbook on jealousy contains several essays suggesting the existence of jealousy in the very young child, so that a careful analysis is necessary to determine if such a view is reasonable.[26]

Sybil Hart's work is a good example of the studies exploring this emotion. In one of her studies infants and their mothers play together and then on signal the mother turns away from her infant and for a few minutes, while ignoring her, attends to and talks to a doll. The 4-month-old infants show such behavior as interest, joy, anger, and sadness as well as intense negative emotionality to their mother's attention to the doll. Infants showed increases in their emotionality and did so more when their mothers expressed more positive than neutral vocal behaviors toward the doll. Such findings were taken to indicate that infants this young show jealousy. However, whether these behaviors reflect jealousy or protest around the loss of the mother's attention is not clear, although I would think protest the more likely.

In studying infants, a child's protest over loss of the attention of others generally has been considered in two ways, either as the departure of the mother, as in the attachment paradigm in which the mother leaves the child alone in a strange room, or when the mother is present but is separated from her child either by a physical barrier or by her not directly attending toward the child as in the still-face paradigm.[27]

In the attachment paradigm, the loss of the mother most often results in protests of sadness and crying, as well as anger, as actions designed to get the mother back.[28] The same behaviors can be seen in situations where the mother is separated from the infant by a see-through barrier. While the 1- and 2-year-olds in the experiments can see their mothers, they cannot get close to them. The behaviors of crying, looking at the mother, and trying to get over the barrier are exhibited.[29] The same can be said for the infant's behavior when the mother turns away from her interaction with the child.[30] Also, looking at the very young infant's response to the frustration of a blocked goal in its object world also shows these same behaviors. Thus, in situations involving the loss of the mother's attention, measured by her nonavailability as when behind a barrier, or by her complete disappearance as in the attachment paradigm, or by her lack of interaction as in the still-face procedure, there are similar infant responses, namely, protest. To call these behaviors "jealousy" seems premature, unless one wishes to attribute mental status to the infant's behavior. Although many would, there is no reason to do so unless one is caught in anthropomorphizing about how the adult would feel in the context of one's loss of one's mother.[31]

As suggested throughout this book, early action patterns, in this case the blockage of a valued object or person, can become the material for a self-conscious emotion once the emergence of the capacity for self-reference appears. Recent work indicating that young children tend to share their toys with others because of a biological disposition and do not show jealousy and possessiveness until the emergence of consciousness around age 2, lends some support for these ideas. It is also at this time that the idea of ownership emerges.[32]

Empathy

Whether empathy is considered an emotion like sympathy or a cognitive act, it seems to involve the ability to place oneself in the role of another. What is important about this ability is the idea that empathy allows for knowing about you, your feelings, what you may be thinking, and what the meaning of your behavior has to you. While we discussed this topic earlier, it is necessary now to think about its development since there is the strong belief that children show empathy long before the emergence of consciousness. Consider, for example, Martin Hoffman's demonstration that in the newborn nursery the crying of one infant elicits the crying of others, or Carolyn Zahn-Waxler's demonstration that the toddler reacts by comforting her mother if she shows distress.[33]

Clearly, if empathy requires taking the perspective of the other, it is difficult to reconcile an infant crying to another infant's cry with this idea. For many of these early matching behaviors the idea of contagion should be considered. It would seem reasonable that all social creatures are by definition affected by the actions of conspecifics and maybe even by the actions of others who resemble them. Contagious behavior is most apparent in the emotional realm, although it can also be seen in other behavior. As we all have experienced, we are likely to feel sad if others around us are crying and to feel happy when others are laughing. The same is true for the emotions of fear, disgust, and anger. The contagious effects of the emotional behavior of others are well known; witness the contagion of yawning or even of the coordination of menstruation of women living together.

Although some claim a form of mentalism for these coordinated emotional action patterns between the baby and the adult, it seems more likely that this coordination reflects contagion as a basic biological necessity of all animals that live with conspecifics. It may even involve the use of motor neurons. It does not involve mentalism, although, as for other action patterns, it may become the material from which mentalism is formed. The simultaneity of action between two people through contagion may be the material out of which adult empathy grows. However, in the mature form of empathy one does not have to be in the presence of the other's distress to feel upset since it is a mental act that does not need the presence of the other's emotional action pattern to produce one's own action pattern.

This, of course, is the problem of much of the research on early empathy. For example, in many studies, the mother pretends that she has pricked her finger on a pin and makes a hurt, sad face and groans in front of the toddler. It is difficult to know whether the toddler's response is caused by contagion or is caused by modeling and learning to comfort another who is showing pain. Indeed, infants often try to comfort their mothers by patting them or hugging them, but at the same time they do not look distressed and may even show a happy-like face. It is necessary to separate out contagion or imitation from empathy around distress in order to see its relation to the emergence of consciousness. Doris Bischof-Kohler demonstrated that empathy around the distress of another represents neither imitation nor contagion *if* the child's behavior is well organized so that both facial expression and behavior are in accord. She was able to show that this occurs only once the child showed self-recognition behaviors.[34] In other words, mentalism is associated with true empathy while its earlier forms are likely to be contagious action patterns. As Frans de Waal has pointed out, elaborate, empathy-like responses certainly can be seen early in the child's life, but the adult human form of the behavior is unlikely to emerge until the development of consciousness.[35]

From a developmental point of view, we are confronted with the conundrum of the same behavior being supported by very different processes, and need to be careful to make sure that we do not commit the error that just because behaviors appear similar on the surface, they are supported by the same underlying process. Indeed, one of the difficulties in the study of development is that, on the one hand, the same process may result in very different behaviors during the developmental sequence, while, on the other hand, the same behavior at different points in time may be supported by very different processes. I think it is safe to conclude that any theory of the development of empathy needs to incorporate the emergence of a self-representation. The distress of the newborn to the cries of other newborns, and the generous charitable donations given by people to the victims of the 2012 Japanese earthquake and tsunami disaster or Hurricane Sandy, should not be considered as having similar underlying processes as the yawning of one person producing yawning in another.

Although other early self-conscious emotions need consideration, what appears to be the case is that all of them are dependent at a minimum on the emergence of consciousness. Few other cognitive capacities besides perception and memory are needed for their emergence, unlike the next set of self-conscious emotions, which rest on the development of complex self-attributions, including self-responsibility, which allows for evaluation of the self in regard to the socialization standards, rules, and goals of family and culture.

THE SELF-CONSCIOUS EVALUATIVE EMOTIONS

Returning to my opening sentence, "I am so ashamed at what I said to him," anchors the discussion of the evaluative self-conscious emotions, since this statement requires consideration of the idea of self-evaluation. When the speaker says that he is ashamed of what he said, it is because of some verbal action on his part that does not meet some standard that he holds. It also implies that he accepts responsibility for his actions. Finally, the experience is his own and while the sentence focuses on his verbal behavior, it is he, his whole self, that is at fault. These aspects of his evaluation lead him to feel ashamed.

Here, now perhaps for the first time in the child's development, the emotional action pattern called shame is elicited by a set of ideas about himself, while most of the earlier action patterns were elicited by the literal properties of the environment. The behaviors and feeling of shame that make up this action pattern are for the most part not learned, but are part of the biological capacity of our species. However, it is the kind of ideas about the self and how the action pattern is expressed that is acquired as part of the child's learning engagement with the social world. The child learns about the standards, rules, and goals of her culture in both direct and indirect ways according to the social nexus in which she is raised. This nexus includes parents, grandparents, siblings, and peers, as well as teachers and others.

These self-conscious evaluative emotions are the bases of our moral behavior, and therefore have been called by some the "moral emotions." While we have seen that the early part of our emotional life is shared with other creatures, and that consciousness and therefore the exposed self-conscious emotions may be shared with the great apes, it is these moral emotions that separate us from all other living creatures that inhabit the planet. The eliciting events of these evaluative self-conscious emotions are ideas about self. While there are theories, such as those of psychoanalysis, that have argued for some universal elicitors of these self-conscious emotions, such as failure at toilet training or exposure of the backside, the idea of an automatic noncognitive elicitor of these evaluative emotions does not seem to make much sense. This does not imply that there are no specific elicitors, rather that the elicitors are the ways we think or what we think about, and there is likely some correspondence between thinking certain thoughts and the occurrence of a particular emotion; however, in the case of this class of emotions, the elicitor is always a way of thinking.[36]

The idea that these emotions are elicited by ways of thinking was recognized by Darwin. However, because he focused on blushing and did not pursue the implications of his idea about thoughts of others and the sensitivity to the opinion of others, whether good or bad, he was not able to differentiate between the various kinds of evaluative self-conscious emotions. This failure restricted his analysis. An additional reason may be that because Darwin was arguing for a connection between the emotions of animals and humans, he might not have wanted to consider the leap that might exist between what animals and humans think. Therefore he did not pursue the idea that humans have the capacity, which animals are unlikely to have, to think about themselves and to think about themselves in ways quite different from how the great apes think about themselves. In part, this might explain his focus on the issue of physical appearance without giving much thought to ideas about standards, rules, and goals.[37]

Let us begin our discussion of the self-conscious evaluative emotions by showing the central role of consciousness in the evaluation process. To summarize what is to follow, let us look at the evaluation of the self. The self-conscious evaluative emotions involve a set of standards, rules, and goals (SRGs). These SRGs are inventions of the culture that are transmitted to children and involve their learning of, and willingness to consider, these SRGs as their own. This process of incorporating SRGs appears to take place by age 3 years, at least in part, since SRGs are constantly being learned throughout life.[38] Moreover, SRGs imply self-evaluation because children need the capacity to evaluate their actions with respect to them. Having self-evaluative capacity allows for two distinct outcomes: the child can evaluate her behavior and hold herself responsible for the action being evaluated or she can hold herself not responsible. In attribution theory, these outcomes have been called an "internal" versus an "external" attribution. If the child concludes that she is not responsible then evaluation of her behavior ceases. However, if she evaluates herself as responsible, then she can evaluate her behavior as successful or not vis-à-vis her SRGs. The determination of success or failure resides within the individual and is based on the nature of the SRGs. For example, if a student believes that only receiving an A on an exam constitutes success, then receiving a B represents a failure for that student; on the other hand, another student may consider a B a great success. Still another type of cognition related to the self has to do with the evaluation of herself in terms of specific or global attributions. "Global self-attributions" refer to the whole self, whereas "specific self-attributions" refer to specific features or actions of the self.[39] It is these types of self-attributions or ideas about the self that give rise to these self-conscious evaluative emotions. Success or failure vis-à-vis an SRG is likely to produce a self-reflection.

This conclusion is consistent with George Mandler's idea that self-reflection is necessary when a plan is formulated and then again when a plan fails or is finished.[40] This self-reflection gives rise to self-attributions and therefore to the specific self-conscious evaluative emotions that occur as a consequence. The importance of such a view suggests three factors. First, the model does not attempt to specify what constitutes a success or a failure, or how the person goes about evaluating success or failure. Second, the model does not specify any particular SRG. In other words, it is not clear whether there are any specific stimuli that uniquely contribute to any of the self-conscious emotions. Third, the model assumes that self-attributions leading to specific emotions are internal events that reside in people themselves, although the SRGs are taught by others. Although this model is based on a phenomenological and cognitive-attributional model, it does not mean that the self-conscious emotions are epiphenomenological or deserve a different status than the cognitive-attributional processes themselves. These self-conscious emotions are action patterns that are innate and are bodily in nature. They are not action patterns that existed earlier, since it is ideas that serve as elicitors of these specific action patterns in the same way as do other stimuli. The important point here is that specific action patterns and therefore emotions can be elicited through a variety of self-attributions.[41]

Such a view stands in contrast to the ideas of Freud and Erikson. Freud discussed the function of guilt but said little about shame. Indeed Freud's avoidance of shame has been linked by Masson to Freud's own problems with shame.[42] However, Freud does discuss two types of guilt, one of which involves the actions of the self, what I will call guilt, and one having to do with the whole self, which I will call shame.[43] For Freud, the superego—the mechanism by which the standards of the parents are incorporated into the self, specifically via the child's fear that the parents will respond to transgression by withdrawal of their love or even by punishment—is the initial source of guilt. Freud's discussion of guilt in relation to the superego is similar to his discussion of guilt in relation to the instinctual drives and their expression. For Freud, anxiety or fear is translatable directly into guilt. The two stages in the development of guilt related to the superego are the fear of authority and the fear of the superego itself once the authority's standards are incorporated. In the well-developed superego, the sense of guilt arises not only when a violation is committed, but even when a violation is being anticipated.

The guilt that Freud focuses on is not a guilt related to the whole self, but rather a guilt related to one's action. For Freud, guilt is a specific and focused response to a transgression that can be rectified by abstinence and penance. However, Freud's discussion of another type of guilt can also be found in his discussion of psychopathology, and it is the guilt resulting from an overdeveloped ego. This guilt is quite like shame. When Freud did mention shame, he usually did so in the context of drives and impulses that require restriction. So, for example, in discussing the impulses having to do with the erogenous zones, he stated that these impulses "evoke opposing mental forces [reacting impulses] which, in order to suppress this displeasure affectively, build up the mental dams of . . . disgust, shame and morality."[44]

Erikson also tried to discuss shame but he had no more success in distinguishing between shame and guilt than the earlier psychoanalysts. Erikson turned more to the Darwinian view when he suggested that shame arises when "one is completely exposed and conscious of being looked at, in a word, self-conscious."[45] Again, Erikson's self-conscious emotion does not differentiate between shame, shyness, embarrassment, and guilt. Erikson tried to differentiate these terms but was not completely successful. For example, he discussed "visual shame" versus "auditory guilt," but he did not develop this distinction. I imagine that the reference to visual shame is based on Darwin's theory that shame derives from being looked at, and that when experiencing shame one wishes to hide one's face and to disappear. Although Erikson held to a view involving the self and self-consciousness, he also indicated that the conditions necessary for feeling shame include being in an upright and exposed position. As he stated, "Clinical observation leads me to believe that shame has much to do with a consciousness of having a front and a back, especially a 'behind.' "[46] Erikson believed that shame is related to specific body acts, in particular toilet functions. Erikson's theory of ego challenges offers his clearest differentiation between shame and guilt, their place in human life, and events likely to elicit them. For example, one of Erikson's developmental challenges was autonomy versus shame and doubt. Autonomy is the attempt of the child to achieve, and is related to the developing sense of the self. Achieving muscular control, including control of the elimination of body waste, is the developmental challenge at this life stage. Shame and doubt arise during this stage as the counterpoints to autonomy and the successful achievement of muscular control. In other words, shame and doubt arise from the child's inability to fully control bodily functions. It is only after this basic ego task that the third ego task, initiative versus guilt, becomes significant. Here Erikson also suggested that guilt has a reparative function. Erikson's developmental sequence indicates a recognition that shame and guilt are different emotions, that shame precedes guilt, and that they are associated in counterpoint with different ego tasks. It also leads to the commonly held psychoanalytic view that guilt is a more mature emotion than shame.

There is very little agreement as to the specific elicitors of shame, guilt, or embarrassment. Many events are capable of eliciting any one of them. No particular stimulus event has been identified as the trigger for shame and guilt. It would be easier to understand these self-conscious emotions if we could specify the class of external events likely to elicit them. If it were true that shame and guilt are similar to anxiety and that they reflect the subject's fear of uncontrollable impulses, then we could consider the causes of shame to be sexual or aggressive impulses. Alternatively, if we could prove that situations having to do with toilet or genital functions are likely to elicit shame, or if we could prove that the way we appear physically, or how we behave in front of others may automatically elicit embarrassment, we could then specify situations that would help us to define these self-conscious emotions and increase our understanding of what causes them. Unfortunately, there is no such clear cause-and-effect pattern, no event that can be used consistently as an elicitor of each of these self-conscious emotions. While there are no known literal events that are likely to cause these self-conscious emotions, certain ideas may have a more universal-like quality of eliciting certain emotions. So, for example, if an attachment figure says to a child, "I do not love you," this statement may well lead to certain negative ideas about the global self, and thus to the emotion of shame, since a global, stable, and negative self-attribution is likely to occur as a consequence of the statement. However, this example has strong cognitive features and is likely therefore to take place after the first year or two of life.

Before we go into the details about the development of these evaluative self-conscious emotions, the formal qualities of the ideas about the self are presented below. My structural model identifies the ideas about the self that serve as the elicitors of each of four self-conscious evaluative emotions. This model is symmetrical with regard to positive and negative self-evaluative emotions in that it accounts not only for shame and guilt in response to failure but also for pride and hubris, sometimes called "alpha" and "beta" pride in response to success.[47] The model also proposes that the immediate elicitors of specific self-evaluative emotions are the qualities of self-related attributions. Given the three sets of judgments shown in Figure 8.1, the model accounts for and distinguishes among four self-conscious evaluative emotions. The immediate elicitors of these are the cognitive self-evaluative processes as described.

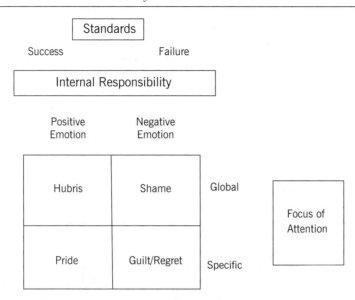

FIGURE 8.1. A model of self-evaluative processes and their relation to four self-evaluative emotions: hubris, shame, pride, and guilt/regret. From Lewis, M., & Sullivan, M. W. (2005). The development of self-conscious emotions. In A. J. Elliot & C. S. Dweck (Eds.), *Handbook of competence and motivation* (p. 189). Copyright 2005 by the Guilford Press. Reprinted by permission of the publisher.

Cognitive Self-Evaluative Processes

Standards, Rules, and Goals

The first feature of the model has to do with the SRGs that govern our behavior. All of us have beliefs about what is acceptable for others and for ourselves in regard to SRGs having to do with actions, thoughts, and emotions. This set of beliefs, or SRGs, constitutes the information the person acquires through culturalization. SRGs differ across different societies, across groups within societies, across different time epochs, and among individuals of different ages. The standards of our culture are varied and complex, yet each of us knows at least some of them. Moreover, each of us has a unique set. To become a member of any group requires one must learn that group's SRGs. SRGs are acquired through a variety of processes. They always are associated with human behavior. They are prescribed by the culture, including the culture at large, as well as by the influences of specific groups, such as clan, peers, and family.

While 1-year-olds are learning about some do's and don'ts, their behavior is controlled by the presence of the adult; the specific do's and don'ts are not incorporated into the child's mental life. Instead, they are likely controlled by direct rewards and punishments. By the second year of life, children show some understanding about appropriate and inappropriate behavior, but these nascent SRGs are not yet incorporated and so still require the presence of an adult. Research indicates that by the end of the second and the beginning of the third year of life children already have incorporated some SRGs and seem to show distress when they violate them.[48] The acquisition of these SRGs continues across the lifespan.

Evaluation

The evaluation of one's actions, thoughts, and feelings in terms of SRGs is the second cognitive-evaluative process that serves as a stimulus. Two major aspects of this process are considered here; the first has to do with responsibility. For the model to work in describing the process of eliciting emotions, responsibility for the success or failure of an SRG is necessary. Individuals differ in their characteristic evaluative responses. Moreover, situations differ in the likelihood that they will cause a particular evaluative response. The second consideration has to do with how individuals make a determination about success or failure in regard to any specific standard.

Responsibility

Within the study of self-attribution, the problem of internal versus external responsibility has received considerable attention. People violate SRGs but often do not attribute the failure to themselves. They may explain their failure in terms of chance or the actions of others. Responsibility evaluations are functions both of situational factors and of individual characteristics. There are people who are likely to blame themselves no matter what happens. Carol Dweck, in studying causes of success and failure, found that many children blamed their success or failure on external forces, not themselves, although there were just as many who were likely to evaluate success and failure in terms of their own actions.[49]

Success or Failure

Another feature of the self-evaluation process has to do with the socialization of what constitutes success or failure. Once one has assumed responsibility, exactly how one comes to evaluate an action, thought, or feeling as a success or a failure is not well understood. This aspect of self-evaluation is particularly important because the same SRGs can result in radically different feelings, depending upon whether success or failure is attributed.

Many factors are involved in producing inaccurate or unique evaluations of success or failure. These include early failures in the self system leading to narcissistic disorders, harsh socialization experiences, and high levels of reward for success or punishment for failure.[50] The evaluation of one's behavior in terms of success and failure is a very important aspect of the emotional response to SRGs, and consequently of the organization of plans and the determination of new goals and plans.

Specific and Global Attributes about the Self

Another attribution in regard to the self has to do with *global* or *specific* self-attribution. "Global" attribution refers to an individual's propensity to focus on the total self. Thus, for any particular behavior violation, some individuals, some of the time, are likely to focus on the totality of the self; they use such self-evaluative phrases as "Because I did this, I am bad or good." Ronnie Janoff-Bulman's distinction between "characterological" and "behavioral" self-blame is particularly relevant here.[51] When a global evaluation is made, the focus is upon the self both as an object and as a subject. The self becomes embroiled in the self. It becomes embroiled because the evaluation of the self by the self is total. There is no way out. The focus is not upon the individual's behavior, but upon the total self. There is little wonder that in using such global attribution one can think of nothing else except the self, and one becomes confused and speechless. Because of this focus on the total self, one is unable to act and is driven from the field of action into hiding or disappearing or wanting to die.

"Specific" attribution refers to individuals' propensity in some situations, some of the time, to focus on specific actions of the self. That is, their self-evaluation is not global, but specific. It is not the total self that has done something good or bad, right or wrong, but instead some particular specific behavior. Notice that for such occurrences, an individual's focus is not on the totality of the self, but on the specific behavior of the self in a specific situation. The focus here is on the behavior of the self in interaction with objects or persons. Here attention is on the actions of the self or the effect on other selves and on reparation.

Global versus specific self-focus may be a personality style. Global attributions for negative events are generally uncorrelated with global attributions for positive events. It is only when positive or negative events are taken into account that relatively stable and consistent attributional patterns are observed. Some individuals are likely to be stable in their global and specific evaluations; under most conditions of success or failure, these subjects are likely to maintain a global or specific posture with respect to self-attribution. In the attribution literature, such dispositional factors have important consequences upon a variety of fixed personality patterns. So, for example, depressed individuals are likely to make stable global attributions, whereas nondepressed individuals are less likely to be stable in their global attributions. These dispositional factors are likely to arise through both temperament and as socialization factors. Both of these factors are considered in the chapters to follow and so are only mentioned here.

In addition to the dispositional factors relating to specific or global attributions, there are likely to be situational constraints as well. Some have called these "prototypic situations." That is, although there are dispositional factors, not all people all the time are involved in either global or specific attributions. Unfortunately, these situational factors have not been well studied. It seems reasonable to believe that certain classes of situations should be more likely than others to elicit a particular focus, but exactly what classes of stimuli are likely to elicit global or specific attributions remain unknown.

These attributions—(1) the establishment of one's SRGs, (2) the evaluation of success or failure of one's actions in regard to these SRGs, and (3) the attributions of the self, with responsibility as either internal or external, as well as either global or specific—give rise to the four evaluative self-conscious emotions presented in the model. It is the cognitive evaluative process of the child himself that elicits these action patterns. Now let us turn to these four self-conscious emotions presented in Figure 8.1.

Shame

Shame is the consequence of a set of complex ideas about the self. First, it is accepting responsibility for a failure in terms of fulfilling SRGs, the consequence of the evaluation of one's actions, thoughts, or feelings. Second, the self-evaluation is global. The phenomenological experience of the person having shame is that of a wish to hide, disappear, or die. It is a highly negative and painful experience and is accompanied by a large increase in the stress hormone cortisol.[52] This painful experience also results in the disruption of ongoing behavior, confusion in thought, and an inability to speak. The other feature of the action pattern accompanying shame includes a shrinking of the body, as in a collapse of the shoulders and head, which is a physical manifestation of the desire to disappear from the eye of the self or the other. Because of the intensity of the action pattern of shame on the whole self, this resulting state is difficult to dissipate. A variety of cognitive strategies, including reinterpretation, forgetting, and conversion are used to cope with the feeling.[53] Shame is often public, but it is just as likely to be private, unlike embarrassment.

In discussing the early form of embarrassment the claim was made that two forms of embarrassment are possible, the first having to do with being the object of another's attention, and the second having to do with self-evaluation. Evaluative embarrassment is often classified as shame.[54] The most notable difference between shame and embarrassment is the intensity level. While shame appears to be associated with an intense and disruptive action pattern, embarrassment is less intense and does not appear to invoke disruption of thought and speech as shame does. Moreover, the bodily action does not show a desire to hide, disappear, or die. Phenomenologically, embarrassment is less differentiated from shame than from guilt. The difference of intensity between shame and embarrassment may be due to the nature of the failed SRG. Some SRGs are closely associated with the core of the self, others less so. Failures associated with core self-evaluations are likely to be more intense than those associated with lesser core values. Moreover, while shame can be experienced in private as well as in public, embarrassment is strictly associated with public events.

Guilt

Guilt also occurs in response to accepting responsibility for a failure of an SRG. It is not as intense a negative emotion as shame, since guilt is the consequence of focus on the child's specific actions that result in the failure rather than on the totality of the self. The action pattern of guilt is directed outward toward reparation rather than inward toward withdrawal as seen in shame's collapse of the body and disruption of thought. In fact the emotion of guilt always seems to have an associated corrective action, something the individual can do to repair the failure.[55]

Guilt can be experienced with different degrees of severity, which are tied to the ease and availability of a corrective action. Should a corrective action not be possible, either in thought, words, or deeds, it is possible that a guilt experience can become one of shame. Here, then, appears another difference between shame and guilt. While it is possible to be ashamed of a guilty action, it is not readily possible to be guilty about being ashamed.[56]

Hubris

Since the English language does not have two different words for pride, that is, pride associated with a task well done, or pride that is arrogant, the term "hubris" is used for the latter, as it represents the pride "that goeth before the fall."[57]

When a child perceives success and assumes total responsibility for it, a global focus on the self leads to hubris, or arrogant pridefulness. Hubris is a highly positive and self-rewarding state; that is, the child feels extremely good about herself. When displaying this emotion, children are often described as "puffed-up," "full of themselves," or even conceited, insolent, or contemptuous. In extreme cases, hubris is associated with grandiosity or with narcissism.[58] Although hubris is felt as a high reward by the person experiencing it, this emotion is unpleasant for others and therefore socially undesirable. Hubristic children have difficulty in their interpersonal relations since their hubris is likely to interfere with the wishes, needs, and desires of others, leading to interpersonal conflict and possibly performance deficits. For example, too much praise of children and their resulting overly high self-esteem can lead to their negative performance.[59] The presumed mechanism in this case might be that excessive pride leads to less effort. Three problems associated with hubris are that (1) it is a transient but addictive emotion; (2) it is unrelated to any specific action, and thus requires continually altering goals or reinterpreting what constitutes success; and (3) it interferes with interpersonal relationships because of its insolent and contemptuous nature.

Pride

Pride is the consequence of a successful evaluation of a specific action. The phenomenological experience is joy over an action, thought, or feeling well done. The focus of pleasure is specific and related to a particular behavior. In pride, the self and the object are separated, as in guilt, and the person focuses attention on the behavior leading to success. Some investigators have likened this state to achievement motivation, an association that seems particularly apt.[60] This form of pride should be related to achievement constructs, such as "efficacy" or "mastery" feelings and "personal satisfaction." Because positive self-evaluative emotion is associated with a particular action, individuals can identify the means by which they can recreate this rewarding state at a future date.

The idea that beliefs and attributions about the self are related to emotions has been proposed by others, although in the past models have been developed primarily for adults and older children, typically with regard to achievement behavior and emotion.[61] However, Carol Dweck, who worked with school-age children, has offered a model similar to mine. She calls global and specific attributions "orientation toward performance" (global) or "orientation toward the task" (specific). Performance-oriented children view failure as the result of an incompetent, stable self, while children with a task orientation focus on "what I did" and tend to not experience their failures as negative, do not blame themselves, and are more confident that they can succeed in similar tasks in the future. They are more likely to believe that ability is "what you learn" with time and experience. Thus, these motivational dispositions appear to capture the responsibility dimension as well as the focus of attention, described in my model.[62] In my view, a performance orientation is consistent with, and perhaps is an early form of, a stable and global attribution and can lead to shame and thus avoidance. Dweck's motivational constructs may measure one or more aspects of emerging attribution processes important to the expression of shame, guilt, pride, and hubris.

Studying Differences in Shame, Embarrassment, and Pride

Individual differences in the self-conscious emotions appear early. There seems to be at least two major sources of individual differences; the first is constitutional and has to do with temperament, while the second is a consequence of the socialization process.

There is evidence that differences in temperament are related to various self-conscious emotions in children. Recent analyses suggest that temperament involves individual differences in the tendency to express positive as well as negative emotion, as well as differences in reactivity level. These aspects of temperament are likely to be related to the self-conscious evaluative emotions. For example, higher anger and fearfulness are associated with later guilt.[63] Reactivity to stress is an important aspect of temperament that is related to negative self-evaluation, such that higher cortisol responses to stress are associated with greater expression of evaluative embarrassment and shame. Collectively, these findings suggest that greater levels of evaluative embarrassment, and shame in particular, are related to temperament through individual differences in self-focus that may arise, in part, because of a lower threshold for pain and an inability to gate or block internal physiological signals. This results in more attention directed toward the self and thus more self-reference. I have proposed that greater stress reactivity leads to greater attention to the self. Following failure, greater self-attention increases the likelihood that children will attribute negative outcomes globally, rather than specifically, thereby increasing the tendency toward shame and/or evaluative embarrassment. Thus, aspects of temperament influence the tendency toward self-attention, which in turn is likely to promote self-conscious evaluative emotions.[64]

Socialization can influence individual differences in the self-conscious emotions in many different ways, including influences in the acquisition of the SRGs, an internal focus of responsibility, and global versus specific focus of attention. The methods used to teach SRGs, that is, how children are rewarded and punished, influence children's style of self-evaluation, and therefore their self-conscious evaluative emotions.

As indicated earlier, the self-conscious emotions have been little studied and their development studied even less. Dweck has studied attributional style, mostly around achievement motivation. Nevertheless, her studies of attribution are one of the essential pieces of data we have. My colleague Margaret Sullivan and I have been studying the development of these emotions by using success and failure on tasks we have given toddlers and young children. While we also have been studying achievement, our focus has not been on achievement per se since we construct our own paradigm for studying these emotions by manipulating whether a child fails or passes some task. The child's response to succeeding or failing gives us the opportunity to study our model of the causes of shame, guilt, pride, and embarrassment.

Given our work on the self-conscious emotions, I want to spend some time giving in detail information about the experimental paradigm we have used to study them. Children 30 months and older are given at least four tasks, one at a time, to complete. These tasks are either matching colors with animals or solving puzzles and are easy—having few items—or more difficult—having many items. We tell the children that the task they are working on is either easy or difficult. In front of the child is a large clock and the child is told that she has to finish each task before the time is up and a loud bell sounds. They are told that if they finish before the bell, they have succeeded, but if they have not finished, they have failed. They are given at least two easy tasks and two difficult tasks.

Because we can manipulate the clock, making it go slower or faster, we can arrange for each child to succeed or fail on each task we give them. By having them fail or succeed by manipulating the clock, we can control their achievement—so their task behavior has nothing to do with their real ability. On half the tasks they succeed and on half they fail. Half of the successes are about easy and half about difficult, while half of the failed tasks are about easy and half about difficult. We measure their action patterns, which include facial expressions and bodily actions. We also ask them a series of questions about their self-attributions after each task. In our studies, children from 30 to 72 months have been seen in this experimental situation. Children do not seem to notice the slowing down or speeding up of the clock, especially given that their attention is directed toward solving the tasks.[65]

It needs to be kept in mind that this manipulation does not always cause shame, embarrassment, or pride. I would estimate that about 55% of the children show these action patterns to our manipulation. Other methods have been tried; for example, we gave the children a doll to play with and after a moment or two of play the arms, legs, and head of the doll fell off. While we could produce failure with this task, we needed another type of task to evaluate the emotional behavior of children when they succeeded. Given that no more children showed shame, guilt, or embarrassment when playing with the dolls than when using our tasks, and since we could produce both success and failure, we have stuck with these tasks.

That not all children show the self-conscious emotions on all the trials again points to the difficulties in studying these emotions. The children's self-conscious emotional responses may or may not be elicited by what we do. For example, if the children did not feel responsible for their success or failure, we do not see these emotions. While there are a few other studies on these emotions in children, my discussion will be for the most part organized around our work. Because of the ages of the children studied, we will be able to examine such issues as the elicitation of these self-conscious emotions, the attributions children give them, and differences between children both as a function of their attributions as well as their histories of socialization.

We observe pride as well as happiness when children of any age succeed. The facial and bodily action patterns are quite clear, with some children jumping up and throwing their hands in the air. They are puffed-up with their chests extended. They also show some embarrassment, but we are not sure as to why. When we observe Japanese children in the success task situations, we also see embarrassment, which is more than what we see for the American children. This behavior may be related to being the object of the attention of the experimenter. Thus, the best guess is that embarrassment during success means that even in situations of success, being the object of attention is likely to produce exposure embarrassment for some children. A good example is that of the school-age child who does well in class, and when the teacher points this out to the other students he becomes embarrassed. Being the object of attention causes embarrassment, especially for some children.[66]

In situations involving failure we observe sadness but also shame and embarrassment, and very rarely guilty behavior. We only see guilt when the child, on hearing the bell ring in the task described earlier, keeps on working even though she knows the time is up. Such children seem to show by their body actions that they need just a little more time to finish their task. This appears to be a form of reparation in response to the fact that they did not finish and therefore had failed the task.[67] Shame is indexed by the dropping of the head, hunched-up shoulders, and a sad or blank facial expression. These physical signs occur very quickly and then readily disappear. We also see embarrassment during failure, which is similar in behavior to the embarrassment we see during success. It differs from shame in the way described earlier: there is no bodily collapse but there is a grin.

While in these studies we cannot see the children's physiological behavior, when we do measure their stress hormones, we find differences between shame and some forms of embarrassment. There are significant increases in cortisol stress response when children fail and show shame and evaluative embarrassment. However, when they show embarrassment at being the object of another's attention they usually do not show cortisol increases. Certainly, they do not show stress hormone increases when they succeed. Such findings should alert us to the powerful effects that shame and evaluative embarrassment can produce.[68]

Individual Differences

We find little change when we observe children's behaviors in these situations over the course of their development from 2½ to 6 years; that is, shame and pride are already present by 2½ and can be elicited by success and failure. However, we do find sex differences, with girls showing more shame and embarrassment across age when they fail than do boys, although there are no sex differences for pride. When we examine these sex differences in shame, we find that girls and boys do not differ in the amount of shame they show when they fail an easy task, but girls show more shame than boys when they fail a difficult task.[69] This result may be due to attribution differences, with girls accounting themselves more responsible for the failure, while boys attribute the failure to the difficulty of the task, a similar finding reported for adult women and men.

Sex differences have been widely reported in internal global attribution styles for negative events. In a study of parental response to children's performance on academic tasks, we found that both mothers and fathers make significantly more specific positive attributions to boys than to girls. Specific positive feedback such as "That's a good way of getting the piece of the puzzle into the box" was higher for 3-year-old boys than for 3-year-old girls. Conversely, specific negative feedback such as "You didn't look for the biggest piece first" was higher for girls. Fathers made more specific attributions than mothers. Mothers and fathers both made more specific attributions to boys than to girls. These findings support the notion that a major difference of attribution style observed between boys and girls is related to these different socialization patterns.[70]

The tendency toward a particular attribution style for failure can also be learned or further consolidated at school. During the elementary school years, teachers are likely to exert considerable influence on children's attribution styles, particularly around achievement. How teachers describe and react to children's actions contributes to their emerging styles and likely influences many of the sex differences observed in achievement-related attributions in later childhood. At least in some studies, most of the criticism that teachers direct at elementary school boys refers to specific instances of misbehavior or lack of effort, that is, to task-specific factors, rather than to negative personality traits or lack of ability. Such feedback patterns promote specific and controllable attributions. In girls, the opposite pattern can be observed. Despite the fact that girls, on average, do better in elementary school than boys, girls are more likely to attribute failures to lack of ability, a global factor.

Teachers' use of evaluative feedback can be a direct cause of either learned helplessness or mastery orientation in children. Once it appears, teachers' criticisms of girls, in contrast to their criticism of boys, almost always indicated that the girls lacked general competence or did not understand the work, which are both global attributions. Thus, there is ample reason to expect sex differences in attribution styles based on the consistent pattern of sex differences observed during early socialization and the school years.[71]

Although information on sex differences constitutes much of what we know about the socialization of attribution styles at home and in school, biological factors that covary with sex cannot be completely ruled out in accounting for some of these differences. For example, Helen Block Lewis has linked a global attribution style to the perceptual and cognitive style of field dependency, which may be related to biological differences. "Field dependence" refers to the ability to separate a perceived object from the context in which it is embedded, with girls more field-dependent than boys.[72]

Learning Standards, Rules, and Goals

In order for success and failure to elicit self-conscious emotions, the child has to internalize SRGs. Several studies have found that around 3 years of age children seem to have acquired some SRGs that they appear to have incorporated into their knowledge system. Deborah Stipek as well as Heinz Heckhausen have shown that independent of an adult's praise or punishment, 3-year-old children seem to know about their performance and even make self-judgments about whether they have succeeded or failed at a task. Jerome Kagan also has shown that by this age, children can identify which pictures they drew at an earlier time.[73] While there is sufficient data to show that children by age 3 years have SRGs, exactly how these are acquired remains relatively unstudied. What is clear, however, is that what constitutes success or failure varies between children. While we will talk about this topic in more detail later, our data also indicate that children this age are likely to show more shame when they fail an easy task than when they fail a difficult task. Moreover, they are likely to show more pride when they succeed in a difficult task rather than in an easy task. When I ask adults when they would feel more shame, it is clear that they would feel more shame if they failed an easy rather than a difficult task. Likewise, they would feel more pride if they solved a difficult rather than an easy task. It seems clear from a variety of data that children by age 3 years already have incorporated some SRGs into their repertoire. Of course the growth of SRGs as a function of socialization and greater cognitive ability is likely to continue.

Evaluative Style

Individual differences in evaluative style have been observed in young children. Sometime between 3 and 6 years, differences in perceptions of personal performance emerge and appear consistent over age. Once learned, these early motivational dispositions may become entrenched as a personality or attribution style, especially in response to negative events. Strong negative events occurring early in children's lives seem to push children toward a global attribution style in a kind of one-trial learning; that is, children exposed to such events will more consistently make global attributions than others under most conditions of failure. Their attributions made in response to success are less likely to be predictable. The intensity and power of negative events acting on a child with still limited coping skills may promote this development. Strong negative emotion swamps any cognitive processing that might override the child's egocentric perceptions about the event. Because the child cannot separate herself from the failure, she focuses on the global self. The range of negative life events that lead to global attributions is in need of further investigation. These events may include negative experiences with parents, with others in the immediate social environment, or with general calamities that impact the self, family, or others. However, a reasonable working hypothesis is that the performance or self-attribution style of failure is created in the cauldron of stress. This topic will be discussed in more detail when we get to Chapter 11 on emotions gone awry.

As we have shown, some attribution can be seen in 3- and 4-year-olds' display of shame and pride as a function of success and failure to easy and difficult tasks. That they behave as we adults do suggests that they evaluate difficult task failures as less their fault than easy task failures, thus exhibiting more shame to the failure of easy tasks. Likewise, success on a difficult task leads to more pride than success on an easy one. In the failure tasks they attribute the failure of an easy task to themselves, thinking something like "After all anyone should have passed it," but at the same time attribute their failure at a difficult task to the task parameters. Such data lead me to believe that they are even at this age already able to evaluate as internally or externally their action response to SRGs.

Let us turn to other individual differences in attribution that may affect the child's emotional behavior. While we have shown that particular evaluative patterns have an impact on children's emotional life, it has also been shown that children's beliefs influence their achievement behaviors and motivation even though they may not yet make adult-like attributions. How, then, can individual young children's evaluative attribution styles be assessed? Paper-and-pencil methods developed for older children and adults are not appropriate with young children. However, there are measurement procedures useful in obtaining individual differences in children's focus either as performance-oriented or task-oriented, how such differences are related to other kinds of evaluative judgments, and how they affect the display of some self-conscious evaluative emotions.

Dweck has obtained performance or task orientations by asking children to work on both solvable and unsolvable tasks and afterward to assess their choice to avoid or return to the unsolved task. Children who choose to avoid the unsolved task and choose instead a task on which they know they have succeeded are considered to be performance-oriented. Their choice of a sure success suggests a motive to avoid a display of incompetence. In order to explore this question further, we have used some of the techniques developed by Dweck but added several others. After each task we ask the children as young as 3 to 4 years a series of questions including whether they would like to do the task again and how they feel about how they did, which they answer by matching their feelings to a series of picture faces going from very sad to very happy. We then score the spontaneous negative or positive statements they make after each task. We also have developed a measure of whether they are task- or performance-oriented.

After each task, children are asked whether the task was easy or difficult. Our focus was on an easy task that they failed. Their response of "easy" or "hard" in the easy failed task informs us about whether they are making a performance- or a task-based evaluation. If they state that it was "hard"—even though in reality it was easy—they are focusing on their performance, which was a failure. If they say "easy," they are focusing on the task despite their own performance. Thus, the easy failed task presents the child with a discrepancy between what the child expects, that is, to do well when it is easy, and the outcome of their behavior, which is a failure. We have found that a child's response reveals whether the child focuses his attention globally on his personal performance, or specifically, on the nature of the task. Our hypothesis is that these judgments in response to the failure at any easy task should predict other self-related evaluations as well as the expression of the self-conscious evaluative emotions.

When we compare the questions we asked the children, we find an interesting coherence between them. The task versus performance measures of easy or difficult were related to whether they wanted to try to do another task. Those children who were task-oriented—that is, who said the task was easy—were significantly more likely to want to try again than were the children who were performance-oriented—that is, who said the task was hard. These data support the idea that performance and task orientation can be measured in 3- to 4-year-olds.[74]

Certain self-attributions lead to more self-conscious emotions. According to our theory, performance-focused children should display more shame following failure than task-focused children and they also should display more pride following success, although this prediction is more tentative because it is not possible to distinguish between hubris and pride at this age. The effect of performance focus on the self-conscious evaluative emotions was observed in two studies. A greater percentage of performance-focused children as opposed to task-focused children showed shame and evaluative embarrassment following failure. While the children showed more shame and embarrassment if they were performance-oriented, they did not show more sadness than the task-oriented children. We also looked at anger in response to failure and here found that performance-oriented children showed more anger than the task-oriented children. As we will see when we discuss emotions gone awry in Chapter 11, performance orientation is likely to lead to more shame, which in some cases leads to the outward deflection of shame into blaming others. Finally, performance orientation affects all the self-conscious emotions more than the early emotions of sadness and joy.

This set of studies reveals that children's task and performance focus following failure on an easy task is related to other evaluative judgments about their performance and to the overt display of their self-conscious evaluative emotions. The consistency of children's answers to questions about an easy failed task can be examined to determine the degree to which they focus on the self when thinking about the failure. A performance focus, as opposed to a task focus following failure, is related to thinking poorly about oneself, to being unwilling to try again, and to being more likely to show shame and evaluative embarrassment following failure. This pattern of negative self-judgments might represent the early precursors of the internal, stable, global attribution styles observed in older children and adults. Such attribution styles for negative events promote shame and thus constitute a risk factor for subsequent maladjustment, a finding discussed later in Chapter 11.

* * *

The emergence of the self-conscious evaluative emotions appears to be dependent on the development of four types of ideas; first is the ability to self-reference, or consciousness; second is the ability to compare one's actions, thoughts, and feelings to the acquired standards, rules, and goals of family and culture; third is the focus of their attention; and fourth is their beliefs about their responsibility for success or failure. While the contents of the ideas are cultural artifacts, the ability to have such ideas and the eliciting effect of them on the self-conscious emotions are likely to be universal, belonging to our species and likely to no other. In the next two chapters we will examine how both socialization functions and temperament affects individual child differences in the development of the early as well as the self-conscious emotions.

CHAPTER 9

Temperament, Emotion, and Stress

I could have subtitled this chapter "The Case of the Rotten Apple" in order to place the idea of temperament within its historical context. At the beginning of the 20th century, prior to the popularity of psychoanalytic and object relations theories, it was said that parents sometimes gave birth to a child who was "a bad apple." Through no fault of their own, and not necessarily as the consequence of bad parenting, one child out of the few a family had just did not turn out well. In a bushel of apples, there was always a rotten one. With the influence of psychoanalytic and object relations theory, this view of the bad apple changed. Now parenting, and mothering in particular, was blamed for the bad apple. Children's social and emotional lives, it was argued, were determined by their attachment to their mothers. Attachment to the mother influenced the child's peer relations, and her emotionality affected the child's emotionality: angry mothers made angry children, depressed mothers made depressed ones. The mother's soothing behavior determined the child's response to stress. I could go on about these beliefs now, but will wait to address them when I talk about the socialization of emotional life.

While Bowlby recognized that the child's characteristics played some role in the forming of the attachment relationship, his emphasis and that of those who agreed with his views has been on the mother–child interaction. If an extraterrestrial observed the last 30 years of research effort, he would find that the overwhelming view held during this period is that if a child "does not turn out well," it is the consequence of poor parenting—even though there was some recognition that the child's characteristics contribute to the problem. This view continues today, with only a limited number of studies looking at child characteristics as they interact with parenting.[1]

Given that we are going to discuss socialization factors in emotional development in Chapter 10, there may be some redundancy here since the interaction between parenting and temperament could be found in either chapter. However, let me state here at the start, the nature–nurture argument is an argument around worldviews. Clearly, the need for parenting is, as Bowlby argued over 40 years ago, both biological and bidirectional.

While most of us now agree that factors other than parenting affect the character of the young child, it is still amazing how little utilization of the individual characteristics of children is factored into the study of social and emotional development. While there are exceptions, most studies of emotional and social development measure the parenting behavior and the attachment relationship and fail to obtain, utilize, or analyze the interactions between the characteristics of the infant and the parenting behavior. Few studies on attachment utilize the child's temperament; rather, they are likely to talk about secure and insecurely attached children as a consequence of how their mothers behave toward them. Mothers who behave in a nonresponsive or ambivalent way are the mothers who produce insecure children. Of particular interest is Jay Belsky's idea that mothers who are intrusive in their interactions produce avoidant children.[2] Although intrusiveness may be the cause of avoidant attachment behaviors, it may be dependent on the child's temperament. For example, in a series of studies, Candice Feiring and I found that a mother's interactive behavior toward her 3-month-old infant was related to whether the child at 1 year was avoidant in her attachment behavior; a mother high in initiating and responsivity to her infant produced an avoidant child. Thus, it is possible to say that such mothers are too intrusive.[3] Fortunately, we also had temperament data about these same children and could look at how the individual characteristics of the children at very early ages might have impacted on their mother's behavior and thereby on their own later attachment behavior. Examination of the avoidant children revealed that at age 3 months, these children preferred to play with the toys and objects around them rather than play with their mothers. It appears that these avoidant 1-year-olds were more object- than person-oriented at 3 months, that is, they seemed to be less social while the other insecurely classified children, the C types, and the securely attached children, the B types, were not.[4] Given the idea that sociability as an individual human temperament characteristic has possible genetic origins, the roles of parenting and temperament and their effect on subsequent emotional and social development become more complex.

About 15–20% of the children in American samples are avoidant in their attachment. It is likely that some of these children are temperamentally asocial, preferring objects to people. They are likely to grow up to be the engineers and "techies" of whom we talk. If they are asocial to begin with, preferring toys to their mothers, their mothers, wanting to engage their inattentive children and get them to pay attention to them (the mothers), try through high levels of interaction to get the children to orient toward them rather than toward objects. The child's temperament rather than maternal behavior may be the cause of their avoidant attachment behavior, or to make the model more interactive, there may be a complex interaction between his temperament and his mother's behavior. Thus, both asocial temperament in the child and the mother's handling of this characteristic may combine to produce the avoidantly attached toddler.

Although we all would agree that the child's temperament must play some role in the child's social and emotional development, it has played and continues to play a relatively minor role in research or in therapy. This lack of concern is puzzling considering that almost 40 years ago Leonard Rosenblum and I published a subsequently highly referenced book, *The Effect of the Infant on Its Caregiver*, in which the infant's characteristics of temperament were shown to interact with parenting behaviors to produce particular developmental outcomes. The best explanation rests on different views of the role of the mother. Until recently, the belief in poor parenting as the cause of differences in the child's emotional life held sway, but now there has been a growing interest in understanding the interaction between biology and experience.[5]

The early chapters of this book have argued for a strong evolutionary adaptive view of the nature of emotional life, where the early action patterns have a strong biological component that may account for individual differences in children. Nevertheless, parenting does make a difference. It is this idea of their interaction that will be the focus of this chapter. In order to carry out the task I consider what is meant by the term "temperament," to expand on the most commonly used constructs, and finally to show how temperament together with socialization may impact on concurrent as well as future emotional life.

THE IDEA OF TEMPERAMENT

While the research literature on emotional development has underutilized the idea of temperament, the idea of innate individual differences now called "temperament" has been accepted both by the general public and by a good number of scientists.[6] Even so, exactly what temperament is and how to measure it has remained somewhat elusive. It is not a cognitive capacity, although temperament may affect individual differences in cognitive ability. Temperament is connected with personality and motor behavior and probably is best seen as some aspect of emotional behavior. Perhaps the best definition comes from a review of the literature, where *temperament* is defined as a "constitutionally based individual difference in emotion, motor, and attentional reactivity and self-regulation."[7] This clearly implicates emotional life.

It is important here, at the beginning of our discussion, to remind ourselves that there is a distinction between transient emotions (elicited by particular events) and moods (long-enduring emotions). Temperament, defined as emotional behavior, represents enduring emotional behavior rather than a transient behavior. We will come back to this idea when we discuss how temperament differences interact with the social environment to produce enduring characteristics in the individual child.

To preview the argument, three features of the nervous system seem to be (1) the threshold to activate the system or how much of the elicitor is needed to produce a response, (2) the intensity of the response, and (3) the regulation of the response, or the time it takes to return to base level. These are features of neurons and synapses, which are not necessarily emotional in nature. The question, then, is how these features interact with the specific emotional action patterns to give rise to different temperaments. Such an idea is not new; however, it provides a somewhat different approach to some other views that include emotions in their definition. As Gordon Allport stated:

> The characteristic phenomena of an individual's emotional nature, including susceptibility to emotional stimulation, his customary strength and speed of response, the qualities of his prevailing mood . . . are dependent upon constitutional make-up and therefore, largely hereditary in origin.[8]

While these three features may be biological and fixed, individual differences in temperament appear to change and are open to environmental influences. Such a view is consistent with Mary Rothbart's idea that temperament can change over time, both as a function of changes in CNS structures and as a function of the effects of the infant's engagement with her social world. For example, young children's ability to moderate their emotional reactivity is due, in part, to the strategies and behaviors that they learn through their interactions with caregivers.[9] A recent study of the change in the trajectory of negative temperament found that both positive maternal behaviors and early negative behavior on the part of the child affect this trajectory.[10]

Without going into the history of the definition of temperament, which includes such early leaders as William Carey, Alexander Thomas, and Stella Chess, there appears to be some confusion for those interested in temperament between two ideas concerning what this innate characteristic is: a processes-like characteristic or a content-focused one. The process group looks to qualities of the nervous system including such aspects as threshold to activate a response, the intensity of a response, and the regulation of the response once it occurs. The content group sees temperament more as a negative emotional response, something like a content analysis that includes fussiness, crying, fearfulness, and introversion, although other process variables such as the ability to be soothed are also included.

While such differences might be reconciled by a careful articulation of how to go from one to the other, along with research to test this process, little attempt has been made to do so. I will try to offer some ideas; however, how to test them is not clear. Researchers agree that temperament in children consists of four factors: (1) fussy/difficult, which includes fussiness, crying, and the ability to be soothed; (2) fearful, which includes negative reactions to places and people and difficulty in adapting to anything new; (3) dull or inhibited, which includes low positive affect and activity, lack of approach, and introversion; and finally, (4) predictable, which includes little rhythmicity and regularity. Nevertheless, there are still some questions about these four factors. These four factors in childhood have been compared to adult dimensions of personality, which have been called the Big Five factors. This work is a reflection of the attempt to connect dimensions of adult personality with corresponding early temperament dimensions.[11] It is important to keep in mind that whatever the set of temperament or personality factors of children and adults, the underlying theme is that there are innate dispositions related to genetic factors, unlearned but potentially modifiable through parenting interactions, a view that stands in strong opposition to the view that parenting factors are the major cause of difference in emotional life.

Given the evidence about individual differences in temperament even in newborns, how to study the number of different types of temperament dimensions, and how they may be related to each other needs to be determined. At a glance, the list of the four dimensions just mentioned seems a bit narrow. Later I will suggest four more, and to these we might add others such as cuddliness. However, the history of interest in temperament, going back to the 1970s, shows that a variety of dimensions have been suggested, from the nine factors that Thomas and Chess posited, to those we have now.[12] The different temperament dimensions have been treated in a variety of ways. One way that was initially used was to take the dimensions and reduce them to some broad categories so that each infant could fit into one or the other. For example, infants could be classified as having easy or difficult temperaments, or even a slow-to-warm-up category. In this way, rather than refer to the ratings of each of Thomas and Chess's nine dimensions, in which there would be scores on each dimension, a simpler way was to classify children within some broad category since this classification has great appeal for clinicians who can talk about the child in some global fashion: "Felicia is a difficult temperament child, while Vivian is an easy temperament child." This kind of shorthand supplied an easily understood classification to aid parents in their caregiving.

More recent parent scales such as the six scales of the Infant Behavior Questionnaire (IBQ) are now used. Again, however, the six scales, while useful, do not give an overall rating of each child. For this purpose, a categorical system again is used whereby scores on the positive scales are summed to generate a positive temperament rating, as they are on the negative items. Specifically, the positive temperament score sums smiling, orienting, and soothability, while the negative temperament score sums the novelty and limitations scales.

The generation of the positive and negative temperament dimensions shares some similarities to the easy and difficult child classification. Given that there are scaled scores, it is possible to look at how an infant's positive and negative temperament scores are related. Obviously, we would think that an infant high in one would be low in the other in the same way we would think that the easy–difficult classification would be mutually exclusive.

To look at this question, we examined the relationship between the positive and negative dimensions based on the IBQ for a group of children seen in the first 6 months of life. The relation between the positive and negative dimensions in our study ranged from a very modest negative correlation at 2 months to a nonsignificant correlation by 6 months. It seems an infant can be high in both positive and negative temperament dimensions.

Because of the lack of a negative association between positive and negative temperament, it was thought possible to create four groups of infants: those who were high in both positive and negative temperament (high reactors), those who were low in both positive and negative temperament (low reactors), those who were high in positive but low in negative temperament (an easy baby), and those who were high in negative and low in positive temperament (difficult baby). These groups constitute two different dimensions of temperament; one we called "reactivity," which has a high and low dimension across both emotional valences, and a positive and a negative valence group. We will call the two dimensions of temperament *emotional tone* as in positive versus negative, which are inversely related, and *emotional intensity*. These two, tone and intensity, turn out to be unrelated. To see the value of this division we examined this classification and how it related to individual children's response to pain. The results confirm that both dimensions are related to the infant's stress response including cortisol increases. The high-intensity infants and the negative-tone infants show the most cortisol response.[13]

While there remains some disagreement as to the various dimensions of temperament, for the most part they are studied by using maternal reports. Although temperament questionnaires that use mothers' reports have been criticized as reflecting maternal biases and perhaps the mother's own temperament, when these questionnaires are compared to actual infant behavior, some agreement, although limited, is found. Mothers can report on what they see their baby doing but they cannot report on internal responses and thus they use only external surface features to report on their infant's temperament. Since the mother is unable to observe the child's internal responses she is unable to report on them as well as she can about behavior. Since individual infants may show temperament dimensions through external as well as internal behaviors, maternal report has to remain limited. Clearly what are needed are independent measures of the child's actual behavior in addition to the maternal report. Jerome Kagan in studying one dimension of temperament, that of inhibitory behaviors, has followed this strategy with considerable success.[14]

SOME MEASURES OF TEMPERAMENT

Although studying temperament through the use of maternal rating scales is valuable, it becomes increasingly clear that if we want to seriously consider temperament we need to go beyond maternal or caregiver report and to measure it directly. I suggest that there are at least three more temperament factors that are different from the four mentioned earlier, although there is some overlap. These temperament factors include sociability, pain sensitivity, and reaction to frustration. While some of these are familiar, new measurements of them are called for.

Sociability

While measures of fearfulness have been considered, sociability, or the orientation to the social as opposed to the nonsocial world, has not received the attention it deserves. This is especially true in considering such cases as children with autism or with Asperger syndrome, two disorders that appear to involve sociability. Moreover, recent work studying the infant's ability to abstract information about others' motives, intentions, desires, and goals needs to consider how individual infant differences in sociability may affect cognitive or mentalistic ability to abstract that knowledge.[15]

In order to study early manifestation of individual differences in sociability, Candice Feiring and I examined a way to measure 3-month-olds' sociability by looking at the amount of time infants played with toys in comparison to the amount of time they spent in interaction with their mothers. We found large differences, with some children preferring to play with toys rather than playing with their mothers and some not. We thought that this difference might reflect a sociability dimension so we compared the children's sociability scores at 3 months with their response to their mother's departure in an attachment paradigm when they were 1 year old. The asocial infants were likely to be less concerned about their mother's departure or reunion in an attachment situation and were scored avoidant. For us, this seemed to indicate that their lack of social focus could be measured across the first years of life.

The sociability factor is often mixed with extroversion; however, it need not be. It might have more to do with empathy or even with individual differences in the cognitive ability to attend to and understand the ideas, desires, motives, and feelings of others. This idea of sociability is more in keeping with what is known about the deficits in people classified as having Asperger syndrome. Perhaps we need to think of sociability as a continuum. At one end may be those who are too social, that is, they are too influenced by others: suggestible, easily susceptible to contagion, or thinking too much about others' opinions and feelings and thus inhibited by their focus on others. On the other end of the continuum there may be those who do not prefer the company of others and who like solitude. At this extreme end are those who are unable to think of others, as in Asperger syndrome. We need to figure out how to measure this factor in infants and children.

Differences in Reaction to Pain

While most studies of temperament rely on maternal report, some investigators have utilized observation of the infant/child's response to particular elicitors. Jerome Kagan has studied what he calls "inhibited temperaments," while Nathan Fox has studied both inhibition and what he calls "exuberance."[16] My colleagues and I have used observational techniques in trying to understand the role of differences in the nervous system and how these early differences are related to temperament, in particular to reactivity and regulation of behaviors, and to see how these qualities affect emotional responses.

From the outset I will argue that there is a difference between "feeling pain" and "being in pain," the subject of a very interesting book by Nikola Grahek, a Yugoslavian philosopher killed in his country's civil war.[17] He argues that pain has an experiential aspect, a conscious state of mind as well as the activity of the neural receptors,[18] something all feelings possess.

We have studied in some detail the child's response to pain as seen in the child's behavioral and physiological response to well-baby inoculation. Facial and bodily activity and cortisol release have been observed in a large set of studies and early individual differences are apparent.[19] Using inoculation—something all infants receive—as the situation to measure pain, Douglas Ramsay and I were able to measure two features of the response to pain, *reactivity* to the needle and *speed of recovery* from it. The initial reaction to the needle prick, which we called reactivity, was observed and large individual differences were seen. We also observed infant dampening response or the ability to regulate, which is how long it takes the child's reactivity to return to the base level. This too showed large individual differences.

Recall that we have suggested that the same emotional action patterns exist from the beginning of life. However, emotional experiences require the emergence of consciousness. Our work on pain with newborn infants and toddlers therefore has more to do with the emotional action patterns—the being in pain—and their relation to temperament. In this work we made a distinction between the external or surface manifestations and the internal manifestations of the action pattern. The external manifestation consists of vocal behavior, in particular crying, as well as bodily movement. The internal manifestation of the pain is the stress response, in particular changes in the hypothalamic-pituitary-adrenal (HPA) axis as measured by cortisol release. Both the internal and the external manifestations are readily measureable and produce a complex set of data that can be used to index the child's response to physical pain.

The first result of our studies is that the internal measure of pain, or cortisol levels, and its external measure, that is, facial/vocal reactivity, are only moderately related, a finding reported by many others.[20] Because the correlation between these two manifestations of pain is only moderate, in studying individual differences in pain it is important to examine not only the amount of pain but how that pain is expressed, either in internal responses or in facial and vocal behavior. The relatedness between these two types of measures may reflect the action of socialization. For example, while external manifestation may be affected by the mother's behavior, internal manifestation may be less affected. In studying this problem we have been able to classify four types of children according to how they manifest pain: High Responders, Low Responders, Stoics, and Cry Babies. The high responders show high levels of both cortisol and facial and vocal behavior while the low responders show low levels of both. Of interest are the Stoics, who show little external reactivity to pain but high internal response of cortisol, and the Cry Babies who show a great deal of crying but little cortisol reactivity. Each of these groups presents problems in terms of emotional development. Since the Stoics do not appear to be in pain they are likely to receive less parental attention. If their mothers cannot see that their cortisol reactions are high, they may not respond to their discomfort. Also of interest are the Cry Babies, who while showing behaviorally that they are in pain, do not internally show any manifestation of it. Perhaps we are looking at the Stoics as the forerunners of those children who will be somatizers while the Cry Babies may be forerunners of hypochondriacs, or those who are emotionally expressive and those who are not.

These individual differences also can be interpreted as cultural differences. A well-known observation has been that Japanese and Chinese children show far less external behavioral manifestation of emotion than American or European children do. Our cross-cultural work looking at infant behavior response to inoculation in Japan and the United States suggests this difference. By using the individual child classification system mentioned earlier, we found that American infants are likely to be either High Responders or Cry Babies while the Japanese infants tend to be Low Responders or Stoics.[21] These differences do not appear to be a function of the caregiving experience across cultures, nor to individual difference within cultures, and therefore may be related of temperament differences. I shall return to this point shortly, since if the claim is that pain responses reflect basic neurological aspects, we should see these differences early, they should have some consistency over time, and they should be for the most part dispositional rather than socialized.

Since pain is likely a nervous system feature, we should be able to measure some of the dimensions we have previously discussed: reactivity, that is, the infant's initial response to the needle prick, and regulation, or the time it takes for the infant to quiet and return to her normal level prior to the inoculation. It is possible to measure both the external behavior and the cortisol response. Reactivity and regulation are not highly related and our observation of the relations of reactivity and regulation both within and between measures reveals little coherence. Not much is known about these differences but they should be further explored, especially since every infant receives inoculation and it would be possible to study large numbers of infants and determine these temperament patterns and their consequences.

A series of studies in our laboratory looking at individual differences across the first 2 years support the idea of individual consistency. While individual differences in reactivity in the newborn period and later have been noted, there are relatively few studies that have looked at the consistency of the nervous system's functioning from birth and those that do have found little stability.[22] However, this may be due to many factors. As a study I did with John Worobey has shown, stability may exist but not for all infants. Looking at neonates' responses to the phenylketonuria (PKU) exam and their response to inoculation 2 months later we found that of the 21 newborns who were high reactors at birth, 18 or 86% remained high reactors at 2 months. In contrast, of the 19 infants who were rated as low or moderate reactors at birth only 45% were likely to be low later. In another set of studies, Douglass Ramsey, David Thomas, and I examined individual differences to the inoculation over the 2- to 24-month period. Here moderate individual consistency was found; infants who took longer to dampen their reaction to the pain were consistent in this response across this age span.[23] The finding for the stability of temperament variable over time is mixed. While some have found stability over time, most have reported little stability. However, these studies often use maternal questionnaires to measure temperament. Direct behavior measures are likely to give better results.[24]

The study of cortisol as a measure of internal stress has to take into account the cortisol maturational factor that is related to the onset of the diurnal cycle, between 2 and 4 months of age. One also has to take into account this cycle once it appears since cortisol release is high in the early morning and becomes lower during the day, only to become higher again during the night and early morning. While the HPA axis matures by about 4 months, at the same time differences in socialization practices around soothing can be seen. However, if infant's reactivity and regulation are due in large part to temperament, maternal responsivity to their children's pain should have only a minor impact on those individual differences. We discuss maternal responsibility in the role of socialization in Chapter 10. Temperament differences to at first physical pain and then later psychological pain need further study, given the centrality of pain in emotional life.

Willfulness

The third temperament dimension we have observed is children's willfulness or children's reaction to frustration. While the term "willful" is no longer generally used, it was used by William James and, as Susan Miller has written, it is a term used by some adults who feel their child is too stubborn or determined and that this stubbornness needs to be controlled. There are childrearing books in which experts have decided that children need to be taught to obey, that is, not to be willful; we are warned "spare the rod and spoil the child." But what of this willfulness? Can there be individual infant differences in it and what role will it play in emotional life?[25] However, if we think of willfulness as agency or as primary narcissism, as Freud wrote, then individual differences in willfulness may play an important role in achievement motivation and may as well be related to an "I can do it" attitude. We all have met people who don't "give up" very easily and others who do. For the most part we think of persistence as a virtue that is taught. This may not be so.

We have been measuring individual differences in persistence through observing infants' behavior during tasks. Given that anger is an approach action pattern elicited by a blocked goal, we use anger and other measures to index differences in willfulness. The particulars of these studies, that is, the learning to pull a string to turn on a picture and the blockage of that learned response, have already been discussed. Briefly, then, infants as young as 2 months of age are taught to pull a string in order to produce a picture on a screen in front of them. After having learned to pull, the pull stops working and no picture appears. Approximately 85% of the children show approach behaviors that include rigorous arm pulling in order to reinstate the picture, angry faces, and an increase in ANS responses such as heart rate, but no increase in stress hormone release. On the other hand, withdrawal responses, seen in the remaining 15%, can be characterized by the lack of increased pulling to reinstate the picture, sad not angry faces, and little increase in heart rate, but a significant increase in stress hormone release. Children at 2 years who show an approach response at 2 months are more persistent when confronted with difficult tasks to solve.

Although there are little data to support the belief, Carol Dweck's finding of differences in young children's attributions about their performance and the role these attributions play in school behavior and emotion may be related to children's temperament.[26] I suspect that "task-oriented children," to use her term, may be high in willful temperament. Willful children should be more likely to be task-oriented especially since even when they fail a task they are willing to try again. The performance-oriented children who are likely not willful are those children who do not choose to try again once they fail. While more study is needed, the observed differences in children's willfulness suggest that this may be another important temperament dimension that can be studied as it relates to infants' emotional behavior, especially the self-conscious emotions.

While cuddliness has not been studied in much detail, the positive emotions' association with physical contact seems to be a likely candidate for an innate disposition that may be linked to tactile receptor differences. Libidinal energy level either about sex or passion in general may have temperament dimensions and also may be innately related to emotional life.

Individual differences in sociability, pain distress, willfulness, and cuddliness appear early. How they are related to the dimensions of temperament discussed by others remains to be seen. What this work does tell us is that we are still in need of a good category system for the temperament dimensions. The individual differences in these dimensions do not seem to be much related to the caregivers' behavior; however, they may be altered subsequently by the infant's social interaction.

TEMPERAMENT AND SOCIALIZATION: THE SPECIAL CASE OF SOOTHING AND DISTRESS

The broad question in regard to the role of socialization in affecting temperament differences has been addressed in the past by looking at the child's distress—usually in everyday situations—and examining the effect of parental soothing on distress. Interestingly, there is more interest in look-ing at the socialization of an infant's distress than on their more positive emotions. This may explain why we do not find more maternal effects on an infant's emotional behavior. Perhaps mothers have more effect on their infant's positive emotions than on their negative emotions! Nevertheless, by examining the relationship between maternal soothing behaviors and infant distress as a consequence of inoculation allows us to study the degree to which infant distress differences, both in the present and in the future, are dependent on the mother's response.

Maternal soothing behavior has been used as a marker for the con-tingency concept.[27] It is recognized that contingency and responsivity are maternal characteristics that facilitate healthy child development. This was predicted on my and John Watson's early studies in which we demonstrated that the contingent responses to infant behavior are critical for the infant's perceptual–cognitive development. This was at the same time that Ain-sworth, Blehar, Waters, and Wall articulated the positive effects of contin-gency on the child's subsequent attachment.[28]

Studies on maternal soothing of infants' everyday distress have mixed results but largely show that infant differences are relatively unaffected by their mothers' behaviors. Ronald Barr and colleagues reported that although maternal soothing reduced the duration of colicky infants' cry bouts, it did not affect the frequency of the cry bouts. Hubbard and van IJzendoorn found no evidence that high maternal responsivity led to less infant crying; in fact, they found a positive relation between more frequent delay of maternal response and a reduced frequency of infant cry bouts. There is no evidence that maternal differences are involved in infant colic or fussiness.[29] Similarly, there is no evidence that maternal differences are involved in various aspects of infant crying behavior such as its increased frequency in the evening hours or its age-related time course, reaching a peak in the second month and little change thereafter.

Infant crying may be related to a variety of biological factors. For example, there is evidence for deregulation in physiological rhythms in col-icky infants, including a flatter circadian rhythm in cortisol production. It is not apparent that the physiological differences could be attributed, to any great extent, to differences in maternal behavior including maternal responsivity to infant distress. Megan Gunnar and her colleagues, using normative samples, found a relation between high cortisol response and proneness to distress at different ages in the first 13 months of life, but no maternal differences. Moreover, infant crying does not seem to be related to differences in the endogenous opioid system. Based on animal findings that the calming effect of sucrose is mediated by the opioid system, Elliot Blass and colleagues have found that sucrose has a calming effect on cry-ing. Moreover, there is a differential calming efficacy of sucrose relative to other stimuli, including pacifiers. In general, in contrast with the finding on the effects of maternal responsivity on infant crying, there is considerable evidence for the efficacy of sucrose in reducing crying in newborn and older infants.[30]

A few studies have examined the impact of maternal behavior on differences in infant adrenocortical response to distress. Spangler and colleagues found that maternal insensitivity was associated with a greater infant cortisol response. Other studies have shown a relation between quality of attachment and cortisol, with insecurely attached infants showing a greater response.[31] While these findings may suggest that maternal behavior affects infant adrenocortical functioning and therefore temperament, they might also indicate that infant differences in adrenocortical reactivity affect maternal behavior.

In order to explore this problem Ramsay and I studied two samples of infants who received inoculation and looked at their mother's response to their pain. We also looked at mother's responses to everyday infant distress as seen during a normal day at home. We found infant's response to inoculation was stable over time, both for their coritsol response and their distress behaviors. We also found stability over time in mother's soothing behavior: high soothing mothers remained so over the months of the study. While there was stability in infant stress and maternal soothing over the first 9 months of life, maternal soothing was not related to infants' cortisol or behavioral responses to pain. This was so when we looked at concurrent soothing and distress as well as at soothing and subsequent distress.

Since soothing to inoculation might be different than soothing to everyday stress, we also measured soothing to everyday distress by observing mothers' behavior at home. Even here, there was no relation between maternal soothing and an infant's everyday stress. The absence of any relation between maternal soothing and infant stress response held, whether we used overall ratings of maternal behavior or a detailed behavioral checklist measure of maternal soothing that included how responsive she was and how contingent her responses were to her infant's distress. As expected, maternal soothing for inoculation was highly related to maternal everyday soothing behavior, although her soothing to inoculation was greater than her soothing to everyday distress.

The results of this work, as well as the results of other studies on the effect of maternal soothing, suggest that individual differences in soothing bear little relation to individual differences in distress. It is this lack of an individual association between distress and soothing that should be our focus. The results of the studies do not speak to the general effect of soothing itself since in order to conclude that soothing has no effect we would need to have a comparison group of infants whose mothers did not sooth them at all. I have no doubt that there would be a difference between groups such that the soothed group would have less stress concurrently and in the future.

The difference between a study of individual differences versus a study of group differences can result in different conclusions. For example, in a well-known study of IQ, genes, and socialization, just such a finding was reported. Children adopted and raised by middle-class mothers had higher IQs than comparable children not so raised. This finding speaks to the effectiveness of socialization on IQ. However, the correlation between the adoptive mother's IQ and the child's IQ was lower than that of the biological mother and the same child. These different results occur when we look at mean differences in groups or when we look at individual differences. Such findings should alert us to carefully consider which analysis is more likely to speak to socialization versus temperament effects. I believe that looking at maternal individual differences in soothing in association with individual differences in distress in their child may be the better way to examine the effects of temperament.[32]

However, the analysis of the effects of socialization on distress is incomplete when we examine only the response to the infant's distress once it occurs. Even though maternal soothing appears to be relatively unimportant, mothers not only soothe their infants when distressed, they also provide positive environments that may *prevent* distress from occurring. Thus, maternal behavior that prevents distress may be more important than maternal soothing in affecting infant stress responses. There are data consistent with the view that a history of positive mother–infant interactions is associated with lowered infant adrenocortical functioning. In this regard, animal research has found that maternal behavior plays an important role in maintaining lowered adrenocortical functioning in the newborn period.[33] Thus, maternal behavior may affect infant cortisol and behavioral stress responses in two ways, by soothing and by preventing distress. Whereas the present findings do not support a soothing function, they do not bear on the same issue of distress prevention, a point we will discuss in Chapter 10 on socialization.

When we talk about the role of socialization in emotional life, we make the point that, while direct maternal soothing might have little effect on infants' response to pain, it might have an effect at a later time, a time when the child can utilize its knowledge of its mother's soothing style to make attributions about his own coping style.

The examination of infant studies of distress suggests too much focus on emotional pain, with relatively little interest, besides our own, on the effects of physical pain. It remains to be determined if there is an association between physical and psychological or emotional pain. Nevertheless, the study of both might profit from more studies on physical pain, especially since all children receive well-baby care (including inoculations, which are almost standard worldwide), making the study of physical pain easy, not only in American babies, but across cultures. Whatever the role maternal behavior may play in an infant's response to pain, the present findings indicate that maternal soothing alone is an insufficient explanation of individual differences in temperament. Perhaps the best view of the regulation of temperament, and therefore of emotional life, is an interaction between characteristics of the child as they interact with socialization.

MOODS AND TEMPERAMENT

If we could scan the emotional life of children, we would see a continuous stream of emotions, the consequence of a particular set of both internal and external elicitors. We believe this set of elicitors is related to the temperamental disposition of the child. In our work we present a particular elicitor, usually for a brief period of time, and watch the child's response—for example, a physiological response such as heart rate to a frightening elicitor. In this type of study emotional responses are seen as transient, that is, as having a specific onset and a brief duration. In addition, the measurement systems employed, whether they be that of Ekman or Izard, require a limited amount of observation time. During that time period, a particular emotion is inferred through the analysis of facial musculature changes along with other behaviors. Thus, emotions are measured as isolated events with fast rise times and are seen as unrelated to preceding emotions. Even though mixtures of emotions may be coded through different facial expressions, in general the emotions are still measured separately and mixed emotions rarely mentioned. Such experimental and measurement methods are not compatible with the view of our experiences of emotions as a stream of events. Theories derived from such studies consequently are limited by an inability to recognize this continuous flow where events influence one another.[34] Earlier in both Chapters 6 and 7 we have seen how a man while driving hits a dog and, in a continuous fashion, first experiences shame which then turns to an experience of anger as his thoughts about his responsibility serve to alter his experiences.

If we imagine emotional life as a continuous stream, three aspects of emotion can be identified that are likely to be related to the sequence: the nature of the elicitor, the consequent action patterns, and the contextual relationship of emotions to preceding and subsequent ones as they relate to the temperament of the child. Having discussed some of these aspects earlier, we will consider how temperament may play a role in this stream. The specific nature of the elicitor affects the emotional action pattern. Certain elicitors are much more likely to elicit some emotions than others; for example, the loss of support or the sensation of falling will most often elicit distress in children at any age. Although this elicitor is usually associated with distress, some children seem to enjoy such situations like riding on a roller-coaster. The understanding of the elicitor–action pattern connection is insufficient to explain individual differences. Action patterns do not occur as single events, yet the effect of an action pattern on subsequent patterns has received relatively little attention, although in Chapter 3 I discussed some of them. Think of an action pattern of joy preceded by another action pattern of joy, which is likely to have different characteristics than an action pattern of joy preceded by fear. Here the issue of temperament and previous experience plays a role. It is likely that for some children their action patterns are more intense and last longer than for other children regardless of the nature of the elicitor or the preceding emotions. The source of such individual differences is part of the dispositional nature of the child. Soothability is a good example: a child who is less likely to be soothed or to sooth herself is likely to be more subject to longer and more intense negative emotional behaviors.

We can think of mood as some enduring feature of emotional life. The chief difference between it and a transient state is its enduring nature. If this is so, each emotional action pattern has a mood; for example, sad has a depressive mood; joy has an exuberance mood; fear has a fearfulness/anxious mood; disgust has a phobia mood; anger has an aggression or persistence mood; interest has a curiosity mood. While some of these connections seem reasonable, some are less so. What seems clear is that moods have some similarity to transient emotions but are not quite the same. These facts need to be further considered, especially since temperament and moods as well as transient emotional responses may all be related.

The temperament scales that are used for the most part speak of fearfulness as a characteristic of the child, allowing us to predict the transient fear response of the child to a transient elicitor. While there is some relation between the two it is not as strong as a one-to-one connection. However, if we wished to measure directly the temperament of fearfulness how might we do so? We know how to measure a transient fear response, or we think we do, and therefore to measure fearfulness as a temperament dimension we might employ two different measuring strategies. First, we could produce a set of transient fearful situations, say four different ones, like the approach of a stranger, the visual cliff, intense and sudden stimulation like loud noises, and so on. If we found that one infant showed a fear response to all four situations, we could say that that child was more fearful than a child who showed only one or no fear responses, and might be temperamentally more fearful. The IBQ scales certainly have a dimension of fearfulness as a temperament feature. Here we rely on a number of occurrences of a transient emotional response to infer a temperament characteristic. Isn't this like what a mother's temperament report is based on?

The second way is a bit more complicated. Since an emotional action pattern is made up of a complex set of behaviors including facial expression, body movement, physiological responses of the ANS and CNS, as well as stress hormone responses, it is likely that the higher the concordance between measures the more intense the emotion.[35] This being the case, individual differences in concordance may reflect temperament differences. The infant showing heart rate increases, fearful face, and high body activity across various situations may be more fearful temperamentally than one who only shows a fear face.

What this discussion raises is whether enduring action patterns or moods are temperament dimensions or not. If they are, then temperament has content. However, we have already stated that temperament may have to do with generally physiological responses such as ease of elicitation, intensity of response, and ability to regulate. These features of temperament are contentless.

The solution to this dilemma is that these contentless temperament dimensions act on transient emotional action patterns to affect moods. This is likely to work as follows: for a difficult-temperament infant the elicitor of fear intersects with ease of eliciting a fear action pattern, the action pattern is more intense, and it is harder to regulate. Given the same number of fear elicitors, the difficult-temperament child is more likely to have a fear mood than a less-difficult-temperament infant. We might think, then, of the following meditational model: fear elicitor in a child with a difficult temperament leads to more of a fear mood than a fear elicitor in an easy temperament child.

Another example is tickling. To do so requires that we once again examine the relationship between elicitors and action patterns, the overall context of this association, and the qualities of the nervous system that underlie temperament. A tickle in the context of a tickle is joyful for an easy-temperament child but aversive for a difficult-temperament one.

This model may seem at first at odds with the more familiar idea of temperament which requires little interaction with the social world since it is considered an innate disposition. While I think that moods are a consequence of the interaction between qualities of the nervous system, they are also related to the type and number of elicitors the infant receives. The type and number that the child receives is a function of the infant's social experiences. *The premise is that emotional action patterns, the consequence of different social experiences, are modulated by qualities of the nervous system, which in turn produce moods. The quality of the nervous system is temperament; however, moods are the result of social experiences and qualities of the nervous system.*

In order to appreciate the relevance of this idea we first need to remember that nervous system qualities are not content-specific. Rather, easy and difficult temperaments need to be redefined as aspects of the nervous system as they interact with specific contexts.[36] Thus, we can say that the nervous system features are the temperament dimensions.

We can now say that both the easy and difficult child, who we will call Gregory and Ben, respectively, possess innate action patterns such as fear and joy. They also possess in different degrees characteristics of their nervous system. Gregory shows low arousal levels, he needs a lot of stimulation to arouse him, and he has a high ability to dampen his responses once they occur. On the other hand, Benjamin shows the reverse: he is easily aroused and has difficulty in dampening his responses once they occur. Both Gregory and Benjamin are exposed to elicitors such as tickling. Gregory responds with joy since he is not overwhelmed by the stimulation, while Benjamin shows fear because he is overwhelmed. The same elicitor produces different emotional action patterns depending on the quality of their nervous systems.

We can further involve the role of socialization by giving to Gregory and Benjamin a different context of the tickling elicitor. Thus, if Gregory receives lots of elicitors of joy while Benjamin receives lots of elicitors of fear, the differences in joy and fear between them will be explained by both differences in their nervous systems and differences in the nature of their social experiences. The role of parenting has to play a role in the presentation of different elicitors to the infant's early action patterns of fear, sadness, happiness, anger, interest, and disgust, as does the quality of his nervous system.[37]

TEMPERAMENT AND CONSCIOUSNESS

Before we leave this topic we need to consider how temperament may affect both the onset of consciousness itself as well as its effect on the self-conscious emotions. As we have mentioned, consciousness, as measured by self-referential behavior, emerges in general between 15 and 24 months and does not appear to be related to socialization factors. It does appear to be related to infants' earlier reactions to pain, which I believe are temperament dimensions. Infants who react with more distress to pain show earlier self-recognition than those who show less distress. This suggests that infants and toddlers who have intense reactions and difficulty regulating pain may have a general problem in gating bodily information. Difficulties in gating internal information result in more attention directed inward and thus to more self-referencing.[38] In terms of the self-conscious emotions there is evidence to suggest that temperament differences may explain some individual differences beyond the socialization experience. Grazyna Kochanska and her colleagues have shown a relationship between temperament and what she calls "internalization" or "moral behavior," what I would consider to be shame and guilt over failure.[39] Moreover, we have been able to relate difficult temperament to differences in the expression of embarrassment.[40]

* * *

While we have yet to discuss socialization factors, it is clear that both need to be considered as they impact the emotional life of the newborn and the child. Temperament has now started to receive the attention it deserves; however, exactly what temperament is remains unanswered. On one hand, it is the qualities of the nervous system having little content. On the other hand, it also is given content. Clearly, more work is needed to address these issues of temperament both as a measure of individual differences and how it interacts with socialization to affect emotional development.

CHAPTER 10

The Socialization of Emotion

This chapter could be subtitled "What My Mother Did to Me," because from the outset I wish to suggest that the idea that what mothers do to their infants and young children largely determines their emotional lives is an overstatement. The psychogenetic mother, what Bruno Bettelheim called the "refrigerator mother," is not the cause of autism, nor is the seductive mother the cause of homosexuality, nor is poor parenting the cause of attention deficit disorder (ADD).[1] While of course what mothers, as well as what fathers, older siblings, and others do to and with the infant will have important effects on him, these effects are not as large as our theories would allow. The role of the family in the socialization of emotion is considerable, but only if we broaden the role of others than mothers, if we look at direct and indirect effects of the family, and if we include temperament and other biological factors as they interact with socialization and mutually influence each other. While biological processes such as temperament are important for the early as well as the later self-conscious emotions, socialization is always a necessary element. This model follows our idea about language development. Language is biologically based; the ability to create grammar and meaning is part of the specific action patterns of humans. But the words we use, the meaning we give to them, the particular forms of grammar that we employ, and the sound of our language are all cultural artifacts to which the infant, entering the social world, must be and is socialized to. So too with the emotional action patterns on which the culture acts. The role of the interaction of socialization with temperament is always necessary.

When over 40 years ago my daughter, Felicia, and my son, Benjamin, were born, their mother and I held strong views about the important role parenting had on their emotional, social, and intellectual lives. We worried about everything we did. In the 1960s the idea of temperament was championed by only a few and the role of the mother was held to be central. While as a parent I believed in my power to seriously affect the child's life, I had noticed when I held each of my children at the time of their birth that Benjamin wrapped his body around me and that Felicia was as stiff as a board. Those early social-like differences continue in some form and to this day there are still traces of them. These personal experiences were a strong force in affecting my ideas about development. The studies of development have moved me to take a more limited view of the role of the mother in a child's development since fathers and siblings are also important in affecting children's emotional lives. While many psychologists who study human development moved toward a more measured view of the role of the mother, our leading theoretical position, that of attachment, still holds to the mother's stronger role. After all, the mother is assumed to be the only attachment figure, and few studies of attachment look at the child's relations with siblings and father in addition to the mother's role in the development of socioemotional competence.[2] On the other hand, few temperament studies use the attachment construct to understand the role of socialization on emotional development. While in the last chapter we focused on temperament, here the focus is on socialization. It is necessary to study both, not only to show how they interact but to show that they are likely inseparable.

THE SOCIAL WORLD

In order to study the role of socialization on emotional life we need to broaden our view of socializing agents to include the entire social nexus, the broad set of needs of the child, and the beliefs and rules of the culture. Unfortunately, there is hardly a book that does not argue for the mother's pivotal role in the emotional development of the child through her attachment to her infant. Let us be clear though: neither the mother nor any other social agent teaches the infant joy or fear, happiness or sadness. These are action patterns innate to our species. Infants can be taught when to be happy or fearful through selection by the social world of particular elicitors that cause action patterns. Infants may be taught how to express these action patterns in various ways, including facial and vocal behavior, and they may be taught about the experiences of them.

Even so, the "idée fixe" about the maternal role in emotional development requires us to reappraise the role of socialization to make sure that both our implicit and our explicit theories about it are understood. To begin, the first of these ideas is that development involves a continuous change, which includes the idea that earlier events influence later ones. This leads readily to stressing the influence of early experiences since it is these early experiences that affect all subsequent development. While this fixed idea holds for all behaviors including cognitive and social ones, it is also true for emotional development.

The second "idée fixe" is that the early mother–child dyad is the only biological unit, and is responsible for the infant and young child's current as well as subsequent emotional development. Not only is the mother central to the child's development, but all others in the child's social world play only a peripheral role. These two ideas are part of what are called the "organismic model," which consists of five features: (1) development is change with a direction and therefore has an end point, (2) earlier events are connected to later ones, (3) change is gradual and a slowly cumulative progression, (4) events that occur in the first few years of life produce the most long-lasting and powerful effects, and (5) mothers alone are the most important element in the child's environment and are more likely than all others to affect their socioemotional well-being, both in childhood and throughout their lives.[3]

To understand the role of socialization requires an examination of existing data. Although there is some support for the organismic model and with it the role of parents, in particular the mother, the support is weak, certainly far weaker than what we believe. In fact, one of the most critical longitudinal studies having an attachment orientation concluded that earlier parenting interacts with later life events and so early attachment is not sufficient to predict later socioemotional outcomes.[4]

A decade ago Judith Rich Harris reviewed the evidence for early parenting in children's development and concluded there was little support for parental effects. Although I disagree with much of what Harris has written, her analysis deserves consideration.[5] The core of her thesis is (1) that there is no or very little support for the proposition that parents—most studies focus on mothers—influence the development of their children; (2) that peers are powerful influences on each other, much more so than parents; and (3) that the peer environment is created by the children themselves. She shows that there is weak evidence to support the idea that parents influence development, including the social, emotional, and intellectual development; her review of the literature reveals correlations that are very weak, accounting for less than 5–10% of the common variance between maternal behavior and child outcomes. There are likely many reasons for this result, including measurement problems; however, the idea as described in the organismic model has weak support. That does not mean that parenting and children's emotional behavior are not related in the here-and-now. What it does mean is that it does not affect future emotional behavior, since environments and children change.

The second point in Harris's book, namely, that peers are more important in the socialization of emotions than parents, raises several other considerations. For the most part, it argues for two ideas. The first is that environmental influences on emotional life are not just those of the child's mother but involve a wide range of people including fathers, siblings, grandparents, peers, and other members of the child's particular social nexus. The fact that others, especially peers, influence the child will require us to consider the difference that now exists between attachment and social network theories. The second major idea, based on her findings that peers influence the child's behavior, is that current environments affect behavior more than does the past environment. The final point she makes, that the child's social environment is produced by the child herself, is consistent with her biological and genetic view, namely, how the biology of the child affects her own emotional life through influencing her social choices of peers.

ATTACHMENT VERSUS
THE SOCIAL NETWORK VIEW

If we are to understand the socialization of emotional life we need to make sure that *all* the social influences on the child are carefully articulated. Most studies on the socialization of emotion, especially in infancy, talk about the mother's interactions with her child. While fathers and siblings, peers and grandparents have received some attention, especially fathers, the overwhelming number of studies focus on mothers.[6] This is no accident, given the influence of attachment theory. However, if others are important, as we believe, we need to consider multiple attachments and with them the various roles that other attachment figures engage the child in. A social network theory will need to be articulated.[7]

Social Networks

While attachment theory in the last half-century has received a good deal of study, theories about the social network of the young child have received relatively little. While Bowlby considered the idea of multiple attachments in the beginning of the first volume of his trilogy, he rejected the idea of multiple attachments in favor of a single attachment, that of the mother. This is not surprising given his psychoanalytic background. Even so, there was no reason for him to do so given his interest in animal imprinting.[8]

At a meeting of the International Society for Human Ethology in Parma, Italy, Konrad Lorenz, one of the discoverers of imprinting, was asked a question that had been of interest to me for some time: whether baby ducks take turns following their mother. If this was the case, and, for example, there were seven ducklings, each duckling would spend one-seventh of the time with its mother and six-sevenths of its time with the other ducklings. If, on the other hand, the ducklings keep to a certain order, one duckling would spend 100% of the time behind its mother and the others 0% of their time. While Lorenz did not know the answer to the question, it is clearly related to the issue of others besides the mother affecting the baby ducklings' development.

In a paper on the social network, we offered the following general propositions that form the basis for a theory of social networks that can serve as an addition to the mother-only attachment perspective:

1. Humans are by nature social animals and from birth enter into a social network.
2. This network is made up of a variety of people, including at least female and male adult caregivers, siblings, other relatives, and friends.
3. Social networks have multiple functions and contexts. Functions include bodily needs such as feeding, bathing, changing, playing, teaching, protection and comfort, as well as affective attention. Contexts, on the other hand, are those physical places where functions are carried out, including various rooms in the house, outdoors, playrooms, and schools.
4. A particular social network of any child is embedded in and varies as a function of a large social environment including family, friends, and culture.
5. The social network changes as a function of the age or development level of the child since new people enter the child's life and new functions occur with development.[9]

Although others, including Urie Bronfenbrenner, have argued for a broader social influence than the mother, to my surprise, the idea of a social network theory with multiple attachments has been unable to compete with attachment theory and its measurement as the important unit of study. Even though the work of Michael Lamb on fathers and Judy Dunn on siblings and peers has been well received, it is the attachment of the child to its mother that has captured our interest.[10]

The social network model, besides suggesting that there are multiple people in the infant's life, also suggests that there are many functions or needs that the infant requires in order for it to survive and become competent. Certainly Bowlby's idea of a secure base is important, but so is play, as is protection from the harm of others, caregiving such as feeding and cleaning, and finally education. While it is assumed that one person, the mother, carries out all these functions, it is clear that play and education may fall to others. As Sarah Blaffer Hrdy has so carefully pointed out in her book

Mothers and Others, it takes more than the mother to raise her children. Given the relatively high rate of birth of children, the probability of a child being born every year or year and a half, Hrdy argues that the mother cannot carry out all the important functions of care by herself; it takes a village to raise her children.[11] The social network theory argues for such a village, a matrix formed by the number of different people in the child's network and the various functions or needs of the child. This matrix changes with development or the age of the child and the nature of the culture in which the child is raised.

If we want to understand the effects of socialization by multiple others on the young child's emotional life, we need to assume that the infant has some perceptual and cognitive capacity that allows him to differentiate the large number of people who populate his social world. We understand that the child can form a model of its mother, but can it form a model of multiple attachments? In a series of papers, my colleagues and I were able to show that infants can discriminate facial features of adults and children on the bases of age and gender. Moreover, on the basis of this distinction, we were able to show that young children have preferences for different people for different functions—just what the social network theory predicts. One article examined young children's preference for various people who could care for their different needs. Since it had already been shown that children as young as 16 months produced the word "baby" to photographs of infants and the word "daddy" or "mommy" to photographs of adults, photographs of these different people were used to question them when they were as young as 3 years old about who they preferred to do different things with. Dolls rather than photographs were used in another study with the same results. The people presented to the children in photographs (or dolls) were an adult male and an adult female, girl and boy children of about the same age as the child, and male and female infants. Each child was given a series of stories around the functions such as (1) getting hurt and asking someone for help, (2) finding a toy and wanting someone to show them how to use it, (3) having extra food and wanting to give or share it, and (4) wanting someone with whom to play. With respect to seeking help, the older persons were the more highly preferred. In terms of play, however, the children tended to prefer peers rather than adults and infants. When seeking someone to show them how to use the toy, the children preferred infants the least, revealing that they had some information about the infant's knowledge level; the three other groups were equally selected.[12]

In a parallel study with 18- to 24-month-olds in a room in which there were two mothers and their two children, we found that while the infants preferred to stay near their own mother, and avoided the other mother, they spent considerable time at play and at looking at the other infant, a consistent finding about early peer interest that we see in studies looking at infants' emotions in response to the approach of an unfamiliar adult and children. Keiko Takahashi, studying Japanese children, also has found this function–person matrix.[13]

The monotropic theory of the mother as the most important person is also likely to restrict our view of the influence of socialization on emotional development. This influence can be seen clearly in the work that exists with nonhuman primates, notably the work of Harry Harlow and his associates. As early as the early 1960s, Harlow's lab had already produced ample evidence that suggested simultaneous and dual affect systems. For example, Harlow and Harlow published a paper that specifically addressed the possibility that there were multiple attachment systems, and argued that there were at least two, one between child and peers, and the other between child and mother. Indeed, even earlier Anna Freud and Sophie Dann discussed the power of peer attachment relationships. Thus, it was and remains possible to broaden attachment theory to make it more compatible with social network theory by reconsidering the monotropic attachment idea.[14]

Teaching or Modeling?

Another problem that often arises in thinking about the socialization of emotion has to do with the direct and indirect effects of others' behavior on the child's emotional life. Whether we focus on the mother–child interaction and relationship or any other person's interactions with the child, we generally consider direct effects. Direct effects have to do with the behavior of the other directed to the child. But there are also indirect effects, those having to do with others not in interaction with the child, but which the infant perceives. Included among indirect effects is the child's perception of what other people do to objects as well as to people. Indirect effects can only be studied through the observation of groups with more than two people. The limitation of observing only dyadic interactions points to the general lack of interest in the various social sources that impact the child. Our lack of an ecological approach limits our theories.

When thinking about more than a single other person's effect on the child's emotions, the indirect effects are in need of consideration. Perhaps a simple example will suffice to show the power of indirect effects. While a mother is yelling at a toddler's older brother for drawing on the wall, the toddler watches intently at the negative emotions being expressed. Although the toddler was not directly acted on—she was not the target of her mother's anger as was her older sibling—still she learns, in an indirect way, not to mark the wall, as well as learns about how angry her mother can be and how her anger made her brother cry. Urie Bronfenbrenner understood the power of the indirect effects when he wrote:

In contrast to the conventional dyadic research model, which is limited to assessing the direct effect of two agents on each other, the design of an ecological experiment must take into account the existence in the setting of systems that include three or more elements and hence permit the indirect influence of anyone there on the direct relations taking place between the others, operating a sub-system.[15]

Children accrue information about emotional life in both direct and indirect ways. Nevertheless, there are relatively few socialization studies that go beyond direct interactions between mother and child. Even those that look at indirect effects have considerable problems in analyzing interactions that go beyond a dyad. We will consider these effects in more detail as they relate to children's emotional development.

Direct Effects

Direct effects can be defined as those interactions that represent the effect or influence of one person on the behaviors of another when both are engaged in mutual interaction. In the study of emotional behavior, direct effects are usually observed in dyadic interactions, for example, in joint attention between the infant and his mother. Direct effects involve information gathered from participation in an interaction with another person or object and always involve the target person as one of the focal participants in the interaction.

> The 3-month-old infant sitting facing her mother, smiles. The mother smiles and vocalizes back. The infant widens her eyes, smiles, and after a pause coos again. Her mother smiles and vocalizes back.

In this example we can see the direct effect of mother on child as well as child on mother. The child's smiling, which may be random at first, is responded to contingently by her mother. The responsivity of mother to child directly affects the rate of infant smiling, and before long the infant smiles in order to produce the maternal response. Besides the direct reinforcement of the smile, the child may have learned a number of different social rules, including that people, at least her mother, are responsive; that she can control her environment, a means and ends rule; and that there is turn taking in emotional exchanges. The learning of these social rules occurs as a direct relationship between the behavior of mother and infant and of each of the participants' behavior.

Historically, direct effects in their simplest form, using the mother–infant interaction data, were represented by the role of the mother's behavior on the infant (M → I). The question usually asked was, for example,

What is the effect of the mother's vocalization on the infant's vocalization, either concurrently or at some future time? As interactional models became more sophisticated, it was recognized that the interaction is reciprocal and that both mother and child influence each other (M $\rightleftarrows$ I). Nonetheless, the kinds of effects studied are still direct.[16]

Indirect Effects

Indirect effects refer to two classes of events. In the first class, indirect effects are those sets of interactions that affect the target child but that occur in the absence of the child. More important for the present discussion is the second class of indirect effects, which refers to interactions among members of the system that occur in the presence of the child even though the interaction is not directed toward or does not involve the child. These kinds of indirect effects are those effects that are based on information on emotion that is gathered from sources other than direct interaction with another person or object. These effects may be the result of observation of another's interaction with persons or objects or may be the result of information gathered from another about emotions, attitudes, behaviors, traits, or actions of a third person. The example of the mother's anger toward the older sibling in the presence of the younger one reflects this type of effect.

Another type of indirect effects is likely to be important. For example, the emotional tone of the family as a unit is likely to have influence on the infant since it is highly salient and observable although not directed toward the infant but toward each other. The emotional expressiveness of the mother, father, and other siblings toward the infant is a measure of direct effects. However, the emotional expressiveness between mother and father, or between parents and other siblings, is just as likely to impact the young child, even though these are indirect effects. Social referencing is another example of this kind of indirect effect.

The toddler can also be indirectly affected by the father's behavior. The father, in the child's absence, makes the mother feel good about herself as a wife and as a mother. The mother's good feeling about her competence influences her responsiveness to the child in a positive way, making her more likely to praise the child's attempts to master the environment. The mother praises the child, which affects the child's smiling behavior. The child's development of smiling has been indirectly influenced by the father. Of the factors that operate when the child is absent and that indirectly affect the mother–child relationship, the husband/father and wife/mother relationship is most salient. In fact the suggestion has been made that the father's influence on early child development is primarily indirect, that is, mediated by the mother, while the mother's effect is more direct.[17]

Still another indirect effect is the infant's learning about emotional behavior through materials he is given by a parent. In this example, the child has learned about her environment not through interaction with her parents but through materials that have been provided by the parent. The mother does not teach 2-year-old Tamara about the animals pictured in the magazine but arranges the environment so as to make the pictures of penguins available for the child's perusal. In a similar fashion the mother's good relationship with her own parents provides the child with an opportunity to interact with adults other than her own parents who are also attentive and responsive to her needs. Thus, the mother indirectly affects the child's development by providing opportunities for the child to interact with varied objects and people. Arrangement of the child's physical, social, and emotional environment is a kind of indirect influence the parent has on the child which does not involve parent–child interaction.

Social referencing is an example of an indirect effect. Social referencing refers to the process whereby an infant utilizes its mother's emotional response to another person to appraise the situation and to learn from it. This process can be seen within the second half of the first year of life.[18] Saul Feinman and I looked at social referencing in 10-month-old infants under four conditions involving a stranger-approach situation. In one condition, the mother spoke to her infant about the approaching stranger in either a happy or a neutral tone, and in another condition the mother spoke to the stranger directly in either a happy or a neutral tone. For the four conditions, infant smiling behavior was used as a measure of the effect of the mother's emotional message. Infants whose mothers spoke to them in a happy and positive way about the stranger smiled at the stranger more than in the neutral condition, although there was no difference in smiling in the positive or neutral condition when the mother spoke to the stranger but not to the infant. The question raised by this study was whether the positive and happy tone the mother used with her infant changed the infant's mood, which is why the infant smiled more to the stranger. Whether the infant was responding to the mother's message is questionable given the child's lack of language ability. The results bear on the topic of how the mother's emotion influences the infant's emotion. Both information exchanges and contagions are possible answers; however, 10-month-olds are less likely to understand a verbal message.

The Role of Emotional Contagion

Although the results show that the mother's positive and happy behavior can affect the child's behavior toward a stranger, it must be her emotional behavior that is attended to and results in the infant's smiling. The studies looking at social referencing would like to claim that there is an information exchange, namely, the mother's behavior references some meaning to the child; it is similar to a cognitive exchange. However, we need to consider the alternative, that of emotional contagion. While contagion is widely observed in animals as well as in people, it is rarely considered when thinking about the effects of socialization on emotional life. Contagion is about an automatic elicitor of a particular action pattern. Think of yawning as an example of contagious behavior. The yawn of one person automatically elicits a yawn in another. Likewise, the cry of one infant produces a cry of another. Being in the company of sad or happy others within the family produces sadness or happiness in a like fashion in the infant.[19] Emotional contagion is an important aspect of adult emotional lives and should also be for infants. It is important to keep in mind that contagion does not reflect empathy, although contagion may be the precursor of empathy. That infants show contagion should not be mistaken for showing empathy since empathetic behaviors presume the maturation of the self system; contagion rather than empathy in infancy is likely to make more sense.

The Feinman and Lewis study also demonstrated the interaction between socialization and temperament There, temperament measures allowed for classifying infants as having easy or difficult temperaments, which could be observed as they interacted with their mother's positive mood. An infant's smiling to the stranger was greater for the easy- than for the difficult-temperament child, thus demonstrating the importance of the interaction of temperament and socialization on the infant's emotional development.[20]

Another question raised about indirect effects is whether the mother's behavior toward a stranger was more effective than a stranger's behavior toward another stranger. In other words, might the mother be more effective than another in affecting the infant's contagious behavior? That is, are we more likely to be affected by a familiar's emotion than by a stranger's? This is another way of demonstrating the effects of multiple people in our life rather than just mothers. In order to address this question we looked at two situations in another study: in the first situation the mother had a positive interaction with stranger B, and in the second situation stranger A had a positive interaction with stranger B. The infant's play interaction to stranger B was the measure of whether the mother or stranger A was more effective in influencing the infant's play behavior with stranger B. For 15-month-olds, both the mother's and stranger A's positive interaction with stranger B affected the toddler's reaction to stranger B. Thus positive behaviors preceding an interaction with a stranger affects the child's positive reaction to that stranger. However, the mother's positive interaction was more effective in producing a positive interaction between the child and stranger B than was stranger A's positive interaction with stranger B. Nevertheless, both were effective in altering the infant's behavior to stranger B when compared to the condition where there was no positive behavior exposure prior to the child's interaction with stranger B. Whether the attachment relationship with the mother, or her history of focusing the infant's attention on important aspects of the environment, or both, affect the infant's behavior to stranger B is open to question. The fact that the infant looked significantly more at stranger B when he was interacting with his mother than when stranger B was interacting with stranger A supports both views. Whatever the cause, an infant's behavior toward another can be affected by the behavior produced by others in the child's environment; this is an indirect effort and supports the view that emotional behavior can be affected by multiple people around the infant.[21]

Although the indirect role of others' emotions on infants' emotions is clear, other indirect features of the environment that are not social also play an important role in emotional development. This is demonstrated by the "broken window theory." In an ingenious set of studies with adults, a street environment was manipulated. In one scenario the street was very neat, while in the other scenario the street was dirty. This setup was designed to test whether the environmental effects of cleanliness would affect people's neatness and cleanliness. A throw-away advertisement was placed on people's bicycles in both conditions. Under the clean conditions, people threw fewer of the ads on the ground, putting them in trash cans instead; the opposite happened in the dirty conditions.[22] With no other information to shape their behavior, people will behave in keeping with the environment that they are in. Extending this finding to children and their emotions, a happy home will have very different effects on the child's emotional life than a sad and upsetting home. As the foregoing examples indicate, indirect effects, whether they are called imitation, modeling, identification, vicarious learning, or observational learning, are probably of considerable importance for the development of emotional life including emotional knowledge, behavior, and expression.[23] It would not be in error to assume that a large degree of culturally appropriate behavior, knowledge, and values are transmitted on the basis of these kinds of indirect effects as well as on the direct ones.

THE SOCIALIZATION OF EMOTIONAL LIFE

The reader has been forewarned about the limitation of research on the socialization of emotion due in large part to our reliance on attachment theory. We have spent some time on the necessity of considering the influences of others besides the mother, and other needs besides attachment such as play and education; indirect influences besides direct ones; and the need to consider the child's effect on the social agent, often its mother. I will return to our structural consideration as to the nature of emotion, namely, those of elicitors, action patterns, and experiences, and show how each might be effected by the social world of the child. Before doing so, however, we need to make clear that other organizing systems can be used.

A good example is Nancy Eisenberg and colleagues' review of parental socialization. Eisenberg et al. divided the socialization literature into four areas, which include parental reactions to children's emotions, parental discussion of emotion and how it is related to children's understanding of emotion (or emotional knowledge), parental expressivity and children's expressivity, and the effects of children's temperament and developmental level on parental behavior. As is often the case, most of the research Eisenberg et al. reviewed focused on enduring rather than transient emotions—for example, focusing on depression rather than sadness. In addition there is a considerable amount of information on children's emotional knowledge or competence as well as on social competence, including emotional regulation, in particular inhibition and aggression. However, in almost all cases it is enduring emotional behavior that is the focus. As discussed in Chapter 3 enduring emotion and emotional behavior may not be the same.[24]

Few studies look at current associations, but instead look more at the predictive effects of socialization. Those that do also suffer from the same problem, the use of questionnaires that ask parents about their behaviors and beliefs and also obtain information from them about their children's behavior. The associations found may have more to do with parental ideas than with the process itself. The use of questionnaires may be helpful in generating hypotheses or in devising models of effect. However, they may well serve poorly as sources of data on parental behaviors as causes of children's outcomes.[25]

Others have explored parents' beliefs and philosophy and feelings about emotions and their children's ability to regulate their emotional life.[26] Consider this example. We asked mothers about whether they are authoritarian or are authoritative, the difference reflecting parents' use of punishment for rule violation. At the same time these mothers were asked about their children's self-regulation behavior or their children's mental health. Let us say that there is a significant, although small, association between authoritarian parenting and lack of self-regulation. While it could mean that this type of parenting leads to lower self-regulation abilities, it could also mean that children with lower self-regulatory abilities cause parents to use more harsh parenting in order to try and regulate an unruly child. Obviously, this kind of data has many problems, not the least of which is parental bias in reporting, as well as the role of the mutual influence of parent on child and child on parent. Some of the child's effect on the parent can be attributable to earlier parental behavior but also perhaps to a greater extent to the child's temperament. For example, it has been found that the 2-year-old child's self-regulation, measured by the delay in reaching for a prohibited cookie, is a function of both biological differences due to environmental toxin exposure when the child was a fetus and parental behavior.[27]

Another issue that is raised by the existing literature is how one looks at socialization practices as they affect emotional life. As mentioned, most studies look at how socialization factors affect children's enduring emotions or personality characteristics. They usually do not look at children's emotional reactions. Thus, an association is implicitly made that emotional interaction differences are the subsequent bases of moods and personality characteristics. While this may be true, there are few data that show how this process comes about. Look at this example from a recent paper by Gisela Trommsdorf:

> Chinese as compared to the U.S. mothers value harmonious and balanced social interactions as goals for emotional development and regulation more highly [here she references Wang and Fivush, 2005]. Among mother–child dyads in the U.S., conversations about past experiences of negative emotions indicate that children are socialized to develop an autonomous sense of self and regulate negative emotions through emotional understanding. In contrast, the conversations of Chinese dyads reveal that emotion regulation is based on relatedness and acceptance of social norms. Such differences in socialization have consequences, for example, for the inhibition of ego-based anger expression due to the social need for harmony and related sensitivity for others' expectations in cultures where the interdependent self-construal prevails.[28]

The question not directly answered is, How does this come about? It could come about through maternal behaviors that organize specific responses in the child or it could come about through the mother's behavior, including her verbal behavior, which teaches the child about cultural ideas and which therefore affect the child's behaviors. One can address cultural differences, say between Japanese and American mothers, by examining the cultural difference as an individual difference in *both* cultures. Taking the example above, one might wish to look at how much conversations by mothers of past negative experiences lead to an autonomous sense of self. If this is the mechanism, then American and Chinese mothers who use the same amount of verbal behavior should have children who are similar. Likewise, the more past negative experience in conversations there was, the more autonomous the behavior of the child should be, independent of the culture. If, after calculating the amount of negative conversations, there are still cultural differences, then this factor cannot be the primary cause. Recently studies have begun to look at the processes by which socialization and culture work. For example, Wang and colleagues found a relation between emotional knowledge in 3-year-olds and their autobiographical memory. Interestingly, when they looked at cultural differences, the processes were the same across Chinese and European Americans.[29] We will come back to this issue when we look at observational studies on the effects of cultural and maternal beliefs as they act on infant distress.

While such studies are harder to do, there are those who use observations to examine the role of parent impact on children's emotional lives. The studies involving social referencing as a stranger approaches or the visual cliff are ways of studying the socialization process as it unfolds. This requires us to know something about parental beliefs, their philosophy about emotional life, and their behavior toward their children as a function of these ideas, as well as the child's behavior, while keeping the child's temperament in mind. Some of the social referencing studies provide good examples of how to observe the child's behavior.

Even better examples are studies that observe the infant in interaction with social and nonsocial events. The work on the observation of infants' responses to frustration as a function of maternal contingency responses is another example. These types of studies are difficult to do since they require hours of careful observation and hours of data analysis to reach any conclusion. Moreover, they require large numbers of infants. It is far easier to hand out questionnaires to large samples.

Given this long list of problems in studying the processes involved in the socialization of emotions, we can see that the task is formidable. As has been pointed out by others, there is much work to be done in order to understand the rules governing the socialization of emotions. Reviews of the literature on socialization practices are limited. In fact, even the study of emotional competence itself is highly dependent on parental values. For example, if parents believe that negative emotion expressions are bad and should be controlled, these parents will punish their children for expressing negative emotions or they will teach their children not to express them, and so make any comprehensive analysis difficult. Also, the need to combine emotional and social competence, while useful, also tends to muddy our ability to draw conclusions. Perhaps the most difficult problem is the focus on the expression of emotion, leaving the experiential aspect of emotion and the relation between self-attributions and socialization somewhat understudied.

Although we have developed some theories about the socialization of emotions, without a scheme to consider the types of emotional behavior specified and how socialization might affect each, progress will be slow. For instance, while we learn something about how parental warmth or abuse affects emotional knowledge of what pictures of emotional faces go with what situations, it does not tell us much about the exact nature of the socialization of facial expressions, or other features of the action patterns. What is needed are more studies that look directly at what mothers, fathers, and others do in interaction with their infants, and how the infants react in terms of their emotion responses to their parents' behavior.

Because of the focus on enduring emotions on socioemotional competence, most of the research to date depends on the use of questionnaires about how much of an emotion the child expresses as it relates to some characteristics of the caregiver or how parental behavior subsequently affects children's mental health. While the enduring emotion, or the level of self-regulation, or even mental health as reported by the mother has some importance, a theory of emotional development and the effects of socialization suggests that we go back to the structural features of emotions, that of elicitors, action patterns, and experiences. Socialization effects may be different for each of these features. I think this is likely to be a more productive way to organize what we know and need to learn about the effects of culture. Before returning to this topic, I would like to offer a word or two about the major premise underlying the model of development of emotions found in this book: *while the role of culture, or socialization, can be seen even at the beginning of life, the role of culture only increases with age.* While early action patterns need little socialization to emerge, the self-conscious emotions are highly dependent on socialization for their occurrence.

As we have tried to make clear, there are some universal practices, both biological and cultural, that transcend specific socialization practices. But at the same time biological effects always take place within a family or culture. The smiling action pattern may have biological causes and therefore may occur across cultures, but how much a child may smile, what kinds of smiles occur and their association with other behavior, and in what contexts smiling occurs are all part of the culture and as such can be said to be either directly or indirectly affected by socialization practices. It is most important to keep in mind that it is not possible to review all the studies that have been done. What we aim to do here is to present a small sample of them in order to highlight some of the important features of socialization. In what follows socialization as it affects elicitors, action patterns, and experiences will be considered. Here we will be talking about the early elicitors, those that give rise to the early action patterns with names like joy, sadness, anger, fear, and the like, and also be talking about the later elicitors that are not literal features of the world but ideas.

Socialization of the Earlier Elicitors

There is support for the belief that elicitor effects, at least in the beginning of life, are not determined by socialization processes. Infants smile to humans' and nonhumans' faces and voices. They cry when they are in pain. Nevertheless, socialization pressures may occur since parents may present more of one type elicitor than another, and since an individual parent may differ from another parent in the amount of any elicitor presented to their infant. For example, in an abusive parenting environment there is likely to be more pain and fewer joy elicitors. Likewise, even in a nonabusive environment, there may be more joy elicitors in one family and fewer in another. Socialization factors are transmitted through the amount and distribution of elicitors, which in turn affect the amount and distribution of the subsequent action patterns.[30]

An example of elicitor differences by culture can be seen in terms of how Japanese and American mothers differ in their physical proximity to their infants. Japanese mothers are more likely to remain in close physical proximity to their infants, even sleeping next to the infant, while American mothers provide less physical proximity. This difference in physical proximity, a function of the parent's ideas about the nature of the parent–child relationship, leads to a different set of potential elicitors. For example, at night the Japanese baby is in close physical proximity to her mother and shares her warmth, and therefore shows fewer distress action patterns than the American infant who sleeps alone and is likely to have more distress-like reactions that go unattended.

While some research indicates differences in parental practices, there are little data showing how these practices lead to different sets of elicitors, and even less evidence about how these elicitors affect the child's action patterns. The practice of leaving the infant alone until it needs to be fed or cleaned should produce different sets of elicitors of action patterns than the practice of being highly attentive to the infant. Nevertheless, given that almost all practices lead to a large class of elicitors and that these different classes are related to different action patterns, all the early emotions are likely to be elicited, although their amount and distribution may be different.

Sara Harkness and Charles Super have suggested the idea of the "developmental niche" as a source of elicitors as a method for the cultural transmission of emotional behavior. For them, the niche consists of the physical and social settings in which the child lives and includes aspects of daily routine such as places where the child is kept, the nature of the social nexus as well as its functions, the system of child care, strategies for meeting the child's needs, and the beliefs and values of the parents. Thus, besides parental behaviors, the physical reality of where the child is situated is important.[31]

A totally different social influence occurs once more cognitive elicitors, or ideas, are added to the literal elicitors, the developmental sequence that we have suggested occurs. Early in life the general classes of elicitors—for example, a blocked goal for an anger action pattern or a loss for a sad action pattern—have in common physically defined events. As cognitions or ideas appear in the developing child, these elicitors as ideas produce the same action pattern; the physical loss of the parent from view that led to sadness is now produced by the idea of the loss of the parent. The loss of the mother by being out of sight or by ceasing to interact with the infant at 12 months now becomes the idea of her loss at 24 months. As Marsha Weinraub and I found many years ago, what the mother says to her 2-year-old when she leaves the child alone in a room makes a big difference in the child's response to her loss. When the mother sneaks out without saying anything, the sense of loss is greater and the distress more than if she tells the child she is leaving, and even less if she tells the child she will be right back and what to do while she is gone.[32]

However, until cognitions emerge, and cognitions about the self and knowledge about parental attitudes and practices about emotions occur, the effects of socialization include how another's behavior shapes the infant's action patterns. This shaping is likely to occur through parental beliefs translated into parental behavior, which in turn affects the child. One example of this is parental contingent reinforcement of certain infant behaviors, with the reinforcement leading to different rates of particular action patterns, such as the contingent reinforcement of crying behavior leading to more crying, or if it is not reinforced to its cessation.[33]

Another example of how others' behavior may affect the infant's early action patterns is through the differential amount of specific elicitors presented to the child. These presentations can be culturally determined, as in the case of Guatemalan Indian mothers placing their infants in dark and quiet rooms and thus decreasing their stimulation—the type and amount of elicitors presented—or by differential behaviors such as those found in an abusive environment.[34] For example, individual infants can differ in the amount of sadness they exhibit because one child may have more situations of loss as a function of parental practices. Individual differences in temperament should also play a role. Nevertheless, the early adaptive associations between elicitors and action patterns should hold until the child's cognitive capacity supports interpretations of elicitors in a different way.

I have already discussed our work on maternal behavior and infants' response to pain elicitors. We have conducted several other studies with infants in the first year of life that suggest the limits of the effectiveness of maternal behavior. We know that infants respond to inoculation with distress. Since it is a common belief that maternal responsiveness can modify infants' distress, we observed infants varying in age from 2 to 18 months in order to see if maternal comforting would affect infants' concurrent as well as future emotional distress. While there is little question that such behaviors as sucking on a pacifier can comfort a distressed child, the question we wanted to answer was whether *individual differences in maternal comfort was related to individual infant differences in distress*. This question had not yet been satisfactorily answered at the individual child level. For example, if comparing two groups of children, with one receiving lots of comforting while the other received less comforting, it is likely, all things being equal, that the group receiving more comfort would show less distress than the group receiving little comfort. In fact, Ronald Barr, working with colicky infants, showed that maternal holding reduced the amount of infants' crying. It should also be mentioned that the placement of sucrose on an infant's lips also decreases distress.[35] However, even in Barr's intervention research with colicky babies, temperament differences were apparent. Thus while holding an infant reduced the total time of distress, it did not affect the number of bouts of distress.

The question that needed to be addressed about soothability is whether an individual's mother's comforting level has a corresponding stress reduction in her infant. In the studies, which measured infants' level of distress by their facial, bodily, and vocal behaviors, as well as by their cortisol stress response, and which also measured the mother's comforting behavior in a wide variety of ways, including her empathic behavior, there was no evidence indicating that an individual difference in a mother's comforting behavior was related to an individual difference in her infant's distress. Maternal comforting also was found to be unrelated both to current and subsequent infant distress.[36]

Maternal comfort behavior is likely to play a role in the child's emotion life, but it may be more complicated than we think. It might have its most significant effect not on the distress action pattern, but on how the child's cognitive processes including memory may interpret the mother's behavior. In the above study, why did some mothers show more comforting behavior than others? To answer this question we needed to turn to maternal comforting characteristics. First, maternal comforting behavior over time appeared stable. Second, since we had data on a mother's response to infant distress in everyday events in addition to when the child was inoculated, we had two different levels of maternal comfort that were dependent on different types of infant distress. Mothers, as expected, showed more soothing behavior to inoculations than to everyday distress.

In addition, we obtained data on maternal style of coping with stress that allowed us to rate the mothers on whether their coping style was to *monitor* the distress or try to ignore or *blunt* it. What we found was an interaction between the mother's coping style and her comforting behavior both in her everyday and in her inoculation stress soothing. Mothers whose coping style was to monitor distress showed no difference in the amount of soothing they showed between everyday and inoculation conditions. In both cases, their soothing response to their infant's distress was very high and did not differ depending upon the level of the stress their infant experienced. However, mothers whose coping style was to blunt their distress showed differential levels of soothing. They showed less soothing to the everyday distress than to the inoculation distress. Moreover, their overall soothing was lower than that of mothers whose coping style was monitoring. Thus, while individual maternal soothing was not related to their particular infant's distress, it was related to maternal coping style.

How might we envision how the interaction between a mother's coping style and her soothing style might affect the child's distress when the child is older? We need to consider how the child might interpret the mother's behavior and how this interpretation might lead to how the child subsequently responds to distress. Imagine a situation in which a child falls and bangs her knee. In one case the mother makes a fuss and shows great concern; in another, she attends to the cut knee but does not make much of a fuss. How does the child interpret these different maternal behaviors once she is able to think about it? In the first case, maternal overconcern might lead the child to interpret her fall as very painful because of her mother's concern. In the second case, the child might interpret her mother's not making a fuss as indicating that her fall was not serious since her mother did not make much of it. Notice that while the maternal soothing behavior did not have much effect on the distress, her soothing behavior as a function of her coping style did affect the child through the child's interpretation of her mother's comforting level. Such possibilities suggest that the role of comforting an infant's distress might involve a maternal personality variable as well as the child's action pattern and most importantly the child's interpretation of her mother's distress through the role of the mother's level of comforting. By age 2 years some of these cognitions have emerged, which could allow the child to use knowledge about parental practices and behaviors to affect her own emotional behavior.

This possibility is strengthened when we look at when a child's emotional knowledge emerges. In a study of 2- to 5-year-olds' emotional knowledge, Linda Michalson and I looked at three features: production of emotional words, understanding of emotional words, and situational knowledge (or what kinds of faces go with what situations). Production of emotional terms is still limited in young children. The 2-year-old's language ability is underdeveloped and only a few children of this age show knowledge of emotional words. Happy and sad appear earliest. However, by age 3 the percentage of correct labels was over 27% for happy, sad, angry, fearful, surprised, and disgusted faces, while by age 5 80% of the children could produce the appropriate words for these emotional faces. However, children's comprehension data is quite different and demonstrates that 2-year-olds already recognize faces that match emotional words. Over 80% of 2-year-olds recognized happy and sad faces while close to 60% recognized surprise, 40% anger, but less than 20% recognized disgust faces. While they can recognize and give labels to faces, 2-year-olds cannot connect faces with situations, something that 3-year-olds do quite well. These data, then, inform us that by age 2 and certainly by age 3 years children already have an idea about the early emotions and what situations are likely to elicit what faces.[37] From a variety of data, therefore, the utilization of ideas as elicitors becomes increasingly important. What reason the mother gives her 2-year-old child for leaving becomes increasingly important in determining the action pattern of sadness at her loss. Even more important, ideas become the elicitors of the self-conscious emotions, which are therefore most open to socialization.

Socialization of Ideas as Elicitors

At about the same time the child's consciousness emerges, so do his ideas of aboutness. This cognitive advancement reflects a transition in emotional life. For example, we have shown that when a 3-year-old fails an easy task he shows more shame than when he fails a difficult task. Likewise, the child shows more pride when succeeding in a difficult task than when succeeding in an easy one. This suggests that by age 3 years the child has ideas about success and failure around his effort, as well as ideas about task difficulty. It is these ideas that become the elicitors of the self-consciousness emotions. Since ideas are cultural construction, they are most open to socialization factors. Nevertheless, these ideas are themselves tied to specific action patterns. Ideas give rise to shame or guilt but shame and guilt, like joy and fear, are not learned; they are action patterns of the human species.

Since beliefs in success or failure on tasks are socialized, children will differ in their evaluation of their behavior and their thoughts about these behaviors. If a child has a standard that only crayoning within the lines of the drawing is a success, then success is staying within the lines and failure is not staying within the lines. On the other hand, if the child holds to no such idea about crayoning outside the lines, then drawing outside the lines is not a failure for her. Success and failure are taught by the culture. Likewise, whether something is a success or a failure due to one's effort is taught by the culture. A child can have the self-attribution that nothing she did caused the success or caused the failure of a particular act. This child is less likely to show pride or shame since her sense of responsibility is undeveloped and cannot generate these self-conscious emotions. Consider winning a lottery. While an adult would be happy at receiving all that money, she is not proud because she did not cause the win.

Studies of parenting behaviors that lead to children's cognitions of self-attributions are few. However, some researchers have looked at abusing parents and suggested that self-attributions are affected by parental behavior.[38] This topic was considered in Chapter 8 but will be discussed further in Chapter 11, on emotions gone awry.

Another self-attribution that is likely to be socialized has to do with the focus of attention, that is, the child's focus on herself or on the task.

Dweck has called these attributions "performance-" or "task-" focused, whereas I have referred to them as "global" or "specific." Whatever we call them, these different focuses result in different emotions—shame in the case of performance or global self focus and guilt/neglect for task or specific focus. Dweck's work on the socialization of these attributions suggests that parents' use of praises may be at fault. The American parental practice of praising the child even though her action may not be particularly praiseworthy is likely to result in a performance self-focus that leads readily to shame when failure occurs rather than to the more productive guilt, which has a repairing action pattern.[39]

It should also be noticed that once the child's cognitive abilities develop, ideas about the early emotions also occur. This allows the child to think about his own behaviors and to make judgments about them. For example, if the parent says something or acts as if the emotion of anger is inappropriate, the child may inhibit the action pattern of anger to frustration, thus disconnecting an elicitor from producing its associated action pattern. Perhaps good examples of this are the studies that report that a parent's behavior that suppresses the child's negative emotion through its negative reaction leads to poor outcomes due to their heightening of the child's emotional arousal and thereby increasing the likelihood of the child's disregulation. On the other hand, Carolyn Saarni found that mothers' restructuring attitudes toward their children's expression of emotions were related to the children's emotional competence.[40] In the same way parents may be able to enhance a pattern if it is considered appropriate. Smiling may be an example of this since the child may be taught to smile without an elicitor being present, such as in a deceptive smile. That girls have been found to smile more than boys when they do not receive an expected prize is likely an example of socialization of deceptive behavior.

Socialization of Action Patterns

Since action patterns include facial, bodily, and physiological organized sets of responses, we need to consider each of these features separately.

Facial expression has received the most attention with respect to socialization. Only a few examples are presented here to show that even in infancy parental behavior can modify children's facial expression as well as their general emotional behavior. However, there are problems with this type of study since infants differ in temperament. Parenting responses as causal agents of these different action patterns are hard to untangle and makes it difficult to separate out socialization and temperament. A crying baby may elicit caregiving that is different from a noncrying baby, and thus different parental behaviors in response to children's expression cannot be readily untangled from the baby's behavior to begin with. Nevertheless, there are some interesting findings. The first is responsivity of the mother to her infant's emotional expression. Susan Goldberg, Deborah Coates, and I have suggested that contingent responding impacts on the infant's behavior. In our studies, we looked at naturally-occurring maternal contingency behavior toward 3-month-old infants' smiling and crying behaviors. Maternal behaviors such as touching, talking to, and smiling at were observed. In 2 hours of at-home observation of mothers, we found that the most contingent maternal response to their infant's crying was kissing, whereas their response of touching and smiling were the most frequent responses to their infant's smiles.[41]

In another study we found that maternal responsivity to 3-month-olds could be divided into proximal and distal responses, with proximal responses including all physical contact while distal responses included vocalization and smiling. Although the child's outcome was not emotional competence, it was found that maternal proximal behavior was positively correlated with current 3-month-old IQ but was negatively correlated with IQ at 6 years. At the same time, distal responsivity was negatively correlated with current IQ and later positively correlated. These findings suggested that the nature of maternal responsivity can affect the child's subsequent ability. More recent studies of parental responses to infant emotional expression are likely to provide the opportunity to selectively promote infants' emotional expressions. The work by Carol Malatesta and Jeannette Haviland seems to show that mothers respond in kind to positive expressions but not negative ones. This suggests that mothers respond to infants' expressions so as to favor positive and discourage negative emotions.[42]

These socialization factors may act in two ways. First, as is often suggested, mothers are able to eliminate or discourage the occurrence of specific facial expressions; that is, by being positive in their interactions and responsivity to positive infant emotions and nonresponsive to the negative ones they can promote the former and suppress the latter. Exactly what does this mean? Does differential reinforcement lead to the reduction of negative emotional facial patterns or to their elimination? Clearly the action patterns such as sadness are not eliminated by reinforcement even though it is possible to socialize the crying response. For example, the sayings "Boys don't cry" or "Big boys don't cry" are used to get boys not to cry; however, these sayings may not eliminate other aspects of the sadness action pattern. On the other hand, if mothers display more positive emotions to their children, the children may be placed in positive situations where not only negative expression is reduced, like crying because they are sad, but the positive parental behavior itself may lead to a positive action pattern in the child.

Once we understand the complexity of an action pattern, facial expression being just one feature, we need to remember that the socialization of this feature may have an impact on the other expressions in the action pattern. Does socialization of one feature of an action pattern affect the entire pattern? Even though there is only limited support for the idea, the possibility exists that affecting one aspect of the action pattern can alter the whole pattern itself. That is, if one smiles even though one is sad, the smiling behavior through a feedback system can change the entire sad pattern. Physiological changes involving the facial musculature, acting on the vagus nerve, can alter the physiology, a theory proposed by Stephen Porges.[43] An alternate explanation is related to the effect of altering the child's facial expression, which then changes other people's behavior toward him. Smiling when sad alters how people regard him, which may alter their response, which alters his action pattern. Finally, by her pretending she is happy when sad, it is possible for her to alter how she thinks about herself and in this way alter the action pattern. In a similar manner, the child can have ideas about sadness, situations that elicit it, and how she is feeling. As such she can act sad even though she is not sad.

This ability to alter features of an action pattern to either suppress or enhance it leads to other problems. What happens when one aspect of the action pattern is socialized while another is not? This has to occur frequently since while facial expression and bodily attributes are visible to the caregiver other parts of the action pattern are not. Because they are not visible any effect on them would be through their interaction with the visible ones. A particular example is the relation between the facial and vocal aspects of distress and the stress hormone cortisol, which is not visible to the caregiver. As I have already mentioned, mothers' ratings of temperament and their infants' behavioral and cortisol stress responses to inoculation showed that there was a small but significant positive association between mothers' report of temperament and the infants' behavioral response to the pain, but little association between the mothers' report and the infants' cortisol response. Obviously, what we cannot see we cannot directly influence.[44]

More central to the issue of socialization of complex action patterns is the question of what happens to aspects of the pattern that are not socialized. Two possibilities exist: first, where the socialization of one alters the others, and second, where the socialization of one aspect has no effect on the other. In both cases, however, the complete action pattern is altered. Some observations of infant behavior may shed light on this question, although more research needs to be done. The first observation involves the infant's response to a stranger, which differs depending on the context in which the stranger appears. If the infant is in a high chair, the infant mostly shows fearfulness or wariness in the face. However, when the same infant is on the floor, the fear action pattern toward the stranger is seen mostly in body movement away from the stranger as the infant moves toward the mother. While the infant moves away there is little facial expression—in fact, looking at the stranger increases. Eliciting events that are produced by the caregiver need to be considered as part of the socialization practices that can affect different aspects of an action pattern.

A more direct example of differential socialization of different aspects of an action pattern involves looking at both outside- and inside-the-body responses that make up the pattern. We can do this by looking at such outside aspects as crying and bodily activity to inoculation and at the same time to the inside aspect of the pattern, such as cortisol stress response. To explore this form of action pattern, Japanese and American babies' response to inoculation was examined. Given the evidence that Japanese infants show less visible distress compared to European-American infants, did they differ in their cortisol stress response? My Japanese colleague Kiyobumi Kawakami and I found that while Japanese infants showed less visible signs of distress they showed significantly greater cortisol response than the American babies.[45] One conclusion of these findings, which is consistent with other results, is that the suppression of one aspect of an action pattern can lead to the increased use of another aspect. This can be seen in the negative association between facial and cortisol reaction for the Japanese babies and the positive association for the American babies. In fact, some recent data on children undergoing suturing procedures for cuts indicate that those who show the most facial, vocal, and bodily distress show little cortisol reaction while those who show the least distress show the highest levels of cortisol. Some researchers have considered individual differences in the visible distress–physiological association to be indicative of affect expressors and repressors. In our own work they were called Cry Babies and Stoics. These differences in how individual children respond internally or externally may have an important association with disease, with external responders showing more cardiovascular problems while internal responders show more strokes.[46]

To summarize the work on the socialization of action patterns, including facial and physiological responses, is not easily done. However, certain facts seem reasonable given the data:

1. At the beginning of life, the adaptive evolutionary-evolved action patterns are complex, with only those aspects of the patterns that are visible to the culture being able to be socialized, those being the facial, vocal, and bodily aspects of the action pattern.
2. The relative effects of socialization and/or temperament on the early action patterns are yet to be determined, but there is strong evidence

to support the proposition that young children's emotions are heavily influenced by their temperament. If anything, parental socialization practices that respond to these differences are most successful.

3. The elicitors of these action patterns have a developmental course for our species. While literal physical events elicit the early action patterns, the development of cognitive capacity allows for ideas as well to become the elicitors of these patterns. At the same time, ideas about the self and ideas about the self in relation to others result in a new set of action patterns that we have called the self-conscious emotions.

4. The child, as an active participant in his own development, uses the socialization practices of his own family and the wider culture as a guide to affect his own behavior. It may also be the case that parental and cultural standards, rules, and goals (SRGs) are relatively successful in altering innate action patterns, enhancing or suppressing features of them depending on parental and cultural rewards and punishments. I prefer, however, to think in terms of the social learning theory idea, namely, socialization must include the child's knowledge of the SRGs of others as well as his knowledge about his own and others' action patterns and eliciting events, all of which the child uses to conform to the social rules of those around him.

Experience and Socialization

The final feature of emotional life is emotional experiences. When we speak of "experience" I hope I have been clear in indicating that there is little socialization involved in the ability to experience oneself. Self-consciousness, or the idea of "me," arises as a function of the maturation of the brain. While elaborate theorizing on the role of socialization in this capacity exists, it is clear that these theories have more to do with the content of the self-consciousness, the "aboutness" of it, than the capacity to experience oneself. Certainly, this appears to be true about self-referential behavior. In all of our studies of toddlers' recognition of themselves in mirrors, we have not been able to get children who do not initially show self-recognition by touching their marked noses to do so, despite our efforts get them to attend to the mark, including getting them to put marks on the experimenters' nose, showing them the red on the experimenters' nose, and even getting them to touch the experimenters' nose. But even after such training, we have not succeeded at persuading the child to touch her own nose when she sees it in the mirror. Such findings as these, as well as work on brain maturation, leads to the belief that the process of acquiring consciousness has relatively little to do with socialization. In fact, there is little evidence linking maternal behavior to self-recognition.[47]

This is not so for the features of the self, the aboutness of me. The study of the self-conscious emotions reveals elaborate socialization regarding how the child thinks about herself. Socialization affects the self-attributions, or ways of thinking about oneself, as has been my claim along with others like Bernard Weiner and Carol Dweck.[48] The SRGs of a society are clearly a feature of how we view ourselves since these SRGs tell us how to behave, think, and feel, and affect how we think about ourselves in terms of success or failure. Clearly SRGs vary by culture, historic time, and individual families. They may also vary by sex. Children by 3 years of age already show that they have acquired some of these SRGs. However, with development more of these SRGs are learned and can be observed. Also, with increased intellectual capacity, children are able to generate SRGs for themselves. Socialization practices can produce too high or too low a set of SRGs. Overachieving parents may set goals and standards too high, and underachieving too low. The consequences of these different levels of SRG's have been suggested; however, it remains unclear whether it is the level of SRGs, their nature, or the punishment or praise they elicit that is the cause of difficulties for the child.

A second aspect of the child's evaluation of herself is whether the child thinks about herself as responsible or not responsible for her actions. Steven Alessandri and I looked at what parents say to young children when they are involved in solving a task. Some parents tend to attribute the child's success or failure to forces outside the child. When the task was to toss a ball into a net, one parent said to her 3-year-old daughter when she failed, "The rim [of the basket] is too small, you can't get the ball in." Such parental statements inform the child that her failure is not related to what she is trying to do but to the nature of the task. Another parent remarked to his son, "You have to practice more to get the ball in," and still another to her daughter, "You're not trying hard enough; try harder and you'll do better." These second examples are intended to focus the child on her own efforts to achieve success and inform her about internal or external self-attributions. There may be sex differences in this socialization task, with girls more likely to see their failure as their own fault while boys do not.[49]

Another self-attribution that is known to be open to socialization is what has been called specific and global attributions or performance and task orientation. There are some socialization data on this attribution, both on biological influences and on socialization ones. The literature on the socialization of guilt can be used as a guide.[50] Parental practices also seem to affect the amount of guilt shown. For example, depressed mothers are likely to blame themselves for their problems, and so these women are likely to make global evaluations of failure to be about themselves and about their children. The children also receive more punishment in the form of love withdrawal and are likely to assume the blame for their parents' problems. It is possible to generalize from these findings, and conclude that parents with all sorts of problems, including alcoholism, drug addiction, fighting or strife with the marital partner, initially produce empathic-like behavior in their children. A child's failure in helping his parent is likely to produce more global attribution about himself. There also is evidence that adults' use of global attributions about the child's behavior may lead to the child's use of global attributions. For example, if a mother says of her daughter's failure "You are not smart," she is doing two things: one, blaming the daughter by making an internal blame statement, and two, making a global self-statement of failure.

I have suggested that the causes of these self-conscious emotions are to be found in the socialization of the child, more specifically in what parents say and do to their children. It is these behaviors that create the self-attributions. Parental language has a strong effect on the child; however, certain parental behaviors above and beyond what they say may have equally profound effects on the child's self-attributions, which in turn affect his emotional life. What I am suggesting is the possibility of acting on the child's self-attributions through parental practices that are not necessarily verbal. Such parental behaviors as humiliation, love withdrawal, and the expression of disgust and contempt may elicit negative self-attributions in the child, and with them the accompanying action patterns associated with shame and guilt.[51] While what parents say to their children elicits the self-conscious emotions, what parents do also elicits these emotions. For example, Hermann Hesse, in "A Child's Heart," writes,

> Would not God find a way out, some superior deception such as the grown-ups . . . , producing one more trump card at the last moment, shaming me after all, not taking me seriously, humiliating me under the damnable mask of kindness.

Parents often humiliate their children under the guise of teasing or teaching them.[52]

Still another example of nonverbal action is the use of contempt, which often occurs without any words being said. Middle-class parents are often pleased with themselves for not using physical punishment; however, they use other techniques including power assertion and love withdrawal. They also use contempt and disgust, which have very similar facial aspects. We frequently observe that contempt and disgust are used as markers of their displeasure. Parents make disgust faces and often accompany them by saying, "That's disgusting" or even "You disgust me." The disgust or contempt face is often used as a means of punishment. It is a very powerful tool in human interactions; for example, as John Gottman has observed, disgust and contempt are overused in marriages that are in trouble.[53]

Finally the use of love withdrawal as a technique to socialize children's emotions needs mentioning. The withdrawal of love as a precipitating event for interpersonal difficulties has received considerable attention from object relations and attachment theorists. Love withdrawal can represent a serious biological loss for the child. More directly relevant is Bowlby's belief that "the model of the attachment figure and the model of the self [self-attributions] are likely to develop so as to be complementary and confirming. Thus, an unwanted [unloved] child is likely not only to feel unwanted . . . but that he is essentially unwantable."[54] That certainly would be a global, negative internal self-attribution, leading in all likelihood to shame and even rage.

While we have been talking about the elicitors and the self-attributions that produce the self-conscious emotions, we have not considered how socialization might affect the experience of the action patterns. This topic has received too little attention and very little research. What does seem reasonable is the idea that socialization can affect how and what we think about our emotions. Parents, through their labeling behavior as well as their responses, may affect the child's experience of his action patterns. For example, we have found that some parents label their child's behavior as indicative of being angry while the same behavior in another child is not so labeled. As Michalson and I have shown, the parent who labels the child's behaviors as anger subsequently has a child who is more angry, while the parent who does not label similar behaviors as anger does not subsequently have an angry child. Thus, how parents interpret and react to their child's action patterns may not only affect the action pattern but the child's experience of his own action patterns.[55]

I have already mentioned cultural differences in labeling behavior, for example, American mothers being more likely to interpret their baby's behaviors as angry than do Japanese mothers. It is also the case that cultures differ in how they interpret children's behaviors. Although American mothers are more likely to interpret child behaviors in emotional terms such as sad or depressed, Chinese mothers are more likely to interpret similar behaviors in physical terms such as the child is tired. The somatization of behaviors, rather than considering them as indexes of emotion, can affect the way the child will experience her behavior.[56] Finally, our ability to change how we feel has to be affected by our social experiences. If, for example, I choose not to feel ashamed by assigning blame or responsibility to others, this flexible ability to alter my experience has to be a function of my attributional system, which is socialized, as well as of other social rules learned through such processes as modeling or indirect learning.

* * *

That socialization plays an important role in the ideas that ultimately elicit the action patterns and thoughts we call emotion cannot be in doubt. Unfortunately, too little is still known about how this comes about, nor do we have enough knowledge about how cultural values are conveyed by parental practices that in turn affect children's ideas and behaviors. We also know relatively little about how the child's knowledge about the SRGs of the family and the larger culture affects the child's ideas as well as her emotional life. What we do know, however, is that the model of a passive child being "shaped" by the actions of her caregiver is a too limited view of the socialization process. Clearly the child is an active and reciprocal member of the socialization process. We also know relatively little about how the temperament characteristics of the child and parent interact, which affects the child's emotional development. We do know that the study of the temperament–socialization interactive process only now is beginning to attract attention, as is our understanding of its role.[57]

Perhaps most important we have little information on how earlier emotional behavior affects later development. I have spent years studying the problem of development, and I think it is safe to say that the belief in the continuity of earlier behavior and individual differences in it are likely not to be seen later unless the environment in which the child becomes the adult remains relatively constant. Even so, the movement from the parent–child cauldron of emotional behavior to that of the child–peer presents new challenges as well as opportunities for change.

CHAPTER 11

Emotional Development
Gone Awry

Having discussed in detail a theory of emotional development in which maturation, temperament, and socialization all play a role, it becomes important now to consider development gone awry. Such a discussion by necessity has to contain some of the material that we have presented earlier, so if some redundancies occur we do so only to set the stage for the discussion of atypical development and what we know about related issues. However, we will avoid the discussion of socialization within the limits we deem normal, discussing only atypical socialization. The elaboration of the theory of the emergence of consciousness as self-referential behavior has allowed us to consider such difficulties associated with its delay or loss, in particular, autism. The same can be said for some of the studies that my colleagues and I—in particular, David Bennett, Margaret Sullivan, Jason Gold, and Candice Feiring—have undertaken in examining the effects of maltreatment, including sexual abuse, on children's emotional life.

Psychopathology and its development have received considerable attention. The theories of Freud and Bowlby, as well as those of others, have been used to describe emotional behavior and its development. These theories, although they are related to emotion and use emotion as the content of interactions with the social world, are not strictly speaking theories of emotional development although they do try to discuss individual differences as they relate to psychopathology. The individual differences they discuss are about enduring emotions, thus, for example, how the loss of the mother, or how having an insecure attachment to the mother, affects the child's depression. Here I think of Bowlby's biography of Darwin, in which he attributes Darwin's lifelong struggle with somatic complaints to his loss of his mother when he was a young child.[1]

The purpose of this chapter is not to reiterate Freud and Bowlby's theories and their schools of thought. Rather, it is to show that a variety of types of atypical development affect the very process of emotional life. Our interest in atypical development includes biologically based causes and how harsh socialization practices, associated with abuse and neglect, impact on children's emotions by affecting their ideas about themselves.

In order to develop a theory of emotional development, we focus on the atypical development of these emotions rather than just on individual differences. One of the central ideas of this book is that all of us develop all the same emotions, and we do so as a species. What we want to argue is that there is a distribution of these emotions among our species; that is, there is a normal range for each one, and it is at the ends of the range where pathology can be located. While the distribution of the early emotions is determined largely by biological differences, some of which have been called temperament, individual differences in the self-conscious emotions are determined largely by the socialization practices of the family and culture.

To begin our consideration of emotions gone awry we need to return to the specific features of an emotion: elicitors, action patterns including expression, and experience. As we have already shown, there is only a loose connection between them.[2]

The dissemblance between elicitors, action patterns including expressions, and experience can itself lead to psychopathology. Clinically we have no difficulty in talking about patients being angry and yet not experiencing their anger; that is, the patient does not know that she is angry. Part of the clinician's task is to make explicit what is the patient's state. The loose connection between experience and expression, like the connection between expression and action pattern, continues through most of our lives and in general is not in itself pathological. While this topic is of inherent interest, we now turn to sources of pathological development in the early emotions and in the development of consciousness and the self-conscious emotions. Each of these contains many possible ways of going awry.

EARLY EMOTIONS AND PATHOLOGY

The first phase of emotional development has to with the primary action patterns, those we have called sadness, fear, interest, disgust, joy, and anger. I have agreed with Darwin's view that these action patterns are evolutionarily adaptive and have evolved to allow for particular actions to take place in particular situations. As we have tried to show, an action pattern of anger on the face, in bodily movements, and in physiological responses is an approach pattern evolved to overcome obstacles that prevent the infant from reaching a desired goal. Fear, as a withdrawal pattern, is an action pattern arising out of situations of uncertainty or of prewired dangerous events like snakes, which evolved to alert the organism to attend to surrounding changes and prepare it for flight. Sadness, a withdrawal pattern, is an action pattern in response to loss. Joy, an approach action pattern, is designed to bring one closer to people and objects that give pleasure. Finally, disgust, a withdrawal action pattern, is designed to rid the mouth of unpleasant smells and tastes. These action patterns involve facial, bodily, and physiological responses and are organized around specific contexts. Let us turn to atypical expression findings since there are data here that may be of use to our discussion.

Some studies of people who are blind suggest that sight-challenged people have no difficulty in voluntarily producing facial expressions.[3] Clearly the production of spontaneous facial expressions does not appear dependent on observational learning. Nevertheless, sight-impaired children's facial expressions deviate from the typical, and there is evidence to suggest that the lack of readability of expressions does affect a mother's behavior toward her child.[4]

Pathology can be seen in these action pattern–situation associations in several ways. To begin, if the facial component of the action pattern is not visible or comprehendible to caregivers, appropriate caregiver responses cannot occur. Lack of a facial component may lead to pathology by affecting the action pattern itself and/or by affecting how the caregiver responds to the infant. As an example of this type of problem we can look at children with cerebral palsy or with Down syndrome. In both clinical examples the neuromusculature of the face may be distorted, preventing that aspect of the action pattern from being produced. If the proprioceptive feedback from the facial neuromusculature is reduced or absent, as both Silvan Tomkins and Jaak Panksepp have argued, this is likely to result in a weaker action pattern since some features of that pattern are absent. The feedback for the proper development of the action pattern is necessary. For example, there is some evidence that the facial expression of fear may lead to more fear and the loss of such neuromuscular feedback can result in less fear. Children with Down syndrome are reported to have different emotional reactions to stimuli that elicit laughter and joy than typically developed children because of their somewhat placid behavior. As a consequence, these children need more stimulation to elicit laughter.[5]

The second difficulty in atypical development has to do with the caregiver's ability to read and react appropriately to the infant's expressive behavior. Some studies support the idea that the failure of the expressive aspect of an emotion, whether through physical, cognitive, or temperamental characteristics, will affect the caregiver–child interaction and the ability to coordinate their behavior, as well as affect the growing attachment relationship.[6]

Another example of development gone awry is the disruption of the association between an action pattern and a particular context. Atypical development here can refer to a child's disposition to approach or avoid stimuli, a characteristic we consider to represent a temperament difference. Some infants with unusual temperaments are likely to react in ways that are inconsistent with the evolutionary adaptive action pattern–context pairing. Thus, an infant with a difficult temperament, and therefore having a low threshold of reactivity, may not have the typical action patterns of expression to a particular elicitor because the elicitor for them is too overwhelming, which might not be the case for an infant with a high reactivity threshold. We have seen that an easily upset infant is less able to respond to strong positive elicitors and therefore is likely to produce a more deviant action pattern than an infant who is not easily upset. We have all observed adults who when laughing too much suddenly begin to cry, and some infants' reaction to tickling become aversive after having initially been pleasurable.

We have reported on this extreme behavior in Chapter 4 when we examined infants' response to a blocked goal. While 10–15% of the infants showed a withdrawal response, 85–90% showed an approach response. Our data show that 2-month-old infants who exhibited withdrawal behaviors to the goal blockage are the same children who showed temper tantrums when they were frustrated in other situations. Such a finding indicates that a large number of these 10–15% of infants who show withdrawal to a blocked goal may be dysregulated.[7] The cause of these individual differences in early action patterns to a blocked goal remains unknown. There is reason to believe that the infant prone to giving up may have differences in serotonin uptake genes and may be more likely under subsequent environmental conditions to be subject to depression.

While we have not fully explored other early action patterns and their relation to particular contexts, we have observed that lack of joy to the appearance of desired objects, or high disgust as a means of the infants ridding themselves of distasteful food, also show a range of individual differences, with some infants overreacting or being too placid.[8] These individual differences, at odds with the adaptive action patterns showed by the majority of infants, suggest the presence of potentially pathological conditions. For example, infants differ in their disgust response to sour tastes, with some showing extreme disgust. These early extreme disgust faces may be indicative of later phobias around contamination.[9] In the case of fear of the stranger, ample evidence suggests individual differences, some of which may be pathological. If our analysis is correct, infants showing extreme fear of a stranger may be at risk for not being able to explore new situations including people since they are overcome by their caution. Indeed, the work on inhibited infants and children suggest just such difficulties.[10] What is important to keep in mind is that while any particular action pattern may be adaptive, extreme forms of the pattern may be an indication of maladaptive behavior. That is, we should expect that action patterns that are absent, extreme, or inappropriate represent individual differences that may result in pathology. While the literature on the negative consequences of difficult temperament is extensive, a recent meta-analysis of the effect of problems in early emotional regulation shows that it is related to subsequent behavioral problems, in particular feeding, sleeping, and crying behavior. Besides the expression of these early action patterns, such studies suggest that their regulation also needs to be considered.[11] As the discussion of temperament made clear, problems in temperament, including threshold of response, as well as the inhibition of a response once it does occur, may play an important role in the individual differences in these action patterns as they are related to particular contexts.

PATHOLOGY IN THE DEVELOPMENT OF CONSCIOUSNESS

The next major milestone in the development of emotional life is the rise of consciousness. Here, the likelihood of development going awry is considerable. As we have already discussed in Chapters 5 and 6 on consciousness, the infant in the second half of the second year of life develops a mental representation of "me." Thus a mental age of 15 to 18 months is necessary for its occurrence. This representation is likely supported by brain maturation as well as by socialization practices. Mental retardation of any sort is likely to delay the emergence of this mental representation. For example, children with Down syndrome need a mental age of 15 to 18 months, regardless of their chronological age, in order to develop a mental representation of themselves. While delays in other areas of functioning accompany the chromosomal abnormality in these children, the mental retardation aspect is clearly related to their ability to develop a mental representation of themselves.[12]

Emotional development gone awry around the problem of a mental representation of the self can also be seen in the research involving children with autism spectrum disorders (ASD). Part of the failure of these children to develop normally is that their self-representation ability is seriously delayed and impaired, resulting in many difficulties including their inability to develop a theory of mind. Therefore they have problems with intersocial behavior like empathy or sharing. We will not repeat what was discussed in the chapters on consciousness but rather examine how this feature goes awry. My colleague Dennis Carmody and I have studied the problem by looking at ASD using measures of self-representation that include mirror recognition, personal pronoun use, and other-directed pretend play. We have shown that these self-referential abilities are related to the maturation of the left hemisphere of the brain, specifically the left temporal area, as well as an overdevelopment of some frontal regions.[13]

The development of self-representation in children with ASD occurs either long after it appears in typically developing children or not at all. There is relatively little evidence on this issue, but that evidence that does exist shows that personal pronoun usage and pretend play involving others is also either delayed or absent. Self-recognition in mirrors has been the most studied. In children with ASD, self-recognition is absent for the most part by 2 years when typically developing children show this ability. It does emerge for some children at later ages, around 4 to 6 years. Those who do not show it have been shown to be the most severely affected by ASD.

That self-representation emerges later has been used to suggest that the lack of self-representation in children with ASD is a function of mental age. For example, Dawson and McKissick, in comparing mirror self-recognition in children with and without ASD, make such a suggestion. However, mental age alone cannot account for the failure to recognize oneself in the mirror. For example, in one study it was found that the mirror self-recognizers had an average mental age of 38 months while nonrecognizers had an average mental age of 22 months. Given repeated demonstrations that show that 80% of typically developing children with a mental age of 21 months show self-recognition, the failure of the subjects to show self-recognition with an average mental age of 22 months does not support the idea that mental age alone accounts for this effect.[14]

Recently we have studied 4-year-old children with ASD and looked at mental age as well as other deficits in communication and social skills, and compared them to typical 2-year-olds. We found that while 100% of typically developing 2-year-old children have mirror recognition, only about half of the children with ASD show it. Moreover, while the great majority of typically developing children show pretend play that involves another, only one-third of children with ASD show this skill. When we examine the children's self-referential deficits, their mental age, and their deficits in communication and social interaction, we find that social skill deficits are the major factor associated with failure to develop a mental representation of the self, not mental age, either alone or in interaction. Clearly mental age is unlikely to account for the deficiencies in children with ASD.[15]

These results address two questions in regard to development gone awry. First, mental age is important in terms of the emergence of the mental representation of "me." It plays a role in typical development, as well as in the development of children with deficits such as Down syndrome, in that one needs a mental age of at least 15 to 18 months for the representation of "me" to emerge. It also plays some role in children with ASD; however, it does not appear to be a major factor. Our findings, as well as those of others, implicate deficits in social skills, for example, in social referencing. Hobson and colleagues believe that the problems of children with ASD are related to poor social interactions. That is, ASD is caused by impoverished experiences of the child in relation to others. It is this early impoverishment that leads to failure in developing self-recognition. This belief is consistent with the idea that self-recognition and consciousness are a function of social experience, something for which there is little supporting evidence.[16]

Because autism presents such a good example of what may occur in the failure of self-representation, we continue to explore the problem by not only observing social deficits but observing brain maturation in these children. Brain-imaging studies of children with autism have revealed atypical growth patterns in the brain relative to the brains of typically developing children. For example, by 2 or 3 years of age, autistic boys have brain volumes larger than average in the cerebrum and cerebellum. This early excessive growth fails to be sustained, however, as the pace of growth for the brains of autistic boys falls significantly below normal development in middle childhood.[17] Not only are these overall differences indicative of different brains in the children with autism relative to those with typical development, but specific brain region differences also have been found. There is some evidence that the frontal lobes are different in children with autism. Remember that we also found that the temporal lobes and some frontal regions are associated with self-referential ability in typical development.[18]

Studying brain region development in children with ASD, Carmody and I used similar MRI procedures as in our earlier studies. We studied myelination differences by region, looking at the medial frontal cortex, the temporal parietal junction, and the temporal poles. Data based on typically developing children served as a reference for age-expected values of maturation for each region. The results showed that for both the left and the right medial frontal cortex, children with ASD showed significant greater maturation than the typically developing children. However, the left temporal parietal junction of the children with ASD showed significant less maturation relative to the typically developing group. The right temporal parietal junction showed no group differences. These data support our contention that children with ASD show specific brain region maturation differences relative to the children without ASD such that the children with ASD show maturation in the frontal region, which is overdeveloped, while they show underdevelopment in the left temporal parietal junction.

These findings of overdevelopment in the medial frontal cortex complement the reports of deviant growth in the frontal region as reported by others.[19] The underdevelopment in the left temporal parietal junction in children with autism is of interest given the relation of this region with the emergence of self-representation and consciousness. These brain regions that show over- and underdevelopment in the autism group are those involved in various tasks of self-representation and the self in comparison to others.[20] More recently we compared the scores on self-referential behavior with some selected brain region volumes in children with ASD and found a significant association with the left temporal pole, the left temporal cortex, and the left medial prefrontal cortex, such that the greater the volume of white matter, the lower the self-referential scores.[21] This demonstration in children with ASD of the relation between the left temporal region with self-recognition, personal pronouns, and pretend play adds further support for the brain maturation hypothesis. The findings that overdevelopment in the frontal regions, accompanied by underdevelopment in the left temporal parietal region, suggests that autism is not a generalized delay of brain maturation, but rather a variation in the timing of maturation that is specific to regions related to consciousness.

Asperger syndrome is considered to be part of ASD, although some have questioned this classification. The chief features of Asperger syndrome are, one, that it can occur in children with normal or even superior intelligence, and two, that it involves deficits in social and emotional behavior. This seems related to the uses of consciousness, as discussed in Chapter 6. It is not a problem in the development of self-recognition, pretend play, and personal pronouns, which appear in children with Asperger syndrome on schedule. Their social and emotional behavior deficit consists of an inability to place themselves in the mind of the other. This failure often takes the form of not knowing what to do socially, which seems to be intuitive in typically developing children. One particular failure is in eye-to-eye contact and the social rules that govern what typically developing children learn or have procedural rules for. These include, for example, knowing that when you talk to another, it is a general rule to look at the other. One teenage child with Asperger and high IQ asked me in clinic, "What is the difference between looking and staring?" He wanted to know how long can you look at another before it becomes a stare. Explaining that a 1- to 2-second look is not a stare was sufficient information for him. Even with his high IQ he was unable to figure this out for himself, but he could learn to do it when instructed.

Another area of deficits is in intuitively knowing about what emotions are likely to occur in what situations and thus what emotion should be expected. Inappropriate expressions often result from the inability to monitor one's own emotions or those of another. Such deficits can and do result in inappropriate emotional behavior, leading to social mismatches. What do these problems have to do with self-representation? As we have seen when we discussed the self-conscious emotions, failures in the self system result in a multitude of problems, in this case, the ability to place oneself in the role of the other, and therefore failures in empathy—to know about what others may know, what they might be thinking of, what their desires are, and in general their inner worlds. That children with Asperger syndrome have facial recognition difficulties is still another problem. The problems of children with Asperger syndrome have little to do with mental age or IQ.

Emotional development gone awry around the development of consciousness has an important impact on the early emotions as well as on the development of the self-conscious emotions. The lack or delay of this development impacts on the early emotional action patterns that we have called the early emotions. Even if these early action patterns themselves have no development gone awry, the delay in consciousness means that the child will have the appropriate action patterns but will not have the appropriate experience of them. The child may be in a state of fear but not experience the fear, since consciousness transforms the action patterns from bodily action into representational realities. Without being able to experience them as a typically developing child, these emotional action patterns are not readily transformed into representations or communicated to others. There can be no real language without the ability to reflect and therefore communicate about oneself either to oneself or to others. Moreover, much of the ability to manipulate emotions by deconstruction, exaggeration, and substitution will be difficult if not impossible.

Without consciousness the child will have difficulty in deceiving himself or others. For example, when we want to appear angrier than we are or to feign surprise or joy, self-reflection is necessary. This is seen in the emotional life of children who do not have a mental age sufficient for consciousness to emerge. A child with Down syndrome, for example, may have the actions associated with joy but not the experiences of their state. Children with ASD may be able to express particular action patterns; however, their inability to experience them properly can result in distortions as well as in dysregulation.

Of particular importance, of course, is the effect of consciousness gone awry on the self-conscious emotions. Here the case is well made by studying children with ASD who show considerable difficulties with these emotions. For example, there is evidence for their developmental failure to show or to recognize such emotions as embarrassment, shame, guilt, and pride in the manner of the typically developing child, even though they do show and recognize happy, anger, and fear faces.

THE SELF-CONSCIOUS EMOTIONS GONE AWRY

The primary emotions show a distribution due to both biological and socialization differences. For the self-conscious emotions, the normal distribution has less to do with biological differences and more to do with socialization factors. Thus in any discussion of the self-conscious emotions gone awry, we return to our interest in socialization factors and the role they play. Since those general factors have been considered in some detail in the discussion of the self-conscious emotions, we will only discuss pathological socialization factors and their impact on them. To begin the discussion, we need to return to their development. As already described, self-conscious emotions imply the development of a mental representation or the idea of me. As Darwin wrote, "The nature of the mental states which induce blushing . . . consist of shyness [what I call embarrassment], shame, and modesty; the essential element in all being *self attention* (italics added)."[22] In order to understand the stimuli that give rise to these self-conscious emotions, the distinction between the early self-conscious emotions, called exposed self-conscious emotions, and the later ones, called the evaluative self-conscious emotions, needs to be made again.

THE EXPOSED SELF-CONSCIOUS EMOTIONS

This class of self-conscious emotions involves, for the most part, the emergence of consciousness, and includes empathy, embarrassment, and jealousy/envy. Atypical development affects each of them.

Empathy

Empathy, by definition, involves the ability of the child to put herself in the role of the other. Recall that we need to distinguish between empathy and contagion. Contagion does not require a mental representation of the self since in contagion the infant's response is automatic, much like the yawn of one person producing a yawn in another. Adult empathy, on the other hand, has the form of "What I know about myself, in terms of my emotions, I also know about you." For example, if I am going to be uneasy in a strange social situation, I can imagine that you too are uneasy in such a situation. The empathic response may not be an accurate one in that what is known about me may not always apply to you. For example, in solving Piagetian perspective-taking tasks, very young children either (1) lack the ability to take the perspective of another (i.e., they take their own perspective); (2) they do not take their own perspective, but they do not correctly identify the perspective of the other; or (3) they do not take their own perspective and correctly identify the perspective of another. The developmental pattern is from 1 to 3.

While effects of socialization are many, the emergence of empathy, not contagion, seems to be a function of the emergence of a self-representation, which leads to mentalism—the idea that you may be like me.

Empathy gone awry may be a function of socialization. Martin Hoffman claims that parental empathic responses model empathy for children, and that individual differences in empathy are largely a function of this type of socialization. This view of socialization is captured by the idea that if we are responsive to our children, we will teach the children to be responsive to others. Thus, a lack of empathy or overuse of empathy as pathology is socialized. The data on socialization of empathy are mixed and certainly our own experiences with children should alert us to child–parent conflict where our responsiveness is not necessarily reciprocated.[23]

Excluding socialization practices for the moment, let us consider that too little empathy and too much are both problems in emotions gone awry. Someone with little empathy has serious interpersonal problems; individuals with Asperger syndrome are an example of this problem in which normal or above-normal intelligent people have trouble with putting themselves in the role of the other. Too much empathy can also cause interpersonal problems. Empathic distress occurs for two reasons: to reduce the other's distress and/or to reduce one's own stress caused by the other's distress. Empathic distress caused by one's own distress at another's distress often leads to maladaptive behavior. Consider parents' concern about their child's distress about not having a job. Parental behavior and advice as a function of their own distress is likely to lead to maladaptive behavior, whereas trying to relieve the distress of the child leads to constructive problem solving.[24] What, besides these factors, might account for differences in empathy? Following Eysenck, we have talked about sociability as a temperament factor that should be related to empathy, much like the child with Asperger syndrome.[25] Without more study, pathology with respect to the development of empathy remains largely unknown.

Embarrassment over Exposure

Embarrassment, of all the early self-conscious exposed emotions, has been the most studied. As we have already discussed, there are two kinds of embarrassment. First, there is exposure embarrassment, which emerges early and is directly related to the emergence of a self-representation. As Darwin noted, exposure embarrassment is caused by the perception of other people's attention. Individual differences in the perception of being the object of other's attention and in the response to that perception are likely to be caused more by biological than by socialization factors. The second kind of embarrassment is embarrassment due to a failed standard. Exposure embarrassment gone awry can occur if self-representation is delayed, as in the case of the child with ASD.

Here, we want to focus on the overexpression of embarrassment. Darwin, who used blushing as a measure of embarrassment, noted large individual differences in response to being the object of another's attention.

Overexpressions of exposure embarrassment may be related to temperament differences. Exposure embarrassment is the emotional response to what has been called shyness or inhibition. For example, Izard considered shyness to be sheepishness, bashfulness, a feeling of uneasiness or psychological discomfort in social situations, an oscillation between fear and interest or between avoidance and approach. In his description, shyness is related to fear and is a nonevaluative emotion centered around the individual's discomfort with others.

Such a description fits Arnold Buss's notion of shyness as an emotional response that is elicited by experiences of conspicuousness. For Buss, shyness and fear are closely related and represent fearfulness toward others. Shyness is readily distinguished from shame in that it appears much earlier than either shame or guilt and has a different behavioral profile.[26] Such an approach to shyness seems reasonable because it fits with other notions relating the self to others, or what we might call the "social self," and is likely related to sociability. Earlier we tried to explain that the elicitor of children's exposure embarrassment is being the object of others' attention. In our studies of exposure embarrassment we have shown that it emerges at the same time as self-representation and that individual differences in exposure embarrassment are associated with difficult temperaments, as measured by maternal report, HR variability changes, and stress cortisol responses. An example of this extreme embarrassment shows this to be the case.[27]

> By the age of 15 months, Toby was extremely fearful of strangers, and was classified as a difficult temperament child, not easily soothed, and a difficult sleeper who could not tolerate being the object of others' attention. She was intolerant of birthdays or events where she was celebrated because as the center of attention, she found such occasions aversive. She could make friends but only one at a time and if her older brother laughed or cried too loud she would flee because she would be in the circle of the attention of others.

Taking these kinds of clinical observations into the laboratory we conducted a series of studies looking at four kinds of situations that might elicit exposure embarrassment. Asking the child to dance, complimenting the child, watching the child look at herself in a mirror, and pointing to the child resulted in the child's discomfort, with the highly embarrassed toddlers showing embarrassment across all the tasks.

Of particular interest in pathological embarrassment was having both the child's mother and the experimenter point to the child and say her name. As a prerequisite the toddler had to recognize herself in the mirror. If the toddler did show self-recognition, she was likely to respond to being pointed to and looked at with embarrassment. While individual differences in embarrassment were evident, related to maternal ratings of difficult temperament, there were some extreme cases. In three cases out of the 20 toddlers we observed, rather than just showing embarrassment to being pointed at and named, they began to cry and had to be consoled by their mothers. These toddlers turned out to be socially isolated, did not like to play in groups, and showed inhibited behavior in social situations like play groups.[28]

In trying to understand these individual differences in embarrassment my colleagues and I have looked at temperament differences as they might relate to embarrassment differences. We found that children who showed self-recognition and were classified as having difficult temperaments, according to both maternal ratings and physiological differences, were over three and a half times more likely to show embarrassment than those not labeled difficult. No differences were found related to maternal behaviors toward the children, however; on the other hand, most infants who showed a high stress hormone response to pain in the first year of life were subsequently more likely to show earlier self-recognition and more importantly to show high levels of embarrassment to exposure events as described above.[29] We would conclude from this evidence that exposure embarrassment gone awry is likely due to biological differences.

Jealousy

Jealousy is another of the exposed self-conscious emotions that has received some attention. However there are few studies on pathological jealousy, although differences between extreme and normal forms of jealousy do exist. Jealousy pertains to wanting what someone else has, while envy pertains to wanting something one does not have. Both terms are often used interchangeably. As with the other exposure, self-conscious emotion, jealousy requires a self-representation. While some have called infant behavior before self-representation development jealousy, it may be a protojealousy, having more to do with protest over loss. The behaviors described when the infant's mother turns her attention away from the child and toward a doll are more protest in nature but may be perceived as jealousy/envy by the mother and those adults observing the scene. This same type of protest behavior can be seen when the mother leaves the child alone in a playroom or when the child is separated from the mother by a barrier. Thus, similar to contagion as the early manifestation of empathy, protest may be the early manifestation of jealousy. Although Sybil Hart reports wide individual child differences, there is little evidence for extreme cases of jealousy. There certainly are clinical reports about parents afraid of leaving their very young infants alone with a toddler sibling for fear the toddler, jealous of the attention the newborn is getting, may harm him. Although there are only clinical suggestions, there is reason to believe that some toddlers exhibit extreme jealousy/envy that may have pathological consequences.[30]

In summary, the early exposed self-conscious emotions that have gone awry have for the most part their origins in the differences of biological action patterns associated with others' distress, as in empathy; focused attention on self, as in embarrassment; and loss of attention, as in jealousy/envy. They can go awry when there is a failure or a delay in self-representations. Moreover, how these differences, which are dispositional or temperamental, are treated by the social environment has an important impact on their development. Sensitive parents, taking these dispositional differences into account, are in some cases able to modify them. Thus while there may be overall little individual consistency in children, toddlers may be relatively unaffected by socialization factors. Identifying the processes between dispositional factors and socialization has yet to be done.

THE EVALUATIVE SELF-CONSCIOUS EMOTIONS

Three points already made need repeating when we discuss the evaluative self-conscious emotions. To begin with, the early action patterns can be measured in facial neuromusculature as well as in bodily and physiological changes. As the emotions become more related to self-representations, they can be observed in bodily actions such as body expansion, as in pride, and in blushing and nervous touching, as in embarrassment, rather than in unique facial patterns. Second, multiple and different elicitors can produce the evaluative emotions since evaluation of success or failure is based on an individual's thoughts about standards, rules, and goals (SRGs). Finally, and perhaps most important, these evaluative self-conscious emotions are produced by ideas rather than by physical stimuli or literal events. These ideas are culturally determined, both within the family through parents, siblings, and kin, and through the larger culture, especially by peers. Thus when we discuss evaluative self-conscious emotions gone awry, by necessity, we must speak more of socializational than dispositional factors as they affect pathology.

Earlier we considered the features of thought that are required to elicit the self-conscious evaluative emotions. Here we will discuss them again only to show how they may go awry. While ways of thinking become the stimulus events that elicit these action patterns, these action patterns of shame and pride themselves are not learned. What is taught is the content or specific ideas that produce these action patterns, and once produced, how to express them. The evolutionary history of our species and their adaptive significance has given rise to the action patterns of shame, guilt, and pride. Moreover, we have shown that these action patterns are species-specific and occur in some form across all cultures. These self-conscious evaluative emotions are as universal as are the early or primary emotions and are part of the species repertoire. When these evaluative self-conscious emotions go awry, they either never occur at all or occur with great frequency or intensity. Their occurrence, either as over- or underuse, becomes the definition of pathology. On the one hand, the person who has never experienced shame is dangerous for he is not limited in what he may do; and on the other hand, if a person has too much shame, there are serious consequences including such pathological conditions as depression and rage. The self system and the self-conscious emotions, and shame pathology in particular, are highly influenced by socialization factors as well as by temperament, although the former seem to be the most associated with these emotions going awry. What, then, are the ways of thinking that are involved in the evaluative self-conscious emotions? Self-conscious evaluative emotions, in addition to consciousness, require other cognitive capacities that were discussed earlier.

In this discussion we consider two issues: how the self-conscious emotions of shame and pride go awry, in terms of maladaptive socialization practices, and how these emotions when they go awry affect the child's social, emotional, and adjustment behavior. To study these two issues with respect to shame we will review how maltreatment, in the form of physical or sexual abuse or neglect, impacts on shame and how high shame and self-attributions affect children's mental health. We will also touch upon stigma and shame and its impact on psychopathology. After considering shame we will briefly turn our attention to guilt and pride where little study has been done. Pride in its more pathological expression as hubris will be considered under the narcissistic disorders.

Shame

In my discussion of maltreatment two major types will be considered: sexual abuse as well as physical abuse and/or neglect. All of these have received both theoretical consideration and empirical study.

Sexual Abuse

Initially Freud considered sexual abuse as the cause of hysteria. However, he soon changed his view, not returning to the connection again.[31] Any kind of abuse, physical or verbal, is likely to lead to attributions about the self and to shame in the child so abused; this is even more the case when there is sexual abuse. These attributions appear to be internal, stable, and global self-views. "This happened because I am a bad person" is the type of thinking about oneself that leads to excessive shame. It seems clear that sexual abuse is likely to lead to shame in the victim and that the shame and the self-attributes are the mediators between the abuse and adjustment, that is, the more shame, the greater the likelihood of poor adjustment.[32] One study of adult women who had been sexually abused during childhood found that the experience of shame was related to the severity of the abuse and to current psychological distress.[33] The traumagenic dynamics of stigmatization around sexual abuse has been linked to shame, but the exact processes have not been explored. However, the literature on shame indicates that the prolonged experience of this emotion leads, in particular, to depression.[34] June Tangney and colleagues have argued that shame-prone individuals may be more vulnerable to depression because of persistent situations in which self-functioning is disrupted, and because the affective experience of shame may contribute to hopelessness.[35]

Problems of dissociation also have been linked to shame. Of interest is the suggestion that sexual abuse may lead to dissociative disorders. It has been suggested that sexual abuse leads to shame in the victim, which leads to dissociation as a defense against this powerfully negative experience. Evidence for the relation between sexual abuse and shame always is evident.[36] Child sexual abuse has been consistently associated with a number of adjustment problems, including depression, posttraumatic stress disorder (PTSD), and poor self-esteem.[37]

The phenomenological experience of shame is a desire to hide the damaged self from others, to disappear, or to die. This is made evident in children who are sexually abused and who display a desire to avoid exposure and to hide themselves when talking about the abuse. Feelings of shame may be heightened by the more severe forms of abuse, such as penetration, and by repeated incidents of abuse. These more severe forms are likely to elicit greater shame as they represent a greater magnitude of transgression from acceptable behavior. Also greater severity may be linked to a sense that the abuse is more uncontrollable, and therefore elicits more shame. Moreover, sexual abuse leads to an increase in self-focus and self-evaluation, making victims more prone to self-conscious emotions, especially those of shame, guilt, and embarrassment. Keep in mind that severity itself affects the level or amount of shame by ways of thinking about the events.

The literature on excessive shame indicates how this emotion can lead to poor adjustment. Because of the negative intensity of the experience of shame, individuals will act to rid themselves of it. However, because shame is a global attack on the self, they have great difficulty in doing so. When shame is excessive, people develop strategies to rid themselves of this feeling, including depression and/or acting-out behaviors.

In order to study this problem we developed a general model that my colleagues and I have applied to a wide variety of traumatic experiences.

In brief, it holds that trauma leads to negative cognitive attributions and shame, which in turn leads to poor adjustment. The model also allows for trauma to directly influence adjustment, although our belief continues to be that the outcomes of trauma are mediated by how the child thinks about the event.

Candice Feiring and I have been able to show the relation among sexual abuse, shame, and adjustment in a longitudinal study of children ages 8 to 15 years who were known to have been sexually abused. We examined the relation between the severity of the sexual abuse, shame, self attribution, and in this case, depression. Our findings indicate that within 6 months of the reported abuse, severity of abuse and amount of shame were both related to depression. However, by 1 year after the reported abuse, only the amount of shame was related to depression. Perhaps more important, children whose experience of shame decreased over the year showed decreases in depression, while children whose shame stayed the same or increased actually showed increases in depression. While no sex differences were reported in this study, gender differences do exist, both in shame-proneness and in manifest psychopathology.[38]

It has been suggested that the need to defend the self against prolonged shame leads to depression in females and rage in males.[39] Females are more likely to experience shame in situations where they perceive they have broken a rule or have not lived up to their own or others' expectations.[40] There is some evidence that shame is more likely in girls because they are more apt to make self-blaming attributions for failure and negative events.[41] Consequently, we expect that abused girls, compared to boys, would be more at risk for shame, a self-blaming attributional style, and the depressive symptoms associated with this style. While we did not find any sex differences in depression, there was some evidence that the boys had more acting-out problems. The lack of outcome measures of aggression and rage in this study meant that we could not examine sex differences when individuals were highly shamed by sexual abuse. However, in another study of children who were maltreated, sex differences as predicted were found.

Physical Abuse and Neglect

The bulk of research on child maltreatment has its theoretical underpinnings in either psychodynamic, sociological, or social learning theories. While all three approaches view child abuse and neglect as multiply determined, they differ substantially in causative emphasis and analysis. However, all of these orientations focus on socialization factors. In the psychodynamic approach, the primary cause of child maltreatment is in the personality disorders of the abusive parent. Investigators have utilized a variety of clinical and standardized testing procedures to delineate the personality characteristics implicated. The resulting lists of traits and typologies have tended to be general, inconclusive, and nondifferentiating. Abusing adults have been variously characterized as immature, impulsive, self-centered, hypersensitive, quick to react with poorly controlled aggression, aimless, psychopathic, antisocial, hostile, passive, dependent, depressed, subject to episodic outburst of loss of control, the need to give nurturance, having intense feelings of self-hatred and worthlessness, and exhibiting a low threshold for frustration.[42]

However, evidence indicates that fewer than 10% of child abusers are diagnosed as mentally ill, and the degree and range of personality disturbance found in abusing parents exist in nonabusing parents as well.[43] The systematic search for personality attributes unique to child abusers has yielded, in fact, only one clear-cut conclusion: that a general defect in character—from whatever source—is present in the abusing parent, allowing aggressive impulses to be expressed too freely. Aggressive parenting behaviors are frequently supported by aggressive childrearing attitudes. Many abusive parents consider physical punishment an appropriate and necessary disciplinary technique. In addition, many have inadequate knowledge of the behaviors and needs that are age-appropriate for their children and hold unrealistic expectations for their performance. Often coupled with misconceptions regarding development is a gross insensitivity to the needs and desires of their children.

Several studies have described a role reversal in abusing and neglecting relations in which the child is treated as an adult and expected to satisfy parental needs for nurturance and good mothering. Moreover, there may exist a general attitude of resentment and rejection toward the child's whole person, or a feeling that the child is unlovable or bad. In such abusing families, one child is selected to be the main or exclusive victim of maltreatment; in most two-parent families, one parent is the active abuser or most obvious neglector, while the other serves to condone the maltreatment by his or her passivity.[44]

The sociological approach defines child maltreatment as a social problem caused by a combination of cultural and socioeconomic factors. The use of force against children in America is seen as a widespread, socially sanctioned childrearing practice embedded in a culture with a tradition of interpersonal violence. As a consequence, child maltreatment exists on two levels in society: the institutional and the familial. It may well be that society as a whole, by permitting millions of children to grow up under conditions of severe deprivation, is a major abuser. On the familial level, studies clearly show that physical punishment is used by parents of all occupations against children of all ages in families at each social-class level.[45] According to the sociological view, what distinguishes the child abuser from the nonabuser is the excessive and inappropriate use of this culturally acceptable disciplinary technique due, in large part, to environmental stresses that increase the strains and frustrations of daily living and weaken mechanisms of self-control. That these stress factors operate with greatest impact and rapidity on the lower socioeconomic classes is a long-held supposition, recently receiving support from demographic studies of child abuse and neglect.[46]

The demographics of abusing and neglecting adults suggest that mothers and younger parents are more likely to be the perpetrators of maltreatment. Family size, as well as the spacing of children within the family, are associated with both abuse and neglect. Abusive families are more likely to be larger, with children born in very close succession. Families headed by females are more likely to be involved in maltreatment. While it remains a belief that abused children make abusing parents, the recent data, controlling for a number of factors, indicate that a history of abuse is an insufficient explanation.[47] While having an abusive experience as a child may produce shame and self-blame when becoming parents, other factors including social learning and perhaps the role of impulse control are more likely factors.

Although blaming the victim is never appropriate, there appear to be child factors that may facilitate child abuse. This suggests that child differences produce the abuse, either from parents, siblings, or peers. For example, maltreatment has been linked to children with difficult temperaments, that is, children who cry excessively, who have feeding disruptions, who make demands for attention, who have toilet-training accidents, who throw temper tantrums, who display irritability, and who manifest unreasonable disobedience are more likely to be abused.[48] Exacerbated by socioeconomic, marital, or personal stresses, the frustrations inherent in raising young children may be potent elicitors of abusive reactions from parents. In those studies in which sex differences have been found, boys are more often reported to be targets of abuse than girls. This may be due to the fact that boys 3 months or younger sleep less and cry and fuss significantly more than girls. Other sex differences in behavior appearing in the preschool years that may have an impact on children's manageability and consequently on child maltreatment include differences in aggression and in compliance, with boys showing more aggression, higher activity levels, and less compliance. Although rates of illegitimacy do not appear to differentiate abused from nonabused children, it is believed that a child resulting from an unplanned or unwanted pregnancy is more likely to be maltreated. In addition, the incidence of prematurity found in samples of abused and neglected children, typically ranging from 22 to 30%, is significantly higher than the 7 to 8% average for the population at large.[49]

Thus, it appears that those infants who are more difficult to care for— who are colicky, irritable, demanding, poor feeders, resistive to physical contact, less adaptable, and hard to satisfy—run an increased risk of being maltreated. The relationship between difficulty in management and child maltreatment continues through childhood, with extremely active, restless, and aggressive children reported to be more vulnerable to abuse and neglect. Kempe and Kempe estimated that 20 to 50% of abused children are significantly neurologically damaged so that they lag behind age mates in language development and the attainment of physical skills, and others have noted the higher incidence of mental retardation, cognitive deficits, and aberrant or defective speech patterns in abused children.[50] By school age, the number of abused and neglected children placed in grades below their age level, in mental institutions, and in special educational classes for the learning-disabled, emotionally disturbed, or mentally retarded is noteworthy. However, the same serious methodological criticisms that can be made of the research aimed at isolating the distinctive personality characteristics of abusive parents apply to an even greater degree to these studies of maltreated children. The lack of representative samples and the failure to use control or comparison groups render these results questionable.

To the problem of deviant parental behavior's effect on emotional life are the additional problems of two types of maltreatment that have been classified as deviant. These are physical abuse and neglect. Furthermore, within the neglect category, some distinctions are made between emotional and maternal neglect. All these types of maltreatment have been found to affect the child's emotional behavior and adjustment. Although there are relatively few studies of comparison, physically abused but not neglected children have a more negative self-representation of themselves including more shame.[51] There is some evidence that physical abuse may be more consistently related to anger and externalizing problems and neglect more related to internalizing problems, although the literature points to a large co-occurrence of abuse and neglect.[50] What, then, is the mechanism that associates maltreatment with increases in the negative self-conscious emotions? Besides the obvious one, namely, the impact on shame and guilt as the consequence of maltreatment on self-attributions, there is also the likelihood that maltreatment disposes the victims to become more vigilant, which means in part that they spend more time thinking about themselves. This overfocus makes them vulnerable to a multitude of problems.

In a series of studies on the emotional lives of abused and neglected children, my colleagues, David Bennett and Margaret Sullivan, and I have looked at mothers' behavior toward their children as a function of the child's gender and of the type of maltreatment the mother had been classified as engaging in. In one study, we found that 4- and 5-year-old maltreated boys showed fewer emotional responses than non-maltreated boys, while for girls, the maltreated girls showed significantly more shame when they failed tasks and less pride when they succeeded in tasks than non-maltreated girls. In a second study, we looked at both physical abuse and neglect and found that for children from 3 to 7 years, neglect rather than physical abuse led to more shame. Moreover, when behavioral problems were examined, it was neglect that predicted more behavioral problems. While there were no gender effects, there was an interesting developmental pattern for the effect of physical abuse. Among younger children, the 3- to 4-four-year olds, physical abuse was directly related to behavioral problems. For the older children, shame and anger were more likely the mediators between the abuse and emotional problems.[52] Observations and parental reports about their punishment styles were used to examine whether there were differences in maternal discipline style between neglecting and physically abusing mothers. While there were reported differences with maltreating mothers in general, reporting more severe punishment than the non-maltreating mothers, there were no differences by type of maltreatment.[53]

The study of maltreatment as a severe form of poor parenting has many problems. To begin with, the legal classification used in most studies has only a weak association to how parents behave when observed or to their reports of their punishment style. Moreover, a legal classification seems to have more to do with being caught than with what they actually do. Also, the data on maltreatment usually involve poverty-level families who have many more problems than just the abuse. There is almost no evidence on the effect of childhood maltreatment by middle-class parents, although recent studies on adoption suggest that early abuse or deprivation may have powerful effects on subsequent developmental problems.[54] Finally, as already mentioned, there is a high comorbidity between physical abuse and certain types of neglect, especially emotional neglect. Although more study is needed, it appears that abuse of any kind produces shame-proneness in children, and this shame-proneness affects their concurrent and subsequent mental health.

Shame and Violence

The effects of abusive parenting and its consequence on shame-proneness and mental health rest on the idea that abuse leads to more shame, negative self-attributes, and self-focus. However, given the destructive nature of too much shame on the psychology of the child, defensive mechanisms are often employed to control the feelings of helplessness, unworthiness, and the desires to hide, disappear, or die. There are a number of such mechanisms, including the conversion of shame into a more tolerable emotion. In the example of the man who killed a dog with his car, discussed in an earlier chapter, the man initially experienced shame, but he quickly reinterpreted the situation so as to make himself not responsible for the accident and thus avoid shame. Helen Block Lewis was one of the first to discuss what she called felt and not-felt shame.[55] As I have thought about this problem, the idea of converted shame makes sense. In converted shame, the experience is no longer one of shame, but instead of another emotion. One way to convert the shame is through blaming others for the failure that initiates shame, rather than blaming oneself for the failure. Indeed, in shame-proneness as a consequence of abusive parenting, the conversion of shame to blame is a highly likely occurrence. This can be seen in the research on violent behavior in children and adolescents who may have too much shame.

The relation between abusive parenting and violent delinquency has been well established. Physical abuse in childhood is consistently identified with increased risk of violent criminal behavior in adolescence and adulthood, as well as with depression. Compared to nonabused adolescents, juveniles exposed to physically abusive and psychologically aggressive parenting have been found to have high rates of self-reported delinquency, involvement in serious and violent delinquent behavior, arrests for criminal acts, and recidivism. Research has confirmed the relation between abusive parenting and violent delinquency in community samples, samples of maltreated children, and in samples of criminal offenders. Abused children are nine times more likely than nonabused children to become involved in criminal activities and to continue their delinquent behavior. These studies highlight the link between abusive parenting and violent delinquent behavior.[56] Given the association between abusive parenting and shame, there is ample evidence to believe that abuse leads to shame, which leads to violence in some children.

If blame of self is converted to blame of others, then aggressive and violent behavior to others may occur. Blaming others for one's own harmful behavior has been linked with delinquent behavior and often provides justification for aggressive responses. John Lochman found that when compared with their nonaggressive peers, delinquent boys were more likely to blame *others* for being aggressive during conflict situations. Research has confirmed the association between violent delinquent behavior and the tendency to blame others in conflict situations. Several authors report that shame-prone individuals tend to exhibit high levels of hostility and abusiveness, and other researchers have identified repeated patterns of shame and rage as "the motor" that drives violent behavior. These studies support our view that abusive parenting leads to converted shame or blaming others to avoid blaming the self, and in turn to aggression and violence.[57] Thus both expressed shame and converted shame have been associated with depression and violence.

One problem with the idea of expressed and converted shame is how to measure them. Having access to a sample of juvenile delinquents, Jason Gold and I were able to give them June Tangney's Test of Self-Conscious

Affect (TOSCA) and they also completed a self-report of how their parents punished them.[58] The TOSCA scales contained scores on expressed shame as well as blaming others. There was a significant negative correlation between expressed shame and blame, which allowed us to create four groups of subjects. A *converted shame group* was made up of those adolescents high in blaming others and low on blaming themselves, while the *expressed shame group* consisted of adolescents who were high on blaming themselves and low on blaming others. The other three groups, high, high and low, low, were of less interest to us. Our prediction in regard to violent crimes was that abusive parenting led to converted shame, which mediated the relationship between abuse and violent crimes. On the other hand, less abusive parenting should lead to expressed shame, which would not be related to violent crimes, but to crimes against property; that is, converted shame prompted actions like physical injury of another, while expressed shame led to actions like robbery. This is exactly what we found. High abusive parenting leads to shame. To avoid this feeling, the individual converts shame of self into blame of others as a mechanism. Converted shame has an object other than the self to blame, and the blaming of others leads to violence. It appears safe to say that adolescents who commit violence, especially to others, as a consequence of abusive parenting, do not have too little shame, but too much. Shame, by being intolerable to the self system, is converted into blame.

Shame and Multiple Personality Disorder

Another consequence of sex abuse on shame-proneness is its relation to multiple personality disorder (MPD). The phenomenon and study of MPD are valuable since they inform us about another way in which the self, to avoid shame, converts it into some other form of pathology. My interest in the topic reflects the belief that we all have about the nature of our selves, especially in Western society. MPD fits with our idea that multiple forces exist within the self and vie for our attention and control. It is the notion of the devil and an angel, one on each shoulder, vying for our souls. The belief that there is "more than one of us in here influencing our behavior" is based on our observation that we often do things we neither want to do nor think of doing. For example, I often promise myself that I will not snack when I am working but then find myself doing so anyway. The belief in good and evil parts of our selves was given a new form by Freud's structural analysis of the personality. The id, ego, and superego battling each other for control of impulses represents a modern, scientific version of the older Christian view of the struggle in the soul between good and evil. The multiple aspects of our personality are well recognized, although always within the idea of the unity of the self.

Even given our ideas of unity, we act in ways that naturally lead to the idea that there are different selves within us. We are aware of some of these processes because they are conscious, and some we are not aware of because they are unconscious. The concept of a unity of self is the construction that explains these diverse and, at times, contradictory actions. Modern neurophysiology supports this view of multiple selves. Split brain research and studies showing hemispheric brain differences in function, both cognitive and affective, have led to the view that there are multiple selves, corresponding to different brain modules that have different functions and needs.[59]

Work on neurophysiology supports the notion of multiple sites of higher mental processing. For example, Joseph LeDoux associates the amygdala in animals with emotional encoding, and similar findings have been reported in humans. These data seem to support the proposition that multiple areas of the brain are capable of processing different kinds of information. Moreover, these different areas may not be in direct communication with one another. If this were true, then we would have evidence to support the idea that humans process information, especially affective information, in a variety of locations in the brain. This idea gives physiological support to our notions of multiple selves and disassociational processes. MPD, then, fits into the new framework of how we view ourselves even though the phenomenon of MPD is somewhat suspect.

Disassociation in its extreme form characterizes MPD. However, disassociation can also occur at less pathological levels. In the simplest case of disassociation, we do not focus on certain aspects of ourselves, for example, automatic processes such as driving to work or skiing.

The older editions of the *Diagnostic and Statistical Manual of Mental Disorders* described MPD as consisting of two features: that there are within the person two or more distinct personalities or personality states, each having its own relatively long-lasting pattern of perception, thought, and relation to the environment; and that at least two of these personalities or personality states periodically take over control of the person's behavior. The reported increase in the diagnosis of this disorder is amazing. Several investigators report an incredible rate of increase in the Western world—for example, less than 40 cases from the period 1901 to 1944, to 6,000 by the middle of the 1980s. This increase may be due to different factors. First, the disorder may be totally new; for whatever cultural reasons, modern times may have produced more instances of multiple personality disorder. Second, the disorder may always have been present, but was not attended to or, if attended to, was seen as a part of another disorder. The last seems the more likely case. MPD may well have been classified under schizophrenia. Remember that the word *schizophrenia* comes from the Greek meaning "split mind." Indeed, schizophrenia was used originally to describe this disorder. Before schizophrenia was introduced as a diagnostic category, there were many reports of MPD. However, when the schizophrenia classification caught on, in the 1920s and early 1930s, there was a sharp drop in the use of the term MPD. Thus, it seems that the multiple personality phenomenon has been around for some time, though previously it was often given a different name. The increase in identified cases of MPD most likely reflects a renewed focus on these patients.

The idea that MPD existed prior to its dramatic increase in the 1980s is supported by a number of sources. Demonic possession, an accusation leading to death at the stake in the Middle Ages and Renaissance, may have been an earlier example of MPD. The classification of MPD is very close to a description of those supposedly possessed by a demonic force. Even the early psychological literature makes reference to multiple personalities. Although William James, at the turn of the century, discussed the various selves that made up the normal self, it is unclear whether he had MPD in mind. Nevertheless, another early psychologist, Morton Prince, first editor of the *Journal of Abnormal Psychology,* wrote about MPD and described a case fitting the description of a multiple personality. Ernest Hilgard has reported on much of this research under the general theme of dissociation. It appears that this disorder is not new, but for some reason it has not received the attention it deserves.[60]

The etiology of MPD has been explored from a clinical perspective. In general, the female to male ratio is on the order of 10:1, although some researchers believe that more men could be identified. The causes of MPD appear to be early childhood trauma, almost always in the form of sexual abuse. The sexual abuse origin of the disorder may be the main reason for the female-to-male ratio, for females are thought to be the more likely targets of such abuse. But recent evidence suggests that boys are sexually abused more often than we used to think. Early childhood sexual trauma may lead to dissociation, with the child in effect saying, "This isn't happening to me." It is important to note that Freud and Breuer originally thought that their female patients had been sexually abused and that symptoms might have been a sign of MPD. "Anna O." was an important patient for their studies on hysteria. Ernest Jones, in his biography of Freud, writing about her, noted: "More interesting, however, was the presence of two distinct states of consciousness: one a fairly normal one, the other that of a naughty and troublesome child, rather like Morton Prince's famous case of Sally Beauchamp. It was thus a case of double personality." Breuer, too, noticed this double personality: "Two entirely distinct states of consciousness were present which alternated very frequently." These studies, as well as the case histories now collected, reveal that sexual abuse can lead to a wide variety of disorders, including such severe dissociative disorders as multiple personality.[61]

Let us, for a moment, accept the idea the disassociation occurs as a consequence of early and severe childhood trauma, usually of a sexual nature. If such events occur and lead to disassociation, we need a mechanism to account for this process. Clearly, a powerful emotion needs to be at work. From our analysis, it seems reasonable to conclude that abuse, sexual or otherwise, leads to shame. The shame produced is too powerful and painful to endure and needs to be transformed or converted. During the shame avoidance process, disassociation occurs. Recall that when shamed, the self attempts to remove itself from the shamed self. One can remove one's self in a variety of ways, many of which I have discussed in *Shame: The Exposed Self.* The easiest ways include forgetting and laughter; a more intense way includes emotional substitution; the most intense way may be the splitting of the self. The etiology of MPD may tell us that prolonged shame experiences, especially around sexual abuse, are likely to lead to this extreme form of dissociation, this fragmentation of the self.

I believe that shame and disassociative processes have some close relation. Under simple and short-lived instances of shame, the dissociative process may be as mild as laughing with the other selves at one's own failure. With more intense shame experiences, the dissociation process becomes more complex; emotional substitution with depression and rage are the likely consequences. Under the most severe and prolonged form of shame, the most intense dissociation occurs, MPD. I suspect that this extreme form of dissociation is not possible for everyone. It is likely that some disposition requirement is necessary for this disorder to appear, the nature of which remains unknown but of interest for further study. Not everyone who suffers extreme and prolonged early childhood trauma develops MPD. Other escapes from prolonged and intense shame are possible, including other psychoses and suicide.

Many theorists think of MPD in terms of conscious versus unconscious processes, but it may actually be an extreme phenomenon of different levels of focal attention. Ross has said, "There is no need for repression or for a concept of an unconscious . . . discarded products of mental consciousness's *dissociative form* are what is being observed." Or, again, when talking about phenomena usually considered as unconsciousness: "for me, multiple personality disorder demonstrates that the so-called unconsciousness is not unconscious at all—it is wide-awake and cognitive in nature, but dissociated." Ross goes on to say that a patient who misses a session is not unconsciously repressing the memory, but rather, it is the work of an "alter," a dissociated other who is part of the self of this patient. This "alter," when contacted, is conscious and will "readily explain her motivation for taking executive control prior to the session and insuring that she [the patient] missed it." The usefulness of a cognitive-levels approach or dissociated approach rests on our willingness to suspend the idea that the unity of self exists.[62] The unity of the self exists but not at the level of the actions of our bodies, including thinking, feeling, and behaving. It exists at the level of our experiential self.

Stigma and Prolonged Shame

While we have been looking at trauma in the child's social interaction as a consequence of prolonged and pathological shame, other factors that are not necessarily related to parenting may affect individual differences. One in particular has to do with children with physical or mental disabilities. The relationship between stigma and shame is another example of how the self-conscious emotions can go awry.

The relation of stigma to shame has been noticed by others, yet the analysis of stigma, at least from Erving Goffman on, has been complicated by the problem of what stigma might be. Clearly, from Goffman's point of view, it is a public mark, something that can be noticed by others and that involves a "spoiled identity." Stigma, for the most part, constitutes a public violation and for a person to fear stigma, it must be transparent, such as in physical appearance. As Goffman points out:

> The immediate presence of normals is likely to reinforce this split between self-demands and self, but, in fact, self-hate and self-degradation only *can occur when he and a mirror are present* (italics added). The awareness of inferiority is what the stigmatized person is unable to keep out of consciousness, the formulation of some chronic feeling of the worst sort of insecurity, the anxiety of being shame.[63]

The literature on stigma and its relation to shame supports the idea of stigma as a cause of shame. To begin with, standards, rules, and goals allow the child to judge whether or not his behavior or appearance meets his standards. From the point of view of standards, it is quite clear that the stigma that a child possesses represents a deviation from the accepted standards of the society. This deviation may be in appearance, behavior, or conduct. Nonetheless, the person is stigmatized by possessing characteristics that do not match the standard.

The second critical feature in the elicitation of shame, as well as the other self-conscious emotions, is the issue of responsibility or self-blame. Here, again, the stigma and shame analyses lead to the same conclusion, the degree to which stigmatized persons can blame themselves or are blamed by others for their condition increases the likelihood of shame. The idea of responsibility and perceived responsibility is central to stigma and shame. In a study that examined the relationship between stigma, perceived responsibility, and emotions, adults rated the following 10 stigmata on a scale of personal responsibility: AIDS, Alzheimer's disease, blindness, cancer, drug addiction, heart disease, obesity, paraplegia, child abuse, and Vietnam War syndrome. Adults also were asked to rate their reactions of anger or sympathy to each condition. The results reveal that six of the stigmata, Alzheimer's disease, blindness, cancer, heart disease, paraplegia, and Vietnam War syndrome, were rated low on perceived personal responsibility, whereas AIDS, abusing children, having a drug addiction, and being obese were rated high on personal responsibility. Conditions for which people were not held responsible elicited pity, but not anger. Therefore, responsibility and self-blame or the blame of others toward the self are very much related. Social rules involve not only standards and rules but also societal beliefs about controllability and therefore responsibility. Responsibility can change as a function of new knowledge and information or a change in social values. When illness was regarded as a form of punishment imposed for wrongdoing, then illness could be thought of as something to be blamed on the person with the illness. However, new scientific knowledge revealed that disease was caused by germs; thus, germs were known to originate outside of the individuals and were therefore not their responsibility. A changing technology changes beliefs about responsibility. As we have noted, responsibility plays an important role in our self-attribution theories about all sorts of violations of SRGs.

Furthermore, one's own perceptions about personal responsibility may conflict with the perceptions that others hold about personal responsibility. For example, a mother who gives birth to a child with mental retardation can blame herself for the condition, believing perhaps that she did not eat well enough or take care of herself during pregnancy, or she can see the child's condition as a chance event with no self-blame. However, we need not only to convince ourselves that we are not responsible, but also to convince others that it is not our fault. An overweight woman may know full well that her condition is glandular and that there is nothing she can do to control her weight; yet, it still remains a stigma for her because she knows others see her as responsible.

Holding oneself responsible is a critical feature in stigma and in the generation of shame, because a violation of the SRGs of society is insufficient to elicit shame unless responsibility can be placed on the self. Stigma may differ from other elicitors of shame in part because it involves a social appearance factor. The degree to which the stigma is socially apparent is the degree to which one must negotiate the issue of blame, not only for oneself but between oneself and others who witness the stigma. Stigmatization is a much more powerful elicitor of shame because it requires a negotiation between oneself and the attributions of others.

Goffman's expression of stigma as a "spoiled identity" makes clear that stigma constitutes a global attribution about the self as bad. A spoiled identity reflects a whole self spoiled by some condition or behavior. Much of the pathology associated with stigma is that the stigma represents the individual; thus, the whole self becomes defined by the stigma. The expressions "the Down syndrome child," "the mentally retarded person," or "the fat lady" all reflect an inescapable realization that the stigma is the defining feature of the self. In this regard, the attempt to alter others' perceptions of people by altering their language, such as referring to "a person who has a disability" rather than "a disabled person," is an attempt to remove the stigma as the defining element of the person and thus to remove the power of the stigma to reflect upon the total self. That the stigma reflects the spoiled identity shows its similarity to our concept of shame and allows us to appreciate how the very act of stigmatization is shame-inducing. It is not surprising to find, in the description of stigma, associated feelings of lack of self-esteem and, with it, depression and acting-out behaviors.[64] Stigma reflects the idea of difference and how difference shames us and those we know.

Stigmatization is a public judgment. The parents of children with a stigma are themselves stigmatized and suffer the same fate as their stigmatized child. For example, the parents of a child who has mental retardation become themselves objects of the stigma. The shame of having such a child lasts a lifetime and leads to many family difficulties, including a high rate of marital discord and divorce, as each parent seeks to blame the other for the stigmatized child. Given the differences between men and women in the acceptance of blame, it is not surprising that husbands tend to blame wives for the stigmatized child and that mothers tend to accept that self-blame more than do fathers. This provides fathers with the opportunity to blame the mother, and thereby to separate themselves from the shame of the stigmatized child.

Although most attention has been paid to the parents of children with stigmas, we should not neglect the impact of stigmas on the other children in the family. The problems for the siblings of children who are stigmatized are manifested in many different ways. Clearly, a child with disabilities is a source of shame to his family, including his brothers or sisters. Siblings of children with a stigma must bear the emotional distress and disappointment of their parents. Their parents' grieving and stress affects them. Moreover, the parents' energy must be directed toward the stigmatized child, thus leaving less time and energy for the typical siblings. In addition, siblings without stigmas are required to share more of the load of family life than they might normally have shouldered. They have to take care of the stigmatized sibling when the parents are not available. The issues of fairness and sibling rivalry also are problems. Parents are likely to favor the stigmatized child when judging the normal competitions between siblings. The sibling who is without stigma is likely not only to be neglected but also to be expected to assume a greater burden and more responsibility within the family. For example, Sarah reported that even when her sister did something wrong, her parents insisted that she, "the normal sister," understand and make allowances for her sister's behavior.

Although no accurate data exist on the effect of the stigma on other members of the family, there can be no question that the stigma associated with having a sibling with difficulties is a burden for the nonaffected siblings, a burden that, given their young age and lack of coping behavior, may be a serious stress for which they are ill-equipped to handle. Moreover, the support system that they might receive from other adults around them is likely to be limited, given the need of the parents to support themselves and the stigmatized child. Thus, the prognosis for the siblings of a stigmatized child appears to be risky, and the little clinical literature on the topic suggests that siblings of children with disabilities are a group particularly at risk for problems related to high standards, self-blame, and the accompanying emotions of shame, embarrassment, and guilt. Atypical emotional development in regard to the child herself or to the child as a function of a sibling rests on the same principles we have been articulating; the self-attributions that support these emotions gone awry are a function of the development of consciousness and then of the impact of socialization, which influences them. Stigma is defined by the social environment.

Emotions gone awry as a function of how we think about ourselves, and the nature of self-attributions, is likely a function of socialization and learning. The example of this is seen most clearly in the studies of the self-conscious emotions of shame and embarrassment. While there is far more information about these emotions than for such emotions as guilt and pride, the same process of socialization is likely to hold for these emotions, which we examine next.

Guilt

The topic of guilt is not easy to discuss since the literature on the topic is substantial, but much of it is really about shame rather than guilt. The confusion over the meaning of these terms is considerable. This confusion goes back to Freud's early writings on guilt, in which he offered the idea of two kinds of guilt: one, now accepted, as having to do with reparation, and the other, more akin to shame, although he did not discuss it as such.

More recently the distinction between guilt and shame has received more attention. As we have shown, guilt or regret is produced when the child evaluates his behavior as a failure but focuses on the specific features of the self or on the self's action that led to the failure, what Dweck might call task focus. Unlike shame, in which the focus is on the global self, with guilt the child focuses on the self's actions and behaviors that are likely to repair the failure. From a phenomenological point of view, a child is pained by his failure and experiences it as a negative feeling, but this pained feeling is directed to the cause of the failure or to the harmed object. Because the cognitive attributional process focuses on the action of the self rather than on the totality of the self, the feeling that is produced is not as intensely negative as shame and does not lead to the same kinds of behavior that shame does. In fact, the emotion of guilt usually has an association with corrective action, something that the child can do—but does not necessarily actually do—to repair the failure. Rectification of the failure and preventing it from occurring again are the two possible corrective paths. Whereas in shame we see the body hunched over itself in an attempt to hide and disappear, in guilt we see children moving in space as if trying to repair their action. The postural differences that accompany shame and guilt are marked and are helpful both in distinguishing these emotions and in measuring child differences.

In our studies of shame and pride we rarely see guilt when the young child fails a task, although the self-attributions we have spoken about, namely, a task versus a performance orientation, suggest that 3-year-old children's response to failure can elicit guilt rather than shame. Recently Eddie Harmon-Jones and colleagues have proposed that guilt should be regarded as an important self-regulatory emotion.[65] They proposed that guilt may function dynamically to provide a negative reinforcement that reduces an approach motivator, which is then transformed when an opportunity for reparation is possible. Because there are few studies looking at reparative guilt gone awry, it is difficult to discuss the problems with guilt that goes awry. Of course one solution is to argue that it is not too much guilt that goes awry but that there is too little guilt and too much shame instead. Although there are only a few studies looking at temperament and guilt, the studies that do exist find an association between difficult temperaments and moral failures, which Grazyna Kochanska calls guilt and conscience.[66] Whether it is guilt or shame she is measuring is not clear; however, in a general sense biological factors need to be explored as a contributing factor in all the problems of the self-conscious emotions that go awry.

Hubris, or Pride Gone Awry

While we all recognize that pride is a powerful emotion, one that gives rise to a positive psychology, we recognize that there may be problems for children with too little pride as well as too much pride. While there is relatively little research that directly speaks to children with too little pride, there is a considerable literature on the topic of too little self-esteem, which might inform us as to the processes that give rise to pride. This discussion of too little self-esteem leads us back to shame.

However, too much pride may be useful to discuss. Given the lack of an English word for too much pride, I have chosen to use the word *hubris* in its place. Hubris is often discussed in terms of narcissism, and therefore it can be thought of as an excess of pride. Before doing so, realize that pride is the consequence of a self-attribution around success, in which the focus is on the specific or task action that leads to this consequence. The phenomenological experience is joy over an action, thought, or feeling well done. The focus on pleasure is specific and related to a particular behavior. In pride, the self and the object are separated as in guilt. It has been related to achievement motivation. Pride is readily observable.[67] We might think of pride as related to guilt as hubris is related to shame, for in hubris, the self-attribution focus is not on the task but on the self. As such we can say that pride gone awry is hubris.

We need to distinguish between narcissism as a description of people's action in the world and narcissism as a disorder since the term can be used both for normal processes and for psychopathology. Freud distinguished two forms of narcissism: "primary narcissism" involved an initial libidinal investment of energy to the as-yet-undifferentiated ego, and "secondary narcissism" made reference to a withdrawal of psychic energy from objects back to the ego. Heinz Kohut, unlike many of the ego psychologists before him, argued that narcissism is not necessarily pathological but instead leads to object love, love for another, at the beginning of life. In its more mature form, narcissism leads to other skills, for example, to creativity, empathy, and humor. We can think of narcissism, at least nonpathological narcissism, as a will to power, assertiveness, or even anger and persistence.[68]

The difficulty in the use of this term for both normal and abnormal processes becomes compounded when we deal with self-psychologies. I think that the term "narcissism" should be reserved for the psychopathological, a belief that dictates my use of terms here. My work with newborns, infants, and children informs me that, from the moment of birth, and perhaps even before, the infant is an active organism in pursuit of biologically adaptive goals. One of the great discoveries of the research effort with infants over the last 30 years has been our recognition of the degree of infant competences. These competences do not become self-reflective until the second half of the second year of life; action patterns, as goal-directed behavior, exist from the beginning of life.

Narcissism as pathology has been defined as a pretentious show of self-importance, such as an obsession with illusions of endless success, rage, subservience, shame, and emptiness, or as a conviction of entitlement, manipulation, overidealization, or deflation, and lack of compassion. This definition appears to be a distillation of a variety of thoughts ranging from

Freud's original statements to Kohut's and Mahler's more recent views. Throughout this volume, we have suggested that a structural approach to the self-conscious emotions might be helpful in defining narcissism. This we have done, arguing that the inability to cope with shame and humiliation underlies this pathological disturbance. The focus of this analysis of narcissism is shame-based. For reasons yet to be considered, narcissists are readily shame-prone and because of this tendency they act to avoid experiencing shame. They avoid shame either by utilizing a set of ideations designed to avoid shame, or, when this process does not work, by engaging in emotional behavior that masks their underlying shame.

Let us start with the most critical feature, namely, that some people are disposed to making global evaluations of themselves, especially around negative events. The underlying cause of narcissism is this propensity to focus on the whole self when evaluating both success and failure. Because of this focus, failure is likely to result in shame, and success is likely to result in hubris. Narcissists are prideful, and their tendency to make a global evaluation affects both their standards and the evaluative process of failure in regard to these standards. A narcissist avoids shame by never experiencing failure, by setting her standards low, so as to never risk the inability to meet them. But low standards, because they are easily met, create the feeling of hubris. Children prone to making global attributions of negative events are likely to set standards that are too low. In a sense, their behavior is sociopathic because their values and goal structures reflect a lower level than those commonly set by people around them. We have the feeling with such personalities that they are willing to try to get away with more.

But global attribution-prone children also set unrealistically high standards, which has the effect of increasing shame. Why, then, should such unrealistic demands be made? Perhaps their expectation of shame leads them to create this raised standard. Alternatively, past successes probably led to hubris, a feeling that they want to reinstate. Finally, and perhaps most likely, they have just not learned to set appropriate standards. If they are readily shamed, they may not have learned how to set realistic goals and therefore they set goals that are either too low or too high.

However, other ideational defenses related to evaluation are also possible. All of us evaluate our behavior relative to a standard in terms of success or failure. But some of us are likely to claim success unrealistically, that is, most others with the same standards who enacted the same behaviors would be likely to evaluate their behavior as failure. An unrealistic evaluation of success is characteristic of grandiosity. Such unrealistic evaluation is designed to increase hubris and to avoid shame. A narcissist evaluates an action that most other people would interpret as a failure as a success. Such unrealistic evaluation marks the self-aggrandizing way in which a narcissist behaves.

If a narcissist cannot judge a particular behavior successful relative to his standard, he enlists other techniques of evaluation in order to avoid shame. For example, the narcissist can recognize failure but still avoid shame by deciding that failure is not his own fault. This form of ideation allows global attribution–prone children to defend against failure by the expedient device of claiming that it was not their fault but instead the fault of someone else, or of chance. Narcissistic personalities exert large amounts of interpersonal control in an attempt to ensure that failure does not occur. The habit of blaming others rather than the self obviously makes for difficult interpersonal relationships. The attributions necessary to avoid shame involve unrealistic standards, blaming others for failure, and claims of success that are out of keeping with group norms.

One final set of behaviors, having to do with control, is also involved in warding off shame. Shame-prone individuals need to control events around them in order to be able to affect the proper attributional stance. They need to pick which standards to accept, which to discard, what behaviors in their service need to be initiated, and who evaluates the outcome. Since they have little control over the global attributional aspect of the process, they attempt to exert control over all other aspects. These features match the characteristics associated with a narcissistic personality. They are related to a global or self-focus evaluation rather than an action focus. Given both the need to avoid shame and the likelihood that shame cannot always be avoided, the narcissistic personality is likely to employ the emotional substitution of depression or rage. Due to our cultural constraints, in general female narcissists are likely to employ depression, while males employ rage. Given that narcissism is the other side of shame, much of what leads to shame going awry also leads to pride going awry. Since our discussion of shame pathology has been extensive, there is no need to repeat it, except to point out the work that Gold and I have reported on juvenile delinquents. It seems obvious that our findings, which demonstrated the rage these subjects experienced as a consequence of their high shame, and converted into blame of others, is a narcissistic-like disorder leading to rage and thus to violence toward others.

While individual differences in pride gone awry are important, I cannot leave this topic without commenting on historical changes in pride. In the last 25 years, there has been a marked increase in the expression of pride. We have only to look at sporting events around the world to see this change. Earlier in the last century, when a sports figure achieved some success, it was thought unsportsman-like to show a display of pride. A baseball player hitting a home run might tip his hat in response to the applause of the crowd with a slight smile on his face. In the past two decades, this public display of pride has radically changed. A full display of pride is now shown, including all the postural features of hands in the air, chest puffed out, and even dancing. This change has occurred quickly, and it holds for men and women and can be seen across America and Europe.

Is this an example of pride gone awry? It is a measure of the sea change in our willingness to express emotions. What is of concern to me is it may be a marker of an increase in narcissism, where the focus has shifted from a job well done—task focus—to I have done well—a performance focus. If this is so, we have cause to worry since such a shift also marks an increase in shame-proneness during failure, and in the desire to avoid shame we alter our self-attributions and even our standards.

Such a shift, if my analysis of shame gone awry is correct, may be a general change in the socialization practices parents have come to use. Increasingly, parents have shifted their focus toward global attributions and away from specific ones. Parents have come to believe that telling children that they love them regardless of what they do, that they are good children even if they do not do good things, is likely to lead to performance orientation, and with it an increase in shame when failure occurs, and narcissism when success occurs. This is likely to play a role in my observation that at a population level pride has gone awry.[69]

* * *

While there is much more to be learned about emotions gone awry, it seems that there is a wide range of causes for failures in emotional development. Certainly biological factors, especially for the early action patterns, have serious consequences, although socialization factors need to be considered as well. Biological factors also most likely account for the development of consciousness or its pathology. The distinction here is in the process of consciousness rather than its aboutness, which is highly influenced by parenting and cultural norms. Here, too, in emotions gone awry, we can see the model that I have offered; namely, with development, the role of biology becomes less important than the role of culture.

While I have tried to look at the process of emotional development from a structural position, there is much to be learned from those researchers interested in developmental psychopathology, where the study of enduring emotions or moods and personality is the major focus. Only when those interested in normal emotional development work together with those interested in psychopathology, can we hope to make progress in our understanding of the development of emotional life.

CHAPTER 12

The Fugue

I have used the musical term *fugue* for this chapter as a metaphor that is intended to capture the complex set of processes that underlie the development of emotional lives. A fugue is made up of multiple and intertwining themes that in a musical piece appear and are replaced or added to by new ones or variations of the old ones. So too are the developmental processes. Our adult ability is to be able to be here and not here—in the past, in the present, and in the future—all at the same time. It is our nature to construct a reality within our literal worlds expressed by metaphors. My use of the term "fugue" as an example of a metaphor is intended to capture the processes that underlie the development of emotional lives. In this book, the fugue has consisted of two themes, first, those action patterns—mostly innate, although some are likely to be predestined to be learned readily—that are connected to specific events in the physical world—and second, the emergence of consciousness, seen first in self-referential behavior and then in self-attributions. These two themes of the fugue were used to explain both phylogenetic and ontogenetic development and at the same time explain how the adult human can be both in the physical world and in the world of ideas at almost the same time.

In terms of evolutionary time, humans possess the action patterns similar in many ways to other animals either as innate or as easily learned behaviors, including those of the face, voice, and body. These action patterns have received attention throughout the book but most notably in Chapters 2 and 4. The theory here presented accepts the view that biological action patterns in response to specific events evolved through adaptive processes—though much more study is needed to clearly demonstrate them. At least for the early action patterns, we have Darwin to thank for pointing out the similarities of these action patterns across animals, including humans. Many animals, at least mammals, share these early action patterns. Where our evolutionary past diverges is that only the great apes and humans show behavior that seems to reflect the emergence of self-referential behavior as in mirror self-recognition. However, we humans diverge again from the great apes since it is only we who seem to have the ability to think about ourselves in relation to our culture, and thus are capable of moral behavior or creating art and religion.

The book has been mostly about the fugue as an ontogenetic process. The infant, certainly by the first half of the first year of life, shows specific action patterns that respond to specific events in the physical world. And by the end of the second year of life the toddler shows the emergence of consciousness as seen in the self-referential behaviors of mirror self-recognition, personal pronoun usage, and pretend play. The emergence of this mental state changes the nature of the earlier action patterns and at the same time creates new ones, some of which we have called the self-conscious emotions. Much of this discussion has been covered in Chapters 5, 6, and 8.

Besides a phylogenetic and ontogenetic history, adult human emotional lives also show this fugue pattern within our daily mental lives. We can drive without thinking about our path to work or home. Or when we learn a new motor skill like skiing, we can ski well without needing to think about the mechanics of skiing. However, at the same time we can think about ourselves and how we did when we wanted to solve a crossword puzzle. The use of consciousness once it emerges has been called a distributive process, indicating that consciousness can be distributed as a function of its need.

We can use the metaphor of the fugue to understand the role of consciousness in the older child and adult humans' mental and emotional lives. We did so in the examples discussed in Chapter 7 on lying and deception and in Chapter 3 on multiple emotions. Understanding what the adult emotional life looks like should aid us in following the developmental path since only when we know better what the adult emotional life is like can we be better able to understand its development. What we know is that for adults we can and at the same time cannot employ our self-referential ability. Joyce Carol Oates's quote at the beginning of Chapter 6 speaks to this adult capacity. "It is our human capacity for being in one place, while having the mental capacity to imagine another place as we have the mental capacity to recall the past, learn from, and calculate the future; that is our species' exceptional talent. All of civilization . . . are the consequence of never being exclusively here, now but having the conscious ability to be there, then."[1]

The problem of the relation between materialism and mind is not new in philosophical thought; we think of it as the mind–body problem.[2] This problem has been presented as a deveopmental one since in our theory we see emotional life as first being materialistic; that is, the action patterns we described become feelings only after the rise of consciousness. However, we see consciousness as an attribute of mind, and we are at a loss to explain how brain maturation becomes self-referential behavior and how these self-referential behaviors become consciousness since this once again confronts us with the mind–body dilemma.

What we have tried to suggest is that from a developmental perspective, the first emerging aspect of mind that arises out of materialism (the brain) is the idea of me that is embedded in self-referential behavior. It is this primary idea, me, however it develops—from brain and social interaction—that becomes the central theme or spine around which all subsequent aspects of mind come to be.

The fugue metaphor also indicates the complex interweaving of a set of themes that make up the word *emotion*. In creating a theory about the development of emotional life we have consulted a wide range of studies with diverse opinions and results. In order to determine what path to take in building a theory of emotional development I would like to pause and summarize these major themes even though they have been articulated throughout this book. Exactly how to do this without much repetition leads us to use two examples of the developmental processes at work. The first vignette describes the transformation of an early action pattern into patterns of thought. To do this we again will take the example of disgust.

The second vignette examines a somewhat different transformation, that from the procedural rules that govern eye regard in the very young infant to its later form of toddler embarrassment as a reaction to others' regard and then to ideas about shared standards, values, and goals that lead to embarrassment and shame by the end of the third year of life.

FROM TASTE TO MORAL DISGUST

Soon after birth, Vivian is given a sour-tasting food. Her nostrils flare, her upper lip raises, and her tongue protrudes from her mouth. "She really doesn't like it," her father says, "What a disgusted face." In fact, the facial coding systems of Izard or Ekman would measure her facial expression as one of disgust. Five years later, after Vivian sees her younger brother throw up, she says, "How disgusting," while at the same time lifting her upper lip and flaring her nostrils. Her facial and motor behavior again would be scored as disgust. She is disgusted by the look of the vomit. At age 13, Vivian watches a TV news report where a Vietnamese army officer raises a pistol to a prisoner's head and shoots him dead. "That's disgusting," she says as she flares her nostrils and raises her upper lip.

In all these instances the observer and Vivian, when she is old enough, report on her disgust as seen on her face. As we have tried to say throughout this book, unlike Gertrude Stein's famous saying about "a rose is a rose is a rose," disgust is not disgust is not disgust. We can see in this vignette the developmental process that our theory of emotional development has needed to attend to. While the action pattern of the facial expression of disgust remains relatively consistent over time, it might have changed for many reasons; thus the same face can have many meanings. For example, in any culture where such facial expressions are frowned upon, the facial movement could be suppressed. Or if Vivian thought that showing a disgust face might hurt her brother's feelings, she might not show it, either by hiding her face or by transforming it into some other facial expression. On the other hand, she might as an adolescent react to the killing with an exaggerated face of disgust in order to impress others as to her feelings about such inhuman behavior as the killing of another person.[3]

This facial expression that we see occur during Vivian's early life has been called action patterns. At the beginning of life these are elicited by specific physical events in the infant's world. However, with maturation and with the effects of the child's social niche, the action pattern is transformed. Vivian's facial movement, as well as other features of her action pattern, are not learned; they are the consequences of the evolved adaptive process, but are highly flexible and are influenced by her history of transactions within her particular social environment. We humans have many of these action patterns, and as we have tried to show they can be found in our emotional, social, and cognitive domains. We have used a variety of names for these action patterns: instincts, innate releasing mechanisms, genotypic behavior, procedural rules, and the machinery of the self, among others. While past developmental theory as understood by Jean Piaget posited that there are no preformed structures in the newborn, arguing instead for the development of structures through the infant's commerce with her physical and social world through processes Piaget called accommodation and assimilation, we now appreciate that the human newborn arrives with a multitude of complex behavioral patterns that connect her to her physical world.

The difficulties with observing these unique action patterns are many. As we have suggested, they include our inability to understand how to parse events in the world in order to look at the infant's response to them. Following Darwin's suggestion that anger is an approach emotion to overcome a specific barrier, my colleagues and I have attempted to study anger by looking at a highly specific event such as the blocking of a previously attained goal. Although we have spent considerable time talking about the anger action pattern, we have in the past looked at other action patterns and found that for the very young infant the action pattern of interest is not learned and consists of receptor orientation, cessation of bodily motion, and heart rate decreases when looking or listening to sounds in the physical world.[4] Moreover, the newborn shows a disgust-like action pattern to something tasting bitter, but as has been shown by Julie Mennella, early exposure to bitter tastes is quite capable of affecting individual differences in the disgust action pattern.[5] While disagreement about these biologically derived action patterns exists, it seems to me that there is sufficient evidence of their existence to use them within the theory of development.

The problem of most concern to me has to do with individual differences in an action pattern that are temperamentally based. Because Vivian has an easy temperament, her disgust face is likely to occur less often than a child who has a difficult temperament. These temperament differences can hold for any action pattern, and we need to study this variation.

Now let us look at the developmental pattern that the vignette about Vivian's disgust reveals. Vivian's early disgust face was to the bitter taste and reflected an unlearned action pattern. All information about the precipitating event and her reaction to it exists for her only at the machine level of self. Vivian's action pattern at 5 years when seeing her brother's upset stomach has the same facial features as when she was a newborn, but now there has been considerable development. She has had many experiences of disgust. Smells and tastes originally produced them but now she can be disgusted by such things as seeing a bug or a snake. Even pictures are capable of producing disgust, as, for example, a picture of a dead or mutilated body, or even feces. The list of events now capable of eliciting disgust has expanded and includes events, including representations of physical events such as pictures of things.

By this age, she has also acquired information about the causes of disgust reactions. She knows that vomiting means that her brother is sick, either from something he has eaten, or some thought that might have caused him discomfort, even like looking at a picture of something she thinks is horribly disgusting like a running nose. She also knows what may happen after he is no longer sick. She also knows about her disgust, and she can remember how she felt when she had been sick. Her disgust, still an action pattern, is now full of ideas including words for it in her language.

Without doubt the most important developmental change that has taken place is that she feels, that is, she has the ability to experience her disgust. She also can give to this feeling all sorts of meaning, including causes and consequences. She knows that she is disgusted, and if she chooses she can mask her facial expression or even exaggerate it depending on whether she wants to make her brother feel better or worse that he has thrown up.

For Vivian, the action pattern and her experiences of it in context have become for her the unit of her emotional life, and these are inseparable.

Important developmental events have occurred that are in need of further study. For example, what was Vivian's history of disgust elicitors? Has she experienced many situations of disgust? What is her temperament like, and how easily is she disgusted? How readily does she recover from a disgust elicitor? What did her parents do or say to her when she was disgusted? Did they use the term "disgusting" in any other context? For example, did they say to her, "You are behaving disgusting"? We also need to know what Vivian knows about disgust. Does she know what events produce it for her? What does she think about others' expression of disgust? It would also be important for any theory of development to study whether individual differences in the disgust action pattern in infancy are maintained after consciousness emerges. The relation between individual difference in early disgust, socialization rules, and the emergence of consciousness are in need of study. To answer these questions requires much more knowledge of the developmental trajectories for individuals in their particular family and culture.

Vivian at 13 exhibits moral disgust. For her, the observation of a moral violation elicits disgust. While someone being shot itself may elicit disgust because of body disfigurement, it is more likely that the cruelty of the action of someone killing another has become the elicitor of her disgust. What is remarkable is that at 13 Vivian shows us the same action pattern, which now is elicited by her ideas of right and wrong. The developmental process appears to utilize this action pattern for a different elicitor—knowledge about rules, goals, and standards that are ideas about what is right or wrong. The utilization of the same action pattern conserves this innate pattern while adding to the physical elicitors ideas as elicitors. It is as if the energy or motive power of the original action pattern has become functionally independent of its original elicitor and now can be used by the culture to enforce its moral codes.

Vivian's trajectory over age allows us to study the possible models of development. We can observe that while new elicitors produce disgust, many of the original ones continue to do so. The model suggested by such a case is one we have called an "additive growth model" wherein the old elicitors are not replaced but new ones are added to them. There is little transformation in the nature of the action pattern. What is transformed is mediated by the emergence of consciousness. With self-reflection Vivian knows that she is disgusted and she knows that if she behaves in a certain way others like her brother will know she is disgusted. The recursive idea of "she knows that he knows that she is disgusted by his vomit" takes place only after the emergence of her consciousness.

This transformation may help our understanding of phylogenetic change. While disgust may be an action pattern existing for many animals besides humans, it is only humans with consciousness who can utilize such ideas. While we have been discussing the disgust action pattern, we could have just as easily considered others. For all action patterns, consciousness brings new elicitors in addition to specific events of the physical world. Sadness over the loss of a desired object becomes sadness over the idea of the potential loss; fear over uncertainty becomes fear over the idea of uncertainty, or its opposite, excitement over what might come next. We know little about these transformations and there is much to learn. What we do know is that these transformations have something to do with the emergent ability to have ideas, ideas about the self and ideas about how the world works. Individual differences in this transformation have to do with both the culture in which the child is embedded and their temperaments. I end discussion of this theme recalling a quote of Edward St. Aubyn that captures this idea of a developmental transformation around the emergence of consciousness by using personal pronouns as an example: "Everything he did at the moment—the fascination with danger, the assertion of ownership, the ritual contradiction, the desire to do things for himself—was about this explosive transition from being 'you' to being 'I,' from seeing himself through his parents' eyes to looking through his own."[6]

EYE REGARD, THE LOOK OF OTHERS, AND EVALUATIVE EMBARRASSMENT

Rana is 3 months old and is sitting in her infant seat looking at her father. Her father smiles and she smiles back at him while still looking at his face. When he turns away, she stops looking and smiling. Unknown to her father, Rana will smile at any configuration that has an oval form and two dark eye-like features although she is likely to smile more at a human face that is animated. Her smile is automatic, it is an action pattern. Faces, human and animal, have great interest for this 3-month-old. When her father looks at an object in her environment, Rana will look in the direction of his look; this joint attention is another of the innate action patterns. Moreover, there is evidence that Rana's eye movements can follow and anticipate where an object is hidden, something that may be akin to the procedural rule related to what will become a theory of mind.[7] The eyes of others and their behavior serve as important elicitors for selected action patterns for 3-month-old Rana.

Humans, more than any other primates, spend a great deal of time in face-to-face interaction. In fact, it has been claimed that a major evolutionary change between humans and other primates is the use of face-to-face interaction, which could have been the precipitant for the increase in the neuromuscular facial emotional patterns seen in humans. Unlike even for the great apes, this eye-to-eye interaction even occurs in humans during sex.[8] Looking behavior is very important for humans and we are quite capable of noticing where another is looking. Just think of the occasions where we notice that someone is looking at our name tag as she is trying to remember our names, which she should have known.

> Rana is 20 months old and she can now look in a mirror. We have placed rouge on her nose and when she looks at the image in the mirror she knows that it is herself as she touches her nose while looking at herself. With the rouge on her nose she no longer touches the image in the mirror but instead looks in the mirror and uses it to touch her own nose. She sees that the image "there" in the mirror is located "here" in the same space where she stands. This ability along with her use of the personal pronouns such as "me" or "mine" and her ability to engage in pretend play suggest that some important developmental change has taken place.

As we have argued, the emergence of consciousness, as measured by her self-referential behavior, has transformed Rana's emotional life. While this emergent capacity is a major milestone, our interest in this vignette has to do with Rana's knowledge that someone is looking at her. While her eye regard ability has existed from the beginning of her life and while she has deep procedural knowledge in this respect, Rana suddenly knows that someone is looking at her. This eye regard of the other now has a meaning that it did not have before; it means that "I know when I look at them, that they are looking at me." From what we know from the research we have talked about earlier this new meaning, "I am being looked at," now results in a new action pattern that I have labeled "exposure embarrassment."

Our studies of embarrassment reveal it to be the first of the self-conscious emotions that appear. Darwin called them such and also saw their emergence after the first 2 years of life. This embarrassment at being looked at reveals Rana's new mental capacity of recursive knowledge, that is, her ability to think about that another is thinking about her. It represents her growing capacity for mentalism and the beginnings of a theory of mind. While at the end of her second year of life her knowledge base is not as elaborated as it will become over time, nonetheless Rana is reacting to others' eye regard toward her. Darwin has described this self-conscious emotion in the following way—for the mental state of embarrassment, he said, "the essential element [is] self-attention."[9]

Here again we can see a similar developmental pattern as we saw for Vivian's disgust. The earlier action pattern or procedural rules around eye regard is with consciousness transformed into mentalism. It is as if Rana has become the object of her own gaze in addition to the gaze of the other, thus producing a new action pattern, that of embarrassment. But again temperament plays an important role. Rana has a difficult temperament and so when she becomes the object of another's attention she becomes quite upset and hides behind her mother; she may even cry at being the object of another's attention. She often becomes inhibited in new situations when she thinks she is the focus of others' eye regard.[10]

Although the data support such a developmental pattern, more study is necessary in order to trace out this changing pattern. As always we need to look at temperament as well as the role of cultural rules about looking since eye regard rules differ by culture. Moreover, it should not go unnoticed that children with autism spectrum disorder have eye regard difficulties and that individual differences have been located in particular brain areas.[11] But the story of Rana's development is not complete since this form of embarrassment is soon to be transformed again.

> By her third year of life, Rana has been taught by her parents, teachers, and peers some of the rules, standards, and goals of her family and friends. She has incorporated them into her cognition structures and, as she is more able to mentalize about her self as well as others, she has acquired self-attributions about her abilities and become able to compare her behavior, feelings, and desires to the standards of others. It has been said that she has incorporated the eyes of the others into herself, and thus does not have a need for the physical presence of others to make these attributions. With these new cognitions Rana's embarrassment at being the object of another's gaze becomes embarrassment as a consequence of her failure vis-à-vis rules, goals, and standards. This new action pattern of embarrassment is more akin to shame or guilt, although the exposure embarrassment still exists.[12]

In both the Vivian and Rana examples, the emergence of consciousness serves as the powerful force of change. Such a developmental course in the human infant is based on the transformation of biologically given action patterns related to the physical world into ideas about the world. While a good deal of evidence supports such a development course, there is much research work to be done. The work toward a theory of emotional development requires that we understand the basic principles of development, some of which we have discussed earlier. Perhaps these principles that we articulate here are a good starting point for the work that needs to be done.

* * *

Because of my interest in the origins of emotional life, I will end by stating in axiomatic form six principles that we may need to guide our continuing research.

1. Any theory about the origins of emotional life requires that we understand that change is at the heart of development.
2. The nature of change can take many forms, at least three in particular. A *transformational model* suggests that the creation of a new behavior or action pattern from an older one results in the loss of the older one. An *accretional model*, also tranformational, suggests that new models allow for the preservation of the older models. And finally, a *model not involving transformation* at all suggests that all action patterns and feelings are there from the beginning. It is likely that all three of these models are at work.
3. The same emotional behavior can be in the services of different processes and motives. Likewise, different behaviors can be in the service of the same emotional processes and motives.
4. Human children are active participants in their emotional development, and this participation is dependent on the emergence of their consciousness.
5. Human emotional development is made up of both evolutionary-derived action patterns and the ability to experience them.
6. Although these emotional action patterns are evolutionarily derived, they are highly adaptable. This adaptability involves both the temperamental features of the child and the environmental niche the child is raised in.

Thus, I think it safe to say that the origins of human emotional development are a fugue made up from many intertwining themes that are connected and reconnected in a complex pattern of change.

Notes

Preface

1. Lewis, M. (1997). *Altering fate: Why the past does not predict the future.* New York: Guilford Press.

2. Kierkegaard, S. (1942). *The present age* (A. Dru, Trans.). New York: Harper Torchbooks. (Original work published 1846)

3. Ainsworth, M. D. S., & Wittig, B. A. (1969). Attachment and exploratory behaviour of one-year-olds in a strange situation. In B. M. Foss (Ed.), *Determinants of infant behaviour* (Vol. 4, pp. 113–136). London: Methuen. Bowlby, J. (1969). *Attachment and loss: Vol. 1. Attachment.* New York: Basic Books. Horney, K. (1939). *New ways in psychoanalysis.* New York: Norton. Klein, M. (1969). *The psycho-analysis of children.* London: Hogarth Press. (Original work published 1932) Sullivan, H. S. (1953). *The interpersonal theory of psychiatry.* New York: Norton. Winnicott, D. W. (1965). A personal view of the Kleinian contribution. In *The maturational processes and the facilitating environment* (pp. 171–178). New York: International Universities Press. (Original work published 1962)

4. Sroufe, L. A. (1983). Infant–caregiver attachment and patterns of adaptation in preschool: The roots of maladaptation and competence. In M. Perlmutter (Ed.), *Minnesota Symposia in Child Psychology* (Vol. 16, pp. 41–83). Hillsdale, NJ: Erlbaum. (p. 74). However, see Sroufe, Coffino, and Carlson [Sroufe, L. A., Coffino, B., & Carlson, E. A. (2010). Conceptualizing the role of early experience: Lessons from the Minnesota Longitudinal Study. *Developmental Review, 30*(1), 36–51.] for a somewhat different view, one where attachment style does change over time.

5. James, W. (1890). *The principles of psychology.* New York: Holt.

6. Gruber, H. E. (1974). *Darwin on man: A psychological study of scientific creativity changes.* Chicago: University of Chicago Press.

7. Darwin, C. R. (1965). *The expression of the emotions in man and animals.* Chicago: University of Chicago Press. (Original work published 1872)

Chapter 1. Studying Emotional Development

1. Daniel Kahneman's [Kahneman, D. (2011). *Thinking, fast and slow*. New York: Farrar, Straus & Giroux.] two types of thoughts, which he labels 1 and 2, captures this bias.

2. See Barrett, L. F. (2012). Emotions are real. *Emotion, 12*(3), 413–429.

3. Darwin, C. R. (1965). *The expression of the emotions in man and animals*. Chicago: University of Chicago Press. (Original work published 1872)

4. Bard, P. (1934). The neuro-hormonal basis of emotional reactions. In C. Murchinson (Ed.), *Handbook of general experimental psychology, Emotion, 1* (pp. 264–311). Worcester, MA: Clark University Press. Cannon, W. B. (1927). The James–Lange theory of emotions: A critical examination and an alternative theory. *American Journal of Psychology, 39*, 106–124. Lewis, M. (2011). Inside and outside: The relation between emotional states and expressions. In M. Lewis (Ed.), Infant emotional development [Special issue], *Emotion Review, 3*(2), 189–196.

5. Frijda, N. H. (1986). *The emotions*. Cambridge, UK: Cambridge University Press. Lewis, M., & Michalson, L. (1983). *Children's emotions and moods: Developmental theory and measurement*. New York: Plenum Press.

6. Lewis, M., Alessandri, S. M., & Sullivan, M. W. (1990). Violation of expectancy, loss of control, and anger in young infants. *Developmental Psychology, 26*(5), 745–751.

7. Gazzaniga, M. S. (1988). Brain modularity: Towards a philosophy of conscious experience. In A. J. Marcel & E. Bisiach (Eds.), *Consciousness in contemporary science* (pp. 218–238). New York: Oxford University Press.

8. Keller, H., Yovai, R., Borke, J., Kartner, J., Jensen, H., & Papaligoura, Z. (2004). Developmental consequences of early parenting experiences: Self-recognition and self-regulation in these cultural communities. *Child Development, 75*, 1745–1760. Markus, H., & Katayama, S. (1991). Culture and the self: Implications for cognition, emotion and motivation. *Psychological Review, 98*, 224–253.

9. Shweder, R. A. (1985). Menstrual pollution, soul loss, and the comparative study of emotions. In M. A. Kleinman & B. Good (Eds.), *Culture and depression* (pp. 182–215). Berkeley and Los Angeles: University of California Press.

10. For example, see Legerstee, M., Ellenbogen, B., Nienhuis, T., & Marsh, H. (2010). Social bonds, triadic relationships, and goals: Preconditions for the emergence of human jealousy. In S. L. Hart & M. Legerstee (Eds.), *Handbook of jealousy: Theory, research, and multidisciplinary approaches* (pp. 163–191). Malden, MA: Wiley–Blackwell (p. 184). Reddy, V. (2010). Green eyes in bio-cultural frames. In S. Hart & M. Legerstee (Eds.), *Handbook of jealousy: Theory, research, and multidisciplinary approaches* (pp. 144–160). Malden, MA: Wiley–Blackwell.

11. Golder, S. A., & Macy, M. W. (2011). Diurnal and seasonal mood vary with work, sleep, and day length across diverse cultures. *Science, 333*, 1878–1881. Hannak, A., Anderson, E., Barrett, L. F., Lehmann, S., Mislove, A., & Riedewald, M. (2012, June). Tweetin' in the rain: Exploring societal-scale effects of weather on mood. *Proceedings of the 6th International AAAI Conference on Weblogs and Social Media (ICWSM '12)*, Dublin, Ireland.

12. Hatfield, E., Cacioppo, J. T., & Rapson, R. L. (1992). Primitive emotional contagion. In M. S. Clark (Ed.), *Emotion and social behavior* (pp. 151–177). Thousand Oaks, CA: Sage.

13. Bridges, K. M. B. (1932). Emotional development in early infancy. *Child Development, 3*, 324–334.

14. Stenberg, C. R., Campos, J. J., & Emde, R. N. (1983). The facial expression of anger in seven-month-old infants. *Child Development, 54*, 178–184.

15. Lewis, M., Alessandri, S. M., & Sullivan, M. W. (1990). Violation of expectancy, loss of control, and anger in young infants. *Developmental Psychology, 26*(5), 745–751. Lewis, M., Sullivan, M. W., Ramsay, D. S., & Alessandri, S. M. (1992). Individual differences in anger and sad expressions during extinction: Antecedents and consequences. *Infant Behavior and Development, 15*, 443–452.

16. Schaffer, H. R. (1974). Cognitive components of the infant's response to strangeness. In M. Lewis & L. A. Rosenblum (Eds.), *The origins of behavior: Vol. 2. The origins of fear* (pp. 11–24). New York: Wiley.

17. Brooks, J., & Lewis, M. (1976). Infants' responses to strangers: Midget, adult and child. *Child Development, 47*, 323–332.

18. Perner, J. (1991). *Understanding the representational mind*. Cambridge, MA: MIT Press. Perner, J. (2010). Who took the cog out of cognitive science?: Mentalism in an era of anti-cognitivism. In P. A. Frensch, & R. Schwarzer (Eds.), *International perspectives on psychological science: Vol. 1. Cognition and neuropsychology* (pp. 241–261). New York: Psychology Press.

19. Oates, J. C. (2011, September 29). The cure!: A review of *Teach us to sit still: A skeptic's search for health and healing,* by Tim Parks. *The New York Review of Books, 58*(14).

20. Sroufe, L. A. (2012, January 29). Ritalin gone wrong. *The New York Times,* p. SR1.

Chapter 2. Deconstructing Emotions

1. Duffy, E. (1934). Emotion: An example of the need for reorientation in psychology. *Psychological Review, 41*(2), 184–198.

2. Gould, S. J. (1981). *The mismeasure of man*. New York: Norton.

3. Lewis, M., & Rosenblum, L. (Eds.). (1974). *The origins of fear: The origins of behavior, 2*. New York: Wiley.

4. Cook, M., & Mineka, S. (1990). Selective associations in the observational conditioning of fear in rhesus monkeys. *Journal of Experimental Psychology: Animal Behavior Processes, 16*(4), 372–389.

5. Hebb, D. O. (1946). On the nature of fear. *Psychological Review, 53*, 259–276.

6. Schaffer, H. R., & Emerson, P. E. (1964). The development of social attachments in infancy. *Monographs of the Society for Research in Child Development, 29*(3, Serial No. 94). Scott, J. P. (1962). Critical periods in behavioral development. *Science, 138*, 949–958.

7. Ainsworth, M. D. S., Blehar, M. C., Waters, E., & Wall, S. (1978). *Patterns of attachment: A psychological study of the strange situation*. Hillsdale, NJ: Erlbaum. Bowlby, J. (1951). Maternal care and mental health. *Bulletin of the World Health Organization, 3*, 355–533.

8. Frijda, N. H. (1986). *The emotions* (p. 41). Cambridge, UK: Cambridge

University Press. Lewis, M., & Michalson, L. (1983). *Children's emotions and moods: Developmental theory and measurement.* New York: Plenum Press.

9. Lewis, M., & Michalson, L. (1983). *Children's emotions and moods: Developmental theory and measurement.* New York: Plenum Press.

10. Recent work by Semin and colleagues has revealed that chemical signals can serve as elicitors since they are associated with specific emotions [de Groot, J. H. B., Smeets, M. A. M., Kaldewaij, A., Duijndam, M. J. A., & Semin, G. R. (2012). Chemosignals communicate human emotions. *Psychological Science, 23*(11), 1417–1424.].

11. Melzack, R., & Wall, P. D. (1965). Pain mechanisms: A new theory. *Science, 150,* 971–979. Wall, P. D., Melzack, R., & Bonica, J. J. (Eds.). (1994). *Textbook of pain* (3rd ed.). Philadelphia: Churchill Livingstone.

12. Izard, C. E. (2004). The generality–specificity issue in infants' emotion responses: A comment on Bennett, Bendersky, and Lewis (2002). *Infancy, 6*(3), 417–423. Izard, C. E., & Dougherty, L. M. (1982). Two complementary systems for measuring facial expressions in infants and children. In C. E. Izard & P. B. Read (Eds.), *Measuring emotions in infants and children* (pp. 97–126). New York: Cambridge University Press (pp. 98, 101).

13. Lazarus, R. S. (1982). Thoughts on the relations between emotion and cognition. *American Psychologist, 37,* 1019–1024.

14. Campos, J., & Stenberg, C. (1981). Perception, appraisal, and emotion: The onset of social referencing. In M. E. Lamb & L. R. Sherrod (Eds.), *Infant social cognition: Empirical and theoretical considerations* (pp. 273–314). Hillsdale, NJ: Erlbaum. Ortony, A., Clore, G. L., & Collins, A. (1988). *The cognitive structure of emotions.* New York: Cambridge University Press. Schachter, S., & Singer, J. E. (1962). Cognitive, social, and physiological determinants of emotional state. *Psychological Review, 69,* 379–399.

15. Such theories have much in common with cognitive attributional theories, which I will return to when I speak of the other feature of emotion, namely, internal experiences. This view of emotion as a general arousal is not new—it goes back almost 50 years. Although the study of Schachter and Singer, which claimed to show that heightening arousal through the use of epinephrine in specific contexts produces a feeling independent of a specific action pattern, has been criticized, it is this type of research together with the weak data on specific elicitor–action pattern connections that give it its appeal. Of course, what does "interpretation of general arousal producing specific emotions" really mean? These types of models suggest that ideas are emotions; that is, fear is an idea as a consequence of the general arousal and context. For them, emotions are mostly ideas with little recourse to elicitor–action pattern connections.

16. To make this discussion clear, I will take as another example pain. Pain can have a cause (or elicitor), for example, a burn on the finger from a hot pot. This is an external elicitor that sets off the firing of specific pain receptors, which produce removal of the hand from the pot, vocal sounds of pain, and perhaps changes in the autonomic nervous system (ANS) and stress hormones. This response is what is called an action pattern. It also sends information toward the brain, where information produces the emotional experience of pain. Notice that the elicitor, the hot pot, triggers the action pattern. Thus, we are in a state of pain, or we are being in pain. Having pain, however, that is, experiencing pain, is dependent on other factors. By rendering the person unconscious, she may be *in pain* but she is not *having pain.* Analgesics taken in the dentist's

office are another example. The elicitor is drilling the teeth, which may produce action patterns of *being in pain*. However, we do not experience the pain, thus we are not *having pain*.

17. Hess, E. H. (1970). Ethology and developmental psychology. In P. Mussen (Ed.), *Carmichael's manual of child psychology* (Vol. 1, pp. 1–38). New York: Wiley.

18. Brooks, J., & Lewis, M. (1976). Infants' responses to strangers: Midget, adult and child. *Child Development, 47,* 323–332. Hess, E. H. (1967). Ethology. In A. M. Freedman & H. I. Kaplan (Eds.), *Comprehensive textbook of psychiatry* (pp. 82–106). Baltimore: Williams & Wilkins.

19. Bowlby, J. (1969). *Attachment and loss: Vol. 1. Attachment.* New York: Basic Books. Spitz, R. A., & Wolf, K. M. (1946). The smiling response: A contribution to the ontogenesis of social relations. *Genetic Psychology Monographs, 34,* 57–125. Wolff, P. H. (1963). Observations on the early development of smiling. In B. M. Foss (Ed.), *Determinants of infant behavior* (Vol. 2, pp. 113–134). New York: Wiley.

20. Hubel, D. H., & Wiesel, T. N. (1962). Receptive fields, binocular interaction, and functional architecture in the cat's visual cortex. *Journal of Physiology, 160,* 106–154.

21. Gross, C. G., Rocha-Miranda, C. E., & Bender, D. B. (1972). Visual properties of neurons in inferotemporal cortex of the macaque. *Journal of Neurophysiology, 35*(1), 96–111.

22. Tomkins, S. S. (1962). *Affect, imagery, consciousness: Vol. 1. The positive affects* (p. 243). New York: Springer.

23. Ekman, P., & Friesen, W. V. (1978). *Facial action coding system: A technique for the measurement of facial movement.* Palo Alto, CA: Consulting Psychologists Press. Izard, C. E. (1979). *The Maximally Discriminative Facial Movement Coding System (MAX).* Newark, DE: University of Delaware, Instructional Resources Center. Tomkins, S. S. (1962). *Affect, imagery, consciousness: Vol. 1. The positive affects.* New York: Springer. Tomkins, S. S. (1963). *Affect, imagery, consciousness: Vol. 2. The negative affects.* New York: Springer.

24. Birdwhistell, R. L. (1974). The language of the body: The natural environment of words. In A. Silverstein (Ed.), *Human communication: Theoretical explorations* (pp. 27–52). Oxford, UK: Erlbaum.

25. While there are few studies involving children looking at decoding body movement, there are a few, for example, that of Boone and Cunningham, which found that 4-year-olds can correctly identify sadness through body activity [Boone, R. T., & Cunningham, J. G. (1998). Children's decoding of emotion in expressive body movement: The development of cue attunement. *Developmental Psychology, 34*(5), 1007–1016.]. Recently Aviezer, Trope, and Todorov reported on the discrimination of positive and negative emotions indicating that bodily cues are better than facial expressions [Aviezer, H., Trope, Y., & Todorov, A. (2012). Body cues, not facial expressions, discriminate between intense positive and negative emotions. *Science, 338,* 1225–1228.

26. Scherer, K. R. (1979). Nonlinguistic vocal indicators of emotion and psychopathology. In C. E. Izard (Ed.), *Emotions in personality and psychopathology* (pp. 495–529). New York: Plenum Press.

27. Hatfield, E., Cacioppo, J. T., & Rapson, R. L. (1992). Primitive emotional contagion. In M. S. Clark (Ed.), *Emotion and social behavior* (pp. 151–177). Thousand Oaks, CA: Sage.

28. Adolph, K. E., Schaffer, H. R., Greenwood, A., & Parry, M. H. (1972). The onset of wariness. *Child Development, 43,* 165–175. Adolph, K. E., Kretch, K. S., & LoBue, V. (in press). Fear of heights in infants? *Current Directions in Psychological Science.*

29. Lewis, M., Ramsay, D. S., & Kawakami, K. (1993). Differences between Japanese infants and Caucasian American infants in behavioral and cortisol response to inoculation. *Child Development, 64,* 1722–1731.

30. Buck, R., Miller, R. E., & Caul, W. F. (1974). Sex, personality, and physiological variables, in the communication of affect via facial expression. *Journal of Personality and Social Psychology, 30*(4), 587–596. Suomi, S. J. (1991). Primate separation models of affective disorders. In J. Madden (Ed.), *Neurobiology of learning, emotion, and affect* (pp. 195–214). New York: Raven Press.

31. Matsumoto, D., Keltner, D., Shiota, M. N., O'Sullivan, M., & Frank, M. (2008). Facial expressions of emotion. In M. Lewis, J. M. Haviland-Jones, & L. Feldman Barrett (Eds.), *Handbook of emotions* (3rd ed., pp. 211–234). New York: Guilford Press.

32. Camras, L. A. (2011). Differentiation, dynamical integration and functional emotional development. In M. Lewis (Ed.), Infant emotional development [Special issue], *Emotion Review, 3*(2), 138–146.

33. It is interesting to note that facial expressions have been the expression of emotion most studied, and it was the advent of these coding systems that led to measures other than self-report or global measures of emotion. The development of the facial coding systems has allowed for the advent of empirical studies, including those with infants and children too young to give or understand verbal report.

34. Otaki, M., Durreit, M., Richards, P., Nyquist, L., & Pennebaker, J. (1986). Maternal and infant behavior in Japan and America. *Journal of Cross-Cultural Psychology, 17,* 251–268.

35. Quinn, P. C., Anzures, G., Izard, C. E., Lee, K., Pascalis, O., Slater, A. M., et al. (2011). Looking across domains to understand infant representation of emotion. *Emotion Review, 3*(2), 197–206.

36. Gibson, J. J. (1960). The concept of the stimulus in psychology. *American Psychologist, 15,* 694–703.

37. Bard, P. (1934). The neuro-hormonal basis of emotional reactions. In C. Murchinson (Ed.), *Handbook of general experimental psychology, Emotion, 1* (pp. 264–311). Worcester, MA: Clark University Press. Cannon, W. B. (1927). The James–Lange theory of emotions: A critical examination and an alternative theory. *American Journal of Psychology, 39,* 106–124. Lindsey, D. B. (1951). Emotion. In S. S. Stevens (Ed.), *Handbook of experimental psychology* (pp. 473–516). New York: Wiley.

38. Lacey, J., Bateman, D., & VanLehn, R. (1953). Autonomic response specificity. *Psychosomatic Medicine, 15,* 8–21.

39. Davidson, R. J. (1994). Complexities in the search for emotion-specific physiology. In P. Ekman & R. J. Davidson (Eds.), *The nature of emotion: Fundamental questions* (pp. 237–242). New York: Oxford University Press.

40. Lewis, M. (2011). Inside and outside: The relation between emotional states and expressions. In M. Lewis (Ed.), Infant Emotional Development [Special issue], *Emotion Review, 3*(2), 189–196. London, UK: Sage. However, also see Bauer, Quas, and Boyce [Bauer, A. M., Quas, J. A., & Boyce, W. T. (2002). Associations between physiological reactivity and children's behavior: Advantages of a multisystem approach. *Developmental and Behavioral Pediatrics, 23,* 102–113.]. and Henry [Henry, J. P.

(1992). Biological basis of the stress response. *Integrative Physiological and Behavioral Science, 27,* 66–83.], who have shown a relation between anger and the autonomic nervous system.

41. Seventy years ago Hull [Hull, C. (1943). *Principles of behavior.* New York: Appleton-Century-Crofts] discussed the notion of retroactive inhibition. More recently, Solomon and Corbit [Solomon, R. L., & Corbit, J. D. (1974). An opponent-process theory of motivation: I. Temporal dynamics of affect. *Psychological Review, 81*(2), 119–145.] proposed a process theory of appetitive behavior, in an attempt to explain how organisms inhibit as well as activate behavior.

42. Campos, J. J., Emde, R. N., Gaensbauer, T. J., & Henderson, C. (1975). Cardiac and behavioral interrelationships in the reactions of infants to strangers. *Developmental Psychology, 11,* 589–601.

43. Prideaux, E. (1920). The psychogalvanic reflex: A review. *Brain, 43,* 50–73.

44. Buck, R., Miller, R. E., & Caul, W. F. (1974). Sex, personality, and physiological variables, in the communication of affect via facial expression. *Journal of Personality and Social Psychology, 30*(4), 587–596.

45. James, W. (1890). *The principles of psychology* (p. 449). New York: Holt.

46. Clore, G. L., & Ortony, A. (2000). Cognition in emotion: Always, sometimes, or never? In R. D. Lane & L. Nadel (Eds.), *Cognitive neuroscience of emotion* (pp. 24–61). New York: Oxford University Press.

47. Izard, C. E. (1971). *The face of emotion.* New York: Appleton-Century-Crofts.

Chapter 3. Multiple Emotions and Moods

1. Russell, J. A. (1991). Natural language concepts of emotion. In D. J. Ozer, J. M. Healy Jr., & A. J. Stewart (Eds.), *Perspectives in personality: Self and emotion* (pp. 119–137). London: Jessica Kingsley.

2. See Magai, C., & Haviland-Jones, J. M. (2002). *The hidden genius of emotion: Lifespan transformations of personality.* New York: Cambridge University Press. Also see Avshalom Caspi [Robins, R. W., John, O. P., & Caspi, A. (1994). Major dimensions of personality in early adolescence: The Big Five and beyond. In C. F. Halverson Jr., G. A. Kohnstamm, & R. P. Martin (Eds.), *The developing structure of temperament and personality from infancy to adulthood* (pp. 267–291). Hillsdale, NJ: Erlbaum.], where enduring emotions are related to personality characteristics such as the Big Five dimensions.

3. Achenbach, T. M. (1991). *Integrative guide for the 1991 CBCL/4-18, YSR, and TRF profiles.* Burlington: University of Vermont, Department of Psychiatry. Achenbach, T. M., & Rescorla, L. A. (2000). *Manual for the ASEBA Preschool Forms & Profiles.* Burlington, VT: University of Vermont, Research Center for Children, Youth, & Families. Achenbach, T. M., & Rescorla, L. A. (2001). *Manual for the ASEBA School-Age Forms & Profiles.* Burlington: University of Vermont, Research Center for Children, Youth, & Families.

4. Izard, C. E. (2010). The many meanings/aspects of emotion: Emotion definitions, functions, activation, and regulation. *Emotion Review, 2,* 363–370. Russell, J. A. (1991). Natural language concepts of emotion. In D. J. Ozer, J. M. Healy Jr., & A. J. Stewart (Eds.), *Perspectives in personality: Self and emotion* (pp. 119–137). London: Jessica Kingsley.

5. Widen, S. C., & Russell, J. A. (2010). Children's scripts for social emotions: Causes and consequences are more central than are facial expressions. *British Journal of Developmental Psychology, 28*, 565–581. (p. 566)

6. Widen, S. C., & Russell, J. A. (2010). Children's scripts for social emotions: Causes and consequences are more central than are facial expressions. *British Journal of Developmental Psychology, 28*, 565–581. (p. 566)

7. Widen, S. C., & Russell, J. A. (2010). Differentiation in preschoolers' categories of emotion. *Emotion, 10*(5), 651–661. Widen, S. C., & Russell, J. A. (2011). In building a script for an emotion, do preschoolers add its cause before its behavior consequence? *Social Development, 20*(3), 471–485.

8. Lewis, M., & Michalson, L. (1983). *Children's emotions and moods: Developmental theory and measurement.* New York: Plenum Press. Michalson, L., & Lewis, M. (1985). What do children know about emotions and when do they know it? In M. Lewis & C. Saarni (Eds.), *The socialization of emotions* (pp. 117–140). New York: Plenum Press. Widen, S. C., & Russell, J. A. (2010). Differentiation in preschoolers' categories of emotion. *Emotion, 10*(5), 651–661.

9. Plutchik used the color wheel to talk about emotional mixture. [Plutchik, R. (1962). *The emotions: Facts, theories and a new model.* New York: Random House.]

10. Rosaldo, M. Z. (1980). *Knowledge and passion: Ilongot notions of self and social life.* New York: Cambridge University Press. Scollon, C. N., Diener, E., Oishi, S., & Biswas-Diener, R. (2004). Emotions across cultures and methods. *Journal of Cross-Cultural Psychology, 35*(3), 304–326.

11. Bennett, D. S., Bendersky, M., & Lewis, M. (2002). Facial expressivity at 4 months: A context by expression analysis. *Infancy, 3*(1), 97–113. Bennett, D. S., Bendersky, M., & Lewis, M. (2005). Does the organization of emotional expression change over time?: Facial expressivity from 4 to 12 months. *Infancy, 8*(2), 167–187.

12. Gibson, J. J. (1960). The concept of the stimulus in psychology. *American Psychologist, 15*, 694–703.

13. Hodson, G., & Costello, K. (2007). Interpersonal disgust, ideological orientations, and dehumanization as predictors of intergroup attitudes. *Psychological Science, 18*, 691–698.

14. Davey, G. C. L., & Marzillier, S. (2009). Disgust and animal phobias. In B. O. Olatunji & D. McKay (Eds.), *Disgust and its disorders: Theory, assessment and treatment implications* (pp. 169–190). Washington, DC: American Psychological Association.

15. Keane, F. (1995). *Season of blood: A Rwandan journey.* New York: Viking Press.

16. Berle, D., & Phillips, E. S. (2006). Disgust and obsessive–compulsive disorder: An update. *Psychiatry, 69*, 228–238. de Jong, P. J. (2007, July). *Vaginismus: Automatic vs. deliberate associations with threat and disgust.* Paper presented at the World Congress of Behavioral and Cognitive Therapies, Barcelona, Spain. de Jong, P. J., van Overveld, M., Weijmar Schultz, W., Peters, M. L., & Buwalda, F. (2009). Disgust and contamination sensitivity in vagismus and dyspareunia. *Archives of Sexual Behavior, 38*(20), 244–252. McKay, D., & Olatunji, B. O. (2009). Disgust and psychopathology: Next steps in an emergent area of treatment and research. In B. O. Olatunji & D. McKay (Eds.), *Disgust and its disorders: Theory, assessment and treatment implications* (pp. 285–292). Washington, DC: American Psychological Association. Neziroglu,

F., Hickey, M., & McKay, D. (2010). Psychophysiological and self-report components of disgust in body dysmorphic disorder: The effects of repeated exposure. *International Journal of Cognitive Therapy, 3*(1), 40–51. Quigley, J., Sherman, M., & Sherman, N. (1997). Personality disorder symptoms, gender, and age as predictors of adolescent disgust sensitivity. *Personality and Individual Differences, 22,* 661–667.

17. Larsen, J. T., McGraw, A. P., & Cacioppo, J. T. (2001). Can people feel happy and sad at the same time? *Journal of Personality and Social Psychology, 81*(4), 684–696.

18. Russell, J. A. (1980). A circumplex model of affect. *Journal of Personality and Social Psychology, 39,* 1161–1178. Russell, J. A., & Carroll, J. M. (1999). On the bipolarity of positive and negative affect. *Psychological Bulletin, 125,* 3–30.

19. Larsen, J. T., & McGraw, A. P. (2011). Further evidence for mixed emotions. *Journal of Personality and Social Psychology, 100*(6), 1095–1110. Larsen, J. T., McGraw, A. P., Mellers, B. A., & Cacioppo, J. T. (2004). The agony of victory and thrill of defeat: Mixed emotional reactions to disappointing wins and relieving losses. *Psychological Science, 15*(5), 325–330.

20. Linda Camras [Camras, L. A., & Fatani, S. S. (2008). The development of facial expressions: Current perspectives on infant emotions. In M. Lewis, J. M. Haviland-Jones, & L. Feldman Barrett (Eds.), *Handbook of emotions* (3rd ed., pp. 291–303). New York: Guilford Press.] and Lisa Feldman Barrett [Lindquist, K. A., & Barrett, L. Feldman (2008). Emotional complexity. In M. Lewis, J. M. Haviland-Jones, & L. Feldman Barrett (Eds.), *Handbook of emotions* (3rd ed., pp. 513–530). New York: Guilford Press.] have argued against the idea of these basic connections preexisting between elicitors and responses and have argued against the Darwinian view supported by Ekman and Izard, for example.

21. Lewis, M., Sullivan, M. W., & Michalson, L. (1984). The cognitive–emotional fugue. In C. E. Izard, J. Kagan, & R. Zajonc (Eds.), *Emotions, cognition, and behavior* (pp. 264–288). New York: Cambridge University Press.

22. Robert Zajonc [Zajonc, R. B. (1980). Feeling and thinking: Preferences need no inferences. *American Psychologist, 35,* 151–175.] and Richard Lazarus [Lazarus, R. S. (1982). Thoughts on the relations between emotion and cognition. *American Psychologist, 37,* 1019–1024.], in highly influential articles, struggled over just such an issue.

23. Wasserman, G. A., & Lewis, M. (1985). Infant sex differences: Ecological effects. *Sex Roles: A Journal of Research, 12,* 665–675.

24. Ainsworth, M. D. S., Bell, S. M., & Stayton, D. J. (1971). Individual differences in strange-situation behavior of one-year-olds. In H. R. Schaffer (Ed.), *The origins of human social relations* (pp. 17–57). Oxford, UK: Academic Press.

25. I am reminded of the work of Harry Helson [Helson, H. (1964). *Adaptation-level theory: An experimental and systematic approach to behavior.* New York: Harper & Row.], who argued for an adaptation model where a response to an event 2 is dependent on the response to event 1. Unfortunately, little is known about this phenomenon when we consider emotions.

26. Such personality traits as conscientiousness are not necessarily emotional.

27. Bowlby, J. (1992). *Charles Darwin: A new life.* New York: Norton.

28. Suomi, S. J. (2005). How gene–environment interactions shape the development of impulsive aggression in rhesus monkeys. In D. M. Stoff & E. J. Sussman (Eds.),

Developmental psychobiology of aggression (pp. 252–268). New York: Cambridge University Press. See also Pluess, M., Belsky, J., Way, B. M., & Taylor, S. E. (2010). 5-HTTLPR moderates effects of current life events on neuroticism: Differential susceptibility to environmental influences. *Progress in Neuro-Psychopharmacology and Biological Psychiatry, 34*(6), 1070–1074.

29. Bates, J. E., Goodnight, J. A., & Fite, J. E. (2008). Temperament and emotion. In M. Lewis, J. M. Haviland-Jones, & L. Feldman Barrett (Eds.), *Handbook of emotions* (3rd ed., pp. 485–496). New York: Guilford Press. Rothbart, M. K., Derryberry, D., & Posner, M. I. (1994). A psychobiological approach to the development of temperament. In J. E. Bates & T. D. Wachs (Eds.), *Temperament: Individual differences at the interface of biology and behavior* (pp. 83–116). Washington, DC: American Psychological Association.

30. DiBiase, R., & Lewis, M. (1997). The relation between temperament and embarrassment. *Cognition and Emotion, 11,* 259–271.

31. Magai, C., & Haviland-Jones, J. M. (2002). *The hidden genius of emotion: Lifespan transformations of personality.* New York: Cambridge University Press.

32. Lewis, M., & Michalson, L. (1983). *Children's emotions and moods: Developmental theory and measurement.* New York: Plenum Press.

33. Another way at getting at duration or intensity would have been to look at the number of behaviors and/or their intensity for any given elicitor. So, for example, the degree of concordance between facial expression, bodily movement, and physiological response could be used to measure intensity.

34. Denham, S. A., & Mitchell-Copeland, J. (1993). Cross-validation of Lewis and Michalson's system for measurement of children's emotional states. *Infant Mental Health Journal, 14*(2), 133–146. Ferri, R. (2011). Personal communication. Sapienza University of Rome, Rome, Italy.

Chapter 4. The Early Emotions

1. Izard, C. E. (1977). *Human emotions.* New York: Plenum Press.

2. Camras, L. A. (2011). Differentiation, dynamical integration and functional emotional development. In M. Lewis (Ed.), Infant emotional development [Special issue], *Emotion Review, 3(2),* 138–146.

3. Malatesta, C. Z., & Haviland, J. M. (1982). Learning display rules: The socialization of emotion expression in infancy. *Child Development, 53*(4), 991–1003.

4. Gallese, V., Fadiga, L., Fogassi, L., & Rizzolatti, G. (1996). Action recognition in the promotor cortex. *Brain, 119,* 593–609.

5. McGurk, H., & Lewis, M. (1974). Space perception in early infancy: Perception within a common auditory–visual space? *Science, 186*(4164), 649–650.

6. Izard, C. E. (1977). *Human emotions.* New York: Plenum Press.

7. Nevertheless, the lack of specificity of action pattern by specific context has made the argument of evolved and adaptive specificity difficult [Kochanska, G., Coy, K. C., Tjebkes, T. L., & Husarek, S. J. (1998). Individual differences in emotionality in infancy. *Child Development, 69*(2), 375–390.].

8. Adolph, K. E., Kretch, K. S., & LoBue, V. (in press). Fear of heights in infants? *Current Directions in Psychological Science.* Braungart-Rieker, J. M., Hill-Soderlund,

A. L., & Karrass, J. (2010). Fear and anger reactivity trajectories from 4 to 16 months: The roles of temperament, regulation, and maternal sensitivity. *Developmental Psychology*, 46(4), 791–804. Lewis, M., Brooks, J., & Haviland, J. M. (1978). Hearts and faces: A study in the measurement of emotion. In M. Lewis & L. Rosenblum (Eds.), *The development of affect: The genesis of behavior, 1* (pp. 77–123). New York: Plenum Press. Lewis, M., & Rosenblum, L. A. (Eds.). (1974). *The origins of fear: The origins of behavior, 2*. New York: Wiley.

    9. Crossman, A. M., Sullivan, M. W., Hitchcock, D., & Lewis, M. (2009). When frustration is repeated: Behavioral and emotion responses during extinction over time. *Emotion*, 9(1), 92–100. Lewis, M., Alessandri, S. M., & Sullivan, M. W. (1990). Violation of expectancy, loss of control, and anger in young infants. *Developmental Psychology*, 26(5), 745–751. Lewis, M., Hitchcock, D. F. A., & Sullivan, M. W. (2004). Physiological and emotional reactivity to learning and frustration. *Infancy*, 6(1), 121–143. Lewis, M., & Ramsay, D. (2004). Infant emotional response to goal blockage, control, and cortisol response. *Emotion Researcher*, 19(2), 8–9. Lewis, M., & Ramsay, D. S. (2005). Infant emotional and cortisol responses to goal blockage. *Child Development*, 76(2), 518–530. Lewis, M., Ramsay, D. S., & Sullivan, M. W. (2006). The relation of ANS and HPA activation to infant anger and sadness response to goal blockage. *Developmental Psychobiology*, 48, 397–405.

    10. Lewis, M., Sullivan, M. W., Ramsay, D. S., & Alessandri, S. M. (1992). Individual differences in anger and sad expressions during extinction: Antecedents and consequences. *Infant Behavior and Development*, 15, 443–452.

    11. While I have stressed that the same context may lead to different action patterns due to temperament, it could be that children, especially older infants and young children, can differentially evaluate the context and thus have different action patterns. This is highly likely to play a role in individual differences in action patterns to the same context.

    12. Lewis, M., Ramsey, D. M. , & Kawakami, K., (1993). Differences between Japanese infants and Caucasian American infants in behavioral and cortical response to inoculation. *Child Development, 64*, 1722–1731.

    13. See Lewis and Michalson [Lewis, M., & Michalson, L. (1983). *Children's emotions and moods: Developmental theory and measurement*. New York: Plenum Press.] for a full description of this measurement strategy.

    14. Bridges, K. M. B. (1932). Emotional development in early infancy. *Child Development*, 3, 324–334.

    15. Schneirla, T. C. (1959). An evolutionary and developmental theory of biphasic processes underlying approach and withdrawal. In M. R. Jones (Ed.), *Nebraska Symposium on Motivation* (Vol. 7, pp. 1–42). Lincoln: University of Nebraska Press. See also Allport, F. H., & Allport, G. W. (1921). Personality traits: Their classification and measurement. *Journal of Abnormal Psychology and Social Psychology*, 16, 6–40. Cannon, W. B. (1927). The James–Lange theory of emotions: A critical examination and an alternative theory. *American Journal of Psychology*, 39, 106–124. Darwin, C. R. (1965). *The expression of the emotions in man and animals*. Chicago: University of Chicago Press. (Original work published 1872). Watson, J. B. (1914). *Behavior: An introduction to comparative psychology*. New York: Holt.

    16. Darwin, C. R. (1965). *The expression of the emotions in man and animals*. Chicago: University of Chicago Press. (Original work published 1872)

17. It is interesting to note that both anger and joy have been associated with activation in the left frontal area of the brain. Studies of the right and left hemispheres suggest that anger and joy approach emotions can be found on the left side, while the withdrawal emotions of sadness and disgust can be found on the right side. That hemisphere's reaction appears to support such a view [Davidson, R. J. (1994). Complexities in the search for emotion-specific physiology. In P. Ekman & R. J. Davidson (Eds.), *The nature of emotion: Fundamental questions* (pp. 237–242). New York: Oxford University Press. Harmon-Jones, E. (2003). Clarifying the emotive functions of asymmetrical frontal cortical activity. *Psychophysiology, 40*(6), 838–848.].

18. Mineka, S., Keir, R., & Price, V. (1980). Fear of snakes in wild- and laboratory-reared rhesus monkeys (Macaca mulatta). *Animal Learning and Behavior, 8*, 653–663.

19. Lacey, J., Bateman, D., & VanLehn, R. (1953). Autonomic response specificity. *Psychosomatic Medicine, 15*, 8–21. Porges, S. W. (2011). *The polyvagal theory: Neurophysiological foundations of emotions, attachment, communication, and self-regulation.* New York: Norton. Porges, S. W. (1986). Respiratory sinus arrhythmia: Physiological basis, quantitative methods, and clinical implications. In P. Grossman, K. Janssen, & D. Vaitl (Eds.), *Cardiorespiratory and cardiosomatic psychophysiology* (pp. 101–115). New York: Plenum Press.

20. Sroufe [Sroufe, L. A. (1996). *Emotional development: The organization of emotional life in the early years.* New York: Cambridge University Press.], while also differentiating a smile from distress, does not consider them emotions, but rather automatic reflexes in response to quantitative rather than qualitative aspects of stimuli, that is, to the temporal and intensity features of arousal. They are not emotions since they do not contain a cognitive component. By 6 months they emerge as basic emotions given the onset of some cognition.

21. Kagan, J., & Lewis, M. (1965). Studies of attention in the human infant. *Merrill–Palmer Quarterly, 11*, 95–127. Lewis, M., Kagan, J., & Kalafat, J. (1966). Patterns of fixation in infants. *Child Development, 37*, 331–341. Lewis, M., Kagan, J., Zavala, F., & Grossberg, R. (1964). Behavioral and cardiac responses to auditory stimulation in the infant. *American Psychologist, 19*, 737 (Abstract). Lewis, M., Meyers, W., Kagan, J., & Grossberg, R. (1963). *Attention to visual patterns in infants.* Paper presented at a symposium on "Studies of Attention in Infants: Methodological Problems and Preliminary Results," American Psychological Association meetings, Philadelphia. Also in *American Psychologist, 18*, 357 (Abstract).

22. Gibson, E. J., & Walk, R. D. (1960). The "visual cliff." *Scientific American, 202*, 67–71.

23. Dodd, C., & Lewis, M. (1969). The magnitude of the orienting response in children as a function of changes in color and contour. *Journal of Experimental Child Psychology, 8*, 296–305.

24. Sroufe, L. A., & Wunsch, J. P. (1972). The development of laughter in the first year of life. *Child Development, 43*(4), 1326–1344.

25. Sroufe, L. A., Waters, E., & Matas, L. (1974). Contextual determinants of infant affective response. In M. Lewis & L. A. Rosenblum (Eds.), *The origins of fear: Vol. 2. The origins of behavior* (pp. 49–72). New York: Wiley.

26. Izard, C. E., Hembree, E. A., & Huebner, R. R. (1987). Infants' emotion expressions to acute pain: Developmental change and stability of individual differences.

Developmental Psychology, 23(1), 105–113. Pavlov, I. P. (1960). *Conditioned reflexes.* New York: Dover Publications. Ramsay, D. S., & Lewis, M. (1994). Developmental change in infant cortisol and behavioral response to inoculation. *Child Development, 65,* 1483–1494. Simonov, P. V. (1964). On the ratio of the motor and vegetative components in the conditioned defensive reflex in man (in Russian). In *Communications Abstracts of the 3rd International Symposium on Central and Peripheral Mechanisms of Motor Activity in Animals and Man,* Moscow (pp. 65–66). Sullivan, M. W., Lewis, M., & Alessandri, S. (1991). Interface between emotion and cognition. In R. M. Downs, L. S. Liben, & D. S. Palermo (Eds.), *Visions of aesthetics, the environment, and development: The legacy of J. F. Wohlwill* (pp. 241–261). Hillsdale, NJ: Erlbaum.

27. Bronson, G. W. (1974). General issues in the study of fear: Section II. In M. Lewis & L. A. Rosenblum (Eds.), *The origins of fear: Vol. 2. The origins of behavior* (pp. 254–258). New York: Wiley. Schaffer, H. R. (1974). Cognitive components of the infant's response to strangeness. In M. Lewis & L. A. Rosenblum (Eds.), *The origins of fear: Vol. 2. The origins of behavior* (pp. 11–24). New York: Wiley. Spitz, R. A. (1965). *The first year of life.* New York: International Universities Press.

28. Lewis, M., & Brooks, J. (1974). Self, others and fear: Infants' reactions to people. In M. Lewis & L. Rosenblum (Eds.), *The origins of fear: Vol. 2. The origins of behavior* (pp. 195–227). New York: Wiley.

29. Campos, J. J., & Stenberg, C. R. (1981). Perception, appraisal, and emotion: The onset of social referencing. In M. E. Lamb & L. R. Sherrod (Eds.), *Infant social cognition: Empirical and theoretical considerations* (pp. 273–314). Hillsdale, NJ: Erlbaum.

30. Lewis, M., Alessandri, S. M. , & Sullivan, M. W. (1990). Violation of expectancy, loss of control, and anger in young infants. *Developmental Psychology, 26*(5), 745–751.

31. Anger at a blocked goal seen in infants as young as 2 months seems to be in contradiction to Piaget's theory that primary circular reactions have not developed that early in the child. However, it may be the case that primary circular reactions can be established through our experimental procedure where we create, through the contingent action of the arm pull and picture outcome, a connection between response and outcome. Gergely and Watson [Gergely, G., & Watson, J. S. (1996). The social biofeedback theory of parental affect-mirroring: The development of emotional self-awareness and self-control in infancy. *International Journal of Psychoanalysis, 77,* 1181–1212.] have argued for such a process established by complex cognitive structures.

32. It is to be noted that the difference between primary and secondary narcissism also addresses this distinction.

33. Ambrose, J. A. (1961). The development of the smiling response in early infancy. In B. M. Foss (Ed.), *Determinants of infant behavior* (pp. 103–105). London: Methuen. Ambrose, A. (1963). The age of onset of ambivalence in early infancy: Indications from the study of laughing. *Journal of Child Psychology and Psychiatry, 4,* 167–181.

34. Fogel, A., Nelson-Goens, G. C., Hsu, H.-C., & Shapiro, A. F. (2000). Do different infant smiles reflect different infant emotions? *Social Development, 9*(4), 497–520. Jones, S. S., Raag, T., & Collins, K. L. (1990). Smiling in older infants: Form and maternal response. *Infant Behavior and Development, 13*(2), 147–165.

35. Blurton-Jones, N. G. (1971). Criteria for use in describing facial expressions of children. *Human Biology, 43*(3), 365–413.

36. Carvajal, F., & Iglesias, J. (1997). Mother and infant smiling exchanges during

face-to-face interaction in infants with and without Down syndrome. *Developmental Psychobiology, 31*(4), 277–286. Kasari, C., & Sigman, M. (1996). Expression and understanding of emotion in atypical development: Autism and Down syndrome. In M. Lewis & M. W. Sullivan (Eds.), *Emotional development in atypical children* (pp. 109–130). Mahwah, NJ: Erlbaum.

37. The argument that one needs to see the expression of another in order to organize one's own expression does not find support here in the case of the blind [Galati, D., Miceli, R., & Sini, B. (2001). Judging and coding facial expression of emotions in congenitally blind children. *International Journal of Behavioral Development, 25*(3), 268–278.].

38. Watson, J. S. (1972). Smiling, cooing, and "The Game." *Merrill–Palmer Quarterly, 18*(4), 323–339.

39. Hitchcock, D. (2002). *The influence of emotional and physiological reactivity on infant memory.* Unpublished doctoral dissertation, Rutgers University, New Brunswick, NJ.

40. Suomi, S. J. (1991). Primate separation models of affective disorders. In J. Madded (Ed.), *Neurobiology of learning, emotion and affect* (pp. 195–213). New York: Raven Press.

41. Bachorowski, J., & Owren, M. J. (2008). Vocal expressions of emotion. In M. Lewis, J. M. Haviland-Jones, & L. Feldman Barrett (Eds.), *Handbook of emotions* (3rd ed., pp. 196–210). New York: Guilford Press.

42. Oster, H. (1978). Facial expression and affect development. In M. Lewis & L. A. Rosenblum (Eds.), *The genesis of behavior: Vol. 1. The development of affect* (pp. 43–76). New York: Plenum Press.

43. While the findings are impressive, the sadness observed may reflect the loss of the interaction rather than a measure of attachment and may reflect the sudden change and loss of something enjoyable; using the paradigm with a stranger might help resolve the problem.

44. Bendersky, M., & Lewis, M. (1998). Arousal modulation in cocaine-exposed infants. *Developmental Psychology, 34*(3), 555–564. Sullivan, M. W., & Lewis, M. (2003). Contextual determinants of anger and other negative expressions in young infants. *Developmental Psychology, 39*(4), 693–705.

45. Rozin, P., Haidt, J., & McCauley, C. R. (2008). Disgust. In M. Lewis, J. M. Haviland-Jones, & L. Feldman Barrett (Eds.), *Handbook of emotions* (3rd ed., pp. 757–776). New York: Guilford Press.

46. Rosenstein, D., & Oster, H. (1988). Differential facial responses to four basic tastes in newborns. *Child Development, 59*(6), 1555–1568.

47. Steiner, J. E. (1979). Human facial expressions in response to taste and smell stimulation. In H. W. Reese & L. P. Lipsitt (Eds.), *Advances in child development and behavior* (Vol. 13, pp. 257–295). New York: Academic Press.

48. Gottman, J. M. (1994). *What predicts divorce?: The relationship between marital processes and marital outcomes.* Hillsdale, NJ: Erlbaum.

Chapter 5. The Rise of Consciousness

1. Block, N. (1995). On a confusion about a function of consciousness. *Behavioral and Brain Sciences, 18,* 227–287. (p. 227)

2. Searle, J. R. (2013, January 10). Can information theory explain consciousness?: Review of *Consciousness: Confessions of a romantic reductionist,* by Christof Koch. *New York Review of Books,* p. 54.

3. Perner, J. (1991). *Understanding the representational mind.* Cambridge, MA: MIT Press.

4. Select portions of this chapter have appeared in Lewis, M. (2010). The emergence of consciousness and its role in human development. In R. M. Lerner & W. F. Overton (Eds.), *The handbook of life-span development: Vol. 1. Cognition, biology, and methods* (pp. 628–670. Hoboken, NJ: Wiley. Copyright 2010 by John Wiley & Sons, Inc. Reprinted by permission of the publisher.

5. Damasio, A. (2010). *Self comes to mind: Constructing the conscious brain.* New York: Pantheon Books/Random House.

6. Hilgard, E. R. (1977). *Divided consciousness: Multiple controls in human thought and action.* New York: Wiley.

7. For other points of view, see Rank, O. (1972). *Will therapy and truth and reality.* New York: Knopf. (Original work published 1945). Rochat, P. (2009). *Others in mind: Social origins of self-consciousness.* New York: Cambridge University Press. Stern, D. N. (1985). *The interpersonal world of the infant.* New York: Basic Books.

8. Hume, D. (1957). *The natural history of religion.* Stanford, CA: Stanford University Press. (Original work published 1757). (p. xix)

9. Cheney, D., & Seyfarth, R. (1990). *How monkeys see the world.* Chicago: University of Chicago Press. Epley, N., Waytz, A., & Cacioppo, J. T. (2007). On seeing human: A three-factor theory of anthropomorphism. *Psychological Review, 114,* 864–886. Morewedge, C. K., Preston, J., & Wegner, D. M. (2007). Timescale bias in the attribution of mind. *Journal of Personality and Social Psychology, 93,* 1–11. Scholl, B. J., & Tremoulet, P. D. (2000). Perceptual causality and animacy. *Trends in Cognitive Sciences, 4,* 299–309.

10. Hecht, J., Miklosi, A., & Gacsi, M. (2012). Behavioral assessment and owner perceptions of behaviors associated with guilt in dogs. *Applied Animal Behavior Science, 139*(1–2), 134–142. Horowitz, A. (2009). Disambiguating the "guilty look": Salient prompts to a familiar dog behavior. *Behavioural Processes, 81*(3), 447–452. Ward, A. G., Olsen, A. S., & Wegner, D. M. (2013). The harm-made mind: Observing victimization augments attribution of minds to vegetative patients, robots and the dead. *Psychological Science.* Published online June 7, doi: 10.1177/0956797612472343.

11. Tronick, E. Z., & Beeghly, M. (2011). Infants' meaning-making and the development of mental health problems. *American Psychologist, 66*(2), 107–119. (p. 113)

12. Gergely and Watson use the infant's action on objects and people as the basis of their claim of early mentalism. This is an important issue to explore since I see these interactions more as action patterns having nothing to do with mentalism. [Gergely, G., & Watson, J. S. (1996). The social biofeedback theory of parental affect-mirroring: The development of emotional self-awareness and self-control in infancy. *International Journal of Psychoanalysis, 77,* 1181–1212.].

13. Lewis, M. (1990). The development of intentionality and the role of consciousness. *Psychological Inquiry, 1*(3), 231–248. Lewis, M. (1990). Intention, consciousness, desires and development. *Psychological Inquiry, 1*(3), 278–283.

14. Newell, A. (1982). The knowledge level. *Artificial Intelligence, 18,* 81–132. Piaget, J. (1952). *The origins of intelligence in children* (M. Cook, Trans.). New York: International Universities Press. (Original work published 1936). Searle, J. R. (1984).

Minds, brains and science. Cambridge, MA: Harvard University Press. Trevarthen, C. B. (1980). The foundations of intersubjectivity: Development of interpersonal and cooperative understanding in infants. In D. R. Olson (Ed.), *The social foundations of language and thought* (pp. 316–342). New York: Norton.

15. Piaget, J. (1952). *The origins of intelligence in children* (M. Cook, Trans.). New York: International Universities Press. (Original work published 1936). Piaget, J., & Inhelder, B. (1969). *The psychology of the child.* New York: Basic Books.

16. Before Piaget Baldwin was also concerned with this issue; see Baldwin, J. M. (1903). *Mental development in the child and the race* (2nd ed.). New York: Macmillan. (Original work published 1894)

17. Dennett, D. C. (2009). *Darwin and the evolution of "why"?* Paper presented at the Darwin Festival, Cambridge, UK. Kagan, J. (2008). In defense of qualitative changes in development. *Child Development, 79*(6), 1606–1624.

18. Lewis, M. (1979). The self as a developmental concept. *Human Development, 22,* 416–419. Neisser, U. (1988). Five kinds of self-knowledge. *Philosophical Psychology, 1,* 35–59. Stern, D. N. (1985). *The interpersonal world of the infant.* New York: Basic Books.

19. For a discussion of this kind of confusion, see Kagan, J. (2008). In defense of qualitative changes in development. *Child Development, 79*(6), 1606–1624. Piaget, J. (1952). *The origins of intelligence in children* (M. Cook, Trans.). New York: International Universities Press. (Original work published 1936)

20. Lewis, M. (1967). The meaning of a response, or why researchers in infant behavior should be oriental metaphysicians. *Merrill–Palmer Quarterly, Behavior and Development, 13*(1), 7–18. Piaget, J. (1952). *The origins of intelligence in children* (M. Cook, Trans.). New York: International Universities Press. (Original work published 1936)

21. Lewis, M., & Michalson, L. (1983). *Children's emotions and moods: Developmental theory and measurement.* New York: Plenum Press.

22. Although most typically developing children show self-recognition by 24 months, several recent reports suggest that cultural differences affect the age for self-recognition. See Courage, M. L., Edison, S. C., & Howe, M. L. (2004). Variability in the early development of visual self-recognition. *Infant Behavior and Development, 27,* 509–532. Keller, H., Kartner, J., Borke, J., Yovsi, R. D., & Kleis, A. (2005). Parenting studies and the development of the categorical self: A longitudinal study on mirror self-recognition in Cameroonian Nso and German families. *International Journal of Behavioral Development, 29*(6), 496–504. Broesch, T., Callaghan, T., Henrich, J., Murphy, C., & Rochat, P. (2010). Cultural variations in children's mirror self-recognition. *Journal of Cross-Cultural Psychology, 42,* 1018–1029.

23. For a broader discussion of the cultural and historical changes, see Lewis, M. (1992). *Shame: The Exposed Self.* New York: Free Press. Also see Geertz, C. (1984). From the native's point of view: On the nature of anthropological understanding. In R. A. Shweder & R. A. Levine (Eds.), *Cultural theory: Essays on mind, self, and emotion* (pp. 123–136). Cambridge, UK: Cambridge University Press. Roland, A. (1988). *In search of self in India and Japan.* Princeton, NJ: Princeton University Press. Shweder, R. A. (2011). Commentary: Ontogenetic cultural psychology. In L. A. Jensen (Ed.), *Bridging cultural and developmental approaches to psychology: New syntheses in theory, research, and policy* (pp. 303–310). New York: Oxford University Press.

24. Lewis, M., Sullivan, M. W., Stanger, C., & Weiss, M. (1989). Self-development and self-conscious emotions. *Child Development, 60*, 146–156.

25. Darwin, C. R. (1965). *The expression of the emotions in man and animals.* Chicago: University of Illinois Press. (Original work published 1872) (p. 327)

26. Lewis, M. (1979). The self as a developmental concept. *Human Development, 22*, 416–419. Lewis, M. (2003). The emergence of consciousness and its role in human development. In J. LeDoux, J. Debiec, & H. Moss (Eds.), *The self: From soul to brain* (Vol. 1001, pp. 104–133). New York: Annals of the New York Academy of Sciences. Also appearing on the ANNALS ONLINE (*www.annalsnyas.org*). Schneider, W. (2011). Memory development in childhood. In U. Goswami (Ed.), *The Wiley–Blackwell handbook of childhood cognitive development* (2nd ed., pp. 347–376). Malden, MA: Wiley–Blackwell.

27. Von Bertalanffy, L. (1967). *Robots, men, and minds.* New York: Brazilles.

28. Gross, J. J. (1999). Emotion and emotion regulation. In L. A. Pervin & O. P. John (Eds.), *Handbook of personality: Theory and research, 2nd edition* (pp. 525–552). New York: Guilford Press.

29. Damasio, A. (2003). *Looking for Spinoza: Joy, sorrow, and the feeling brain.* London: Heinemann. Damasio, A. (2010). *Self comes to mind: Constructing the conscious brain.* New York: Pantheon Books/Random House.

30. Wegner, D. M. (2009). How to think, say, or do precisely the worst thing for any occasion. *Science, 325*, 48–50.

31. Gazzaniga, M. S. (1988). Brain modularity: Towards a philosophy of conscious experience. In A. J. Marcel & E. Bisiach (Eds.), *Consciousness in contemporary science* (pp. 218–238). New York: Oxford University Press. For a historical review of this topic, see Wylie, R. C. (1961). *A self-concept: A critical survey of pertinent research literature.* Lincoln, NE: University of Nebraska Press.

32. Pribram, K. H. (1984). Emotion: A neurobehavioral analysis. In K. R. Scherer & P. Ekman (Eds.), *Approaches to emotion* (pp. 13–38). Hillsdale, NJ: Erlbaum. (p. 25)

33. Lewis, M., Stanger, C., & Sullivan, M. W. (1989). Deception in three-year-olds. *Developmental Psychology, 25*(3), 439–443. Wellman, H. M. (1990). *The child's theory of mind.* Cambridge, MA: MIT Press. Moses, J., & Chandler, M. J. (1992). Traveler's guide to children's theories of mind. *Psychological Inquiry, 3*, 285–301.

34. For a discussion of this type of problem, see Putnam, H. (1981). *Reason, truth, and history.* New York: Cambridge University Press.

35. Harter, S. (1983). Developmental perspectives on the self-system. In E. M. Hetherington (Ed.), *Handbook of child psychology: Vol. 4. Socialization, personality and social development* (pp. 275–385). New York: Wiley. Hobson, R. P. (1990). On the origins of self and the case of autism. *Development and Psychopathology, 2*, 163–181.

36. St. Aubyn, E. (2005). *Mother's milk.* New York: Open City Books. (pp. 577–578)

37. The ability to use the mirror to reference himself has been mistaken for the child's understanding of the reflective property of mirrors. There is ample evidence that although children are able to produce self-referential behavior through the use of the mirror-mark technique, they do not know many of the properties of reflected surfaces; for example, they cannot use the mirror to find an object reflected in its surface [Butterworth, G. (1990). Origins of self-perception in infancy. In D. Cicchetti & M. Beeghly (Eds.), *The self in transition: Infancy to childhood* (pp. 119–137). Chicago: University

of Chicago Press.]. What is important about the self-referential behaviors in the mirror is that they need not be a marker of general knowledge about reflected surfaces, but rather a marker for the child's knowledge about himself. They are the equivalent of the phrase "That's me." This recognition, if put into words, says "is this me over there, is this me here."

38. Leslie, A. M. (1987). Pretense and representation: The origin of "theory of mind." *Psychological Review, 94,* 412–426.

39. Fein, G. G. (1975). A transformational analysis of pretending. *Developmental Psychology, 11,* 291–296. Flavell, J. H. (1988). The development of children's knowledge about the mind: From cognitive connections to mental representations. In J. W. Astington, P. L. Harris, & D. R. Olson (Eds.), *Developing theories of mind* (pp. 244–267). Cambridge, UK: Cambridge University Press. Huttenlocher, J., & Higgins, E. T. (1978). Issues in the study of symbolic development. In W. Collins (Ed.), *Minnesota Symposia on Child Psychology* (Vol. 11, pp. 98–140). Hillsdale, NJ: Erlbaum. Lowe, M. (1975). Trends in the development of representational play in infants from one to three years: An observational study. *Journal of Child Psychology and Psychiatry, 16,* 33–47. McCune, L. (1995). A normative study of representation play at the transition to language. *Developmental Psychology, 31,* 198–206. McCune-Nicolich, L. (1981). Toward symbolic functioning: Structure of early pretend games and potential parallels with language. *Child Development, 52*(3), 785–797. Nicolich, L. (1977). Beyond sensorimotor intelligence: Assessment of symbolic maturity through analysis of pretend play. *Merrill–Palmer Quarterly, 23,* 89–102. Piaget, J. (1962). *Play, dreams, and imitation in childhood* (C. Gatlegno & F. M. Hodgson, Trans.). New York: Norton. (Original work published 1951 in French). Rosen, C. S., Schwebel, D. C., & Singer, J. L. (1997). Preschoolers' attributions of mental states in pretense. *Child Development, 68,* 1133–1142. Wellman, H. M. (1990). *The child's theory of mind.* Cambridge, MA: MIT Press. Wimmer, H., & Perner, J. (1983). Beliefs about beliefs: Representation and constraining function of wrong beliefs in young children's understanding of deception. *Cognition, 13,* 103–128.

40. Lewis, M., & Ramsay, D. S. (2004). Development of self-recognition, personal pronoun use, and pretend play during the 2nd year. *Child Development, 75*(6), 1821–1831.

41. Lewis, M., Sullivan, M. W., Stanger, C., & Weiss, M. (1989). Self-development and self-conscious emotions. *Child Development, 60,* 146–156.

42. Zahn-Waxler, C., Radke-Yarrow, M., Wagner, E., & Chapman, M. (1992). Development of concern for others. *Developmental Psychology, 28,* 126–136.

43. Bischof-Kohler, D. (1994). Self-objectification and other-oriented emotions: Self-recognition, empathy, and prosocial behavior in the second year. *Zeitschrift für Psychologie, 202,* 349–377.

44. Harley, K., & Reese, E. (1999). Origins of autobiographical memory. *Developmental Psychology, 35,* 1338–1348.

45. Asendorpf, J. B. (2002). Self-awareness and secondary representation. In A. N. Meltzoff & W. Prinz (Eds.), *The imitative mind: Development, evolution, and brain bases. Cambridge studies in cognitive perceptual development* (pp. 63–73). New York: Cambridge University Press. Asendorpf, J. B., & Baudonniere, P. M. (1993). Self-awareness and other-awareness: Mirror self-recognition and synchronic imitation among unfamiliar peers. *Developmental Psychology, 29*(1), 88–95. Asendorpf, J.

B., Warkentin, V., & Baudonniere, P. M. (1996). Self-awareness and other-awareness: II. Mirror self-recognition, social contingency awareness, and synchronic imitation. *Developmental Psychology, 32*(2), 313–321.

46. Bertenthal, B. L., & Fischer, K. W. (1978). Development of self-recognition in the infant. *Developmental Psychology, 14,* 44–50. Carmody, D. P., & Lewis, M. (2010). Regional white matter development in children with autism spectrum disorders. *Developmental Psychobiology, 52*(8), 755–763. Published online June 16, 2010. Fischer, K. (1980). A theory of cognitive development: The control and construction of hierarchies of skills. *Psychological Review, 87,* 477–531. Also see Mascolo, M. P., & Fischer, K. W. (2010). The dynamic development of thinking, feeling, and acting over the life span. In W. F. Overton & R. M. Lerner (Eds.), *The handbook of life-span development: Vol. 1. Cognition, biology and methods* (pp. 149–194). Hoboken, NJ: Wiley. Pipp, S., Fischer, K. W., & Jennings, S. (1987). Acquisition of self- and mother knowledge in infancy. *Developmental Psychology, 23,* 86–96.

47. Hobson, R. P. (1990). On the origins of self and the case of autism. *Development and Psychopathology, 2,* 163–181. Lewis, M., & Carmody, D. (2008). Self-representation and brain development. *Developmental Psychology, 44*(5), 1329–1334.

48. Gallup, G. G. Jr. (1970). Chimpanzees: Self-recognition. *Science, 167*(3914), 86–87. Gallup, G. G. Jr. (1991). Toward a comparative psychology of self-awareness: Species limitations and cognitive consequences. In G. R. Goethals & J. Strauss (Eds.), *The self: An interdisciplinary approach* (pp. 121–135). New York: Springer-Verlag.

49. Fletcher, P. C., Happe, F., Frith, U., Baker, S. C., Dolan R. J., Frackowiak, R. S., et al. (1995). Other minds in the brain: A functional imaging study of "theory of mind" in story comprehension. *Cognition, 57*(2), 109–128. Fossati, P., Hevenor, S. J., Graham, S. J., Grady, C., Keightley, M. L., Craik, F., et al. (2003). In search of the emotional self: An fMRI study using positive and negative emotional words. *American Journal of Psychiatry, 160*(11), 1938–1945. Frith, C. D., & Frith, U. (2006). The neural basis of mentalizing. *Neuron, 50*(4), 531–534. Frith, U., & Frith, C. D. (2003). Development and neurophysiology of mentalizing. *Philosophical Transactions of the Royal Society of London B: Biological Sciences, 358*(1431), 459–473. Gallagher, H. L., Happe, F., Brunswick, N., Fletcher, P. C., Frith, U., & Frith, C. D. (2000). Reading the mind in cartoons and stories: An fMRI study of "theory of mind" in verbal and nonverbal tasks. *Neuropsychologia, 38*(1), 11–21. Kampe, K. K., Frith, C. D., & Frith, U. (2003). "Hey John": Signals conveying communicative intention toward the self activate brain regions associated with "mentalizing," regardless of modality. *Journal of Neuroscience, 23*(12), 5258–5263. Macrae, C. N., Moran, J. M., Heatherton, T. F., Banfield, J. F., & Kelley, W. M. (2004). Medial prefrontal activity predicts memory for self. *Cerebral Cortex, 14*(6), 647–654. Mitchell, J. P., Heatherton, T. F., & Macrae, C. N. (2002). Distinct neural systems subserve person and object knowledge. *Proceedings of the National Academy of Sciences of the USA, 99*(23), 15238–15243. Pfeifer, J. H., & Peake, S. J. (2012). Self-development: Integrating cognitive, socioemotional, and neuroimaging perspectives. *Developmental Cognitive Neuroscience, 2*(1), 55–69.

50. Fletcher, P. C., Happe, F., Frith, U., Baker, S. C., Dolan R. J., Frackowiak, R. S., et al. (1995). Other minds in the brain: A functional imaging study of "theory of mind" in story comprehension. *Cognition, 57*(2), 109–128. Fossati, P., Hevenor, S. J., Graham, S. J., Grady, C., Keightley, M. L., Craik, F., et al. (2003). In search of the emotional self: An fMRI study using positive and negative emotional words. *American*

Journal of Psychiatry, 160(11), 1938–1945. Frith, C. D., & Frith, U. (2006). The neural basis of mentalizing. *Neuron, 50*(4), 531–534. Frith, U., & Frith, C. D. (2003). Development and neurophysiology of mentalizing. *Philosophical Transactions of the Royal Society of London B: Biological Sciences, 358*(1431), 459–473. Gallagher, H. L., Happe, F., Brunswick, N., Fletcher, P. C., Frith, U., & Frith, C. D. (2000). Reading the mind in cartoons and stories: An fMRI study of "theory of mind" in verbal and nonverbal tasks. *Neuropsychologia, 38*(1), 11–21. Kampe, K. K., Frith, C. D., & Frith, U. (2003). "Hey John": Signals conveying communicative intention toward the self activate brain regions associated with "mentalizing," regardless of modality. *Journal of Neuroscience, 23*(12), 5258–5263. Macrae, C. N., Moran, J. M., Heatherton, T. F., Banfield, J. F., & Kelley, W. M. (2004). Medial prefrontal activity predicts memory for self. *Cerebral Cortex, 14*(6), 647–654. Mitchell, J. P., Heatherton, T. F., & Macrae, C. N. (2002). Distinct neural systems subserve person and object knowledge. *Proceedings of the National Academy of Sciences of the USA, 99*(23), 15238–15243. Pfeifer, J. H., & Peake, S. J. (2012). Self-development: Integrating cognitive, socioemotional, and neuroimaging perspectives. *Developmental Cognitive Neuroscience, 2*(1), 55–69.

51. Saxe, R., Carey, S., & Kanwisher, N. (2004). Understanding other minds: Linking developmental psychology and functional neuroimaging. *Annual Review of Psychology, 55,* 87–124. Souweidane, M. M., Kim, K. H., McDowall, R., Ruge, M. I., Lis, E., Krol, G., et al. (1999). Brain mapping in sedated infants and young children with passive-functional magnetic resonance imaging. *Pediatric Neurosurgery, 30*(2), 86–92.

52. Anjari, M., Srinivasan, L., Allsop, J. M., Hajnal, J. V., Rutherford, M. A., Edwards, A. D., et al. (2007). Diffusion tensor imaging with tract-based spatial statistics reveals local white matter abnormalities in preterm infants. *Neuroimage, 35*(3), 1021–1027. Carmody, D. P, Dunn, S. M., Boddie-Willis, A. S., DeMarco, J. K., & Lewis, M. (2004). A quantitative measure of myelination development in infants, using MR images. *Neuroradiology, 46,* 781–786. Dubois, J., Hertz-Pannier, L., Dehaene-Lambertz, G., Cointepas, Y., & Le Bihan, D. (2006). Assessment of the early organization and maturation of infants' cerebral white matter fiber bundles: A feasibility study using quantitative diffusion tensor imagining and tractography. *Neuroimage, 30*(4), 1121–1132. Giedd, J. N., Blumenthal, J., Jeffries, N. O., Castellanos, F. X., Liu, H., Zijdenbos, A., et al. (1999). Brain development during childhood and adolescence: A longitudinal MRI study. *Nature Neuroscience, 2*(10), 861–863. Hermoye, L., Saint-Martin, C., Cosnard, G., Lee, S. K., Kim, J., Nassogne, M. C., et al. (2006). Pediatric diffusion tensor imaging: Normal database and observation of the white matter maturation in early childhood. *Neuroimage, 29*(2), 493–504. Mukherjee, P., Miller, J. H., Shimony, J. S., Conturo, T. E., Lee, B. C., Almli, C. R., et al. (2001). Normal brain maturation during childhood: Developmental trends characterized with diffusion-tensor MR imaging. *Radiology, 221*(2), 349–358. Thompson, D. K., Warfield, S. K., Carlin, J. B., Pavlovic, M., Wang, H. X., Bear, M., et al. (2007). Perinatal risk factors altering regional brain structure in the preterm infant. *Brain, 130,* 667–677.

53. Carmody, D. P., Dunn, S. M., & Lewis, M. (2003). Brain activity during auditory name recognition: A functional MRI study. *Academic Radiology, 10,* 952–953. Carmody, D. P., & Lewis, M. (2006). Brain activation when hearing one's own and others' names. *Brain Research, 1116,* 153–158. Carmody, D. P., & Lewis, M. (2012). Self representation in children with and without autism spectrum disorders. *Child*

Psychiatry and Human Development, 43(2), 227–237. Carmody, D. P., & Lewis, M. (in preparation) Self representation and brain enlargement in children with autism spectrum disorders. Lewis, M., & Carmody, D. P. (2008). Self representation and brain development. *Developmental Psychology, 44*(5), 1329–1334. Some studies have found evidence for both left- and right-hemisphere involvement in self-representation; however, the left hemisphere shows greater activation on tasks involving self-representation, whereas the right hemisphere shows activation in tasks involving self in comparison with others. For example, Ruby and Decety [Ruby, P., & Decety, J. (2001). Effect of subjective perspective taking during simulation of action: A PET investigation of agency. *Nature Neuroscience, 4*(5), 546–550.], using PET, reported left parietal activation when subjects mentally simulated an action with a first-person perspective and right parietal activation when subjects simulated an action with a third-person perspective. See also Frith, C. D., & Frith, U. (2006). The neural basis of mentalizing. *Neuron, 50*(4), 531–534. Frith, U., & Frith, C. D. (2003). Development and neurophysiology of mentalizing. *Philosophical Transactions of the Royal Society of London B: Biological Sciences, 358*(1431), 459–473.

54. Frith, C. D., & Frith, U. (2006). The neural basis of mentalizing. *Neuron, 50*(4), 531–534. Frith, U., & Frith, C. D. (2003). Development and neurophysiology of mentalizing. *Philosophical Transactions of the Royal Society of London B: Biological Sciences, 358*(1431), 459–473.

55. In fact the various ideas about social interaction can lead to different conclusions. For Freud or John Watson, imperfect contingency is necessary for its development, while for others, for example, Edward Z. Tronick, the most efficient parenting involves the most responsive, a view also shared by Cooley.

56. James, W. (1890). *The principles of psychology.* New York: Holt. (p. 43)

57. See Overton, W. F. (2006). Developmental psychology: Philosophy, concepts, methodology. In R. M. Lerner & W. Damon (Eds.), *Handbook of child psychology: Vol. 1. Theoretical models of human development* (6th ed., pp. 18–88). Hoboken, NJ: Wiley.

58. It should be noted that new ideas about pain also make the distinction between the bodily experience and the idea or experience of pain. See Grahek, N. (2001). *Feeling pain and being in pain.* Oldenburg, Germany: BIS-Verlag.

59. Piaget, J. (1960). *The psychology of intelligence.* New York: Littlefield Adams. (p. 39)

60. Mead, G. H. (1934). *Mind, self, and society: From the standpoint of a social behaviorist.* Chicago: University of Chicago Press. (p. 135)

61. Winnicott, D. W. (1965). A personal view of the Kleinian contribution. In D. W. Winnicott, *The maturational processes and the facilitating environment: Studies in the theory of emotional development* (pp. 171–178). Oxford, UK: International Universities Press. (p. 177)

62. Mahler, M. S., Pine, F., & Bergman, A. (1975). *The psychological birth of the infant.* New York: Basic Books.

63. In our study of attachment and the child's development of consciousness as measured in self-reflected behaviors, we have not found any relation. See Lewis, M., Brooks-Gunn, J., & Jaskir, J. (1985). Individual differences in visual self recognition as a function of mother–infant attachment relationship. *Developmental Psychology, 21*, 1181–1187. Pipp, S., Fischer, K. W., & Jennings, S. (1987). Acquisition of self- and mother knowledge in infancy. *Developmental Psychology, 23*, 86–96.

64. Bannister, D., & Agnew, J. (1977). The child's construing of self. In J. K. Cole & A. W. Landfield (Eds.), *Nebraska Symposium on Motivation: Vol. 24. 1976 Personal construct psychology*. Lincoln: University of Nebraska Press. (p. 99)

65. Merleau-Ponty, M. (1964). *Primacy of perception* (J. Eddie, Ed.; W. Cobb, Trans.). Evanston, IL: Northwestern University Press. (p. 113)

66. Asch, S. E. (1952). *Social psychology*. Englewood Cliffs, NJ: Prentice-Hall. Heider, F. (1958). *The psychology of interpersonal relations*. New York: Wiley. (p. 33)

67. Although Duval and Wicklund's argument seems reasonable, there are some difficulties with it. For example, take their point 1 about an entity who has a different point of view than the child. How can the child know there is a different point of view without knowing his own point of view, implying self-reflection in the creation of consciousness, which is what consciousness is about?

68. Gergely and Watson use the child's action on objects and people as the basis of their claim of early mentalism. This becomes an important issue to explore [Gergely, G., & Watson, J. S. (1996). The social biofeedback theory of parental affect-mirroring: The development of emotional self-awareness and self-control in infancy. *International Journal of Psychoanalysis, 77*, 1181–1212.].

69. Margalit, A. (2005, October 20). The genius of Spinoza. A review of *Spinoza and Spinozism*, by Stuart Hampshire. *The New York Review of Books*, p. 50.

Chapter 6. The Transforming Role of Consciousness

1. From Oates, J. C. (2011, September 29). The cure! A review of *Teach us to sit still: A skeptic's search for health and healing*, by Tim Parks. *The New York Review of Books, 58*(14).

2. The idea of procedural rules can be found in an excellent paper by Perner [Perner, J. (2010). Who took the cog out of cog*nitive* science?: Mentalism in an era of anti-cognitivism. In P. A. Frensch & R. Schwarzer (Eds.), *International perspectives on psychological science: Vol. 1. Cognition and neuropsychology* (pp. 241–261). New York: Psychology Press.].

3. Gazzaniga, M. S. (1985). *The social brain: Discovering the networks of the mind*. New York: Basic Books.

4. LeDoux, J. (1990). Cognitive and emotional interactions in the brain. *Cognition and Emotions, 3*(4), 265–289. Weiskrantz, L. (1986). *Blindsight: A case study and implications*. Oxford, UK: Oxford University Press.

5. Charcot, J. M. (1889). *Clinical lectures on diseases of the nervous system*. London: New Sydenham Society. Hilgard, E. R. (1977). *Divided consciousness: Multiple controls in human thought and action*. New York: Wiley. Janet, P. (1929). *Major symptoms of hysteria*. New York: Hafner.

6. Werner, H. (1948). *Comparative psychology of mental development*. Oxford, UK: Follett.

7. Much of this section appeared in Lewis, M. (2010). The emergence of consciousness and its role in human development. In R. M. Lerner & W. F. Overton (Eds.), *The handbook of lifespan development: Vol. 1. Cognition, biology, and methods* (pp. 628–670). Hoboken, NJ: Wiley. Copyright 2010 by John Wiley & Sons, Inc. Reprinted by permission of the publisher.

8. Durant, W. (1954). *The story of philosophy*. New York: Pocket Books. (pp. 121, 129)

9. Clark, R. W. (1972). *Einstein: The life and times*. New York: Avon. (p. 58)

10. Clark, R. W. (1972). *Einstein: The life and times*. New York: Avon. (p. 119)

11. Clark, R. W. (1972). *Einstein: The life and times*. New York: Avon. (p. 120)

12. Clark, R. W. (1972). *Einstein: The life and times*. New York: Avon. (p. 120)

13. Zukav, G. (1979). *The dancing Wu Li masters*. New York: Morrow. (p. 54)

14. Zukav, G. (1979). *The dancing Wu Li masters*. New York: Morrow. (p. 110)

15. Merleau-Ponty, M. (1964). *Primacy of perception* (J. Eddie, Ed.; W. Cobb, Trans.). Evanston, IL: Northwestern University Press. Overton, W. F. (2006). Developmental psychology: Philosophy, concepts, methodology. In R. M. Lerner & W. Damon (Eds.), *Handbook of child psychology: Vol. 1. Theoretical models of human development* (6th ed., pp. 18–88). Hoboken, NJ: Wiley. Piaget, J. (1960). *The psychology of intelligence*. New York: Littlefield Adams. Polyani, M. (1958). *Personal language: Toward a post-critical philosophy*. London: Routledge & Kegan Paul.

16. Hamlyn, D. W. (1974). Person-perception and our understanding of others. In T. Mischel (Ed.), *Understanding other persons* (pp. 1–36). Oxford, UK: Rowman & Littlefield.

17. Merleau-Ponty, M. (1964). *Primacy of perception* (J. Eddie, Ed.; W. Cobb, Trans.). Evanston, IL: Northwestern University Press. (p. 113)

18. Gallup, G. G. Jr. (1991). Toward a comparative psychology of self-awareness: Species limitations and cognitive consequences. In G. R. Goethals & J. Strauss (Eds.), *The self: An interdisciplinary approach* (pp. 121–135). New York: Springer-Verlag. Leslie, A. M. (1987). Pretense and representation: The origin of "theory of mind." *Psychological Review, 94*, 412–426. Povinelli, D. J., & Eddy, T. J. (1996). What young chimpanzees know about seeing. *Monographs of the Society for Research in Child Development* (Serial No. 247, Vol. 61, No. 3). Premack, D., & Woodruff, G. (1978). Does the chimpanzee have a theory of mind? *The Brain and Behavioral Sciences, 4*, 515–526. Shantz, C. U. (1975). *The development of social cognition*. Chicago: University of Chicago Press. Youniss, J. (1975). Another perspective on social cognition. In A. D. Pick (Ed.), *Minnesota Symposium on Child Psychology, Vol. 9* (pp. 173–196). Minneapolis: University of Minnesota Press.

19. Leslie, A. M. (1987). Pretense and representation: The origin of "theory of mind." *Psychological Review, 94*, 412–426.

20. Baillargeon, R., Li, J., Gertner, Y., & Wu, D. (2011). How do infants reason about physical events? In U. Goswami (Ed.), *The Wiley–Blackwell handbook of childhood cognitive development, 2nd edition* (pp. 11–48). Malden, MA: Wiley–Blackwell.

21. Asch, S. E. (1952). *Social psychology*. Englewood Cliffs, NJ: Prentice-Hall. (p. 212)

22. Bannister, D., & Agnew, J. (1977). The child's construing of self. In J. K. Cole & A. W. Landfield (Eds.), *Nebraska Symposium on Motivation: Vol. 24. 1976, Personal construct psychology* (pp. 99–125). Lincoln: University of Nebraska Press. (p. 101)

23. Hinde, R. N. (1976). Interactions, relationships and social structure. *Man, 11*, 1–17. Hinde, R. N. (1979). *Towards understanding relationships*. London: Academic Press.

24. Buber, M. (1958). *I & thou* (2nd ed.) (R. G. Smith, Trans.). New York:

Scribners. Emde, R. N. (1988). Developmental terminable and interminable: II. Recent psychoanalytical theory and therapeutic considerations. *International Journal of Psychoanalysis, 69,* 283–296. Sullivan, H. S. (1953). *The interpersonal theory of psychiatry.* New York: Norton.

25. Borke, H. (1971). Interpersonal perception of young children: Egocentricism or empathy. *Developmental Psychology, 5,* 263–269. Zahn-Waxler, C., & Radke-Yarrow, M. (1981). The development of prosocial behavior: Alternative research strategies. In N. Eisenberg-Berg (Ed.), *The development of prosocial behavior* (pp. 109–138). New York: Academic Press.

26. Mahler, M. S., Pine, F., & Bergman, A. (1975). *The psychological birth of the infant.* New York: Basic Books.

27. Bretherton, I. (1987). New perspectives on attachment relations: Security, communication, and internal working models. In J. D. Osofsky (Ed.), *Handbook of infant development* (2nd ed., pp. 1061–1100). New York: Wiley. Main, M., Kaplan, N., & Cassidy, J. (1985). Security in infancy, childhood, and adulthood: A move to the level of representation. In I. Bretherton & W. Waters (Eds.), Growing points of attachment theory and research. *Monographs of the Society for Research in Child Development,* 50, (1–2, Serial No. 209), 66–104.

28. Bowlby, J. (1973). *Attachment and loss: Vol. 2. Separation: Anxiety and anger.* New York: Basic Books.

29. Lewis, M., Feiring, C., & Rosenthal, S. (2000). Attachment over time. *Child Development, 71*(3), 707–720. Sroufe, L. A., Coffino, B., & Carlson, E. A. (2010). Conceptualizing the role of early experience: Lessons from the Minnesota Longitudinal Study. *Developmental Review, 30*(1), 36–51.

30. Rozin, P., Haidt, J., & McCauley, C. R. (2008). Disgust. In M. Lewis, J. M. Haviland-Jones, & L. Feldman Barrett (Eds.), *Handbook of emotions, 3rd edition* (pp. 757–776). New York: Guilford Press.

31. Daniel Dennett and others (see, e.g., Hilary Putnam) have tried to make a distinction between competence and comprehension, the former reflecting complex action patterns with little associative meaning, while the latter include these action patterns with mental ability including consciousness, as well as ideas about the world. I have made this distinction in trying to explain the difference between machinery of the self as in action patterns and consciousness which is about an idea of me. To restate the developmental process as I see it involves the movement from action patterns to ideas, in terms of both the nature of elicitors of emotional life and the nature of the type of emotional response found in the culture where development takes place [Dennett, D. C. (2009, July). *Darwin and the evolution of "why"?* Paper presented at the Darwin Festival, Cambridge, UK. Putnam, H. (1963). Brains and behavior. In R. J. Butler (Ed.), *Analytical philosophy, second series* (pp. 211–235). Oxford, UK: Basil Blackwell.].

32. See Bischof-Kohler, D. (1991). The development of empathy in infants. In M. E. Lamb & H. Keller (Eds.), *Development: Perspectives from German-speaking countries* (pp. 245–273). Hillsdale, NJ: Erlbaum. Halperin, M. (1989, April). *Empathy and self-awareness.* Paper presented at the Society for Research in Child Development meeting, Kansas City.

33. Hart, S. L. (2010). The ontogenesis of jealousy in the first year of life: A theory of jealousy as a biologically-based dimension of temperament. In S. L. Hart & M. Legerstee (Eds.), *Handbook of jealousy: Theory, research, and multidisciplinary approaches*

(pp. 57–82). Malden, MA: Blackwell/Wiley. Lewis, M. (2010). Loss, protest, and emotional development. In S. Hart & M. Legerstee (Eds.), *Handbook of jealousy: Theory, research, and multidisciplinary approaches* (pp. 27–39). Malden, MA: Blackwell/Wiley. Masciuch, S., & Kienapple, K. (1993). The emergence of jealousy in children 4 months to 7 years of age. *Journal of Social and Personal Relationships, 10,* 421–435.

34. Beck, A. T. (1979). *Cognitive therapy and the emotional disorders.* New York: Meridian. Nolen-Hoeksema, S., Wolfson, A., Mumme, D., & Guskin, K. (1995). Helplessness in children of depressed and nondepressed mothers. *Developmental Psychology, 31(3),* 377–387. Seligman, M. E. P. (1975). *Helplessness: On depression, development, and death.* San Francisco: Freeman.

35. Darwin, C. R. (1965). *The expression of the emotions in man and animals.* Chicago: University of Illinois Press. (Original work published 1872) (p. 325)

Chapter 7. Lying and Deception in Emotional Life

1. Lewis, M. (1993). The development of deception. In M. Lewis & C. Saarni (Eds.), *Lying and deception in everyday life* (pp. 90–105). New York: Guilford Press.

2. Mitchell, R. W. (1993). Animals as liars: The human face of nonhuman duplicity. In M. Lewis & C. Saarni (Eds.), *Lying and deception in everyday life* (pp. 59–89). New York: Guilford Press.

3. Ekman, P., & Friesen, W. V. (1975). *Unmasking the face: A guide to recognizing emotions from facial clues.* Englewood Cliffs, NJ: Prentice-Hall. Izard, C. (1977). *Human emotions.* New York: Plenum Press.

4. Ekman, P. (1985). *Telling lies.* New York: Norton.

5. Lewis, M., & Saarni, C. (Eds.). (1993). *Lying and deception in everyday life.* New York: Guilford Press. Saarni, C., & Lewis, M. (1993). Deceit and illusion in human affairs. In M. Lewis & C. Saarni (Eds.), *Lying and deception in everyday life* (pp. 1–29). New York: Guilford Press.

6. Bond, C. F., & DePaulo, B. M. (2006). Accuracy of deception judgments. *Personality and Social Psychology Review, 10,* 214–234. Ekman, P., & O'Sullivan, M. (1991). Who can catch a liar? *American Psychologist, 46(9),* 913–920. Porter, S., & ten Brinke, L. (2008). Reading between the lies: Identifying concealed and falsified emotions in universal facial expressions. *Psychological Science, 19(5),* 508–514. Vrij, A. (2000). *Detecting lies and deceit: The psychology of lying and the implications for professional practice.* Chichester, UK: Wiley. Vrij, A. (2008). *Detecting lies and deceit: Pitfalls and opportunities.* Chichester, UK: Wiley.

7. Trivers, R. L. (2011). *The folly of fools: The logic of deceit and self-deception in human life.* New York: Basic Books.

8. Some studies of adults suggest that people show increases in negative emotions when they are challenged with difficult tasks (see Maya Tamir's work [e.g., Ford, B. Q., & Tamir, M. (2012). When getting angry is smart: Emotional preferences and emotional intelligence. *Emotion, 12(4),* 685–689.]. Perhaps a more accurate picture would be that too much of negative emotions such as shame may be harmful, while moderate amounts may not be (see, e.g., Dacher Keltner and Ann Kring's paper on this topic [Keltner, D., & Kring, A. M. (1998). Emotion, social function, and psychopathology. *Review of General Psychology, 2(3),* 320–342.].

9. See also Byrne, R. W., & Corp, N. (2004). Neocortex size predicts deception rate in primates. *Proceedings of the Royal Society of London B: Biological Sciences, 271,* 1693–1699. Otter, Z., & Egan, V. (2007). The evolutionary role of self-deceptive enhancement as a protective factor against antisocial cognitions. *Personality and Individual Differences, 43,* 2258–2269.

10. Hilgard, E. R. (1977). *Divided consciousness: Multiple controls in human thought and action.* New York: Wiley. Janet, P. (1929). *Major symptoms of hysteria.* New York: Hafner.

11. Crossman, A. M., & Lewis, M. (2006). Adults' ability to detect children's lying. *Behavioral Sciences and the Law, 24,* 703–715.

12. Ambrose, J. A. (1961). The development of the smiling response in early infancy. In B. Foss (Ed.), *Determinants of infant behaviour* (Vol. 1, pp. 179–196). New York: Wiley. Gewirtz, J. L. (1965). The course of smiling by groups of Israeli infants in the first 18 months of life. *Scripta Hierosolymitana, 14,* 9–58. Wolff, P. H. (1963). Observations on the early development of smiling. In B. M. Foss (Ed.), *Determinants of infant behavior* (Vol. 2, pp. 113–138). London: Methuen.

13. See Anderson, M. C., & Levy, B. J. (2009). Suppressing unwanted memories. *Current Directions in Psychological Science, 18*(4), 189–194. Fazio, L. K., & Marsh, E. J. (2010). Correcting false memories. *Psychological Science, 21*(6), 801–803. Lindsay, D. S., Hagen, L., Read, J. D., Wade, K. A., & Garry, M. (2004). True photographs and false memories. *Psychological Science, 15*(3), 149–154. Mazzoni, G., Scoboria, A., & Harvey, L. (2010). Nonbelieved memories. *Psychological Science, 21*(9), 1334–1340.

14. Saarni, C. (1984). An observational study of children's attempts to monitor their expressive behavior. *Child Development, 55,* 1504–1513.

15. Cole, P. M. (1986). Children's spontaneous control of facial expression. *Child Development, 57,* 1309–1321.

16. See the work of Victoria Talwar and Kang Lee [Talwar, V., Murphy, S. M., & Lee, K. (2007). White lie-telling in children for politeness purposes. *International Journal of Behavioral Development, 31*(1), 1–11.].

17. See also Garner, P. W., & Power, T. G. (1996). Preschoolers' emotional control in the disappointment paradigm and its relation to temperament, emotional knowledge, and family expressiveness. *Child Development, 67,* 1406–1419. Talwar, V., & Lee, K. (2002). Emergence of white lie-telling in children between 3 and 7 years of age. *Merrill–Palmer Quarterly, 48,* 160–181. Talwar, V., Murphy, S. M., & Lee, K. (2007). White lie-telling in children for politeness purposes. *International Journal of Behavioral Development, 31*(1), 1–11.

18. Braten, S. (2009). *The intersubjective mirror in infant learning and evolution of speech.* Amsterdam, The Netherlands: Benjamins.

19. Brighi, A. (2011). Personal communication. University of Bologna, Italy.

20. Lewis, M. (1993). The development of deception. In M. Lewis & C. Saarni (Eds.), *Lying and deception in everyday life* (pp. 90–105). New York: Guilford Press. Lewis, M., Stanger, C., & Sullivan, M. W. (1989). Deception in three-year-olds. *Developmental Psychology, 25*(3), 439–443. Polak, A., & Harris, P. L. (1999). Deception by young children following noncompliance. *Developmental Psychology, 35,* 561–568.

21. Lewis, M. (1993). The development of deception. In M. Lewis & C. Saarni (Eds.), *Lying and deception in everyday life* (pp. 90–105). New York: Guilford Press. Lewis, M. (2008). The emergence of human emotions. In M. Lewis, J. M. Haviland-Jones,

& L. Feldman Barrett (Eds.), *Handbook of emotions, 3rd edition* (pp. 304–319). New York: Guilford Press. Talwar, V., & Lee, K. (2008). Social and cognitive correlates of children's lying behavior. *Child Development, 79*(4), 866–881.

22. Mischel, W., & Metzner, R. (1962). Preference for delayed reward as a function of age, intelligence, and length of delay interval. *Journal of Abnormal and Social Psychology, 64*(6), 425–431.

23. Talwar, V., & Lee, K. (2008). Social and cognitive correlates of children's lying behavior. *Child Development, 79*(4), 866–881.

24. Leslie, A. M. (1987). Pretense and representation: The origins of "theory of mind." *Psychological Review, 94*(4), 412–426. Piaget, J. (1962). *Play, dreams, and imitation in childhood* (C. Gatlegno & F. M. Hodgson, Trans.). New York: Norton. (Original work published 1951 in French)

25. Carmody, D. P., & Lewis, M. (2012). Self representation in children with and without autism spectrum disorders. *Child Psychiatry and Human Development, 43*(2), 227–237.

26. See Lewis, M., & Ramsay, D. S. (2004). Development of self-recognition, personal pronoun use, and pretend play in the second year. *Child Development, 75*(6), 1821–1831.

27. Piaget, J. (1954). *Construction of reality in the child*. Paterson, NJ: Littlefield, Adams.

28. Kropp, P. R., & Rogers, R. (1993). Understanding malingering: Motivation, method, and detection. In M. Lewis & C. Saarni (Eds.), *Lying and deception in everyday life* (pp. 201–216). New York: Guilford Press.

29. Self-deception in older children has been studied but will not be reviewed here as it is not central to our discussion of the role of deception in the young child's emotional life. See Baumeister, R. F. (1993). Lying to yourself: The enigma of self-deception. In M. Lewis & C. Saarni (Eds.), *Lying and deception in everyday life* (pp. 166–183). New York: Guilford Press. Solomon, R. C. (1993). What a tangled web: Deception and self-deception in philosophy. In M. Lewis & C. Saarni (Eds.), *Lying and deception in everyday life* (pp. 30–58). New York: Guilford Press. Sigmon, S. T., & Snyder, C. R. (1993). Looking at oneself in a rose-colored mirror: The role of excuses in the negotiation of personal reality. In M. Lewis & C. Saarni (Eds.), *Lying and deception in everyday life* (pp. 148–165). New York: Guilford Press.

Chapter 8. The Self-Conscious Emotions

1. It should be pointed out again that once ideas emerge these ideas can also be the elicitors of the early emotional action patterns. Sadness at *actual* loss of the mother in the literal world now can be sadness caused by the *idea* of her loss in the mind.

2. The word "hubris" is used to denote pride that is not focused on actions but on the global self.

3. Masciuch, S., & Kienapple, K. (1993). The emergence of jealousy in children 4 months to 7 years of age. *Journal of Social and Personal Relationships, 10*, 421–435.

4. Darwin, C. R. (1965). *The expression of the emotions in man and animals*. Chicago: University of Chicago Press. (Original work published 1872) (pp. 326–327)

5. Plutchik, R. (1980). A general psychoevolutionary theory of emotion. In R.

Plutchik & H. Kellerman (Eds.), *Emotion: Theory, research, and experience: Vol. 1. Theories of emotion* (pp. 3–33). New York: Academic Press.

6. Lewis, M., Sullivan, M. W., Stanger, C., & Weiss, M. (1989). Self-development and self-conscious emotions. *Child Development, 60,* 146–156.

7. For exceptions, see Broucek, F. J. (1991*). Shame and the self.* New York: Guilford Press. Lewis, H. B. (1971). *Shame and guilt in neurosis.* New York: International Universities Press. Morrison, A. P. (1989). *Shame: The underside of narcissism.* Hillsdale, NJ: Analytic Press.

8. Goffman, E. (1959). *Presentation of self in everyday life.* Garden City, NY: Doubleday.

9. Dann, O. T. (1977). A case study of embarrassment. *Journal of the American Psychoanalytic Association, 25,* 453–470. Edelmann, R. J. (1987). *The psychology of embarrassment.* Chichester, UK: Wiley (p. 14). Modigliani, A. (1968). Embarrassment and embarrassability. *Sociometry, 31,* 313–326.

10. See Lewis, H. B. (1971). *Shame and guilt in neurosis.* New York: International Universities Press. Semin, G. R., & Manstead, A. S. R. (1981). The beholder beheld: A study in social emotionality. *European Journal of Social Psychology, 11,* 253–265. Izard, C. E. (1977). *Human emotions.* New York: Plenum Press. Tomkins, S. S. (1963). *Affect, imagery, and consciousness: Vol. 2. The negative affects.* New York: Tavistock/Routledge.

11. Eysenck, H. J. (1956). The questionnaire measurement of neuroticism and extraversion. *Revista Psicologia, 50,* 113–140.

12. Kagan, J., Snidman, N., Arcus, D., & Reznick, J. S. (1994). *Galen's prophecy: Temperament in human nature.* New York: Basic Books.

13. Zimbardo, P. G. (1977). *Shyness.* Reading, MA: Addison-Wesley. Also see Jones, W. H., Cheek, J. M., & Briggs, S. R. (Eds.). (1986). *Shyness: Perspectives on research and treatment.* New York: Plenum Press.

14. Buss, A. H. (1980). *Self-consciousness and social anxiety.* San Francisco: Freeman. Cheek, J. M., & Buss, A. H. (1981). Shyness and sociability. *Journal of Personality and Social Psychology, 41,* 330–339. Fenigstein, A., Scheier, M. F., & Buss, A. H. (1975). Public and private self-consciousness: Assessment and theory. *Journal of Consulting and Clinical Psychology, 43,* 522–527.

15. Buss, A. H. (1980). *Self-consciousness and social anxiety.* San Francisco: Freeman. Geppert, U. (1986). *A coding system for analyzing behavioral expressions of self-evaluative emotions* [Technical manual]. Munich: Max-Planck Institute for Psychological Research.

16. Blushing, which received so much attention in Darwin's analysis, would be a likely candidate for indexing embarrassment. However, blushing does not always occur because there are large individual differences in the likelihood of this response. Differences may be due, in part, to different physiology; it is certainly related to skin coloration, with light-skinned people blushing more visibly than dark-skinned people. In our research on self-conscious emotions, blushing in children is a relatively infrequent event. Even when children above the age of 3 show embarrassment in terms of other behaviors, it is rare to observe blushing in those children. This should not be surprising since it is relatively unusual to see blushing in adults. Given the self-reports indicating the high incidence of embarrassment, it is interesting to note that the occasions of blushing seem to be disproportionately low. [See Leary, M. R., & Meadows, S. (1991).

Predictors, elicitors and concomitants of social blushing. *Journal of Personality and Social Psychology, 60*(2), 254–262.].

17. Izard, C. E., & Tyson, M. C. (1986). Shyness as a discrete emotion. In W. H. Jones, J. M. Cheek, & S. R. Briggs (Eds.), *Shyness: Perspectives on research and treatment* (pp. 147–160). New York: Plenum Press.

18. Eysenck, H. J. (1956). The questionnaire measurement of neuroticism and extraversion. *Revista Psicologia, 50*, 113–140. Kagan, J., Reznick, J. S., & Snedman, N. (1988). Biological bases of childhood shyness. *Science, 240*, 167–171.

19. Izard, C. E. (1979). *The Maximally Discriminative Facial Movement Coding System (MAX)*. Newark: University of Delaware, Instructional Resources Center. Tomkins, S. S. (1963). *Affect, imagery, and consciousness: Vol. 2. The negative affects*. New York: Tavistock/Routledge.

20. Lewis, M., Stanger, C., Sullivan, M. W., & Barone, P. (1991). Changes in embarrassment as a function of age, sex and situation. *British Journal of Developmental Psychology, 9*, 485–492.

21. DiBiase, R., & Lewis, M. (1997). The relation between temperament and embarrassment. *Cognition and Emotion, 11*, 259–271. Lewis, M., & Ramsay, D. (2002). Cortisol response to embarrassment and shame. *Child Development, 73*(4), 1034–1045.

22. Meares, R. (1992). *The metaphor of play on self: The secret and borderline experience*. Melbourne, Australia: Hill of Content.

23. Csikszentmihalyi, M., & Csikszentmihalyi, I. S. (1988). *Optimal experience: Psychological studies of flow in consciousness*. New York: Cambridge University Press.

24. Rozin suggests that disgust also has this developmental pattern [Rozin, P., Haidt, J., & McCauley, C. R. (1993). Disgust. In M. Lewis & J. M. Haviland (Eds.), *Handbook of emotions* (pp. 575–594). New York: Guilford Press.].

25. Harris, C. R. (2006). Embarrassment: A form of social pain. *American Scientist, 94*, 524–533.

26. Hart, S. L., & Legerstee, M. (Eds.). (2010). *Handbook of jealousy: Theory, research, and multidisciplinary approaches*. Malden, MA: Blackwell/Wiley.

27. Ainsworth, M. D. S., & Bell, S. M. (1970). Attachment, exploration, and separation: Illustrated by the behavior of one-year-olds in a strange situation. *Child Development, 41*, 49–67. Lewis, M., & Ramsay, D. S. (2005). Infant emotional and cortisol responses to goal blockage. *Child Development, 76*(2), 518–530. Weinberg, K. M., & Tronick, E. Z. (1996). Infant affective reactions to the resumption of maternal interaction after the still-face. *Child Development, 67*, 905–914.

28. Weinraub, M., & Lewis, M. (1977). The determinants of children's responses to separation. *Monographs of the Society for Research in Child Development, 42*(4, Serial No. 172), 1–78.

29. Feiring, C., & Lewis, M. (1979). Sex and age differences in young children's reactions to frustration: A further look at the Goldberg and Lewis (1969) subjects. *Child Development, 50*, 848–853. Goldberg, S., & Lewis, M. (1969). Play behavior in the year-old infant: Early sex differences. *Child Development, 40*, 21–31. Wasserman, G. A., & Lewis, M. (1985). Infant sex differences: Ecological effects. *Sex Roles: A Journal of Research, 12*, 665–675.

30. Lewis, M., & Ramsay, D. S. (2004). Infant emotional response to goal

blockage, control, and cortisol response. *Emotion Researcher, 19*(2), 8–9. Tronick, E. Z., Als, H., Adamson, L., Wise, S., & Brazelton, T. B. (1978). The infant's response to entrapment between contradictory messages in face-to-face interaction. *Journal of the American Academy of Child Psychiatry, 17*, 1–13.

31. Bradley, B. S. (2010). Jealousy in infant–peer trios: From narcissism to culture. In S. L. Hart & M. Legerstee (Eds.), *Handbook of jealousy: Theory, research, and multidisciplinary approaches* (pp. 192–234). Malden, MA: Blackwell/Wiley. Hobson, R. P. (2010). Is jealousy a complex emotion? In S. L. Hart & M. Legerstee (Eds.), *Handbook of jealousy: Theory, research, and multidisciplinary approaches* (pp. 293–311). Malden, MA: Blackwell/Wiley. Keller, H., & Lamm, B. (2010). Culture, parenting, and the development of jealousy. In S. L. Hart & M. Legerstee (Eds.), *Handbook of jealousy: Theory, research, and multidisciplinary approaches* (pp. 477–497). Malden, MA: Blackwell/Wiley. Trevarthen, C. B., & Aitken, K. J. (2001). Infant intersubjectivity: Research, theory and clinical applications. *Journal of Child Psychology and Psychiatry, 42*, 3–48.

32. Braten, S. (2009). *The intersubjective mirror in infant learning and evolution of speech.* Amsterdam, The Netherlands: Benjamins. Friedman, O. (2011, October). *Principles guiding young children's reasoning about ownership.* Presentation at the Rutgers University Center for Cognitive Science Colloquium Series, New Brunswick, NJ.

33. Sagi, A., & Hoffman, M. L. (1976). Empathic distress in the newborn. *Developmental Psychology, 12*(2), 175–176. Roth-Hanania, R., Davidov, M., & Zahn-Waxler, C. (2011). Empathy development from 8 to 16 months: Early signs of concern for others. *Infant Behavior and Development, 34*, 447–458.

34. Bischof-Kohler, D. (1991). The development of empathy in infants. In M. E. Lamb & H. Keller (Eds.), *Infant development: Perspectives from German-speaking countries* (pp. 245–273). Hillsdale, NJ: Erlbaum.

35. Preston, S. D., & de Waal, F. B. M. (2002). Empathy: Its ultimate and proximate bases. *Behavioral and Brain Sciences, 25*, 1–71.

36. This does not mean that the earlier emotions, those called primary or basic, are elicited by noncognitive events. Cognitive factors may play a role in the elicitation of any emotion; however, the nature of cognitive events are much less articulated and differentiated in the earlier ones [see Plutchik, R. (1980). A general psychoevolutionary theory of emotion. In R. Plutchik & H. Kellerman (Eds.), *Emotion: Theory, research, and experience: Vol. 1. Theories of emotion* (pp. 3–33). New York: Academic Press.].

37. Herrmann, E., Hernandez-Lloreda, M. V., Call, J., Hare, B., & Tomasello, M. (2010). The structure of individual differences in the cognitive abilities of children and chimpanzees. *Psychological Science, 21*(1), 102–110. Premack, D. (2010). Why humans are unique: Three theories. *Perspectives on Psychological Science, 5*(1), 22–32.

38. Stipek, D. J., Recchia, S., & McClintic, S. (1992). Self evaluation in young children. *Monographs of the Society for Research in Child Development, 57*(1, Serial No. 226).

39. Dweck, C. S., & Leggett, E. L. (1988). A social cognitive approach to motivation and personality. *Psychological Review, 95*, 256–273. Weiner, B. (1986). *An attributional theory of motivation and emotion.* New York: Springer-Verlag.

40. Mandler, G. (1975). *Mind and emotion.* New York: Wiley.

41. The idea that cognitions can lead to emotions has been poorly received by some, who believe that this idea implies that cognitions have real status whereas emotions are

epiphenomenological [Schachter, S., & Singer, J. E. (1962). Cognitive, social, and physiological determinants of emotional state. *Psychological Review, 69*, 379–399.]. I mean to give emotions that same status as cognitions. Just as cognitions can lead to emotions, emotions can lead to cognitions. The theory implies no status difference.

42. Masson, J. M. (1984). *The assault on the truth: Freud's suppression of the seduction theory.* New York: Farrar, Straus and Giroux.

43. Tangney has tried to study the two types of guilt as suggested by Freud, but has had little success in differentiating shame from the first type of guilt. [Tangney, J. P. (1995). Shame and guilt in interpersonal relationships. In J. P. Tangney & K. W. Fischer (Eds.), *Self-conscious emotions: The psychology of shame, guilt, embarrassment, and pride* (pp. 114–139). New York: Guilford Press.].

44. Freud, S. (1953). Three essays on the theory of sexuality. In J. Strachey (Ed. and Trans.), *The standard edition of the complete psychological works of Sigmund Freud* (Vol. 7, pp. 153–243). London: Hogarth Press. (Original work published 1905) (p. 178)

45. Erikson, E. H. (1950). *Childhood and society.* New York: Norton. (pp. 223–224)

46. Erikson, E. H. (1950). *Childhood and society.* New York: Norton. (pp. 223–224)

47. Heckhausen, H. (1984). Emergent achievement behavior: Some early developments. In J. Nicholls (Ed.), *The development of achievement motivation* (pp. 1–32). Greenwich, CT: JAI Press. Stipek, D. J. (1983). A developmental analysis of pride and shame. *Human Development, 26*(1), 42–54.

48. Stipek, D. J., Recchia, S., & McClintic, S. (1992). Self evaluation in young children. *Monographs of the Society for Research in Child Development, 57*(1, Serial No. 226).

49. See Dweck, C. S. (1991). Self-theories and goals: Their role in motivation, personality and development. In R. Dienstbeir (Ed.), *Nebraska Symposium on Motivation* (Vol. 36, pp. 199–236). Lincoln: University of Nebraska Press. Dweck, C. S., & Leggett, E. L. (1988). A social cognitive approach to motivation and personality. *Psychological Review, 95*, 256–273. Seligman, M. E. P., Peterson, C., Kaslow, N., Tannenbaum, R., Alloy, L., & Abramson, L. (1984). Attributional style and depressive symptoms among children. *Journal of Abnormal Psychology, 39*, 235–238. Weiner, B. (1986) *An attributional theory of motivation and emotion.* New York: Springer-Verlag.

50. See Alessandri, S. M., & Lewis, M. (1996). Differences in pride and shame in maltreated and non-maltreated preschoolers. *Child Development, 67*, 1857–1869. Morrison, A. P. (1989). *Shame: The underside of narcissism.* Hillsdale, NJ: Analytic Press.

51. Beck, A. T. (1979). *Cognitive therapy and emotional disorders.* New York: Times Mirror. Dweck, C. S. (1991). Self-theories and goals: Their role in motivation, personality and development. In R. Dienstbeir (Ed.), *Nebraska Symposium on Motivation* (Vol. 36, pp. 199–236). Lincoln: University of Nebraska Press. Janoff-Bulman, R. (1979). Characterological versus behavioral self-blame: Inquiries into depression and rape. *Journal of Personality and Social Psychology, 37*, 1798–1809. Lewis, H. B. (1971). *Shame and guilt in neurosis.* New York: International Universities Press. Weiner, B. (1986). *An attributional theory of motivation and emotion.* New York: Springer-Verlag.

52. Gruenewald, T. L., Kemeny, M. E., Aziz, N., & Fahey, J. L. (2004). Acute threat to the social self: Shame, social self-esteem, and cortisol activity. *Psychosomatic Medicine, 66*, 915–924. Lewis, M., & Ramsay, D. (2002). Cortisol response to embarrassment and shame. *Child Development, 73*(4), 1034–1045.

53. Lewis, H. B. (1971). *Shame and guilt in neurosis.* New York: International Universities Press. Lewis, M. (1992). *Shame: The exposed self.* New York: Free Press.

54. Izard, C. E. (1979). *The Maximally Discriminative Facial Movement Coding System (MAX).* Newark: University of Delaware, Instructional Resources Center. Tomkins, S. S. (1963). *Affect, imagery, and consciousness: Vol. 2. The negative affects.* New York: Tavistock/Routledge.

55. Cole, P. M., Barrett, K. C., & Zahn-Waxler, C. (1992). Emotion displays in two-year-olds. *Child Development, 63*, 314–324.

56. Freud's two types of guilt appear to conform to the differences between shame and guilt.

57. Tracy, J. L., & Robins, R. W. (2007). The psychological structure of pride: A tale of two facets. *Journal of Personality and Social Psychology, 92*(3), 506–525. I have also described these two types of pride and shown that children can discriminate between them.

58. Morrison, A. P. (1989). *Shame: The underside of narcissism.* Hillsdale, NJ: Analytic Press.

59. Baumeister, R. F., Campbell, J., Kreuger, J., & Vohs, K. D. (2003). Does high self-esteem cause better performance, interpersonal success, happiness, or healthier lifestyles? *Psychological Science in the Public Interest, 4*(1), 1–44. Kamins, M. L., & Dweck, C. S. (1999). Person versus process praise and criticism: Implications for contingent self-worth and coping. *Developmental Psychology, 35*, 835–847. Mueller, C. M., & Dweck, C. S. (1998). Praise for intelligence can undermine children's motivation and performance. *Journal of Personality and Social Psychology, 75*, 33–52.

60. Heckhausen, H. (1984). Emergent achievement behavior: Some early developments. In J. Nicholls (Ed.), *The development of achievement motivation* (pp. 1–32). Greenwich, CT: JAI Press. Stipek, D. J., Recchia, S., & McClintic, S. (1992). Self-evaluation in young children. *Monographs of the Society for Research in Child Development, 57*(1, Serial No. 226).

61. See Beck, A. T. (1979). *Cognitive therapy and emotional disorders.* New York: Times Mirror. Lewis, H. B. (1987). Shame: The "sleeper" in psychopathology. In H. B. Lewis (Ed.), *The role of shame in symptom formation* (pp. 1–28). Hillsdale, NJ: Erlbaum. Nolen-Hoeksema, S., Girgus, J. S., & Seligman, M. E. P. (1992). Predictors and consequences of childhood depressive symptoms: A 5-year longitudinal study. *Journal of Abnormal Psychology, 101*, 405–422. Nolen-Hoeksema, S., Wolfson, A., Mumme, D., & Guskin, K. (1995). Helplessness in children of depressed and nondepressed mothers. *Developmental Psychology, 31*, 377–387. Seligman, M. E. P. (1975). *Helplessness: On depression, development, and death.* San Francisco: Freeman. Weiner, B., & Graham, S. (1989). Understanding the motivational role of affect: Life-span research from an attributional perspective. *Cognition and Emotion, 3*, 401–419.

62. Dweck, C. S. (1991). Self-theories and goals: Their role in motivation, personality and development. In R. Dienstbeir (Ed.), *Nebraska Symposium on Motivation* (Vol. 36, pp. 199–236). Lincoln: University of Nebraska Press. Dweck, C. S., Chiu, C., & Hong, Y. (1995). Implicit theories and their role in judgments and reactions: A world

from two perspectives. *Psychological Inquiry, 6,* 267–285. Smiley, P. A., & Dweck, C. S. (1995). Individual differences in achievement goals among young children. *Child Development, 65,* 1723–1743.

63. Kochanska, G. (1995). Children's temperament, mothers' discipline, and security of attachment: Multiple pathways to emerging internalization. *Child Development, 66*(3), 597–615. Kochanska, G., Coy, K. C., & Murray, K. T. (2001). The development of self-regulation in the first 4 years of life. *Child Development, 72,* 1091–1111. Kochanska, G., DeVet, K., Goldman, M., Murray, K. T., & Putnam, S. P. (1994). Maternal reports of conscience development and temperament in young children. *Child Development, 65*(3), 852–868. Ramsay, D., & Lewis, M. (2001). Temperament, stress, and soothing. In T. D. Wachs & G. A. Kohnstamm (Eds.), *Temperament in context* (pp. 23–41). Mahwah, NJ: Erlbaum. Rothbart, M. K., Ahadi, S. A., & Hershey, K. L. (1994). Temperament and social behavior in childhood. *Merrill–Palmer Quarterly, 40,* 21–39.

64. Csikszentmihalyi, M. (1991). *Flow: The psychology of optimal experience.* New York: Harper Collins. Lewis, M., & Ramsay, D. S. (1997). Stress reactivity and self-recognition. *Child Development, 68,* 621–629. Lewis, M., & Ramsay, D. (2002). Cortisol response to embarrassment and shame. *Child Development, 73*(4), 1034–1045.

65. Bennett, D. S., Sullivan, M. W., & Lewis, M. (2010). Neglected children, shame-proneness and depressive symptoms. *Child Maltreatment, 15*(4), 305–314. Lewis, M., Alessandri, S. M. , & Sullivan, M. W. (1992). Differences in shame and pride as a function of children's gender and task difficulty. *Child Development, 63,* 630–638. Lewis, M., & Sullivan, M. (2005). The development of self-conscious emotions. In A. Elliott & C. Dweck (Eds.), *Handbook of competence and motivation* (pp. 185–201). New York: Guilford Press.

66. Lewis, M., Takai-Kawakami, K., Kawakami, K., & Sullivan, M. (2010). Cultural differences in emotional responses to success and failure. *International Journal of Behavioral Development, 34*(1), 53–61.

67. Alessandri, S. M., & Lewis, M. (1993). Parental evaluation and its relation to shame and pride in young children. *Sex Roles, 29*(5–6), 335–343.

68. Lewis, M., & Ramsay, D. S. (2002). Cortisol response to embarrassment and shame. *Child Development, 73*(4), 1034–1045.

69. Lewis, M., Alessandri, S. M., & Sullivan, M. W. (1992). Differences in shame and pride as a function of children's gender and task difficulty. *Child Development, 63,* 630–638.

70. See Levine, L. E., & Conway, J. M. (2010). Self–other awareness and peer relationships in toddlers: Gender comparisons. *Infant and Child Development, 19,* 455–464.

71. Lewis, H. B. (1976). *Psychic war in men and women.* New York: New York University Press. Witkin, H. (1965). Psychological differentiation and forms of pathology. *Journal of Abnormal Psychology, 70,* 317–336.

72. Lewis, H. B. (1976). *Psychic war in men and women.* New York: New York University Press. Witkin, H. (1965). Psychological differentiation and forms of pathology. *Journal of Abnormal Psychology, 70,* 317–336.

73. Heckhausen, H. (1984). Emergent achievement behavior: Some early developments. In J. Nicholls (Ed.), *The development of achievement motivation* (pp. 1–32).

Greenwich, CT: JAI Press. Nolan, E., Adams, S., & Kagan, J. (1980). Children's recognition memory for their drawings. *Journal of Genetic Psychology: Research and Theory on Human Development, 137*(1), 11–15. Stipek, D. J., Recchia, S., & McClintic, S. (1992). Self evaluation in young children. *Monographs of the Society for Research in Child Development, 57*(1, Serial No. 226).

74. Matthews, T. A., Sullivan, M. W., & Lewis, M. (2013, March 1–4). Young children's self-evaluation and emotional behavior during achievement tasks. Poster presented at the Annual Meeting of the Eastern Psychological Association, New York, NY.

Chapter 9. Temperament, Emotion, and Stress

1. Blandon, A. Y., Calkins, S. D., Kean, S. P., & O'Brien, M. (2010). Contributions of child's physiology and maternal behavior to children's trajectories of temperamental reactivity. *Developmental Psychology, 46*(5), 1089–1102. Volbrecht, M. M., & Goldsmith, H. H. (2010). Early temperamental and family predictors of shyness and anxiety. *Developmental Psychology, 46*(5), 1192–1205.

2. Belsky, J., Rovine, M., & Taylor, D. (1984). The Pennsylvania Infant and Family Development Project: III. The origins of individual differences in infant–mother attachment: Maternal and infant contributions. *Child Development, 55*, 718–728.

3. Mothers who were minimally interactive, both in terms of initiating and responding, had children who were ambivalently attached, while mothers neither overly nor under interactive produced securely attached 1-year-olds.

4. Lewis, M., & Feiring, C. (1989). Infant, mother and mother–infant interaction behavior and subsequent attachment. *Child Development, 60*, 831–837.

5. See the epigenetic work of Zhang, T.-Y., & Meaney, M. J. (2010). Epigenetics and the environmental regulation of the genome and its function. *Annual Review of Psychology, 61*, 439–466.

6. Bates, J. E., Schermerhorn, A. C., & Petersen, I. T. (2012). Temperament and parenting in developmental perspective. In M. Zentner & R. L. Shiner (Eds.), *The handbook of temperament* (pp. 425–441). New York: Guilford Press. Caspi, A., & Shiner, R. L. (2006). *Personality development*. Hoboken, NJ: Wiley. Klein, D. L., Dyson, M. W., Kujawa, A. J., & Kotov, R. (2012). Temperament and internalizing disorders. In M. Zentner & R. L. Shiner (Eds.), *The handbook of temperament* (pp. 541–561). New York: Guilford Press.

7. Bates, J. E., Schermerhorn, A. C., & Petersen, I. T. (in press). Temperament concepts in developmental psychopathology. In M. Lewis & K. Rudolph (Eds.), *Handbook of developmental psychopathology, 3rd edition*. New York: Springer. Rothbart, M. K., & Bates, J. E. (1998). Temperament. In W. Damon & N. Eisenberg (Eds.), *Handbook of child psychology* (5th ed.): *Vol. 3. Social, emotional, and personality development* (pp. 105–176). Hoboken, NJ: Wiley. (p. 109)

8. Allport, G. W. (1961). *Pattern and growth in personality*. New York: Rinehart & Winston. (p. 34)

9. See Calkins, S. D., & Hill, A. (2007). Caregiver influences on emerging emotion regulation: Biological and environmental transactions in early development. In J. J. Gross (Ed.), *Handbook of emotion regulation* (pp. 229–248). New York: Guilford Press.

10. See Blandon, A. Y., Calkins, S. D., Kean, S. P., & O'Brien, M. (2010). Contributions of child's physiology and maternal behavior to children's trajectories of temperamental reactivity. *Developmental Psychology, 46*(5), 1089–1102. Volbrecht, M. M., & Goldsmith, H. H. (2010). Early temperamental and family predictors of shyness and anxiety. *Developmental Psychology, 46*(5), 1192–1205.

11. Goldberg, L. R. (1993). The structure of phenotypic personality traits. *American Psychologist, 48*, 26–34.

12. Thomas, A., & Chess, S. (1977). *Temperament and development.* New York: Brunner/Mazel.

13. Ramsay, D. S., & Lewis, M. (2001). Temperament, stress, and soothing. In T. D. Wachs & G. A. Kohnstamm (Eds.), *Temperament in context* (pp. 23–41). Mahwah, NJ: Erlbaum.

14. Kagan, J., Snidman, N., Arcus, D., & Reznick, J. S. (1994). *Galen's prophecy: Temperament in human nature.* New York: Basic Books.

15. Lewis and Ramsay on pain and self-recognition: Lewis, M., & Ramsay, D. S. (1997). Stress reactivity and self-recognition. *Child Development, 68*, 621–629. Also: Baillargeon, R., Li, J., Gertner, Y., & Wu, D. (2011). How do infants reason about physical events? In U. Goswami (Ed.), *The Wiley–Blackwell handbook of childhood cognitive development, second edition* (pp. 11–48). Malden, MA: Wiley/Blackwell. While a mother's direct response to her infant's pain seems to be unrelated to the infant's pain response, either concurrent or subsequently, her response may signal the child, later in his development, to attend to or not attend to his own pain.

16. Kagan, J., Snidman, N., Arcus, D., & Reznick, J. S. (1994). *Galen's prophecy: Temperament in human nature.* New York: Basic Books. Fox, N. A., Henderson, H. A., Rubin, K. H., Calkins, S. D., & Schmidt, L. A. (2001). Continuity and discontinuity of behavioral inhibition and exuberance: Psychological and behavioral influences across the first four years of life. *Child Development, 72*(1), 1–21.

17. Grahek, N. (2001). *Feeling pain and being in pain.* Oldenburg, Germany: BIS-Verlag.

18. A recent study reports that cannabis can make patients less bothered by pain although the pain itself is not less [Lee, M. C., Ploner, M., Wiech, K., Bingel, U., Waniqasekera, V., Brooks, J., et al. (2013). Amygdala activity contributes to the dissociative effect of cannabis on pain perception. *Pain, 154*(1), 124–134.].

19. See Lewis on culture and biology [Lewis, M. (1989). Culture and biology: The role of temperament. In P. R. Zelazo & R. G. Barr (Eds.), *Challenges to developmental paradigms* (pp. 203–223). Hillsdale, NJ: Erlbaum.]. Kochanska, G., Coy, K. C., Tjebkes, T. L., & Husarek, S. J. (1998). Individual differences in emotionality in infancy. *Child Development, 69*(2), 375–390. Lewis, M., Worobey, J., & Thomas, D. (1989). Behavioral features of early reactivity: Antecedents and consequences. In M. Lewis & J. Worobey (Eds.), *New directions for child development: Infant stress and coping* (pp. 33–46). San Francisco: Jossey-Bass.

20. Gunnar, M. R., Talge, N. M., & Herrera, A. (2009). Stressor paradigms in developmental studies: What does and does not work to produce mean increases in salivary cortisol. *Psychoneuroendocrinology, 34*, 953–967.

21. Lewis, M., Ramsay, D. S., & Kawakami, K. (1993). Differences between Japanese infants and Caucasian American infants in behavioral and cortisol response to inoculation. *Child Development, 64*, 1722–1731.

22. Goldsmith, H. H., & Campos, J. J. (1982). Toward a theory of infant temperament. In R. N. Emde & R. J. Harmon (Eds.), *The development of attachment and affiliative systems* (pp. 161–193). New York: Plenum Press. Hubert, N. C., Wachs, T. D., Peters-Martin, P., & Gandour, M. J. (1982). The study of early temperament: Measurement and conceptual issues. *Child Development, 53,* 571–600. Isabella, R. A., Ward, M. J., & Belsky, J. (1985). Convergence of multiple sources of information on infant individuality: Neonatal behavior, infant behavior, and temperament reports. *Infant Behavior and Development, 8*(3), 283–291. Matheny, A. P. Jr., Riese, M. L., & Wilson, R. S. (1985). Rudiments of infant temperament: Newborn to 9 months. *Developmental Psychology, 21,* 486–494.

23. Lewis, M., & Ramsay, D. S. (1995). Stability and change in cortisol and behavioral responses to stress during the first 18 months of life. *Developmental Psychobiology, 28*(8), 419–428. Lewis, M., & Thomas, D. (1990). Cortisol release in infants in response to inoculation. *Child Development, 61,* 50–59. Ramsay, D., & Lewis, M. (2001). Temperament, stress, and soothing. In T. D. Wachs & G. A. Kohnstamm (Eds.), *Temperament in context* (pp. 23–41). Mahwah, NJ: Erlbaum. Worobey, J., & Lewis, M. (1989). Individual differences in the reactivity of young infants. *Developmental Psychology, 25*(4), 663–667. Kagan also has found more stability in the same high inhibited children. This suggests that the environmental effects may be greater on high rather than low reactivity children [Kagan, J., Snidman, N., Arcus, D., & Reznick, J. S. (1994). *Galen's prophecy: Temperament in human nature.* New York: Basic Books.].

24. Birns, B., Barten, S., & Bridger, W. (1969). Individual differences in temperamental characteristics of infants. *Transactions of the New York Academy of Sciences, 31,* 1071–1082. Fox, N. A., Henderson, H. A., Rubin, K. H., Calkins, S. D., & Schmidt, L. A. (2001). Continuity and discontinuity of behavioral inhibition and exuberance: Psychological and behavioral influences across the first four years of life. *Child Development, 72*(1), 1–21. Goldsmith, H. H., & Campos, J. J. (1982). Toward a theory of infant temperament. In R. N. Emde & R. J. Harmon (Eds.), *The development of attachment and affiliative systems* (pp. 161–193). New York: Plenum Press. Hubert, N. C., Wachs, T. D., Peters-Martin, P., & Gandour, M. J. (1982). The study of early temperament: Measurement and conceptual issues. *Child Development, 53,* 571–600. Isabella, R. A., Ward, M. J., & Belsky, J. (1985). Convergence of multiple sources of information on infant individuality: Neonatal behavior, infant behavior, and temperament reports. *Infant Behavior and Development, 8*(3), 283–291. Kagan, J., Snidman, N., Arcus, D., & Reznick, J. S. (1994). *Galen's prophecy: Temperament in human nature.* New York: Basic Books. Lewis, M., & Ramsay, D. S. (1995). Stability and change in cortisol and behavioral responses to stress during the first 18 months of life. *Developmental Psychobiology, 28*(8), 419–428. Matheny, A. P. Jr., Riese, M. L., & Wilson, R. S. (1985). Rudiments of infant temperament: Newborn to 9 months. *Developmental Psychology, 21,* 486–494. Riese, M. L. (1987). Temperament stability between the neonatal period and 24 months. *Developmental Psychology, 23,* 216–222.

25. Eckholm, E. (2011, November 7). Preaching virtue of spanking, even as deaths fuel debate. *New York Times,* p. A1. Miller, S. (1985). *The shame experience.* Hillsdale, NJ: Erlbaum. See also Biringen, Z., Emde, R. N., Campos, J. J., & Appelbaum, M. I. (1995). Affective reorganization in the infant, the mother, and the dyad: The role of upright locomotion and its timing. *Child Development, 66*(2), 499–514.

26. Dweck, C. S., & Leggett, E. L. (1988). A social cognitive approach to motivation and personality. *Psychological Review, 95*, 256–273.

27. Sroufe, L. A. (1996). *Emotional development: The organization of emotional life in the early years.* New York: Cambridge University Press. Tronick, E. (1989). Emotions and emotional communication in infants. *American Psychologist, 44*, 112–119.

28. Ainsworth, M. D. S., Blehar, M. C., Waters, E., & Wall, S. (1978). *Patterns of attachment: A psychological study of the strange situation.* Hillsdale, NJ: Erlbaum. Lewis, M. (1978). The infant and its caregiver: The role of contingency. *Allied Health and Behavioral Sciences, 1*(4), 469–474. Lewis, M., & Goldberg, S. (1969). Perceptual–cognitive development in infancy: A generalized expectancy model as a function of the mother–infant interaction. *Merrill–Palmer Quarterly, 15*(1), 81–100. Watson, J. S. (1966). The development and generalization of "contingency awareness" in early infancy: Some hypotheses. *Merrill–Palmer Quarterly, 12*, 123–135.

29. Barr, R. G. (1989). Recasting a clinical enigma: The case of infant crying. In P. R. Zelazo & R. G. Barr (Eds.), *Challenges to developmental paradigms: Implications for theory, assessment and treatment* (pp. 43–64). Hillsdale, NJ: Erlbaum. Emde, R. N., Gaensbauer, T. J., & Harmon, R. J. (1976). Emotional expression in infancy: A biobehavioral study. *Psychological Issues, 10*(1, Monograph 37). New York: International Universities Press. Hubbard, F. O. A., & van IJzendoorn, M. H. (1991). Maternal unresponsiveness and infant crying across the first 9 months: A naturalistic longitudinal study. *Infant Behavior and Development, 14*, 299–312. Hunziker, U. A., & Barr, R. G. (1986). Increased carrying reduces infant crying: A randomized control trial. *Pediatrics, 77*, 641–648.

30. Barr, R. G., Young, S. N., Wright, J. H., Cassidy, K. L., Hendricks, L., Bedard, Y., et al. (1995). "Sucrose analgesia" and diphtheria–tetanus–pertussis immunizations at 2 and 4 months. *Developmental and Behavioral Pediatrics, 16*, 220–225. Blass, E. M. (1997). Infant formula quiets crying human newborns. *Developmental and Behavioral Pediatrics, 18*, 162–165. Blass, E. M., & Ciaramitaro, V. (1994). A new look at some old mechanisms in human newborns: Taste and tactile determinants of state, affect, and action. *Monographs of the Society for Research in Child Development, 59*(Serial No. 239), 1–101. Gunnar, M. R., Brodersen, L., Krueger, K., & Rigatuso, J. (1996). Dampening of adrenocortical responses during infancy: Normative changes and individual differences. *Child Development, 67*, 877–889. Gunnar, M. R., Larson, M. C., Hertsgaard, L., Harris, M. L., & Brodersen, L. (1992). The stressfulness of separation among nine-month-old infants: Effects of social context variables and infant temperament. *Child Development, 63*, 290–303. Gunnar, M. R., Mangelsdorf, S., Larson, M. C., & Hertsgaard, L. (1989). Attachment, temperament, and adrenocortical activity in infancy: A study of psychoendocrine regulation. *Developmental Psychology, 25*, 355–363. White, B. P., Donzella, B., Vraa, R., Armasti, M., Robison, K., & Barr, R. G. (1997, April). *Evidence of sleep differences and possible dysregulation of daily cortisol activity in infants with colic.* Poster session presented at the biennial meeting of the Society for Research in Child Development, Washington, DC.

31. Nachmias, M., Gunnar, M., Mangelsdorf, S., Parritz, R. H., & Buss, K. (1996). Behavioral inhibition and stress reactivity: The moderating role of attachment security. *Child Development, 67*, 508–522. Spangler, G., Schieche, M., Ilg, U., Maier, U., & Ackermann, C. (1994). Maternal sensitivity as an external organizer for biobehavioral regulation in infancy. *Developmental Psychobiology, 27*, 425–437.

32. Richardson, K., & Norgate, S. H. (2006). A critical analysis of IQ studies of adopted children. *Human Development, 49*, 319–335.

33. See Rosenfield, Suchecki, and Levine [Rosenfield, P., Suchecki, D., & Levine, S. (1992). Multifactorial regulation of the hypothalamic–pituitary–adrenal axis during development. *Neuroscience and Behavioral Reviews, 16*, 553–568.] for a review of this literature.

34. James Russell and his colleagues found that the labeling of an emotional expression was highly influenced by the set of emotions given to be labeled. Such findings suggest the idea of flow of emotions [Pochedly, J. T., Widen, S. C., & Russell, J. A. (2012). What emotion does the "facial expression of disgust" express? *Emotion, 12*(6), 1315–1319.].

35. Lewis, M. (2011). Inside and outside: The relation between emotional states and expressions. In M. Lewis (Ed.), Infant emotional development [Special issue], *Emotion Review, 3*(2), 189–196.

36. Rothbart, M. K., Sheese, B. E., Rueda, M. R., & Posner, M. I. (2011). Developing mechanisms of self-regulation in early life. In M. Lewis (Ed.), Infant emotional development [Special issue], *Emotion Review, 3*(2), 207–213.

37. Bates, J. E. (1987). Temperament in infancy. In J. D. Osofsky (Ed.), *Handbook of infant development, second edition* (pp. 1101–1149). New York: Wiley. Goldsmith, H. H., & Campos, J. J. (1986). Fundamental issues in the study of early temperament: The Denver Twin Temperament Study. In M. E. Lamb, A. L. Brown, & B. Rogoff (Eds.), *Advances in developmental psychology* (Vol. 4, pp. 231–283). Hillsdale, NJ: Erlbaum. Gunnar, M. R., Brodersen, L., Krueger, K., & Rigatuso, J. (1996). Dampening of adrenocortical responses during infancy: Normative changes and individual differences. *Child Development, 67*, 877–889. Gunnar, M. R., Larson, M. C., Hertsgaard, L., Harris, M. L., & Brodersen, L. (1992). The stressfulness of separation among nine-month-old infants: Effects of social context variables and infant temperament. *Child Development, 63*, 290–303. Ramsay, D., & Lewis, M. (2001). Temperament, stress, and soothing. In T. D. Wachs & G. A. Kohnstamm (Eds.), *Temperament in context* (pp. 23–41). Mahwah, NJ: Erlbaum.

38. Lewis and Ramsay on pain and self-recognition: Lewis, M., & Ramsay, D. S. (1997). Stress reactivity and self-recognition. *Child Development, 68*, 621–629.

39. Kochanska, G., Coy, K. C., & Murray, K. T. (2001). The development of self-regulation in the first 4 years of life. *Child Development, 72*, 1091–1111. Rothbart, M. K., Ahadi, S. A., & Hershey, K. L. (1994). Temperament and social behavior in childhood. *Merrill–Palmer Quarterly, 40*, 21–39.

40. DiBiase, R., & Lewis, M. (1997). The relation between temperament and embarrassment. *Cognition and Emotion, 11*, 259–271.

Chapter 10. The Socialization of Emotion

1. Bettelheim, B. (1967). *The empty fortress: Infantile autism and the birth of the self.* Oxford, UK: Free Press of Glencoe. Sroufe, L. A. (2012, January 28). Ritalin gone wrong. *New York Times*, p. SR1.

2. Bowlby, J. (1969). *Attachment and loss: Vol. 1. Attachment.* New York: Basic Books.

3. Lewis, M. (1997). *Altering fate: Why the past does not predict the future.* New York: Guilford Press.

4. Sroufe, L. A., Coffino, B., & Carlson, E. A. (2010). Conceptualizing the role of early experience: Lessons from the Minnesota Longitudinal Study. *Developmental Review, 30*(1), 36–51.

5. Harris's original paper, before it was expanded into a book, was well received in the psychological community, winning a prestigious award from the American Psychological Association [Harris, J. R. (1995). Where is the child's environment?: A group socialization theory of development. *Psychological Review, 102*(3), 458–489. Harris, J. R. (1998). *The nurture assumption: Why children turn out the way they do.* New York: Free Press.]. The reader interested in this problem should read my critique of Harris's book as well as *Altering Fate*, where I describe this issue in more detail than I need to here [Lewis, M. (1999). Do environments matter at all? (Review of *The nurture assumption: Why children turn out the way they do,* by Judith Rich Harris), *Social Policy, Summer,* 34–43. Lewis, M. (1997). *Altering fate: Why the past does not predict the future.* New York: Guilford Press.].

6. While mothers are the most readily available parent for study, the absence of father–infant studies cannot be due to the fact that fathers work away from home and mothers do not. Given the large number of working mothers in the work force, it is more likely that father-absent studies are due more to theoretical considerations.

7. Bronfenbrenner, U. (1979). *The ecology of development.* Cambridge, MA: Harvard University Press.

8. Bowlby, J. (1969). *Attachment and loss: Vol. 1. Attachment.* New York: Basic Books.

9. Weinraub, M., Brooks, J., & Lewis, M. (1977). The social network: A reconsideration of the concept of attachment. *Human Development, 20,* 31–47.

10. Dunn, J. (1993). *Young children's close relationships: Beyond attachment.* Thousand Oaks, CA: Sage. Lamb, M. E. (Ed.). (2004). *The role of the father in child development, 4th ed.* Hoboken, NJ: Wiley.

11. Hrdy, S. B. (2009). *Mothers and others: The evolutionary origins of mutual understanding.* Cambridge, MA: Harvard University Press.

12. In fact, Walden and Kim showed that infants selectively looked at a stranger adult rather than the parent when the stranger adult was perceived as having more knowledge about the situation [Walden, T. A., & Kim, G. (2005). Infants' social looking toward mothers and strangers. *International Journal of Behavioral Development, 29*(5), 356–360.].

13. Brooks, J., & Lewis, M. (1976). Infants' responses to strangers: Midget, adult and child. *Child Development, 47,* 323–332. Edwards, C. P., & Lewis, M. (1979). Young children's concepts of social relations: Social functions and social objects. In M. Lewis & L. A. Rosenblum (Eds.), *The child and its family: The genesis of behavior 2* (pp. 245–266). New York: Plenum Press. Lewis, M., Young, G., Brooks, J., & Michalson, L. (1975). The beginning of friendship. In M. Lewis & L. A. Rosenblum (Eds.), *Friendship and peer relations: The origins of behavior 4* (pp. 27–65). New York: Wiley. Takahashi, K., & Hatano, G. (1980–1981). Extension of attachment objects among Japanese toddlers. *Research and Clinical Center for Child Development, Annual Report 1980–1981,* 9–18.

14. Foss, B. M. (Ed.). (1961). *Determinants of infant behaviour.* Oxford, UK:

Wiley. Foss, B. M. (Ed.). (1963). *Determinants of infant behavior: II.* Oxford, UK: Wiley. Foss, B. M. (Ed.). (1966). *Determinants of infant behavior: III.* Oxford, UK: Wiley. Foss, B. M. (Ed.). (1969). *Determinants of infant behavior: IV.* New York: Methuen. Freud, A., & Dann, S. (1951). An experiment in group upbringing. In R. Eissler, A. Freud, H. Hartman, & E. Kris (Eds.), *The psychoanalytic study of the child* (Vol. 6, pp. 127–168). New York: International Universities Press. Harlow, H. F., & Harlow, M. K. (1965). The affectional systems. In A. M. Schrier, H. F. Harlow, & F. Stollnitz (Eds.), *Behavior of nonhuman primates* (Vol. 2, pp. 287–334). New York: Academic Press. Ruppenthal, G. C., Arling, G. L., Harlow, H. F., Sackett, G. P., & Suomi, S. J. (1976). 10-year perspective of motherless-mother monkey behavior. *Journal of Abnormal Psychology, 85,* 341–349.

15. Bronfenbrenner, U. (1976). The experimental ecology of education. *Teachers College Record, 78*(2), 157–204. (p. 178)

16. Brazelton, T. B., Koslowski, B., & Main, M. (1974). The origins of reciprocity: The early mother–infant interaction. In M. Lewis & L. Rosenblum (Eds.), *The effect of the infant on its caregiver: The origins of behavior, Vol. 1* (pp. 49–76). New York: Wiley. Lewis, M. (1972). State as an infant–environment interaction: An analysis of mother–infant interaction as a function of sex. *Merrill–Palmer Quarterly, 18,* 95–121. Lewis, M., & Rosenblum, L. A. (Eds.). (1974). *The effect of the infant on its caregiver: The origins of behavior, Vol. 1.* New York: Wiley. Stern, D. N. (1974). Mother and infant at play: The dyadic interaction involving facial, vocal, and gaze behavior. In M. Lewis & L. A. Rosenblum (Eds.), *The effect of the infant on its caregiver: The origins of behavior, Vol. 1* (pp. 187–213). New York: Wiley.

17. Clarke-Stewart, K. A. (1978). Recasting the lone stranger. In J. Glick & K. A. Clarke-Stewart (Eds.), *The development of social understanding* (pp. 109–175). Oxford, UK: Gardner. Lamb, M. E. (1975, April). *Infants, fathers, and mothers: Interaction at 8 months of age in the home and in the laboratory.* Paper presented at the meetings of the Eastern Psychological Association, New York. Lewis, M., & Weinraub, M. (1976). The father's role in the infant's social network. In M. Lamb (Ed.), *The role of the father in child development,* (pp. 157–184). New York: Wiley.

18. Campos, J. J., & Stenberg, C. R. (1981). Perception, appraisal, and emotion: The onset of social referencing. In M. Lamb & L. R. Sherrod (Eds.), *Infant social cognition: Empirical and theoretical considerations* (pp. 273–314). Hillsdale, NJ: Erlbaum. Feinman, S., & Lewis, M. (1983). Social referencing and second order effects in ten-month-old infants. *Child Development, 54,* 878–887.

19. I am reminded of Gunter Grass's book *The Tin Drum,* where he describes how adults went to a theater to cry and where the crying of others facilitated crying behavior [Grass, G. (1961). *The tin drum.* New York: Random House.], or the canned laughter on TV comedy shows designed to facilitate laughter in the TV viewer.

20. See Kochanska, G. (1993). Toward a synthesis of parental socialization and child temperament in early development of conscience. *Child Development, 64*(2), 325–347.

21. Feiring, C., Lewis, M., & Starr, M. D. (1984). Indirect effects and infants' reaction to strangers. *Developmental Psychology, 20,* 485–491. See also the paper by Repacholi, Meltzoff, and Olsen, who showed that toddlers were less likely to explore an object after just witnessing an adult scolding another adult for exploring the object [Repacholi, B. M., Meltzoff, A. N., & Olsen, B. (2008). Infants' understanding of the

link between visual perception and emotion: "If she can't see me doing it, she won't get angry." *Developmental Psychology, 44*(2), 561–574.].

22. Keizer, K., Lindenberg, S., & Steg, L. (2008, December 12). The spreading of disorder. *Science, 322*(5908), 1681–1685.

23. See, for example, Bandura, A. (1969). *Principles of behavior modification.* New York: Holt, Rinehart, & Winston. Bandura, A. (1973). *Aggression: A social learning analysis.* Englewood Cliffs, NJ: Prentice-Hall. Freud, S. (1953). Three essays on the theory of sexuality. In J. Strachey (Ed. & Trans.), in collaboration with A. Freud, *The standard edition of the complete psychological works of Sigmund Freud* (Vol. 7, pp. 269–279). London: Hogarth Press and the Institute of Psychoanalysis. (Originally published 1905) Guillaume, D. (1971). *Imitation in children* (E. P. Halperin, Trans.). Chicago: University of Chicago Press. (Originally published 1926) Hagen, J., & Hale, G. (1973). The development of attention in children. In A. D. Pick (Ed.), *Minnesota Symposia on Child Psychology* (Vol. 7, pp. 117–140). Minneapolis: University of Minnesota Press. Hartup, W. W., & Coates, B. (1970). The role of imitation in childhood socialization. In R. A. Hoppe, G. A. Milton, & E. C. Simmel (Eds.), *Early experiences and the processes of socialization* (pp. 109–142). New York: Academic Press. Lewis, M. (1979, March). *Issues in the study of imitation.* Paper presented at a Symposium on Imitation in Infancy: What, When, and How, at the meetings of the Society for Research in Child Development, San Francisco. Also in ERIC's Resources in Education (RIE), #ED 171-394. Parke, R. D., Power, T. G., & Gottman, J. M. (1979). Conceptualizing and quantifying influence patterns in the family triad. In M. E. Lamb, S. J. Suomi, & G. R. Stephenson (Eds.), *Social interaction analysis* (pp. 231–253). Madison: University of Wisconsin Press. Piaget, J. (1962). *Play, dreams, and imitation in childhood* (C. Gatlegno & F. M. Hodgson, Trans.). New York: Norton. (Original work published 1951 in French). Yando, R., Seitz, V., & Zigler, E. (1978). *Imitation: A developmental perspective.* Hillsdale, NJ: Erlbaum.

24. Eisenberg, N., Cumberland, A., & Spinrad, T. L. (1998). Parental socialization of emotion. *Psychological Inquiry, 9*(4), 241–273.

25. For criticism of maternal report, see Kagan, J. (1998). Biology and the child. In W. Damon & N. Eisenberg (Eds.), *Handbook of child psychology* (5th ed.): *Vol. 3. Social, emotional, and personality development* (pp. 177–235). Hoboken, NJ: Wiley. Rothbart, M. K., & Bates, J. E. (2006). Temperament. In N. Eisenberg, W. Damon, & R. M. Lerner (Eds.), *Handbook of child psychology* (6th ed.): *Vol. 3. Social, emotional, and personality development* (pp. 99–166). Hoboken, NJ: Wiley.

26. Eisenberg, N. (2000). Emotion, regulation, and moral development. *Annual Review of Psychology, 51*, 665–697. Eisenberg, N., Fabes, R. A., & Murphy, B. C. (1996). Parents' reactions to children's negative emotions: Relations to children's social competence and comforting behavior. *Child Development, 67*, 2227–2247. Gottman, J. M., Katz, L. F., & Hooven, C. (1997). *Meta-emotion: How families communicate emotionally.* Hillsdale, NJ: Erlbaum. Kochanska, G., Tjebkes, T. L., & Forman, D. R. (1998). Children's emerging regulation of conduct: Restraint, compliance, and internalization from infancy to the second year. *Child Development, 69*(5), 1378–1389.

27. Bendersky, M., & Lewis, M. (1998). Prenatal cocaine exposure and impulse control at two years. *Annals of the New York Academy of Sciences, 846*, 365–367.

28. Trommsdorff, G. (2006). Development of emotions as organized by culture. *International Society for the Study of Behavioural Development Newsletter, 1*(49),

1–4. [Supplement to *International Journal of Behavioral Development, 30*(3), May 2006.] (p. 3)

29. Wang, Q., & Fivush, R. (2005). Mother–child conversations of emotionally salient events: Exploring the functions of emotional reminiscing in European-American and Chinese families. *Social Development, 14*(3), 473–495.

30. We need always to keep in mind that the child's temperament also interacts with any elicitor, producing different consequences in different children. The temperamental difficult child can be overwhelmed by the intensity of an elicitor, such as tickling, while another less temperamental child is not.

31. Harkness, S., & Super, C. M. (1985). Child–environment interactions in the socialization of affect. In M. Lewis & C. Saarni (Eds.), *The socialization of emotions* (pp. 21–36). New York: Plenum Press.

32. Weinraub, M., & Lewis, M. (1977). The determinants of children's responses to separation. *Monographs of the Society for Research in Child Development, 42*(4, Serial No. 172).

33. Gewirtz, J. L., & Boyd, E. F. (1977). Does maternal responding imply reduced infant crying?: A critique of the 1972 Bell and Ainsworth report. *Child Development, 48*, 1200–1207.

34. Kagan, J., & Klein, R. E. (1973). Cross-cultural perspectives on early development. *American Psychologist, 28*(11), 947–961.

35. Barr, R. G., Young, S. N., Wright, J. H., Cassidy, K.L, Hendricks, L., Bedard, Y., et al. (1995). "Sucrose analgesia" and diphtheria–tetanus–pertussis immunizations at 2 and 4 months. *Developmental and Behavioral Pediatrics, 16*, 220–225. Blass, E. M. (1997). Infant formula quiets crying human newborns. *Developmental and Behavioral Pediatrics, 18,* 162–165.

36. The data on maternal response to distress is not as clear as many think. In a study by Bell and Ainsworth [Bell, S. M., & Ainsworth, M. D. S. (1972). Infant crying and maternal responsiveness. *Child Development, 43*, 1171–1190.], the claim was made that maternal response to the infant's distress did not lead to more crying at later ages, but less. However, Gewirtz [Gewirtz, J. L., & Boyd, E. F. (1977). Does maternal responding imply reduced infant crying?: A critique of the 1972 Bell and Ainsworth report. *Child Development, 48*, 1200–1207.], in a critique of the findings, demonstrates that their results and conclusion were not valid. Even so, the Bell and Ainsworth study is considered to be a classic in the literature. See Lewis and Ramsay for details [Lewis, M., & Ramsay, D. S. (1999). Effect of maternal soothing on infant stress reactivity. *Child Development, 70*(1), 11–20.].

37. Lewis, M., & Michalson, L. (1985). Faces as signs and symbols. In G. Zivin (Ed.), *Development of expressive behavior: Biology–environmental interaction* (pp. 153–182). New York: Academic Press. Michalson, L., & Lewis, M. (1985). What do children know about emotions and when do they know it? In M. Lewis & C. Saarni (Eds.), *The socialization of emotions* (pp. 117–140). New York: Plenum Press.

38. Alessandri, S. M., & Lewis, M. (1996). Differences in pride and shame in maltreated and non-maltreated preschoolers. *Child Development, 67*, 1857–1869. Alessandri, S. M., & Lewis, M. (1996). Development of the self-conscious emotions in maltreated children. In M. Lewis & M. W. Sullivan (Eds.), *Emotional development in atypical children* (pp. 185–202). Mahwah, NJ: Erlbaum.

39. Dweck, C. S. (2006). *Mindset: The new psychology of success*. New York:

Random House. Lewis, M. (1995). *Shame: The exposed self* (Paperback edition). New York: Free Press.

40. Denham, S. A. (1993). Maternal emotional responsiveness and toddlers' social–emotional competence. *Journal of Child Psychology and Psychiatry, 34,* 715–728. Eisenberg, N., Fabes, R. A., & Murphy, B. C. (1996). Parents' reactions to children's negative emotions: Relations to children's social competence and comforting behavior. *Child Development, 67,* 2227–2247. Saarni, C. (1985). Indirect processes in affect socialization. In M. Lewis & C. Saarni (Eds.), *The socialization of emotions* (pp. 187–209). New York: Plenum Press. Roberts, W., & Strayer, J. (1987). Parents' responses to the emotional distress of their children: Relations with children's competence. *Developmental Psychology, 23,* 415–432.

41. It should be noted that the at-home observed rate of maternal responsivity to infant smiling and crying accounted for under 20% of the infant's behavior [Coates, D., & Lewis, M. (1984). Early mother–infant interaction and infant cognitive status as predictors of school performance and cognitive behavior in six year olds. *Child Development, 55,* 1219–1230. Lewis, M., & Coates, D. L. (1980). Mother–infant interactions and cognitive development in twelve-week-old infants. *Infant Behavior and Development, 3,* 95–105. Lewis, M., & Goldberg, S. (1969). Perceptual–cognitive development in infancy: A generalized expectancy model as a function of the mother–infant interaction. *Merrill–Palmer Quarterly, 15*(1), 81–100.].

42. Capatides, J. B., & Bloom, L. (1993). Underlying process in the socialization of emotion. *Advances in Infancy Research, 8,* 99–135. Malatesta, C. Z., Grigoryev, P., Lamb, C., Albin, M., & Culver, C. (1986). Emotion socialization and expressive development in preterm and full-term infants. *Child Development, 57,* 316–330. Malatesta, C. Z., & Haviland, J. M. (1982). Learning display rules: The socialization of emotion expression in infancy. *Child Development, 53*(4), 991–1003. Malatesta, C. Z., & Haviland, J. M. (1985). Signals, symbols and socialization: The modification of emotional expression in human development. In M. Lewis & C. Saarni (Eds.), *The socialization of emotions* (pp. 89–116). New York: Plenum Press.

43. Porges, S. W. (2011*). The polyvagal theory: Neurophysiological foundations of emotions, attachment, communication, and self-regulation.* New York: Norton.

44. Ramsay, D. S., & Lewis, M. (2001). Temperament, stress, and soothing. In T. D. Wachs & G. A. Kohnstamm (Eds.), *Temperament in context* (pp. 23–41). Mahwah, NJ: Erlbaum.

45. Lewis, M., Ramsay, D. S., & Kawakami, K. (1993). Differences between Japanese infants and Caucasian American infants in behavioral and cortisol response to inoculation. *Child Development, 64,* 1722–1731.

46. Lewis, M. (2011). Inside and outside: The relation between emotional states and expressions. In M. Lewis (Ed.), Infant emotional development [Special issue]. *Emotion Review, 3*(2), 189–196.

47. Earlier I mentioned the work of Keller that seems to show cultural differences in the age of self-recognition. These differences, if they can be replicated, are likely due to cultural differences in getting children to conform to the experimenter's requests.

48. Dweck, C. S., & Leggett, E. L. (1988). A social cognitive approach to motivation and personality. *Psychological Review, 95,* 256–273. Weiner, B. (1986). *An attributional theory of motivation and emotion.* New York: Springer-Verlag.

49. Alessandri, S. M., & Lewis, M. (1993). Parental evaluation and its relation to

shame and pride in young children. *Sex Roles, 29*(5–6), 335–343. Lewis, M. (1995). *Shame: The exposed self* (Paperback edition). New York: Free Press.

50. See Kochanska [Kochanska, G. (1991). Socialization and temperament in the development of guilt and conscience. *Child Development, 62,* 1379–1392.], who argues that temperament in combination with socialization affects the self-conscious emotions.

51. Lewis, M. (1995). *Shame: The exposed self* (Paperback edition). New York: Free Press.

52. Hesse, H. (1970). A child's heart. In H. Hesse (R. Winston & C. Winston, Trans.), *Klingsor's last summer.* New York: Farrar, Straus and Giroux. (Original work published 1920 in German)

53. Gottman, J. M. (1994). *What predicts divorce?: The relationship between marital processes and marital outcomes.* Hillsdale, NJ: Erlbaum.

54. Bowlby, J. (1973). *Attachment and loss: Vol. 2. Separation: Anxiety and anger.* New York: Basic Books. (p. 204)

55. Lewis, M., & Michalson, L. (1983). *Children's emotions and moods: Developmental theory and measurement.* New York: Plenum Press. Lewis, M., & Michalson, L. (Eds.). (1984). Emotional development and infant mental health [Special issue], *Infant Mental Health Journal, 5*(3).

56. I knew a mother who was a physician whose specialty was allergies. Once, when we arrived at her home, her 8-year-old daughter greeted us with whining behavior for some unknown reason. Her mother's response to her whining was "She is having a cerebral allergy." I am sure that the somatization of emotional behavior is widespread and that some cultures use more of it than others.

57. Nederhof, E., Belsky, J., Ormel, J., & Oldehinkel, A. J. (2012). Effects of divorce on Dutch boys' and girls' externalizing behavior in gene x environment perspective: Diathesis stress or differential susceptibility in the Dutch Tracking Adolescents' Individual Lives Survey study? *Development and Psychopathology, 24*(3), 929–939. O'Connor, T. G., Caspi, A., DeFries, J. C., & Plomin, R. (2000). Are associations between parental divorce and children's adjustment genetically mediated?: An adoption study. *Developmental Psychology, 36*(4), 429–437. O'Connor, T. G., Deater-Deckard, K., Fulker, D., Rutter, M., & Plomin, R. (1998). Genotype–environment correlations in late childhood and early adolescence: Antisocial behavioral problems and coercive parenting. *Developmental Psychology, 34*(5), 970–981. van IJzendoorn, M. H., Belsky, J., & Bakermans-Kranenburg, M. J. (2012). Serotonin transporter genotypes. 5HTTLPR as a marker of differential susceptibility?: A meta-analysis of child and adolescent gene-by-environment studies. *Translational Psychiatry, 2,* e147.

Chapter 11. Emotional Development Gone Awry

1. Bowlby, J. (1992). *Charles Darwin: A new life.* New York: Norton.

2. For example, Izard and Ekman, the originators of two elaborate facial coding systems, themselves predicated on the work of Tomkins and Darwin, have argued that facial expressions bear a one-to-one relation to internal states. This argument has led to the belief that it is possible for experts to detect lying by carefully studying facial expressions. As we have seen in Chapter 7, on deception, the association between expression and internal state is rather low, which is why lying is possible. Likewise, research data

presented in Chapter 10, on temperament, indicate that internal manifestations of pain and distress bear only a moderate association to facial expressions, psychological manifestations, and vocal expressions. This moderate association between facial expressions of emotions and internal states leads me to assume that there are important socialization factors at work that dissemble facial expressions from internal states. My work, as well as that of Carolyn Saarni, Pamela Cole, Paul Harris, and Kang Lee, clearly indicates a dissemblance of emotional expression from an emotional action pattern.

The same might be held for the association between emotional action patterns and experiences. Indeed, from a developmental perspective, one would expect experiences, conscious manifestations of action patterns, and the patterns themselves to be unrelated early in life, since the child does not develop a representation of himself until 18 months or so and thus cannot have experiences about himself.

3. Galati, D., Scherer, K. R., & Ricci-Bitti, P. E. (1997). Voluntary facial expression of emotion: Comparing congenitally blind with normally sighted encoders. *Journal of Personality and Social Psychology, 73*(6), 1363–1379. Galati, D., Sini, B., Schmidt, S., & Tinti, C. (2003). Spontaneous facial expressions in congenitally blind and sighted children aged 8–11. *Journal of Visual Impairment and Blindness, 97,* 418–428. Matsumoto, D., & Willingham, B. (2009). Spontaneous facial expressions of emotion of congenitally and noncongenitally blind individuals. *Journal of Personality and Social Psychology, 96*(1), 1–10.

4. Umbel, V. M., & LaVoie, L. (1988, April). *The IMCE: An attempt at the measurement of the mutual contingency experience.* Poster presented at the International Conference on Infant Studies, Washington, DC. Walden, T. A., & Knieps, L. (1996). Reading and responding to social signals. In M. Lewis & M. W. Sullivan (Eds.), *Emotional development in atypical children* (pp. 29–42). Mahwah, NJ: Erlbaum.

5. Cicchetti, D., & Sroufe, L. A. (1978). An organizational view of affect: Illustration from the study of Down's syndrome infants. In M. Lewis & L. A. Rosenblum (Eds.), *The development of affect* (Vol. 1, pp. 309–350). New York: Plenum Press. Field, T. (1996). Expressivity in physically and emotionally handicapped children. In M. Lewis & M. W. Sullivan (Eds.), *Emotional development in atypical children* (pp. 1–27). Mahwah, NJ: Erlbaum. Panksepp, J. (2008). The affective brain and core consciousness: How does neural activity generate emotional feelings? In M. Lewis, J. M. Haviland-Jones, & L. Feldman Barrett (Eds.), *Handbook of emotions* (3rd ed., pp. 47–67). New York: Guilford Press. Tomkins, S. S. (1962). *Affect, imagery, consciousness: Vol. 1. The positive affects.* New York: Springer. Also see Lewis, M., & Sullivan, M. W. (Eds.), (1996). *Emotional development in atypical children.* Mahwah, NJ: Erlbaum.

6. Goldberg, S. (1997). Attachment and childhood behavior problems in normal, at-risk and clinical samples. In L. Atkinson & K. J. Zucker (Eds.), *Attachment and psychopathology* (pp. 171–195). New York: Guilford Press. Mundy, P., & Willoughby, J. (1996). Nonverbal communication, joint attention, and early socioemotional development. In M. Lewis & M. W. Sullivan (Eds.), *Emotional development in atypical children* (pp. 65–87). Mahwah, NJ: Erlbaum. Stern, D. N. (1985). *The interpersonal world of the infant.* New York: Basic Books.

7. Sullivan, M. W., & Lewis, M. (2012). Relations of early goal-blockage response and gender to subsequent tantrum behavior. *Infancy, 17*(2), 159–178.

8. Bennett, D. S., Bendersky, M., & Lewis, M. (2002). Facial expressivity at 4 months: A context by expression analysis. *Infancy, 3*(1), 97–113.

9. Rozin, P., Haidt, J., & McCauley, C. R. (2009). Disgust: The body and soul emotion in the 21st century. In B. O. Olatunji & D. McKay (Eds.), *Disgust and its disorders: Theory, assessment, and treatment implications* (pp. 9–29). Washington, DC: American Psychological Association.

10. Kagan, J. (2003). Behavioral inhibition as a temperamental category. In R. J. Davidson, K. R. Scherer, & H. H. Goldsmith (Eds.), *Handbook of affective sciences* (pp. 320–331). New York: Oxford University Press.

11. Hemmi, M. H., Wolke, D., & Schneider, S. (2011). Associations between problems with crying, sleeping and/or feeding in infancy and long-term behavioural outcomes in childhood: A meta-analysis. *Archives of Disease in Childhood, 96*(7), 622–629.

12. Brooks-Gunn, J., & Lewis, M. (1982). Temperament and affective interaction in handicapped infants. *Journal of Division of Early Childhood, 5,* 31–41.

13. Lewis, M., & Carmody, D. (2008). Self representation and brain development. *Developmental Psychology, 44*(5), 1329–1334.

14. Dawson, G., & McKissick, F. C. (1984). Self-recognition in autistic children. *Journal of Autism and Developmental Disorders, 14,* 383–394. Ferrari, M., & Matthews, W. S. (1983). Self-recognition deficits in autism: Syndrome-specific or general developmental delay? *Journal of Autism and Developmental Disorders, 13,* 317–324.

15. Carmody, D. P., & Lewis, M. (2012). Self representation in children with and without autism spectrum disorders. *Child Psychiatry and Human Development, 43*(2), 227–237.

16. Hobson, R. P., Chidambi, G., Lee, A., & Meyer, J. (2006). Foundations for self-awareness: An exploration through autism. *Monographs of the Society for Research in Child Development, 71*(2, Serial No. 284), 120–166. Mundy, P. (1995). Joint attention and social emotional approach behavior in children with autism. *Development and Psychopathology, 7,* 63–82.

17. Amaral, D. G., Schumann, C. M., & Nordahl, C. W. (2008). Neuroanatomy of autism. *Trends in Neurosciences, 31*(3), 137–145. Bauman, M. L., & Kemper, T. L. (2005). Neuroanatomic observations of the brain in autism: A review and future directions. *International Journal of Developmental Neuroscience, 23*(2–3), 183–187.

18. Samson, D., Apperly, I. A., Chiavarion, C., & Humphreys, G. W. (2004). Left temporoparietal junction is necessary for representing someone else's belief. *Nature Neuroscience, 7,* 499–500. Saxe, R., Carey, S., & Kanwisher, N. (2004). Understanding other minds: Linking developmental psychology and functional neuroimaging. *Annual Review of Psychology, 55,* 87–124.

19. Amaral, D. G., Schumann, C. M., & Nordahl, C. W. (2008). Neuroanatomy of autism. *Trends in Neurosciences, 31*(3), 137–145.

20. Frith, U. (2001). Mind blindness and the brain in autism. *Neuron, 32*(6), 969–979.

21. Carmody, D. P., & Lewis, M. (in preparation). *Self representation and brain enlargement in children with autism spectrum disorders.*

22. Darwin, C. R. (1965). *The expression of emotions in man and animals.* Chicago: University of Chicago Press. (Original work published 1872) (p. 325)

23. Hoffman, M. L. (2008). Empathy and prosocial behavior. In M. Lewis, J. M. Haviland-Jones, & L. Feldman Barrett (Eds.), *Handbook of emotions* (3rd ed., pp. 440–455). New York: Guilford Press. Trivers, R. L. (1974). Parent–offspring conflict. *American Zoologist, 14*(1), 249–264.

24. Eisenberg, N., Fabes, R. A., Murphy, B. C., Karbon, M., Maszk, P., Smith, M., et al. (1994). The relations of emotionality and regulation to dispositional and situational empathy-related responding. *Journal of Personality and Social Psychology, 66*(4), 776–797.

25. Eysenck, H. J. (1954). *The psychology of politics.* London: Routledge & Kegan Paul.

26. Buss, A. H. (1980). *Self-consciousness and social anxiety.* San Francisco: Freeman. Izard, C. E., & Tyson, M. C. (1986). Shyness as a discrete emotion. In W. H. Jones, J. M. Cheek, & S. R. Briggs (Eds.), *Shyness: Perspectives on research and treatment* (pp. 147–160). New York: Plenum Press. Lewis, M. (1992). *Shame: The exposed self.* New York: Free Press.

27. DiBiase, R., & Lewis, M. (1997). The relation between temperament and embarrassment. *Cognition and Emotion, 11,* 259–271. Eysenck, H. J. (1954). *The psychology of politics.* London: Routledge & Kegan Paul. Kagan, J., Snidman, N., Arcus, D., & Reznick, J. S. (1994). *Galen's prophecy: Temperament in human nature.* New York: Basic Books. Lewis, M., & Ramsay, D. S. (1997). Stress reactivity and self-recognition. *Child Development, 68,* 621–629.

28. Amazingly, once the children showed self-recognition, a measure of the emerging representation of self, they showed embarrassment. However, not all children who show self-recognition show embarrassment, just in the same way that not all adults blush. This distribution is quite marked, however; some show none, most show some, and a few show extreme embarrassment, defined by showing embarrassment to every situation, even becoming upset when pointed to.

29. DiBiase, R., & Lewis, M. (1997). The relation between temperament and embarrassment. *Cognition and Emotion, 11,* 259–271.

30. Hart, S. L., & Legerstee, M. (Eds.). (2010). *Handbook of jealousy: Theory, research, and multidisciplinary approaches.* Malden, MA: Blackwell/Wiley. Feiring, C., & Lewis, M. (1979). Sex and age differences in young children's reactions to frustration: A further look at the Goldberg and Lewis (1969) subjects. *Child Development, 50,* 848–853. Lewis, M. (2010). Loss, protest, and emotional development. In S. Hart & M. Legerstee (Eds.), *Handbook of jealousy: Theory, research, and multidisciplinary approaches* (pp. 27–39). Malden, MA: Blackwell/Wiley.

31. Masson, J. M. (1984). *The assault on truth: Freud's suppression of the seduction theory.* New York: Farrar, Straus and Giroux.

32. Lewis, M. (1992). *Shame: The exposed self.* New York: Free Press. Ross, C. A. (1989). *Multiple personality disorder.* New York: Wiley. Tangney, J. P., Wagner, P. E., & Gramzow, R. (1990, June). *Shame-proneness, but not guilt-proneness, is linked to psychological maladjustment.* Poster presented at the annual meeting of the American Psychological Society, Dallas, TX.

33. Bousha, D., & Twentyman, C. T. (1984). Mother–child interactional style in abuse, neglect, and control groups: Naturalistic observations in the home. *Journal of Abnormal Psychology, 93,* 106–114. Coffey, P., Leitenberg, H., Henning, K., Turner, T., & Bennett, R. T. (1996). Mediators of the long-term impact of child sexual abuse: Perceived stigma, betrayal, powerlessness, and self-blame. *Child Abuse and Neglect, 20*(5), 447–455. Elliott, D. M., Briere, J., McNeil, D., Cox, J., & Bauman, D. (1995, July). *Multivariate impacts of sexual molestation, physical abuse and neglect in a forensic sample.* Paper presented at the Fourth International

Family Violence Research Conference, Durham, NH. Fantuzzo, J. W., Weiss, A. D., Atkins, M., Meyers, R., & Noone, M. (1998). A contextually relevant assessment of the impact of child maltreatment on the social competencies of low-income urban children. *Journal of the American Academy of Child and Adolescent Psychiatry, 37*, 1201–1208. Hoffman-Plotkin, D., & Twentyman, C. T. (1984). A multimodal assessment of behavioral and cognitive deficits in abused and neglected preschoolers. *Child Development, 55*, 794–802. Lynch, M., & Cicchetti, D. (1998). An ecological–transactional analysis of children and contexts: The longitudinal interplay among child maltreatment, community violence, and children's symptomatology. *Development and Psychopathology, 10*, 235–257. Manly, J. T., Kim, J. E., Rogosch, F. A., & Cicchetti, D. (2001). Dimensions of child maltreatment and children's adjustment: Contributions of developmental timing and subtype. *Development and Psychopathology, 13*, 759–782.

34. Harder, D. W., & Lewis, S. J. (1986). The assessment of shame and guilt. In J. N. Butcher & C. D. Spielberger (Eds.), *Advances in personality assessment: Vol. 6* (pp. 89–114). Hillsdale, NJ: Erlbaum. Lewis, H. B. (1987). The role of shame in depression over the lifespan. In H. B. Lewis (Ed.), *The role of shame in symptom formation* (pp. 29–50). Hillsdale, NJ: Erlbaum.

35. Tangney, J. P., Burggraf, S. A., & Wagner, P. E. (1995). Shame-proneness, guilt-proneness, and psychological symptoms. In J. P. Tangney & K. W. Fischer (Eds.), *Self-conscious emotions: The psychology of shame, guilt, embarrassment and pride* (pp. 343–367). New York: Guilford Press.

36. Lewis, M. (1992). *Shame: The exposed self.* New York: Free Press. Ross, C. A. (1989). *Multiple personality disorder.* New York: Wiley.

37. Feiring, C., Taska, L., & Lewis, M. (1998). The role of shame and attributional style in children's and adolescents' adaptation to sexual abuse. *Child Maltreatment, 3*(2), 129–142. Feiring, C., Taska, L., & Lewis, M. (1999). Age and gender differences in children's and adolescents' adaptation to sexual abuse. *Child Abuse and Neglect, 23*, 115–128. Widom, C. S. (1999). Posttraumatic stress disorder in abused and neglected children grown up. *American Journal of Psychiatry, 156*(8), 1223–1229.

38. Feiring, C., Taska, L., & Lewis, M. (1998). The role of shame and attributional style in children's and adolescents' adaptation to sexual abuse. *Child Maltreatment, 3*(2), 129–142. Feiring, C., Taska, L., & Lewis, M. (1999). Age and gender differences in children's and adolescents' adaptation to sexual abuse. *Child Abuse and Neglect, 23*, 115–128.

39. Feiring, C., Taska, L., & Lewis, M. (1998). The role of shame and attributional style in children's and adolescents' adaptation to sexual abuse. *Child Maltreatment, 3*(2), 129–142. Feiring, C., Taska, L., & Lewis, M. (1999). Age and gender differences in children's and adolescents' adaptation to sexual abuse. *Child Abuse and Neglect, 23*, 115–128.

40. Cutler, S. E., & Nolen-Hoeksema, S. (1991). Accounting for sex differences in depression through female victimization: Childhood sexual abuse. *Sex Roles, 24*, 425–438. Friedrich, W. N., Beilke, R. L., & Urquiza, A. J. (1988). Behavior problems in young sexually abused boys. *Journal of Interpersonal Violence, 3*, 21–28. Lewis, H. B. (1971). *Shame and guilt in neurosis.* New York: International Universities Press. Retzinger, S. M. (1987). Resentment of laughter: Video studies of the shame–rage spiral. In H. B. Lewis (Ed.), *The role of shame in symptom formation* (pp. 151–181). Hillsdale,

NJ: Erlbaum. Tangney, J. P. (1991). Moral affect: The good, the bad, and the ugly. *Journal of Personality and Social Psychology, 61,* 598–607.

41. Dweck, C. S., & Leggett, E. L. (1988). A social cognitive approach to motivation and personality. *Psychological Review, 95,* 256–273.

42. Elmer, E. (1977). Follow-up study of traumatized children. *Child Abuse and Neglect, 1*(1), 105–109. Gil, D. (1970). *Violence against children: Physical child abuse in the United States.* Cambridge, MA: Harvard University Press. Kempe, C. H. (1973). A practical approach to the protection of the abused child and rehabilitation of the abusing parent. *Pediatrics, 51*(4), 804–809.

43. Walters, D. R. (1975). *Physical and sexual abuse of children: Causes and treatment.* Bloomington: Indiana University Press.

44. Brown, J. A., & Daniels, R. (1968). Some observations on abusive parents. *Child Welfare, 47,* 89–94. Kempe, C. H., Silverman, F. N., Steele, B. F., Droegemueller, W., & Silver, H. K. (1962). The battered child syndrome. *Journal of the American Medical Association, 181,* 17–24.

45. Parke, R. D., & Collmer, C. W. (1975). Child abuse: An interdisciplinary analysis. In E. M. Hetherington (Ed.), *Review of child development research* (Vol. 5, pp. 509–590). Chicago: University of Chicago Press.

46. National Academy of Sciences. (1976). *Toward a national policy for children and families.* Washington, DC: U.S. Government Printing Office.

47. Widom, C. S. (1989). The cycle of violence. *Science, 244,* 160–166. See also the work on observing mother monkeys: Ruppenthal, G. C., Arling, G. L., Harlow, H. F., Sackett, G. P., & Suomi, S. J. (1976). A 10-year perspective of motherless-mother monkey behavior. *Journal of Abnormal Psychology, 85,* 341–349.

48. Blumberg, M. L. (1974). Psychopathology of the abusing parent. *American Journal of Psychotherapy, 28,* 21–29. Kempe, R. S., & Kempe, C. H. (1978). *Child abuse.* Cambridge, MA: Harvard University Press. Weston, J. T. (1968). The pathology of child abuse. In R. E. Helfer & C. H. Kempe (Eds.), *The battered child* (pp. 77–100). Chicago: University of Chicago Press.

49. Gelles, R. J. (1973). Child abuse as psychopathology: A sociological critique and reformulation. *American Journal of Orthopsychiatry, 43,* 611–621. Jacobs, R. A., & Kent, J. T. (1977). Psychosocial profiles of families of failure to thrive infants—Preliminary report. *Child Abuse and Neglect, 1*(2–4), 469–477. Klein, M., & Stern, L. (1971). Low birth weight and the battered child syndrome. *American Journal of Diseases of Childhood, 122,* 15–18.

50. Kempe, R. S., & Kempe, C. H. (1978). *Child abuse.* Cambridge, MA: Harvard University Press.

51. Fantuzzo, J. W., Weiss, A. D., Atkins, M., Meyers, R., & Noone, M. (1998). A contextually relevant assessment of the impact of child maltreatment on the social competencies of low-income urban children. *Journal of the American Academy of Child and Adolescent Psychiatry, 37,* 1201–1208. Lynch, M., & Cicchetti, D. (1998). An ecological–transactional analysis of children and contexts: The longitudinal interplay among child maltreatment, community violence, and children's symptomatology. *Development and Psychopathology, 10,* 235–257. Manly, J. T., Kim, J. E., Rogosch, F. A., & Cicchetti, D. (2001). Dimensions of child maltreatment and children's adjustment: Contributions of developmental timing and subtype. *Development and Psychopathology, 13,* 759–782.

52. Bennett, D. S., Sullivan, M. W., & Lewis, M. (2005). Young children's adjustment as a function of maltreatment, shame, and anger. *Child Maltreatment, 10*(4), 311–323.

53. Bennett, D. S., Sullivan, M. W., & Lewis, M. (2006). Relations of parental report and observation of parenting to maltreatment history. *Child Maltreatment, 11*(1), 63–75.

54. Rutter, M., Beckett, C., Castle, J., Colvert, E., Kreppner, J., Mehta, M., et al. (2007). Effects of profound early institutional deprivation: An overview of findings from a UK longitudinal study of Romanian adoptees. *European Journal of Developmental Psychology, 4*(3), 332–350.

55. Lewis, H. B. (1971). *Shame and guilt in neurosis.* New York: International Universities Press.

56. Cicchetti, D., & Manly, J. T. (2001). Operationalizing child maltreatment: Developmental processes and outcomes. *Developmental Psychopathology, 13*(4), 755–757. Crowley, T. J., Mikulich, S. K., Ehlers, K. M., Hall, S. K., & Whitmore, E. A. (2003). Discriminative validity and clinical utility of an abuse-neglect interview for adolescents with conduct and substance abuse problems. *American Journal of Psychiatry, 160*(8), 1461–1469. Dodge, K. A., Pettit, G. S., Bates, J. E., & Valente, E. (1995). Social information-processing patterns partially mediate the effect of early physical abuse on later conduct problems. *Journal of Abnormal Psychology, 104*, 632–643. Kelley, B. T., Thornberry, T. P., & Smith, C. A. (1997). *In the wake of childhood maltreatment.* Washington, DC: U.S. Department of Justice, Office of Justice Programs, Office of Juvenile Justice and Delinquency Prevention. Lansford, J. E., Dodge, K. A., Pettit, G. S., Bates, J. E., Crozier, J., & Kaplow, J. (2002). A 12-year prospective study of the long-term effects of early child physical maltreatment on psychological, behavioral, and academic problems in adolescence. *Archive of Pediatric and Adolescent Medicine, 156*(8), 824–830. Loeber, R., & Stouthamer-Loeber, M. (1998). Development of juvenile aggression and violence: Some common misconceptions and controversies. *American Psychologist, 53*(2), 242–259. Mayfield, M. G., & Widom, C. S. (1996). The cycle of violence. *Archives of Pediatric and Adolescent Medicine, 150*, 390–395. McCord, J. (1991). Questioning the value of punishment. *Social Problems, 38*(2), 167–179. National Council on Crime and Delinquency. (1999). *Development of an empirically based risk assessment instrument for the Virginia Department of Juvenile Justice: Final report.* Madison, WI : Virginia Department of Juvenile Justice. Patterson, G. R. (Ed.). (1995). *Coercion—A basis for early age of onset for arrest.* New York: Cambridge University Press. Widom, C. S. (1992). *The cycle of violence: Research in brief.* Washington, DC: U.S. Department of Justice, Office of Justice Programs, National Institute of Justice. Wiebush, R., Freitag, R., & Baird, C. (2001, June). *Preventing delinquency through improved child protective services.* Washington, DC: U.S. Department of Justice, Office of Juvenile Justice and Delinquency Prevention, Office of Justice Programs.

57. Averill, J. R. (1982). *Anger and aggression.* New York: Springer-Verlag. Cramer, P., & Kelly, F. D. (2004). Defense mechanisms in adolescent conduct disorder and adjustment reaction. *Journal of Nervous and Mental Disorders, 192*(2), 139–145. Dodge, K. A., McClaskey, C. L., & Feldman, E. (1985). Situational approach to the assessment of social competence in children. *Journal of Consulting and Clinical Psychology, 53*(3), 344–353. Dutton, C. G. (2002). Personality dynamics of intimate abusiveness. *Journal of Psychiatric Practice, 8*(4), 216–228. Lochman, J. E. (1987).

Self- and peer perceptions and attributional biases of aggressive and nonaggressive boys in dyadic interactions. *Journal of Consulting and Clinical Psychology, 55*(3), 404–410. Retzinger, S. M. (1991). *Violent emotions: Shame and rage in marital quarrels.* London: Sage. Scheff, T. J. (2001). Working class emotions and relationships: Secondary analysis of classic texts by Sennett, R., Cobb, J., and Willis, P. Internet paper accessible at *www.soc.ucsb.edu/faculty/scheff/22.html.* Tangney, J. P., & Dearing, R. L. (2002). *Shame and guilt.* New York: Guilford Press. Tangney, J. P., Wagner, P. E., Hill-Barlow, D., Marschall, D. E., & Gramzow, R. (1996). Relation of shame and guilt to constructive versus destructive responses to anger across the lifespan. *Journal of Personality and Social Psychology, 70*(4), 797–809. Zelli, A., Dodge, K. A., Lochman, J. E., Laird, R. D., & Conduct Problems Prevention Research Group. (1999). The distinction between beliefs legitimizing aggression and deviant processing of social cues: Testing measurement validity and the hypothesis that biased processing mediates the effects of beliefs on aggression. *Journal of Personality and Social Psychology, 77*(1), 150–166.

58. Gold, J., Sullivan, M. W., & Lewis, M. (2011). The relation between abuse and violent delinquency: The conversion of shame to blame in juvenile offenders. *Child Abuse and Neglect, 35*(7), 459–467.

59. Gazzaniga, M. S. (1988). Brain modularity: Towards a philosophy of conscious experience. In A. J. Marcel & E. Bisiach (Eds.), *Consciousness in contemporary science* (pp. 218–238). New York: Oxford University Press. Ross, C. A. (1989). *Multiple personality disorder.* New York: Wiley.

60. Hilgard, E. R. (1977). *Divided consciousness: Multiple controls in human thought and action.* New York: Wiley. Prince, M. (1978). *The dissociation of a personality.* New York: Oxford University Press. (Original work published 1906)

61. Breuer, J., & Freud, S. (1986). Studies on hysteria. In J. Strachey (Ed. and Trans.), *The standard edition of the complete psychological works of Sigmund Freud* (Vol. 2, p. 76). London: Hogarth Press. (Original work published 1895) Jones, E. M. (1953). *Sigmund Freud: Life and work* (Vol. 1, p. 246). London: Hogarth Press.

62. Ross, C. A. (1989). *Multiple personality disorder.* New York: Wiley. (p. 218)

63. Goffman, E. (1963). *Stigma: Notes on the management of a spoiled identity.* Englewood Cliffs, NJ: Prentice-Hall. (p. 7)

64. Angrosino, M. V. (1992). Metaphors of stigma: How deinstitutionalized mentally retarded adults see themselves. *Journal of Contemporary Ethnography, 21*(2), 171–199. Gibbons, F. X. (1985). Stigma perception: Social comparison among mentally retarded persons. *American Journal of Mental Deficiency, 90*(1), 98–106. Lewis, M. (1998). Shame and stigma. In P. Gilbert & B. Andrews (Eds.), *Shame: Interpersonal behavior, psychopathology, and culture* (pp. 126–140). New York: Oxford University Press. Reiss, S., & Benson, B. A. (1984). Awareness of negative social conditions among mentally retarded, emotionally disturbed outpatients. *American Journal of Psychiatry, 141*(1), 88–90. Rogers, S. J. (1991). Observation of emotional functioning in young handicapped children. *Child Care Health and Development, 17,* 303–312. Szivos-Bach, S. E. (1993). Social comparisons, stigma and mainstreaming: The self-esteem of young adults with a mild mental handicap. *Mental Handicap Research, 6*(3), 217–236. Taylor, A. R., Asher, S. R., & Williams, G. A. (1987). The social adaptation of mainstreamed mildly retarded children. *Child Development, 58,* 1321–1334. Varni, J. W., Setoguchi, Y., Rappaport, L. R., & Talbot, D. (1992). Psychological adjustment and perceived social support in children with congenital/acquired limb deficiencies. *Journal*

of Behavioral Medicine, 15(1), 31–44. Weiner, B. (1993). On sin versus sickness: A theory of perceived responsibility and social motivation. *American Psychologist, 48*(9), 957–965.

65. Amodio, D. M., Devine, P. G., & Harmon-Jones, E. (2007). A dynamic model of guilt: Implications for motivation and self-regulation in the context of prejudice. *Psychological Science, 18*(6), 524–530.

66. Kochanska, G. (1991). Socialization and temperament in the development of guilt and conscience. *Child Development, 62*, 1379–1392. Kochanska, G. (1997). Multiple pathways to conscience for children with different temperaments: From toddlerhood to age 5. *Developmental Psychology, 33*, 597–615.

67. Lewis, M., Alessandri, S. M., & Sullivan, M. W. (1992). Differences in shame and pride as a function of children's gender and task difficulty. *Child Development, 63*, 630–638. Tracy, J. L., & Robins, R. W. (2004). Show your pride: Evidence for a discrete emotion expression. *Psychological Science, 15*(3), 194–197. Tracy, J. L., Robins, R. W., & Lagattuta, K. H. (2005). Can children recognize pride? *Emotion, 5*(3), 251–257.

68. Kohut, H. (1966). Forms and transformations of narcissism. *Journal of the American Psychoanalytic Association, 14*(2), 243–272.

69. Brummelman, E., Thomaes, S., Overbeek, G., de Castro, B. O., van den Hout, M. A., & Bushman, B. J. (2013). On feeding those hungry for praise: Person praise backfires in children with low self-esteem. *Journal of Experimental Psychology: General.* Published online Feb. 18. doi: 10.1037/a0031917. See also Dweck, C. S. (2006). *Mindset: The new psychology of success.* New York: Random House.

Chapter 12. The Fugue

1. From Oates, J. C. (2011, September 29). The cure! A review of *Teach us to sit still: A skeptic's search for health and healing,* by Tim Parks. *New York Review of Books, 58*(14).

2. Descartes, R. (1984). *The philosophical writings of Descartes, Vol. I* (J. Cottingham, R. Stoothoff, & D. Murdoch, Trans.). Cambridge, UK: Cambridge University Press. Descartes, R. (1985). *The philosophical writings of Descartes, Vol. 2* (J. Cottingham, R. Stoothoff, & D. Murdoch, Trans.). Cambridge, UK: Cambridge University Press. Descartes, R. (1991). *The philosophical writings of Descartes, Vol. 3; The correspondence* (J. Cottingham, R. Stoothoff, D. Murdoch, & A. Kenny, Trans.). Cambridge, UK: Cambridge University Press.

3. In a study of nurses, Ekman [Ekman, P. (1985). *Telling lies.* New York: Norton.] suggested that in order to properly care for patients, nurses needed to suppress their disgust looks. While he claimed that they could do so, the data he presents is somewhat questionable.

4. Kagan, J., & Lewis, M. (1965). Studies of attention in the human infant. *Merrill–Palmer Quarterly, 11*, 95–127. Lewis, M., Kagan, J., & Kalafat, J. (1966). Patterns of fixation in infants. *Child Development, 37*, 331–341. Lewis, M., Kagan, J., Kalafat, J., & Campbell, H. (1966). The cardiac response as a correlate of attention in infants. *Child Development, 37*, 63–71.

5. Mennella, J. (2012, March). *Sensitive periods in flavor learning.* Paper presented at the Roger Fine and George Heinrich Brown Bag Series at the Institute for the

Study of Child Development, Department of Pediatrics, UMDNJ-RWJMS, New Brunswick, NJ.

6. St. Aubyn, E. (2005). *Mother's milk*. New York: Open City Books. (pp. 577–578)

7. Baillargeon, R., Li, J., Gertner, Y., & Wu, D. (2011). How do infants reason about physical events? In U. Goswami (Ed.), *The Wiley–Blackwell handbook of childhood cognitive development* (2nd ed., pp. 11–48). Malden, MA: Wiley–Blackwell. Also see Metcalfe and Terrace ([Metcalfe, J., & Terrace, H. S. (Eds.). (2013)]. *Agency and joint attention*. New York: Oxford University Press) for a discussion of joint attention.

8. Morris, D. (1967). *The naked ape: A zoologist's study of the human animal*. London: Jonathan Cape.

9. Darwin, C. R. (1965). *The expression of the emotions in man and animals*. Chicago: University of Chicago Press. (Original work published 1872) (p. 325)

10. DiBiase, R., & Lewis, M. (1997). The relation between temperament and embarrassment. *Cognition and Emotion, 11*, 259–271.

11. Liu, J., Harris, A., & Kanwisher, N. (2002). Stages of processing in face perception: An MEG study. *Nature Neuroscience, 5*(9), 910–916.

12. Lewis, M. (1992). *Shame: The Exposed Self*. New York: Free Press.

Author Index

Abramson, L., 303
Achenbach, T. M., 279
Ackermann, C., 309
Adams, S., 306
Adamson, L., 302
Adolph, K. E., 278, 282
Agnew, J., 106, 120, 294, 295
Ahadi, S. A., 305, 310
Ainsworth, M. D. S., x, 57, 189, 273, 275, 281, 301, 309, 314
Aitken, K. J., 302
Albin, M., 315
Alessandri, S. M., 223, 274, 275, 283, 285, 303, 305, 314, 315, 324
Alloy, L., 303
Allport, F. H., 72, 283
Allport, G. W., 180, 283, 306
Allsop, J. M., 292
Almli, C. R., 292
Als, H., 302
Amaral, D. G., 318
Ambrose, J. A., 285, 298
Amodio, D. M., 324
Anderson, E., 274
Anderson, M. C., 298
Andrews, B., 323
Angrosino, M. V., 323
Anjari, M., 292
Anzures, G., 278
Appelbaum, M. I., 308
Apperly, I. A., 318
Arcus, D., 300, 307, 308, 319
Arling, G. L., 312, 321
Armasti, M., 309
Asch, S. E., 106, 120, 294, 295
Asendorpf, J. B., 290
Asher, S. R., 323
Astington, J. W., 290
Atkins, M., 320, 321
Atkinson, L., 317

Averill, J. R., 322
Aviezer, H., 277
Aziz, N., 304

Bachorowski, J., 286
Baillargeon, R., 295, 307, 325
Baird, C., 322
Baker, S. C., 291
Bakermans-Kranenburg, M. J., 316
Baldwin, J. M., 103, 288
Bandura, A., 313
Banfield, J. F., 291, 292
Bannister, D., 106, 120, 294, 295
Bard, P., 274, 278
Barone, P., 301
Barr, R. G., 189, 215, 307, 309, 314
Barrett, K. C., 304
Barrett, L. F., 274, 278, 281
Barten, S., 308
Bateman, D., 278, 284
Bates, J. E., 282, 306, 310, 313, 322
Baudonniere, P. M., 290, 291
Bauer, A. M, 278
Bauman, D., 319
Bauman, M. L., 318
Baumeister, R. F., 299, 304
Bear, M., 292
Beck, A. T., 128, 297, 303, 304
Beckett, C., 322
Bedard, Y., 309, 314
Beeghly, M., 90, 287, 289
Beilke, R. L., 320
Bell, S. M., 281, 301, 314
Belsky, J., 178, 282, 306, 308, 316
Bender, D. B., 277
Bendersky, M., 280, 286, 313, 317
Bennett, D. S., 227, 246, 280, 305, 317, 322
Bennett, R. T., 319
Benson, B. A., 323
Bergman, A., 293, 296

Berle, D., 280
Bertenthal, B. L., 291
Bettelheim, B., 197, 310
Bingel, U., 307
Birdwhistell, R. L., 35, 277
Biringen, Z., 308
Birns, B., 308
Bischof-Kohler, D., 157, 290, 296, 302
Bisiach, E., 274, 289, 323
Biswas-Diener, R., 280
Blandon, A. Y., 306, 307
Blass, E. M., 189, 309, 314
Blehar, M. C., 189, 275, 309
Block, N., 86, 286
Bloom, L., 315
Blumberg, M. L., 321
Blumenthal, J., 292
Blurton Jones, N. G, 285
Boddie-Willis, A. S., 292
Bond, C. F., 297
Bonica, J. J., 276
Boone, R. T., 277
Borke, H., 296
Borke, J., 274, 288
Bousha, D., 319
Bowlby, J., x, xi, 33, 58, 59, 75, 122–123, 177,
    178, 200, 201, 225, 227–228, 273, 275,
    277, 281, 296, 310, 311, 316
Boyce, W. T., 278
Boyd, E. F., 314
Bradley, B. S., 302
Braten, S., 140, 298, 302
Braungart-Rieker, J. M., 282
Brazelton, T. B., 302, 312
Bretherton, I., 296
Breuer, J., 251, 323
Bridger, W., 308
Bridges, K. M. B., 18, 71, 275, 283
Briere, J., 319
Briggs, S. R., 300, 301, 319
Brighi, A., 298
Brodersen, L., 309, 310
Broesch, T., 288
Bronfenbrenner, U., 201, 203, 311, 312
Bronson, G. W., 77, 285
Brooks, J., 275, 277, 283, 285, 307, 311
Brooks-Gunn, J., xiii, 293, 318
Broucek, F. J., 300
Brown, A. L., 310
Brown, J. A., 321
Brummelman, E., 324
Brunswick, N., 291, 292
Buber, M., 122, 295
Buck, R., 278, 279
Burggraf, S. A., 320
Bushman, B. J., 324
Buss, A. H., 238, 300, 319
Buss, K., 309
Butcher, J. N., 320
Butler, R. J., 296

Butterworth, G., 289
Buwalda, F., 280
Byrne, R. W., 132, 298

Cacioppo, J. T., 54, 274, 277, 281, 287
Calkins, S. D., 306, 307, 308
Call, J., 302
Callaghan, T., 288
Campbell, H., 324
Campbell, J., 304
Campos, J. J., 31, 42, 275, 276, 279, 285, 308,
    310, 312
Camras, L. A., 38, 55, 65, 278, 281, 282
Cannon, W. B., 72, 274, 278, 283
Capatides, J. B., 315
Carey, S., 292, 318
Carey, W., 180
Carlin, J. B., 292
Carlson, E. A., 273, 296, 311
Carmody, D. P., 101, 102, 231, 233, 291, 292,
    293, 299, 318
Carroll, J. M., 281
Carvajal, F., 285
Caspi, A., 279, 306, 316
Cassidy, J., 296
Cassidy, K. L., 309, 314
Castellanos, F. X., 292
Castle, J., 322
Caul, W. F., 278, 279
Chandler, M. J., 289
Chapman, M., 290
Charcot, J. M., 112, 294
Cheek, J. M., 300, 301, 319
Cheney, D., 287
Chess, S., 180, 181, 307
Chiavarion, C., 318
Chidambi, G., 318
Cicchetti, D., 289, 317, 320, 321, 322
Clark, R. W., 295
Clarke-Stewart, K. A., 312
Clore, G. L., 276, 279
Coates, B., 313
Coates, D., 219, 315
Cobb, J., 323
Cobb, W., 294, 295
Coffey, P., 319
Coffino, B., 273, 296, 311
Cointepas, Y., 292
Cole, J. K., 294, 295
Cole, P. M., 139, 298, 304, 317
Collins, A., 276
Collins, K. L., 285
Collins, W., 290
Collmer, C. W., 321
Colvert, E., 322
Conduct Problems Prevention Research Group,
    323
Conturo, T. E., 292
Conway, J. M., 305
Cook, M., 275, 287, 288

Cooley, C., 104, 105, 293
Corbit, J. D., 279
Corp, N., 298
Cosnard, G., 292
Costello, K., 280
Cottingham, J., 324
Coup, N., 132
Courage, M. L., 288
Cox, J., 319
Coy, K. C., 282, 305, 307, 310
Craik, F., 291
Cramer, P., 322
Crossman, A. M., 283, 298
Crowley, T. J., 322
Crozier, J., 322
Csikszentmihalyi, I. S., 153, 301
Csikszentmihalyi, M., 153, 301, 305
Culver, C., 315
Cumberland, A., 313
Cunningham, J. G., 277
Cutler, S. E., 320

Damasio, A., 287, 289
Damon, W., 293, 295, 306, 313
Daniels, R., 321
Dann, O. T., 300
Dann, S., 203, 312
Darwin, C. R., xii, xiii, 2, 3, 13–14, 17, 20, 21, 22, 35, 38, 52, 55, 58, 63, 66, 68, 70, 72, 74, 81, 82, 95, 104, 124, 128, 146–147, 148, 149, 159, 161, 227, 228, 236, 237, 262, 265, 269, 273, 274, 283, 289, 297, 299, 300, 316, 318, 325
Davey, G. C. L., 280
Davidov, M., 302
Davidson, R. J., 278, 284, 318
Dawson, G., 232, 318
Dearing, R. L., 323
Deater-Deckard, K., 316
Debiec, J., 289
Decarie, T., 76
de Castro, B. O., 324
Decety, J., 293
DeFries, J. C., 316
de Groot, J. H. B., 276
Dehaene-Lambertz, G., 292
de Jong, P. J., 280
DeMarco, J. K., 292
Denham, S. A., 62, 282, 315
Dennett, D. C., 288, 296
DePaulo, B. M., 297
Derryberry, D., 282
Descartes, R., 324
DeVet, K., 305
Devine, P. G., 324
de Waal, F. B. M., 157, 302
DiBiase, R., 282, 301, 310, 319, 325
Diener, E., 280
Dienstbeir, R., 303
Dodd, C., 284

Dodge, K. A., 322, 323
Dolan R. J., 291
Donzella, B., 309
Downs, R. M., 285
Droegemueller, W., 321
Dru, A., 273
Dubois, J., 292
Duffy, E., 25, 275
Duijndam, M. J. A., 276
Dunn, J., 201, 311
Dunn, S. M., 292
Durant, W., 295
Durreit, M., 278
Dutton, C. G., 322
Duval, S., 106, 294
Dweck, C. S., 128, 164, 168, 169, 175, 188, 218, 223, 256, 302, 303, 304, 305, 309, 314, 315, 321, 324
Dyson, M. W., 306

Eckholm, E., 308
Eddie, J., 294, 295
Eddington, A., 116
Eddy, T. J., 295
Edelmann, R. J., 300
Edison, S. C., 288
Edwards, A. D., 292
Edwards, C. P., 311
Egan, V., 298
Ehlers, K. M., 322
Eisenberg, N., 209, 306, 313, 315, 319
Eisenberg-Berg, N., 296
Eissler, R., 312
Ekman, P., 35, 66, 67, 80–81, 130, 192, 264, 277, 278, 284, 289, 297, 316, 324
Ellenbogen, B., 274
Elliott, A., 305
Elliott, D. M., 319
Elmer, E., 321
Emde, R. N., 122, 275, 279, 296, 308, 309
Emerson, P. E., 275
Epley, N., 287
Erikson, E. H., 161–162, 303
Eysenck, H. J., 237, 300, 301, 319

Fabes, R. A., 313, 315, 319
Fadiga, L., 282
Fahey, J. L., 304
Fantuzzo, J. W., 320, 321
Fatani, S. S., 281
Fazio, L. K., 298
Fein, G. G., 290
Feinman, S., 206, 207, 312
Feiring, C., 178, 183, 227, 243, 296, 301, 306, 312, 319, 320
Feldman, E., 322
Feldman Barrett, L., 282, 286, 296, 299, 317, 318
Fenigstein, A., 300
Ferrari, M., 318

Ferri, R., 62, 282
Fischer, K. W., 100, 291, 293, 303, 320
Fite, J. E., 282
Fivush, R., 210, 314
Flavell, J. H., 290
Fletcher, P. C., 291, 292
Fogassi, L., 282
Fogel, A., 285
Ford, B. Q., 297
Forman, D. R., 313
Foss, B. M., 273, 277, 285, 298, 311–312
Fossati, P., 291
Fox, N. A., 184, 307, 308
Frackowiak, R. S., 291
Frank, M., 278
Freedman, A. M., 277
Freitag, R., 322
Frensch, P. A., 275, 294
Freud, A., 203, 312, 313
Freud, S., x, xi, 8, 58, 104–105, 112, 146,
    148, 160–161, 187, 227-228, 241, 249,
    251, 256, 258, 259, 303, 304, 293, 313,
    323
Friedman, O., 302
Friedrich, W. N., 320
Friesen, W. V., 35, 277, 297
Frijda, N. H., 29, 274, 275
Frith, C. D., 102, 291, 292, 293
Frith, U., 102, 291, 292, 293, 318
Fulker, D., 316

Gacsi, M., 287
Gaensbauer, T. J., 279, 309
Galati, D., 286, 317
Gallagher, H. L., 291, 292
Gallese, V., 282
Gallup, G. G. Jr., 291, 295
Gandour, M. J., 308
Garner, P. W., 298
Garry, M., 298
Gatlegno, C., 290, 299, 313
Gazzaniga, M. S., 7, 112, 274, 289, 294, 323
Geertz, C., 288
Gelles, R. J., 321
Gergely, G., 107, 285, 287, 294
Gertner, Y., 295, 307, 325
Gewirtz, J. L., 298, 314
Gibbons, F. X., 323
Gibson, E. J., 75, 284
Gibson, J. J., 40, 52, 278, 280
Giedd, J. N., 292
Gil, D., 321
Gilbert, P., 323
Girgus, J. S., 304
Glick, J., 312
Goethals, G. R., 291, 295
Goffman, E., 148, 253, 254, 300, 323
Gold, J., 53, 227, 248, 260, 323
Goldberg, L. R., 307
Goldberg, S., 219, 301, 309, 315, 317, 319

Golder, S. A., 274
Goldman, M., 305
Goldsmith, H. H., 306, 307, 308, 310, 318
Good, B., 274
Goodnight, J. A., 282
Goswami, U., 289, 295, 307, 325
Gottman, J. M., 84, 225, 286, 313, 316
Gould, S. J., 275
Grady, C., 291
Graham, S., 304
Graham, S. J., 291
Grahek, N., 184, 293, 307
Gramzow, R., 319, 323
Grass, G., 312
Greenwood, A., 278
Grigoryev, P., 315
Gross, C. G., 277
Gross, J. J., 289, 306
Grossberg, R., 284
Grossman, P., 284
Gruber, H. E., xii, 273
Gruenewald, T. L, 304
Guillaume, D., 313
Gunnar, M. R., 189, 307, 309, 310
Guskin, K., 297, 304

Hagen, J., 313
Hagen, L., 298
Haidt, J., 286, 296, 301, 318
Hajnal, J. V., 292
Hale, G., 313
Hall, S. K., 322
Halperin, E. P., 313
Halperin, M., 296
Halverson, C. F., Jr., 279
Hamlyn, D. W., 118, 295
Hampshire, S., 294
Hannak, A., 274
Happe, F., 291, 292
Harder, D. W., 320
Hare, B., 302
Harkness, S., 213, 314
Harley, K., 290
Harlow, H. F., 203, 312, 321
Harlow, M. K., 203, 312
Harmon, R. J., 308, 309
Harmon-Jones, E., 257, 284, 324
Harris, A., 325
Harris, C. R., 301
Harris, M. L., 309, 310
Harris, P. L., 290, 298, 317
Hart, S. L., 155, 239, 274, 296, 297, 301, 302,
    319
Harter, S., 289
Hartman, H., 312
Hartup, W. W., 313
Harvey, L., 298
Hatano, G., 311
Hatfield, E., 274, 277
Haviland, J. M., 59, 219, 282, 283, 301, 315

Haviland-Jones, J. M., 278, 279, 281, 282, 286, 296, 298, 317, 318
Healy, J. M., Jr., 279
Heatherton, T. F., 291, 292
Hebb, D. O., 27, 275
Hecht, J., 89, 287
Heckhausen, H., 173, 303, 304, 305
Heider, F., 106, 294
Helfer, R. E., 321
Helson, H., 281
Hembree, E. A., 284
Hemmi, M. H., 318
Henderson, C., 279
Henderson, H. A., 307, 308
Hendricks, L., 309, 314
Henning, K., 319
Henrich, J., 288
Henry, J. P., 278
Hermoye, L., 292
Hernandez-Lloreda, M. V., 302
Herrera, A., 307
Herrmann, E., 302
Hershey, K. L., 305, 310
Hertsgaard, L., 309, 310
Hertz-Pannier, L., 292
Hess, E. H., 277
Hesse, H., 224, 316
Hetherington, E. M., 289, 321
Hevenor, S. J., 291
Hickey, M., 281
Higgins, E. T., 290
Hilgard, E. R., 88, 111, 112, 134, 251, 287, 294, 298, 323
Hill, A., 306
Hill-Barlow, D., 323
Hill-Soderlund, A. L., 282–283
Hinde, R. N., 121, 295
Hitchcock, D., 283, 286
Hobson, R. P., 233, 289, 291, 302, 318
Hodgson, F. M., 290, 299, 313
Hodson, G., 280
Hoffman, M. L., 156, 237, 302, 318
Hoffman-Plotkin, D., 320
Hooven, C., 313
Hoppe, R. A., 313
Horney, K., x, 273
Horowitz, A., 89, 287
Howe M. L., 288
Hrdy, S. B., 201–202, 311
Hsu, H.-C., 285
Hubbard, F. O. A., 189, 309
Hubel, D. H., 33, 277
Hubert, N. C., 308
Huebner, R. R., 284
Hull, C., 279
Hume, D., 89, 287
Humphreys, G. W., 318
Hunziker, U. A., 309
Husarek, S. J., 282, 307
Huttenlocher, J., 290

Iglesias, J., 285
Ilg, U., 309
Inhelder, B., 288
Isabella, R. A., 308
Izard, C. E., ix, 25, 31, 35, 44, 49, 63, 66, 67, 70, 76, 130, 150, 192, 238, 264, 276, 277, 278, 279, 281, 282, 284, 297, 300, 301, 304, 316, 319

Jacobs, R. A., 321
James, W., xi, 2, 11, 41, 43–44, 69, 102–103, 111, 187, 251, 273, 279, 293
Janet, P., 111, 112, 134, 294, 298
Janoff-Bulman, R., 165, 303
Janssen, K., 284
Jaskir, J., 293
Jeffries, N. O., 292
Jennings, S., 291, 293
Jensen, H., 274
Jensen, L. A., 288
John, O. P., 279, 289
Jones, E. M., 251, 323
Jones, M. R., 283
Jones, S. S., 285
Jones, W. H., 300, 301, 319

Kagan, J., xi, 75, 149, 173, 183, 184, 281, 284, 288, 300, 301, 306, 307, 308, 313, 314, 318, 319, 324
Kahneman, D., 274
Kalafat, J., 284, 324
Kaldewaij, A., 276
Kamins, M. L., 304
Kampe, K. K., 291, 292
Kanwisher, N., 292, 318, 325
Kaplan, H. I., 277
Kaplan, N., 296
Kaplow, J., 322
Karbon, M., 319
Karrass, J., 283
Kartner, J., 274, 288
Kasari, C., 286
Kaslow, N., 303
Katayama, S, 274
Katz, L. F., 313
Kawakami, K., 221, 278, 283, 305, 307, 315
Kean, S. P., 306, 307
Keane, F., 280
Keightley, M. L., 291
Keir, R., 284
Keizer, K., 313
Keller, H., 274, 288, 296, 302
Kellerman, H., 300, 302
Kelley, B. T., 322
Kelley, W. M., 291, 292
Kelly, F. D., 322
Keltner, D., 37, 278, 297
Kemeny, M. E., 304
Kempe, C. H., 246, 321
Kempe, R. S., 246, 321

Kemper, T. L., 318
Kenny, A., 324
Kent, J. T., 321
Kienapple, K., 297, 299
Kierkegaard, S., 273
Kim, G., 311
Kim, J., 292
Kim, J. E., 320, 321
Kim, K. H., 292
Klein, D. L., 306
Klein, M., x, 105, 273, 321
Klein, R. E., 314
Kleinman, M. A., 274
Kleis, A., 288
Knieps, L., 317
Koch, C., 287
Kochanska, G., 195, 257, 282, 305, 307, 310, 312, 313, 316, 324
Kohnstamm, G. A., 279, 305, 307, 308, 310, 315
Kohut, H., 258, 259, 324
Koslowski, B., 312
Kotov, R., 306
Kreppner, J., 322
Kretch, K. S., 278, 282
Kreuger, J., 304
Kring, A. M., 297
Kris, E., 312
Krol, G., 292
Kropp, P. R., 299
Krueger, K., 309, 310
Kujawa, A. J., 306

Lacey, J., 41, 278, 284
Lagattuta, K. H., 324
Laird, R. D., 323
Lamb, C., 315
Lamb, M. E., 201, 276, 285, 296, 302, 310, 311, 312, 313
Lamm, B., 302
Landfield, A. W., 294, 295
Lange, C., 41, 274, 278, 283
Lane, R. D., 279
Lansford, J. E., 322
Larsen, J. T., 54, 55, 281
Larson, M. C., 309, 310
LaVoie, L., 317
Lazarus, R. S., 4, 44, 276, 281
Leary, M. R., 300
Le Bihan, D., 292
LeDoux, J., 112, 250, 289, 294
Lee, A., 318
Lee, B. C., 292
Lee, K., 141, 278, 298, 299, 317
Lee, M. C., 307
Lee, S. K., 292
Legerstee, M., 274, 296, 297, 301, 302, 319
Leggett, E. L., 302, 303, 309, 315, 321
Lehmann, S., 274
Leitenberg, H., 319

Lerner, R. M., 287, 291, 293, 294, 295, 313
Leslie, A. M., 99, 142, 143, 290, 295, 299
Levine, L. E., 305
Levine, R. A., 288
Levine, S., 310
Levy, B. J., 298
Lewis, H. B., 173, 247–248, 300, 303, 304, 305, 320, 322
Lewis, M., 19, 50, 52, 62, 163, 207, 273, 274, 275, 276, 277, 278, 280, 281, 282, 283, 284, 285, 286, 287, 288, 289, 290, 291, 292, 293, 294, 296, 297, 298, 299, 300, 301, 303, 304, 305, 306, 307, 308, 309, 310, 311, 312, 313, 314, 315, 316, 317, 318, 319, 320, 322, 323, 324, 325
Lewis, S. J., 320
Li, J., 295, 307, 325
Liben, L. S., 285
Lindenberg, S., 313
Lindquist, K. A, 281
Lindsay, D. S., 298
Lindsey, D. B., 278
Lipsitt, L. P., 286
Lis, E., 292
Liu, H., 292
Liu, J., 325
LoBue, V., 278, 282
Lochman, J. E., 248, 322, 323
Loeber, R., 322
Lorenz, K., 200–201
Lowe, M., 290
Lynch, M., 320, 321

Mach, E., 116
Macrae, C. N., 291, 292
Macy, M. W., 274
Madden, J., 278
Magai, C., 59, 279, 282
Mahler, M. S., 105, 122, 293, 296
Maier, U., 309
Main, M., 122, 296, 312
Malatesta, C. Z., 219, 282, 315
Mandler, G., 160, 302
Mangelsdorf, S., 309
Manly, J. T., 320, 321, 322
Manstead, A. S. R., 300
Marcel, A. J., 274, 289, 323
Margalit, A., 108, 294
Markus, H., 274
Marschall, D. E., 323
Marsh, E. J., 298
Marsh, H., 274
Martin, R. P., 279
Marzillier, S., 280
Masciuch, S., 297, 299
Mascolo, M. P., 291
Masson, J. M., 160, 303, 319
Maszk, P., 319
Matas, L., 284
Matheny, A. P. Jr., 308

Matsumoto, D., 278, 317
Matthews, T. A., 306
Matthews, W. S., 318
Mayfield, M. G., 322
Mazzoni, G., 298
McCauley, C. R., 286, 296, 301, 318
McClaskey, C. L., 322
McClintic, S., 302, 303, 304, 306
McCord, J., 322
McCune, L., 290
McCune-Nicolich, L., 290
McDowall, R., 292
McGraw, A. P., 281
McGurk, H., 65, 282
McKay, D., 280, 281, 318
McKissick, F. C., 232, 318
McNeil, D., 319
Mead, G. H., 104, 105, 106, 293
Meadows, S., 300
Meaney, M. J., 306
Meares, R., 301
Mehta, M., 322
Mellers, B. A., 281
Meltzoff, A. N., 290, 312
Melzack, R., 30, 276
Mennella, J., 266, 324
Merleau-Ponty, M., 106, 118, 294, 295
Metcalfe, J., 325
Metzner, R., 299
Meyer, J., 318
Meyers, R., 320, 321
Meyers, W., 284
Miceli, R., 286
Michalson, L., 47, 50, 52, 59, 62, 216, 225,
    274, 276, 280, 281, 282, 283, 288, 311,
    314, 316
Miklosi, A., 287
Mikulich, S. K., 322
Miller, J. H., 292
Miller, R. E., 278, 279
Miller, S., 187, 308
Milton, G. A., 313
Mineka, S., 27, 275, 284
Mischel, T., 295
Mischel, W., 299
Mislove, A., 274
Mitchell, J. P., 291, 292
Mitchell, R. W., 130, 297
Mitchell-Copeland, J., 282
Modigliani, A., 300
Moran, J. M., 291, 292
Morewedge, C. K., 287
Morris, D., 325
Morrison, A. P., 300, 303, 304
Moses, J., 289
Moss, H., 289
Mueller, C. M., 304
Mukherjee, P., 292
Mumme, D., 297, 304
Mundy, P., 317, 318

Murchinson, C., 274, 278
Murdoch, D., 324
Murphy, B. C., 313, 315, 319
Murphy, C., 288
Murphy, S. M., 298
Murray, K. T., 305, 310
Mussen, P., 277

Nachmias, M., 309
Nadel, L., 279
Nassogne, M. C., 292
National Academy of Sciences, 321
Nederhof, E., 316
Neisser, U., 288
Nelson-Goens, G. C., 285
Newell, A., 287
Neziroglu, F., 280–281
Nicholls, J., 304, 305
Nicolich, L., 290
Nienhuis, T., 274
Nolan, E., 306
Nolen-Hoeksema, S., 297, 304, 320
Noone, M., 320, 321
Nordahl, C. W., 318
Norgate, S. H., 310
Nyquist, L., 278

Oates, J. C., 22, 109, 111, 263, 275, 294, 324
O'Brien, M., 306, 307
O'Connor, T. G., 316
Oishi, S., 280
Olatunji, B. O., 280, 318
Oldehinkel, A. J., 316
Olsen, A. S., 287
Olsen, B., 312
Olson, D. R., 288, 290
Ormel, J., 316
Ortony, A., 31, 276, 279
Osofsky, J. D., 296, 310
Oster, H., 286
O'Sullivan, M., 278, 297
Otaki, M., 278
Otter, Z., 298
Overbeek, G., 324
Overton, W. F., 287, 291, 293, 294, 295
Owren, M. J., 286
Ozer, D. J., 279

Palermo, D. S., 285
Panksepp, J., 229, 317
Papaligoura, Z., 274
Parke, R. D., 321
Parritz, R. H., 309
Parry, M. H., 278
Pascalis, O., 278
Patterson, G. R., 322
Pavlov, I. P., 76, 285
Pavlovic, M., 292
Peake, S. J., 291, 292
Pennebaker, J., 278

Perlmutter, M., 273
Perner, J., 22, 118, 275, 287, 290, 294
Pervin, L. A., 289
Peters, M. L., 280
Petersen, I. T., 306
Peters-Martin, P., 308
Peterson, C., 303
Pettit, G. S., 322
Pfeifer, J. H., 291, 292
Phillips, E. S., 280
Piaget, J., 91, 92, 100, 103, 142, 265, 287, 288,
    293, 295, 299, 313
Pick, A. D., 295, 313
Pine, F., 293, 296
Pipp, S., 291, 293
Plomin, R., 316
Ploner, M., 307
Pluess, M., 282
Plutchik, R., 280, 299–300, 302
Pochedly, J. T., 310
Poincaré, H., 116
Polak, A., 298
Polyani, M., 295
Porges, S. W., 220, 284, 315
Porter, S., 297
Posner, M. I., 282, 310
Povinelli, D. J., 295
Power, T. G., 298, 313
Premack, D., 295, 302
Preston, J., 287
Preston, S. D., 302
Pribram, K. H., 97, 289
Price, V., 284
Prideaux, E., 42, 279
Prince, M., 251, 323
Prinz, W., 290
Putnam, H., 289, 296
Putnam, S. P., 305

Quas, J. A., 278
Quigley, J., 281
Quinn, P. C., 278

Raag, T., 285
Radke-Yarrow, M., 290, 296
Ramsay, D. S., 184, 186, 190, 275, 278, 283,
    285, 290, 299, 301, 304, 305, 307, 308,
    310, 314, 315, 319
Rank, O., 287
Rappaport, L. R., 323
Rapson, R. L., 274, 277
Read, J. D., 298
Read, P. B., 276
Recchia, S., 302, 303, 304, 306
Reddy, V., 274
Reese, E., 290
Reese, H. W., 286
Reiss, S., 323
Repacholi, B. M., 312
Rescorla, L. A., 279

Retzinger, S. M., 320, 323
Reznick, J. S., 300, 301, 307, 308, 319
Ricci-Bitti, P. E., 317
Richards, P., 278
Richardson, K., 310
Riedewald, M., 274
Riese, M. L., 308
Rigatuso, J., 309, 310
Rizzolatti, G., 282
Roberts, W., 315
Robins, R. W., 279, 304, 324
Robison, K., 309
Rocha-Miranda, C. E., 277
Rochat, P., 287, 288
Rogers, R., 299
Rogers, S. J., 323
Rogoff, B., 310
Rogosch, F. A., 320, 321
Roland, A., 288
Rosaldo, M. Z., 280
Rosen, C. S., 290
Rosenblum, L. A., 179, 275, 283, 284, 285,
    286, 311, 312, 317
Rosenfield, P., 310
Rosenstein, D., 286
Rosenthal, S., 296
Ross, C. A., 252, 319, 320, 323
Rothbart, M. K., 180, 282, 305, 306, 310, 313
Roth-Hanania, R., 302
Rovine, M., 306
Rozin, P., 84, 286, 296, 301, 318
Ruby, P., 293
Rudolph, K., 306
Rueda, M. R., 310
Ruge, M. I., 292
Ruppenthal, G. C., 312, 321
Russell, J. A., 46, 49, 50, 52, 54, 279, 280,
    281, 310
Rutherford, M. A., 292
Rutter, M., 316, 322

Saarni, C., 139, 218, 280, 297, 298, 299, 314,
    315, 317
Sackett, G. P., 312, 321
Sagi, A., 302
St. Aubyn, E., 99, 268, 289, 325
Saint-Martin, C., 292
Samson, D., 318
Saxe, R., 292, 318
Schachter, S., 31, 276, 303
Schaffer, H. R., 19, 275, 278, 281, 285
Scheff, T. J., 323
Scheier, M. F., 300
Scherer, K. R., 36, 277, 289, 317, 318
Schermerhorn, A. C., 306
Schieche, M., 309
Schmidt, L. A., 307, 308
Schmidt, S., 317
Schneider, S., 318

Schneider, W., 289
Schneirla, T. C., 72, 283
Scholl, B. J., 287
Schrier, A. M., 312
Schumann, C. M., 318
Schwarzer, R., 275, 294
Schwebel, D. C., 290
Scoboria, A., 298
Scollon, C. N., 280
Scott, J. P., 275
Searle, J. R., 86, 287
Seitz, V., 313
Seligman, M. E. P., 128, 297, 303, 304
Semin, G. R., 276, 300
Sennett, R., 323
Setoguchi, Y., 323
Seyfarth, R., 287
Shantz, C. U., 118, 295
Shapiro, A. F., 285
Sheese, B. E., 310
Sherman, M., 281
Sherman, N., 281
Sherrod, L. R., 276, 285, 312
Shimony, J. S., 292
Shiner, R. L., 306
Shiota, M. N., 278
Shweder, R. A., 10, 274, 288
Sigman, M., 286
Sigmon, S. T., 299
Silver, H. K., 321
Silverman, F. N., 321
Silverstein, A., 277
Simmel, E. C., 313
Simonov, P. V., 76, 285
Singer, J. E., 276, 303
Singer, J. L., 290
Sini, B., 286, 317
Slater, A. M., 278
Smeets, M. A. M., 276
Smiley, P. A., 305
Smith, C. A., 322
Smith, M., 319
Smith, R. G., 295
Snedman, N., 301
Snidman, N., 300, 307, 308, 319
Snyder, C. R., 299
Solomon, R. C., 299
Solomon, R. L., 279
Souweidane, M. M., 292
Spangler, G., 309
Spielberger, C. D., 320
Spinrad, T. L., 313
Spitz, R. A., 277, 285
Srinivasan, L., 292
Sroufe, L. A., x–xi, 76, 273, 275, 284, 296, 309, 310, 311, 317
Stanger, C., 289, 290, 298, 300, 301
Starr, M. D., 312
Stayton, D. J., 281
Steele, B. F., 321

Steg, L., 313
Stein, G., 265
Steiner, J. E., 83, 286
Stenberg, C. R., 275, 276, 285, 312
Stephenson, G. R., 313
Stern, D. N., 105, 287, 288, 312, 317
Stern, L., 321
Stevens, S. S., 278
Stewart, A. J., 279
Stipek, D. J., 173, 302, 303, 304, 306
Stoff, D. M., 281
Stollnitz, F., 312
Stoothoff, R., 324
Stouthamer-Loeber, M., 322
Strachey, J., 303, 313, 323
Strauss, J., 291, 295
Strayer, J., 315
Suchecki, D., 310
Sullivan, H. S., x, 121, 273, 296
Sullivan, M. W., xiii, 52, 163, 169, 227, 246, 274, 275, 281, 283, 285, 286, 289, 290, 298, 300, 301, 305, 306, 314, 317, 322, 323, 324
Suomi, S. J., 37, 59, 81, 278, 281, 286, 312, 313, 321
Super, C. M., 213, 314
Sussman, E. J., 281
Szivos- Bach, S. E., 323

Takahashi, K., 203, 311
Takai-Kawakami, K., 305
Talbot, D., 323
Talge, N. M., 307
Talwar, V., 141, 298, 299
Tamir, M., 297
Tanaka, J. W., 278
Tangney, J. P., 248, 303, 319, 320, 321, 323
Tannenbaum, R., 303
Taska, L., 320
Taylor, A. R., 323
Taylor, D., 306
Taylor, S. E., 282
ten Brinke, L., 297
Terrace, H. S., 325
Thomaes, S., 324
Thomas, A., 180, 181, 307
Thomas, D., 186, 307, 308
Thompson, D. K., 292
Thornberry, T. P., 322
Tinti, C., 317
Tjebkes, T. L., 282, 307, 313
Todorov, A., 277
Tomasello, M., 302
Tomkins, S. S., 34, 35, 146, 229, 277, 300, 301, 304, 316, 317
Tracy, J. L., 304, 324
Tremoulet, P. D., 287
Trevarthen, C. B., 288, 302
Trivers, R. L., 131, 297, 318
Trommsdorff, G., 210, 313

Tronick, E. Z., 90, 287, 293, 301, 302
Trope, Y., 277
Turner, T., 319
Twentyman, C. T., 319, 320
Tyson, M. C., 150, 301, 319

Umbel, V. M., 317
Urquiza, A. J., 320

Vaitl, D., 284
Valente, E., 322
van den Hout, M. A., 324
van IJzendoorn, M. H., 189, 309, 316
VanLehn, R., 278, 284
van Overveld, M., 280
Varni, J. W., 323
Vohs, K. D., 304
Volbrecht, M. M., 306, 307
Von Bertalanffy, L., 289
Vraa, R., 309
Vrij, A., 297

Wachs, T. D., 282, 305, 307, 308, 310, 315
Wade, K. A., 298
Wagner, E., 290
Wagner, P. E., 319, 320, 323
Walden, T. A., 311, 317
Walk, R. D., 284
Wall, P. D., 30, 276
Wall, S., 189, 275, 309
Walters, D. R., 321
Wang, H. X., 292
Wang, Q., 210, 314
Waniqasekera, V., 307
Ward, A. G., 89, 287
Ward, M. J., 308
Warfield, S. K., 292
Warkentin, V., 291
Wasserman, G. A., 57, 281, 301
Waters, E., 189, 275, 284, 309
Waters, W., 296
Watson, J. B., 72, 283
Watson, J. S., 107, 189, 285, 286, 287, 293, 294, 309
Way, B. M., 282
Waytz, A., 287
Wegner, D. M., 89, 96, 287, 289
Weijmar Schultz, W., 280
Weinberg, K. M., 301
Weiner, B., 223, 302, 303, 304, 315, 324
Weinraub, M., 214, 301, 311, 312, 314
Weisel, T. N., 277
Weiskrantz, L., 112, 294
Weiss, A. D., 320, 321
Weiss, M., 289, 290, 300

Wellman, H. M., 289, 290
Werner, B., 128
Werner, H., 113, 294
Weston, J. T., 321
Wheeler, J., 117
White, B. P., 309
Whitmore, E. A., 322
Wicklund, R., 106, 294
Widen, S. C., 49, 50, 52, 280, 310
Widom, C. S., 320, 321, 322
Wiebush, R., 322
Wiech, K., 307
Wiesel, T. N., 33
Williams, G. A., 323
Willingham, B., 317
Willis, P., 323
Willoughby, J., 317
Wilson, R. S., 308
Wimmer, H., 290
Winnicott, D. W., x, 105, 273, 293
Winston, C., 316
Winston, R., 316
Wise, S., 302
Witkin, H., 305
Wittig, B. A., 273
Wolf, K. M., 277
Wolff, P. H., 277, 298
Wolfson, A., 297, 304
Wolke, D., 318
Woodruff, G., 295
Worobey, J., 186, 307, 308
Wright, J. H., 309, 314
Wu, D., 295, 307, 325
Wunsch, J. P., 284
Wylie, R. C., 289

Yando, R., 313
Young, G., 311
Young, S. N., 309, 314
Youniss, J., 118, 295
Yovai, R., 274
Yovsi, R. D., 288

Zahn-Waxler, C., 156, 290, 296, 302, 304
Zajonc, R. B., 4, 281
Zavala, F., 284
Zelazo, P. R., 307, 309
Zelli, A., 323
Zentner, M., 306
Zhang, T.-Y., 306
Zigler, E., 313
Zijdenbos, A., 292
Zimbardo, P. G., 149, 300
Zivin, G., 314
Zucker, K. J., 317
Zukav, G., 118, 295

Subject Index

Abuse and neglect, 24, 227, 241–249
  content of consciousness in, 94
  elicitors and action patterns in, 213, 214
  emotional knowledge in, 211
  legal classification of, 247
  multiple personality disorder in, 249, 251, 252
  personality of child in, 60–61
  personality of parents in, 243–244, 246
  self-attributions in, 217, 241–242, 243, 246
  sexual abuse in, 241–243
  shame in, 241–249, 252
  socialization in, 24, 211, 213, 214, 217, 228, 241–247
  violence in, 248–249
Accommodation process, 265
Accretional model, 271
Achievement. See also Success or failure
  attributions on, 128, 169, 172–173, 174
  in experimental tasks, 170
  and pride, 168, 258
Action patterns, 1–6, 8, 34–43
  adaptive, 17, 20, 21, 31, 42–43, 66
  in adults and children, comparison of, 3
  of approach. See Approach emotions or action patterns
  atypical development of, 23–24, 230–231
  circular, 91, 285
  and consciousness, xv, 17, 123–126, 296
  context of, 1, 2, 63–64, 67, 68–69, 282
  Darwin on, 2, 3, 17, 20, 35, 38, 52, 55, 66, 70, 72, 74, 81, 228, 262
  deactivation of, 30
  definition of, 5, 35, 40
  differentiated from mental acts, 91
  of disgust, 18, 52, 125, 265
  duration of, 46, 47, 56, 194

  early, 11, 21–22, 63–85. See also Early emotions and action patterns
  elicitors of, 29–34. See also Elicitors
  and emotional experience, 4, 44, 48, 111, 228
  and emotional expression, 33–43
  emotional receptors affecting, 33–34
  environmental influences on, 18, 20, 23
  evolution of, 1, 5, 15, 21, 31, 40, 42, 55, 262–263, 271
  and facial expressions, 130–131, 136–137, 228–229
  flexibility and plasticity of, 5, 6, 15
  individual differences in, 12, 40, 42, 55–56, 60, 63, 69–70, 266, 283
  inhibition of, 30, 37, 42, 231, 279
  as innate responses, 11, 18, 66–68, 110, 118, 198
  intentions and intentionality in, 90–91
  later development of, 18
  learning of, 64–66
  manipulation of, 124–125, 129–144
  and moods, 47, 193, 194
  observation of, 47, 59–62
  in pain, 30, 276–277
  parent interpretation and response to, 225
  previous, effect on subsequent patterns, 193
  as procedural rules, 17, 110, 118, 119, 294
  self-conscious, 18
  socialization of, 48, 70, 218–222
  and temperament, 11, 40, 56, 69–70, 76, 195, 221–222, 230, 266, 283
  and theory of mind, 119
  of withdrawal. See Withdrawal emotions or action patterns
Adaptation model, 281

Adjustment, sexual abuse affecting, 242, 243
Adrenocortical response to distress, 190, 191
The Advancement of Learning (Bacon), 115
Affiliation, 62
Aggressive parenting behaviors, 244
Akrasia, 8, 96–97
Alienation and embarrassment, 148
*Altering Fate: Why the Past Does Not
    Predict the Future* (Lewis), vii
Amygdala, 33, 96, 112, 250
Anger, 17
    of abused children, 247
    as adaptive pattern, 78
    as approach pattern, 69, 70, 72, 73, 78
    in arm restraint response of infant, 13,
        67, 78
    in blocked goal, 5, 17, 32, 48, 55, 68–69,
        70, 78, 265, 285
    brain activity in, 284
    consciousness affecting action pattern of,
        126
    cultural influences on, 39, 48, 78, 93, 129,
        225
    Darwin on, 68, 265
    deception about, 137
    and disgust, 53
    as early emotion, 18–19, 22, 72, 73,
        78–79
    elicitors of, 5, 32
    experience of, 48, 228
    facial patterns in, 67, 68
    in failure, 176
    labeling behavior as, 93, 225
    observation and measurement of, 59, 61, 62
    parent reports of, 39, 48, 78, 93
    and rage, 79
    socialization affecting expression and
        experience of, 39, 48, 129, 218, 225
Animals, 17
    anthropomorphization of, 89, 287
    attachment of, 203
    body movements and postures of, 36
    deception by, 130, 132
    early action patterns of, 14, 262–263
    emotional contagion in, 207
    eye-to-eye interactions of, 268
    facial neuromusculature of, 35
    fearful-like behavior of, 27
    gene–environment interactions in, 59
    imprinting of, 200–201
    sadness as withdrawal pattern of, 81
    self-conscious emotions of, 14, 158–159
    self-recognition of, 100, 263
    self-referential behaviors of, 109, 263
    soothing behavior of mothers, 191
    stress hormones in, 37, 191
    visual cortex of, 34

Anthropomorphization, 89–90, 92, 156, 287
Apes, chimpanzees, and monkeys
    early action patterns of, 14, 262–263
    eye-to-eye interactions of, 268
    facial neuromusculature of, 35
    fearful-like behavior of, 27
    gene–environment interactions in, 59
    self-conscious emotions of, 14, 158, 159
    self-recognition of, 100, 263
    self-referential behaviors of, 109, 263
    stress hormones and emotional expression
        of, 37
    visual cortex of, 34
Approach emotions or action patterns, 22,
        72–73, 110, 229
    in anger, 69, 70, 72, 73, 78
    in "babyishness" quality, 33
    in blocked goal, 188, 230
    cerebral hemisphere differences in, 33
    consciousness affecting, 125–126
    curiosity as, 16
    emotional expressions in, 36, 40
    with withdrawal pattern in fear, 22,
        73–74, 76
Arm pulling task with visual reward, 68–69
    anger in, 68–69
    disgust in, 84
    pleasure from learning in, 69, 80
    sadness in, 82
    willfulness in, 187–188
Arm restraint, infant response to, 13, 67, 78
Arousal, 31, 42, 276
Asperger syndrome, 183, 184, 234–235,
        237
Assimilation process, 265
Attachment, x–xi, 177
    attributions on, 90
    avoidant, 178–179
    Bowlby on, x, 122–123, 177, 200, 201,
        225
    and consciousness, 105, 293
    and cortisol levels in distress, 190
    early, impact on later relationships, 123
    and jealousy, 155–156
    locomotion in expression of, 36
    multiple, 200–203
    and parenting practices, 178–179
    and sadness, 82
    in social networks, 200–203
    and social relationships, 121, 122–123
    and stranger fear, 28
    and temperament, 59, 178–179, 198
    working model of, 122, 123
Attention and interest
    as approach pattern, 73
    body movement and posture in, 35
    consciousness affecting, 126

Attention and interest (*continued*)
  as early emotion or action pattern, 18, 22,
    71, 73, 75
  embarrassment in, 127, 149, 151–152,
    171, 237–239, 269–270
  and eye regard of others, 268–270
  inward and outward focus of, 4, 93,
    110–111, 112–113, 153, 263
  jealousy about, 155–156, 239
  joint, of infant and others, 268
  types of, xi
Attention deficit disorder, 23, 197
Attractors in complexity theory, 66
Attributions, 23, 29
  in abuse and neglect, 217, 241–242, 243,
    246
  anthropomorphization in, 89–90, 92–
    93
  on arousal, 31
  disposition affecting, 165–166
  as elicitors, 31, 128
  gender differences in, 172–173, 223
  global and specific, 128, 160, 165–166,
    218, 223–224
  in guilt, 128, 218, 223–224, 257
  in hubris, 258
  impact on emotional development, 93
  internal and external, 159
  in narcissism, 259, 260
  observations as basis of, 26
  parenting practices affecting, 217–218,
    223–225
  of parents and caregivers, 6, 26, 93, 172,
    261
  in pride, 128, 168–169, 258
  on responsibility, 14, 23, 128, 159, 164,
    223
  and self-deception, 133
  self-referential ability required for, 126
  in shame, 128, 133, 146, 241–242,
    254–255
  socialization affecting, 172–173, 217–218,
    223–225
  on success or failure, 14, 128, 159–160,
    164–165, 169, 172–173, 174, 217–218,
    223
  on very young infants, 89–90, 92–93
  and willfulness, 188
Atypical development, 23–24, 227–261
Autism spectrum disorders, 23, 197,
    231–235
  brain development in, 102, 232, 233–234,
    291, 292–293
  eye regard difficulties in, 270
  mental age in, 100, 232
  pretense and pretend play in, 100, 143,
    231, 232, 234
  self-referential behaviors in, 100, 102,
    143, 231–235, 292–293
  sociability in, 183
Autonomic nervous system, 41, 42, 276
Autonomy, 161

Bacon, Francis, 115, 117
Bard, Philip, 41
Biblical story of Adam and Eve, 16
Big Five dimensions of personality, 181
Blame
  in child abuse, 245, 249
  and global attributions of parents,
    223–224
  in narcissism, 260
  in shame, 248, 249, 253–254, 255
  in stigmatization, 253–254, 255
Blindness, facial expressions in, 80, 229,
    286
Blocked goal
  anger in, 5, 17, 32, 48, 55, 68–69, 70, 78,
    265, 285
  approach and withdrawal patterns in,
    188, 230
  individual differences in response to,
    69–70
  physiologic responses in, 68
  sadness in, 69, 82
  socialization affecting response to, 70
  willfulness in, 187–188
Blushing, 95, 146–147, 148, 149, 236, 237,
    300
Body movements and postures, 35–37, 277
  in embarrassment, 149, 150, 171
  in guilt, 171, 257
  in pride, 35, 171, 260–261
  in shame, 35, 150, 166, 171, 257
Bohr, Niels, 115, 117
Bowlby, John, x, xi, 33, 59, 178, 227–
    228
  on attachment, x, 122–123, 177, 200,
    201, 225
  on Darwin, 58, 227
  on fear response of infants, 75
  on smiling of infants, 33
Brain
  in anger and joy, 284
  in approach and withdrawal action
    patterns, 33
  association between emotions and
    physiologic changes in, 33, 41
  in autism spectrum disorders, 102, 232,
    233–234, 291, 292–293
  in emotional experiences, 44
  gray and white matter in, 101
  hemispheric differences in function, 33,
    41, 64, 73, 74, 232, 250, 284, 293

maturation of, and rise of consciousness, 22, 94, 101–102, 107–108, 222, 232, 233–234, 291–293
modularity of functions, 112
in multiple personality disorder, 250
visual cortex of, 33–34

Cannon, Walter, 41
Caregivers. *See* Parents and caregivers
Central nervous system, 33–34, 41. *See also* Brain
Cerebral hemispheres, 33, 41, 64, 73, 74, 232, 250, 284, 293
Cerebral palsy, facial expressions in, 229
Chemical signals as elicitors, 276
Child abuse and neglect. *See* Abuse and neglect
Child Behavior Checklist, 47
Children's Emotions and Moods (Lewis & Michalson), 4
China, culture and socialization in, 210, 211, 225
Cognitive development, 14
    consciousness in, 113, 114, 118–120
    elicitor changes in, 32–33
    emotional experience in, 44
    and language development, 120
    self-conscious emotions in, 16–17, 20–21
Colic, maternal soothing behavior in, 189, 215
Comfort measures in soothing of infant, 214–216
Communication
    crying in, 81, 82, 83, 134
    facial expressions in, 31, 37
    nonverbal, of newborn, 92
Comparison ability, and fear, 19, 28, 76
Competence
    comprehension compared to, 296
    observation and measurement of, 59, 60, 62
    performance compared to, 26
    socioemotional, 198, 199, 211, 212
Complexity theory, 65–66
Compliments, embarrassment from, 151
Comprehension, differentiated from competence, 296
Conditioned response to elicitors, 30
Conscience, and guilt, 257
Consciousness, viii, 8–10, 86, 87, 88
    and action patterns, xiii, 17–18, 123–126, 296
    adaptive and nonadaptive aspects of, 93, 113
    atypical development of, 231–235
    bidirectional interactions in, 118
    and brain maturation, 22, 94, 101–102, 107–108, 291–293

and cognitive development, 113, 114, 118–120
collective, 10
cultural differences in, 10, 94
and decentering, 103
and deception, 129–144
distribution process, 4, 9, 93, 110–111, 112–113, 153, 263
divided, 111–113, 134
and emotional life, 88–92, 123–124
and experience, 7–8, 43, 48, 86–87, 235
and feelings, 1, 7, 43–44, 86
idea of "me" in. *See* Idea of "me"
and identity, 10
implicit and explicit, 134
inward and outward focus of attention in, 4, 93, 110–111, 112–113, 153
lack of, in young infants, 7–8, 89–91, 104
measures of, 8, 9, 22, 93, 98–100
model of, 19, 113–114
perspective taking in, 103, 104, 106, 118, 120
rise of, xii–xiii, 8–10, 22, 86–108, 110, 146
and self-conscious emotions. *See* Self-conscious emotions
and self-referential behavior. *See* Self-referential behavior
and self system, 91–97
and social world, 102–107, 118, 120–123, 293, 294
and temperament, 195–196
and theory of mind, 118–120
transforming role of, 22, 109–128
use of term, 2, 6, 8, 86–87
Contagion, emotional, vii, 206–208
    differentiated from empathy, 127, 156–157, 207, 236
    geography as factor in, 13
    vocal expressions in, 36
Contempt, 83, 224–225
Contingent responses to infant behavior, 189
    in crying, 214, 219, 315
    in smiling, 204, 219, 315
Control
    attributions on, 128
    loss of, 27, 82
Coping style, maternal, 215–216
Corpus callosum, 7, 112
Cortisol levels
    daily variations in, 187
    and facial expressions, 37, 221
    in inoculation and pain response, 37, 184, 185, 186, 187, 190, 220, 221
    and maternal soothing behavior, 189, 190, 215

Cortisol levels (*continued*)
  in shame and embarrassment, 132, 169,
    171–172
  and temperament, 182
Creativity, xii, 15, 126, 258
Cry Babies, 185, 186, 221
Crying, vii, 36
  calming effect of sucrose in, 189–190,
    215
  communication function of, 81, 82, 83,
    134
  contingent response to, 214, 219, 314
  emotional contagion in, 207
  gender differences in, 70, 71, 129
  in happiness, 71
  maternal soothing in, 189, 215
  of newborn, 156
  in pain, 134, 185
  in sadness, 70, 71, 81, 82, 83
  socialization affecting, 70, 71, 129, 219
  temperament differences in, 185, 186, 221
Cuddliness, 188
Culture, xii
  and action patterns, 70
  and anger in children, 39, 48, 78, 93, 129,
    225
  child maltreatment and abuse in, 244
  and consciousness, 10, 94
  and deception, 15, 136, 141
  elicitors in, 213
  and emotional experience, 49–50
  and emotional expression, 36, 39
  and emotional mixture words, 51
  and evaluative self-conscious emotions,
    14, 163
  and eye regard of others, 270
  and inoculation and pain response, 37, 70,
    186, 221
  and labeling of behavior, 225
  and self-referential behavior, 94, 288
  and socialization, 210–211
  standards, rules, and goals in, 14,
    159–160, 163–164. See also Standards,
    rules, and goals
Curiosity, 16

Darwin, Charles
  on action patterns, 2, 3, 17, 20, 35, 38,
    52, 55, 66, 70, 72, 74, 81, 228, 262
  on anger in blocked goal, 68, 265
  on approach and withdrawal patterns,
    72, 81
  on blushing, 95, 146–147, 149, 236, 237,
    300
  Bowlby on, 58, 227
  on embarrassment, 22, 95, 148, 236, 237,
    269

  on emotional development of humans and
    animals, 13–14, 17, 63
  emotional life of, 58, 227
  *The Expression of the Emotions in Man
    and Animals*, 2
  on facial expressions, 35
  Gruber on, xii
  influence on Mead, 104
  on sadness, 72, 81, 82
  on self-conscious emotions, xiii, 21, 22,
    95, 124, 128, 159, 161, 236
  on shame, 161, 236
Daycare setting, observation of action
    patterns in, 60–62
Decentering, 103
Deception, 15, 22–23, 71, 98, 129–144
  as adaptive, 131–132, 136, 139, 141,
    142
  to avoid punishment, 140–142, 143
  delay in consciousness development
    affecting, 235
  detection of, 131, 136
  development of, 134–136, 138–144
  on disgust, 137, 265, 324
  environmental influences in, 137–138
  facial expression in, 3, 37–38, 130, 131
  on fear, 124–125
  to hurt others, 143
  knowledge required for, 119, 134
  motives for, 138–144
  and pretend play, 143, 144
  to protect feelings of others, 131,
    132–133, 138–140
  of self. See Self-deception
  smiling in, 138, 140, 218, 220
Depression, 61–62, 242, 243, 260
Descartes, 3, 103
Developmental niche, 213
Differential emotions theory, 66
Difficult temperament, 181, 182, 194, 195
  abuse in, 245–246
  embarrassment in, 59, 239
Disabilities, stigma of, 253, 255
Disappointment, deception about, 138–140,
    298
Discrepancy
  fearful response to, 27, 76, 77
  joy-like response to, 76, 79
Disgust, 52–54, 264–268, 301
  action pattern of, 18, 52, 125, 265
  atypical response, 230
  consciousness affecting, 125
  deception about, 137, 265, 324
  as early emotion, 18, 22, 73, 83–85
  elicitors of, 18, 52–54, 266–267
  facial expression of, 18, 52, 83, 84,
    264–266

individual differences in, 83–84, 267
moral, 18, 85, 125, 126, 267
multiple emotions associated with, 53–54
negative feelings in response to, 84
parent expression of, 224–225
as withdrawal pattern, 22, 73, 83, 84,
    125–126, 229
Dissociation, 112
multiple personality disorder in, 250,
    251–252
in sexual abuse, 242
Distress, 18. *See also* Stress
adrenocortical response to, 190, 191
empathic, 237
maternal coping styles in, 215–216
maternal soothing behavior in, 188–192,
    214–216, 314
sucrose in, 189–190, 215
temperament differences in, 188–192, 221
Down syndrome, 23
emotional experience in, 235
facial expressions in, 79–80, 229, 286
laughter in, 229
mental age in, 79, 231, 232
mental representation of self in, 231
smiling in, 79–80, 286
Duchenne smile, 80–81
Dull temperament, 181
Dynamic systems approach to organization
    of emotional expression, 38

Early emotions and action patterns, xii,
    18–20, 21–22, 63–85, 110, 145–146
anger, 18–19, 22, 72, 73, 78–79
in apes and humans, 14, 262–263
approach and withdrawal types, 72–74
atypical development of, 23–24, 228–231
in biblical story of Adam and Eve, 16–17
Darwin on, 13–14, 17, 63
development of, 71
disgust, 18, 22, 73, 83–85
elicitors of, 11, 20, 21, 31–32, 147, 302
fear, 19, 26–28, 73–74, 75–78
individual differences in, 13, 69–71
as innate response, 18, 66–68
interest, 18, 22, 73, 75
joy, 18, 22, 72, 73, 79–81
learning of, 30, 31–32, 64–66
in newborn, 71–73
sadness, 11, 18, 22, 72, 73, 81–83
socialization of, 212–217
specific context of, 63–64, 67, 68–69
Easy temperament, 181–182, 194, 195
The Effect of the Infant on Its Caregiver
    (Rosenblum), 179
Effort attributions, 128
Ego, 104–105, 107, 146, 249

in guilt, 161
in narcissism, 258
Egocentric errors, 119
Einstein, Albert, 115, 116, 117
Ekman, Paul
on Duchenne smile, 80–81
on facial expressions, 35, 66, 67, 130,
    192, 264, 316
Elicitors, 3, 29–34
of anger, 5, 32
arousal attributional model of, 31
association with specific action pattern, 5,
    21, 30, 31, 32, 33
chemical signals as, 276
cognitive development affecting, 32–33
conditioned response to, 30
cultural differences in, 213
definition of, 30
of disgust, 18, 52–54, 266–267
of early action patterns, 11, 20, 21,
    31–32, 147, 302
of embarrassment, 147, 152, 153, 162
of emotional expression, 38–39, 40
and emotional receptors, 33–34
of enduring action patterns, 47
external and internal, 29–30, 276
of fear, 26–28, 32, 39, 147, 194
of guilt, 33, 147, 162
ideas as. *See* Ideas as elicitors
individual differences in, 33
influence of earlier elicitors on subsequent
    experiences, 57
intensity of response to, 282
and multiple emotions, 21, 50–51
nature of stimulus from, 40, 52
observation of response to, 47, 59–62,
    282
of pain, 276–277
of sadness, 11, 32, 33, 213–214, 299
of shame, 33, 146, 147, 158, 162
socialization affecting response to, 195,
    212–218
Embarrassment, 14, 20, 269–270
behaviors associated with, 149–150, 171
blushing in, 95, 147, 148, 149, 237, 300
from compliments, 151
Darwin on, 22, 95, 148, 236, 237, 269
elicitors of, 147, 152, 153, 162
and emergence of consciousness, 153
evaluative, 23, 126–127, 146, 152–153,
    154
exposed, 14, 22, 95, 126–127, 146,
    148–154, 237–239, 269, 270
functional significance of, 153–154
gender differences in, 172
individual differences in, 60, 151–152,
    154

Embarrassment (*continued*)
  of Japanese children, 171
  measures of, 20, 149–150
  in performance orientation, 176
  and shame, 148, 149, 150, 166–167
  and shyness, 148, 149, 150, 151, 238
  stress response in, 132, 169, 171–172
  studying differences in, 169–176
  in success, 171
  and temperament, 59, 151–152, 154, 238,
    239, 269–270
Emotional experience, 4, 43–45
  and action patterns, 4, 44, 48, 111, 228
  of anger, 48, 228
  cognitive development affecting, 44
  and consciousness, 7–8, 43, 48, 86–87,
    235
  of fear, 3, 4, 26, 124
  influence on subsequent events, 57–58
  and language development, 49
  of pain, 103, 184, 276–277, 293
  in self-deception, 130, 133
  and socialization, 48–49, 222–225
  use of term, 2, 6–7, 8, 43, 86–87
Emotional expression, 33–43
  body movements and posture in, 35–36.
    See also Body movements and postures
  development of, 39–40
  dynamic systems approach to, 38
  elicitors of, 38–39, 40
  facial, 35. See also Facial expressions
  internal and external, 42
  interpretation of, 39, 229
  measurement and coding of, 38–39, 278
  in multiple emotions, 52
  problems in caregiver reaction to, 229
  vocal, 36
Emotional intensity, 182
Emotional tone, 182
Emotion Review, 25
Emotions
  atypical development of, 23–24, 227–261
  components of, 3, 4–5, 16, 21, 25–45,
    47–48, 56
  definition of, 1–2, 25–26, 29, 43
  duration of, 21, 56, 58–59, 62, 282
  early or primary. See Early emotions and
    action patterns
  elicitors of. See Elicitors
  features of, 29
  individual differences in, 3
  and moods, 21, 47, 56–58
  multiple. See Multiple emotions
  and personality, 58–59
  self-conscious. See Self-conscious emotions
  as thoughts, 1, 2, 3
  use of term, 2, 4, 45

Emotions and Moods (Lewis & Michalson),
    47
Empathy, 14
  atypical, 236–237
  development of, 22, 122, 157
  differentiated from contagion, 127,
    156–157, 207, 236
  as exposed self-conscious emotion, 14, 22,
    95, 126, 127, 146, 156–158, 236–237
  and self-referential behavior, 127
Endocrine system, 41, 42
  cortisol in. See Cortisol levels
  and facial expressions, 37, 41, 221
Enjoyment. See Joy
Environmental influences, 18, 20, 23
  culture in. See Culture
  in deception, 137–138
  developmental niche in, 213
  family in. See Family
Envy, 14, 22, 148, 155, 239
Evaluative self-conscious emotions, 18, 19,
    20, 124, 127–128, 146, 158–176
  atypical, 240–261
  compared to exposed self-conscious
    emotions, 126–127, 146
  elicitors of, 162, 240
  embarrassment, 23, 126–127, 146,
    152–153, 154
  guilt, 14, 23, 95, 126, 127, 146, 167,
    256–257
  hubris, 146, 162, 167–168, 257–261
  individual differences in, 169, 172–173
  model of, 163–166
  as moral emotions, 14–15
  in performance and task orientation,
    175–176
  pride, 14, 23, 95, 126, 127, 146, 168–
    169
  shame, 14, 23, 95, 126, 127, 146, 158,
    166–167, 241–256
  shyness, 149
  standards, rules, and goals in, 14,
    159–160, 163–166, 167, 169, 173
  studying differences in, 169–176
Evolution
  of action patterns, 1, 5, 15, 21, 31, 40, 42,
    55, 262–263, 271
  of consciousness, 9
  of deception, 131–132, 139
  of facial expressions, 31, 35
Existential contingency, ix–x
Experience, emotional. See Emotional
  experience
Exposed self-conscious emotions, 18, 19, 20,
    124, 146, 148–158
  in apes and humans, 14
  atypical, 236–240

compared to evaluative self-conscious emotions, 126–127, 146
embarrassment, 14, 22, 95, 126–127, 146, 148–154, 237–239, 269
empathy, 14, 22, 95, 126, 127, 146, 156–158, 236–237
jealousy, 14, 22, 126, 127, 146, 155–156, 239–240
Expression, emotional. *See* Emotional expression
The Expression of the Emotions in Man and Animals (Darwin), 2
Extroversion, 184
Eye regard of others, 268–270

Facial expressions, 2–3, 5, 18, 31, 35, 65–66
in anger, 67, 68
appropriate for situation, 50, 135
communication function of, 31, 37
complexity theory of, 65–66
correspondence to action pattern or experience, 130–131, 136–137, 228–229, 316–317
deception in, 3, 37–38, 130, 131
discrimination and preference of infants, 39–40, 202
in disgust, 18, 52, 83, 84, 264–266
in Down syndrome, 79–80, 229, 286
early recognition of, 49
elicitors of, 40
emotions associated with, 31
evolution of, 31, 35
in fear, 64, 229
and hormone system, 37, 41, 221
interpretation of, 39
measurement and coding of, 35, 36, 38, 52, 130, 264, 278, 316
in multiple emotions, 52, 55
of newborn, 130
in pain, 37, 185, 220, 221
and posture, 35
produced on request, 134–135
relationship to other modalities of emotional expression, 36–37
in sadness, 11, 40, 82
smiling in, 79–81. *See also* Smiling
socialization of, 137, 218, 219–220
in stranger approach, 37, 39, 64, 67, 221
in visual impairment, 80, 229, 286
Failure. *See* Success or failure
False beliefs, 119, 120
Family
child abuse and neglect in, 245
deception in, 137, 138–139
father–child interactions in, 198, 200, 201, 205, 311
indirect effects of interactions in, 205–206

individual differences in, 12
mother–child interactions in. *See* Mother–child interactions
in socialization, 200
of stigmatized child, 255–256
Father–child interactions, 198, 200, 201, 311
indirect effects in, 205
Fear, 3, 4, 17
approach and withdrawal patterns in, 22, 73–74, 76
and comparison ability, 19, 28, 76
consciousness affecting action pattern of, 124–125, 126
context of, ix
deception about, 124–125, 137
in discrepancy, 27, 76, 77
and disgust, 53
as early emotion, 19, 26–28, 73–74, 75–78
elicitors of, 26–28, 32, 39, 147, 194
emotional expressions of, 36, 39
experience of, 3, 4, 26, 124
facial expression of, 64, 229
individual differences in, 13, 77
as innate response, 198, 228–229
learning of, 27, 28
in loss of control, 27
observation and measurement of, 59, 60, 61, 62
of pain, 28, 76
shyness in, 238
in stranger approach. *See* Stranger approach
and temperament, 27, 76, 181, 193, 194
in visual cliff studies, 13, 75–76
Feelings, 3, 6–8
and consciousness, 1, 7, 43–44, 86
and deception for hurting others, 143
and deception for protection of others, 131, 132–133, 138–140
empathy about, 156
of pain, 6, 7, 184
use of term, 2, 6–7, 8, 43
Field dependency, 173
Flow state, 153
Freud, Sigmund, x, xi, 112, 227–228, 303
on guilt, 146, 160–161, 256, 303, 304
on id, ego, and superego, 104–105, 249
on narcissism, 258, 259
on repression, 112
on sexual abuse, 241, 251
on shame, 146, 148, 160, 304
theory of developmental psychopathology, 58
on unconscious processes, 8
on willfulness, 187

Frontal region of brain
in autism spectrum disorders, 102, 233, 234
in self-referential behavior, 101, 232, 233, 234
Frustration, willfulness in reaction to, 187–188
Fugue, 5, 56, 57, 58, 262–271
use of term, 262
Fussy temperament, 181

Galvanic skin response, 41, 42
Gaze
in embarrassment, 149, 150
and eye regard of others, 268–270
Gender differences
in abused children, 245, 246
in crying, 70, 71, 129
in deception, 139–140, 218
in multiple personality disorder, 251
in narcissism, 260
in shame, 172, 243
in socialization, 223
Genetic factors, 34, 59, 181, 191, 230
Geographic influences on emotional expression, 12–13
Global attributions, 128, 160, 165–166, 174, 218
gender differences in, 172, 173
guilt and blame in, 223–224
in narcissism, 259, 260
of parents, 261
in stigmatization, 254–255
Goals
blocked. See Blocked goal
and intentions, 90–91
standards, rules, and. See Standards, rules, and goals
Grandparents, 200
Gray matter, 101
Green Eggs and Ham (Seuss), 8
Grief, 103
Guatemalan Indians, 214
Guilt, 20
in abuse and neglect, 246
action pattern of, 167, 240–241
attributions in, 128, 218, 223–224, 257
atypical, 256–257
blushing in, 149
body movements and posture in, 171, 257
and conscience, 257
in dogs, 89, 287
elicitors of, 33, 147, 162
as evaluative self-conscious emotion, 14, 23, 95, 126, 127, 146, 167, 256–257
Freud on, 146, 160–161, 256, 303, 304
and shame, 161–162, 167, 218, 256–257

socialization of, 223–224
in task orientation, 218, 256, 257

Hady, as term for happiness and sadness, 51, 55
Hand gestures in embarrassment, 149, 150
Happiness, 6, 18
consciousness affecting action pattern of, 126
crying in, 71
deception about, 137
elicitors of, 147
facial expression of, 40
as innate response, 198
observation and measurement of, 59, 61, 62
with sadness, 51, 54, 55
in success, 33
Harris, Judith Rich, 199–200, 311
High Responders, 185, 186
Homosexuality, 23, 197
Hormones, 41, 42
cortisol. See Cortisol levels
and facial expressions, 37, 41, 221
Hubris, 126, 128, 257–261
atypical development of, 257–261
as evaluative self-conscious emotion, 146, 162, 167–168, 257–261
and narcissism, 258–260
use of term, 167, 299
Humiliation
of child by parents, 224
self-deception to avoid, 142

Id, 104–105, 107, 249
Idea of "me," 17, 92
adaptive and nonadaptive aspects of, 93
atypical development of, 231–235
brain maturation affecting, 22, 94, 101–102
emergence of, 17–18, 22, 89
measures of, 88, 98–100
and self-conscious emotions, 17–18, 20, 146
and self-referential behavior, 20, 22, 88
in self system, 96
unity and continuity in, 10
and unknown parts of self, 87–88
use of term, 86–87
Ideas as elicitors, 17–18, 30–31, 159, 162, 240, 299, 302–303
in abuse and neglect, 24
compared to earlier literal elicitors, 11, 18, 31, 145, 147
development required for, 11, 21, 31, 32, 145
self-attributions in, 128, 160

of shame, 146
socialization of, 24, 213–214, 217–218, 240
Identity, 10
stigmatization affecting, 253, 254–255
Ilongot people, 51
Imitation, vii, 10, 65, 92
and empathy, 157
Immune system, stress affecting, 132
Imprinting, 200–201
Individuation, 105, 122
Infant Behavior Questionnaire, 182, 193
Inhibited temperament, 181, 184
Innate releasing mechanisms (IRMs), 74
Innate responses, 5, 9, 110
action patterns as, 11, 18, 66–68, 110, 118, 198
fear in, 27, 73–74
multiple emotions in, 5
receptors in, 34
sadness in, 3, 198
smiling in, 33, 137, 268
Inoculation response, 191–192
cortisol levels in, 37, 184, 190, 220, 221
cultural differences in, 37, 70, 186, 221
fear faces in, 76
maternal soothing behavior in, 190, 214–215
pain reactivity in, 184–185
stability over time, 186–187
Instincts, 9
Intelligence quotient, 26, 141, 191, 219
in Asperger syndrome, 234, 235
Intentions and intentionality, 90–91, 92, 95, 96–97
Interest. See Attention and interest
Izard, Carroll
on action patterns, 31, 44, 49, 63, 70
on coding of facial expressions, 35, 67, 130, 192, 264, 316
differential emotions theory of, 66
on fear faces of infants in inoculation, 76
on shyness, 150, 238
survey research on emotions, xi, 25

James, William
on attention, xi
definition of emotions, 2, 43
on duality of self, 102–103, 251
on emotional experience or feeling, 43–44, 111
on infant behavior, 11
theory of emotions, 41, 43–44
on willfulness 69,187
Japan
emotional expression and geography of, 12
self in culture of, 94

Japanese children
anger of, 39, 48, 78, 129, 225
deception by, 38, 141
embarrassment of, 171
emotional expression of, 37, 38, 39
inoculation response of, 37, 70, 221
pain response of, 37, 70, 186
physical proximity to mothers, 213
Jealousy, 20
atypical development of, 239–240
compared to envy, 155, 239
as exposed self-conscious emotion, 14, 22, 126, 127, 146, 155–156, 239–240
and self-referential behavior, 127
Joy
as approach pattern, 72, 73, 229
brain activity in, 284
in discrepancy, 76
as early emotion, 18, 22, 72, 73, 79–81
as innate response, 198
in learning, 69, 80
smiling in, 79–81

Kierkegaard, S., vii–viii
Knowledge
about self, in idea of me. See Idea of "me"
and deception, 119, 134, 142–143
role of knower in, 114–120
social, 120–121
and theory of mind, 118–120

Labeling, 93, 225
Lange, Carl, 41
Language development, 197
affecting measures of consciousness, 98–99
and cognitive development, 120
and emotional experience, 49
and emotional expression, 6
and multiple emotions, 51
personal pronoun use in. See Personal pronoun use
production and understanding of emotional words in, 216
Laughter, 76, 79
in Down syndrome, 229
Learning
in arm pulling task with visual reward, 68–69
of deception, 136, 139, 140
of early action patterns, 30, 31–32, 64–66
of emotional experience, 44
of fear response, 27, 28
pleasure in, 69, 80
in social referencing, 206
of standards, rules, and goals, 159, 163–164, 173, 222, 223

"Little white lies," 138–140
Locomotion
    emotional expression in, 36–37
    and movement away in stranger approach,
        37, 64, 77–78
Loss
    of control, 27, 82
    in love withdrawal, 225
    sadness in, 3, 17, 32, 73, 81, 82, 213–214,
        229, 286
Love withdrawal by parents, 224, 225
Low Responders, 185, 186
Lying, 22, 71, 129–144. *See also* Deception

Machinery of self, 9, 22, 89, 94, 95, 97,
        107, 110
Mammals, emotional development in, 14
Mastery, and joy in learning, 69, 80
Materialism, 263–264
Memory
    and self-deception, 130, 138, 142
    and theory of mind, 119
Mental age, 235
    in autism spectrum disorders, 100, 232
    in Down syndrome, 79, 231, 232
    and self-referential behavior, 100, 231, 232
Mentalism, 8, 20, 22, 43, 52, 157, 269, 287
Mental representations
    idea of "me" in. *See* Idea of "me"
    in imitation, 92
    and intentionality, 91
    of mother–child relationship, x
Mental retardation
    and abuse, 246
    delay in mental self-representation in, 231
    stigma of, 254, 255
Mind–body problem, 263–264
Mirror neurons, 65
Mirror self-recognition, 222, 269, 289–290
    in autism spectrum disorders, 231, 232,
        234
    brain regions in, 102, 222
    cultural differences in, 288
    and embarrassment, 238, 239
    as measure of self-referential behavior, 8,
        9, 22, 93, 99, 100, 102, 269, 289–290
    mental age in, 100, 232
    observation of, 99
    and pain response, 195
    and self-conscious emotions, 127
Moods, 21, 47, 56–58
    and action patterns, 47, 193, 194
    and personality, 47, 56, 58
    and temperament, 47, 180, 192–195
Moral emotions, 14–15, 23, 158–159
    disgust in, 18, 85, 125, 126, 267
Moro reflex, 30

Mother–child interactions
    abuse and neglect in, 245, 246–247
    attachment in. *See* Attachment
    contingency responses in, 189, 204, 214,
        219
    and development of consciousness, 105,
        293
    direct effects of, 203, 204–205
    empathy in, 156, 157
    indirect effects in, 203, 205–206
    mental representation of, x
    organismic model on, 199
    as relationship, 121–123
    and sadness response of infant, 82, 286
    in separation, 105, 155–156, 214, 239
    smiling of infant affecting, 33, 204, 219,
        315
    socialization role of, x, 23, 197–226
    soothing behavior in, 189–192, 214–216
    and stranger response of infants, 42
    temperament of child affecting, 23,
        178–179
    working model of, 122, 123
Mothers and Others (Hrdy), 202
Motivation
    attributions affecting, 128, 168–169
    for deception, 138–144
Multiple emotions, 5, 21, 46–56
    in arm restraint, 5, 13, 55
    disgust in, 53–54
    facial expressions in, 52, 55
    language terms in, 51, 55
    as sequential or simultaneous, 54–55
    situations eliciting, 50–51
Multiple personality disorder, 249–253
Myelination of brain in autism spectrum
        disorder, 102, 233

Name recognition
    brain activation in, 101, 292
    as measure of consciousness, 98
Narcissism, 168, 187, 258–260, 285
Neglect. *See* Abuse and neglect
Neocortex size, and deception, 132, 298
Nervous system, 41, 42
    autonomic, 41, 42, 276
    central, 33–34, 41. *See also* Brain
    emotional receptors in, 33–34
    mirror neurons in, 65
    in moods, 194–195
    in pain response, 276
    in temperament, 180, 194–195
Neurons, mirror, 65
Newborn
    crying of, 156
    development of differentiated action
        patterns in, 71–73

disgust of, 83–84
facial expressions of, 130
imitation by, 92
nonverbal communication by, 92
pain of, 6, 185, 186
temperament of, 181
Newton, Isaac, 115–116, 117
Niche
    developmental, 213
    social, 1, 2
Novum Organum (Bacon), 115

Object relations theory, 177
Observation of enduring emotions, 47,
    59–62
Obsessive–compulsive disorders, 54
Ontogenetic development, 13–14, 262, 263
    of deception, 130
    of facial expressions, 31
    of self-consciousness, 101
    of self-recognition, 100
Organismic model, 199
The Origins of Fear (Lewis & Rosenblum),
    26
Ownership, emergence of idea of, 156

Pain, 6–7
    cortisol levels in, 37, 184, 185, 186, 187,
        190
    crying in, 134, 185
    cultural differences in response to, 37, 70,
        186, 221
    deactivation of action pattern in, 30
    elicitor and action pattern in, 276–277
    facial expressions in, 37, 185, 220, 221
    fear of, 28, 76
    feeling or experience of, 6, 7, 103, 184,
        276–277, 293
    in inoculations, 184–185. *See also*
        Inoculation response
    maternal soothing behavior in, 190,
        191–192, 214–215
    of newborn, 6, 185, 186
    reactivity to, 37, 70, 184–187, 307
    self-recognition affecting response to, 195
    speed of recovery from, 184–185
    stability over time of response to, 186–187
Parenting practices
    elicitor differences in, 212–213
    and self-attributions of child, 107,
        217–218, 223–225
    self-report measures on, 209
    and temperament of child, 177–179, 180
Parents and caregivers
    abuse and neglect by, 243–247. *See also*
        Abuse and neglect
    attachment to. *See* Attachment

attributions of, 6, 26, 93, 172, 261
contingent responses to infant behavior,
    189, 204, 214, 219, 315
crying as signal to, 81, 82, 83, 134
deception learned from, 139, 140
and emergence of consciousness in child,
    94, 107
empathy modeled by, 237
and father–child interactions, 198, 200,
    201, 205, 311
inability to react to expressive behavior of
    infant, 229
infant observation of facial patterns of,
    65, 66
labeling by, 93, 225
and mother–child interactions. *See*
    Mother–child interactions
observation of child interactions with,
    60–62
proximal and distal responsivity of, 219
reaction to disgust action pattern of child,
    84
reports on anger in infants, 39, 48, 78,
    93
socialization role of, 43, 197–226
of stigmatized child, 255
Parietal region of brain, 101, 233
Peeking/no peeking task, deception in,
    135–136, 140–141
Peers
    attachment relationship with, 203
    and infant interest in other infants, 77,
        202–203
    influence in socialization, 199–200, 201
Performance, compared to competence,
    26
Performance orientation, 14, 128, 218
    compared to task orientation, 175–176
    and willfulness, 188
Personality, 58–62
    of abusive parents, 243–244, 246
    Big Five dimensions of, 181
    definition of, 58
    and global or specific attributions,
        165–166
    and individual differences in emotional
        behavior, 59–62
    and moods, 47, 56, 58
    and multiple personality disorder,
        249–253
Personal pronoun use
    in autism spectrum disorders, 231, 232,
        234
    brain regions in, 102
    as measure of self-referential behavior, 8,
        9, 22, 93, 98–99, 100, 102, 268, 269
Phobias, disgust and fear in, 53

Phylogenetic development, 13–14, 262
  of disgust, 267
  of facial expressions, 35
  of self-consciousness, 101
  of self-recognition, 100
Physical appearance, and shame in
    stigmatization, 253
Planck, Max, 115
Play, pretend. *See* Pretend play
Play face, 79
Posture. *See* Body movements and postures
Predictable temperament, 181
Prefrontal cortex in autism spectrum
    disorders, 102, 234
Prematurity, abuse and neglect in, 245
Pretend play, 15
  in autism spectrum disorders, 100, 143,
    231, 232, 234
  brain regions in, 102
  and deception, 143, 144
  as measure of self-referential behavior, 8,
    9, 22, 93, 99–100, 102, 143, 269
  with objects, 142
  with others, 143
Pretense, 15, 99–100, 142–143, 144
Pride, 20
  action pattern of, 240–241
  attributions in, 128, 168–169, 258
  elicitors of, 33, 147
  as evaluative self-conscious emotion, 14,
    23, 95, 126, 127, 146, 168–169
  gender differences in, 172
  and hubris, 167–168, 257–261
  posture in, 35, 171, 260–261
  studying differences in, 169–176
  task difficulty affecting, 174, 217
Procedural rules, 8, 22, 264, 268
  action patterns as, 17, 110, 118, 119, 294
Pronouns, personal. *See* Personal pronoun
    use
Psychoanalytic theory, 104–105, 106–107,
    177
Psychodynamic theory on child abuse,
    243–244
Psychopathology, 53, 54, 58, 227
Psychotherapy, 59
Punishment
  by abusive parents, 244, 247, 249
  lying to avoid, 140–142, 143

Quantum mechanics, 115–117

Rage, 79
  in narcissism, 260
  and shame of abused children, 243, 248
Reactivity
  caregiver interactions affecting, 180
  emotional tone and intensity in, 182

facial expression and cortisol levels in, 37,
    184, 185
  and inhibition of action patterns, 42, 231
  maternal response to, 190, 191
  to pain, 37, 70, 184–187, 307
  speed of recovery in, 184
  to stress, 169, 220
  and temperament, 59, 169, 180, 182,
    184–187
  threshold in, 169, 180, 231
Receptors
  emotional, 33–34
  in pain response, 276
Reflexive behavior, 92
Reinforcement of infant behaviors, 214
  contingent responses in, 189, 204, 214,
    219, 315
Relationships, 121–123
Relativity theory, 116, 117
Repression, 252
Responsibility
  attributions on, 14, 23, 128, 159, 164,
    223
  and guilt, 167
  and hubris, 167
  and shame, 133, 166, 247, 253–254
  in stigmatization, 253–254

Sadness
  and anger of infant in arm restraint, 13
  in blocked goal, 69, 82
  body cues of, 277
  consciousness affecting action pattern of,
    126
  contagious nature of, 36
  crying in, 70, 71, 81, 82, 83
  cultural influences on expression of, 129
  Darwin on, 72, 81, 82
  deception about, 137
  duration of, 47, 56, 57, 58, 61
  as early emotion, 11, 17, 18, 22, 72, 73,
    81–83
  elicitors of, 11, 32, 33, 213–214, 299
  experience of, 44
  facial expression of, 11, 40, 82
  with happiness, 51, 54, 55
  individual differences in, 3
  influence of earlier events on subsequent
    experiences, 57
  as innate response, 3, 198
  in loss, 3, 17, 32, 73, 81, 82, 213–214,
    229, 286
  observation of, 61–62
  in separation from mother, 18, 155, 214
  as withdrawal pattern, 22, 69, 72, 73, 81,
    229
Schema, 27
Schizophrenia, 250–251

Scientific method, 114–117
Scripts, 49, 280
Self, 91–97
  cultural and historical differences in idea
    of, 93–94
  duality of, 102–103, 104
  and idea of "me." *See* Idea of "me"
  machinery of, 9, 22, 89, 94, 95, 97, 107,
    110
  measurement of, 93
  in multiple personality disorder, 249–250,
    253
  as system, 95–97
  unity of, 10, 249–250, 253
Self-conscious emotions, xiii, 75, 89,
    145–176. *See also specific emotions.*
  in abuse and neglect, 241–249
  in animals and humans, comparison of,
    14–15, 17, 158–159
  attributions in, 126, 127, 128, 159–160
  atypical development of, 24, 235–261
  cognitive development affecting, 16–17,
    20–21
  embarrassment, 148–154
  emergence of, 22, 126–128, 148
  evaluative, 158–176
  exposed, 148–158
  ideas as elicitors of. *See* Ideas as elicitors
  individual differences in, 169, 172–173
  lack of research on, 147
  moral, 14–15, 23, 158–159
  and self-referential behavior, 20–21, 22,
    126, 148
  shame, 241–256
  socialization of, 169, 212, 217–218,
    235–237, 240
  and temperament, 169, 195–196
Self-deception, 15, 22–23, 132–134,
    142–143
  and complexity of self-system, 97
  cultural influences on, 129
  emotional experience in, 130, 133
  evolutionary and adaptive function of,
    131, 132
  and memory, 130, 138, 142
  in older children, 299
  and pretend play, 143, 144
Self–other differentiation, 95, 96
Self-recognition in mirror. *See* Mirror self-
    recognition
Self-referential behavior, viii, 1, 6, 19, 22,
    86, 87, 88
  in autism spectrum disorders, 100, 102,
    143, 231–235, 292–293
  in brain maturation, 94, 107–108, 222,
    233–234, 291–293
  cultural differences in, 94, 288
  and deception, 143

  and embarrassment, 151, 153–154
  lack of, in young infants, 7–8
  mirror self-recognition in. *See* Mirror self-
    recognition
  personal pronoun use in. *See* Personal
    pronoun use
  pretend play in. *See* Pretend play
  rise of, 1, 8–10, 86–108, 263
  and self-conscious emotions, 20–21, 22,
    126, 148
Self-reflection, 96
  capacity for and content of, 107
  consciousness as, 97, 103, 145
  Darwin on, 128
  embarrassment in, 148, 151, 153–154
  self-conscious emotions in, 128, 145, 148,
    160
  on success or failure, 160
  temporary loss of, 153–154
Self-regulation, 94–95, 96
  guilt in, 257
  limitations of existing research on,
    209–210
Self system, 91–97
  complexity of, 110
Separation of mother and child
  and individuation, 105
  jealousy in, 155–156, 239
  sadness in, 18, 155, 214
Sexual abuse, 241–243
  multiple personality disorder in, 249, 251,
    252
Shame
  in abuse and neglect, 241–249, 252
  action pattern in, 166, 240–241
  attributions in, 128, 133, 146, 241–242,
    254–255
  atypical development of, 241–256
  in biblical story of Adam and Eve, 16–
    17
  and blame, 248, 249, 253–254, 255
  blushing in, 149
  body movements and posture in, 35, 150,
    166, 171, 257
  consciousness required for, 89, 145
  converted to another emotion, 133,
    247–249, 252
  coping with, 166
  differentiated from disgust, 83
  elicitors of, 33, 146, 147, 158, 162
  and embarrassment, 148, 149, 150,
    166–167
  as evaluative self-conscious emotion,
    14, 20, 23, 95, 126, 127, 146, 158,
    166–167, 240, 241–256
  Freud on, 146, 148, 160, 304
  gender differences in, 172, 243
  and guilt, 161–162, 167, 218, 256–257

Shame (*continued*)
  and multiple personality disorder,
    249–253
  and narcissism, 259, 260
  as negative emotion, 132, 297
  in performance orientation, 175, 176, 218
  rage in, 79, 248
  responsibility in, 133, 166, 247, 253–254
  self-deception to avoid, 132, 133, 142
  and self-referential behavior, 9
  standards, rules, and goals in, xiii, 145,
    253, 254
  in stigmatization, 253–256
  stress response in, 132, 169, 171–172
  studying differences in, 169–176
  task difficulty affecting, 174, 217
  and violence, 247–249
  visual, 161
Shyness, 150
  and embarrassment, 148, 149, 150, 151,
    238
Siblings, 198, 200, 201
  indirect effects of parent interactions with,
    205
  of stigmatized child, 255–256
Signs and signals, differentiation of, 125
Sleep, 71, 73
Smell, and disgust pattern, 84, 125
Smiling
  contingent response to, 204, 219, 315
  in deceptive behavior, 138, 140, 218, 220
  in Down syndrome, 79–80, 286
  Duchenne smile in, 80–81
  in embarrassment, 149
  as innate response, 33, 137, 268
  and joy, 79–81
  learning and reinforcement of, 204
  in pleasure, 18
  social, 79, 80
  socialization affecting, 212
  synchrony with action patterns, 137
Sociability, 59, 183–184, 237
Social biofeedback theory, 294
Social cognition, 118
Social interactions
  in autism spectrum disorders, deficits in,
    232, 233
  bidirectional, 118, 122, 205
  deception to protect feelings of others in,
    131, 132–133, 138–140
  and development of consciousness, 101,
    102–107, 118, 293, 294
  direct effects of, 203, 204–205
  indirect effects of, 203–204, 205–208
  relationships in, 120–123
  sadness in, 82–83
  separation and individuation in, 105, 122

shyness in, 149
smiling in, 79, 80
Socialization, 5, 15, 23, 24, 197–226
  in abuse and neglect, 24, 211, 213, 214,
    217, 228, 241–247
  of action patterns, 48, 70, 136, 218–
    222
  of anger expression and experience, 39,
    48, 129, 218, 225
  behavioral scripts in, 31
  cultural differences in, 210–211
  deception in, 136, 137, 140
  direct effects of interactions in, 203,
    204–205
  of early elicitors, 212–217
  and emotional experience, 48–49,
    222–225
  emotional expressions in, 36, 37, 39
  of empathy, 236–237
  and evaluation of success or failure,
    164–165, 172–173, 217–218
  of facial expression, 137, 218, 219–220
  of ideas as elicitors, 24, 213–214,
    217–218, 240
  indirect effects of interactions in,
    203–204, 205–208
  individual differences in, 12, 13, 17
  limitations of existing research on,
    208–212
  peer influences in, 199–200
  role of mother in, x, 23, 197–226
  and self-attributions, 172–173, 217–218,
    223–225
  of self-conscious emotions, 169, 212,
    217–218, 235–237, 240
  social networks in, 200–203
  and temperament, 12, 13, 188–192, 197,
    207
Social learning theory, 222, 245
Social networks, 200–208, 311
Social niche, 1, 2
Social referencing, 205, 206, 211
Social relationships, 120–123
Social smiling, 79, 80
Sociological approach to child abuse,
    244–245
Somatization of behaviors, 225, 316
Soothing, 189–192, 214–216, 314
  in inoculation, 190, 214–215
  previous experience affecting, 193
  temperament affecting, 181, 182,
    189–192, 215
Specific attributions, 128, 160, 165–166,
    218, 223
  gender differences in, 172
Spinoza, Baruch, 108
Stability attributions, 128

Standards, rules, and goals (SRGs), 222
  and evaluative self-conscious emotions,
    14, 159–160, 163–166, 167, 169
  learning of, 159, 163–164, 173, 222, 223
  and shame, xiii, 145, 253, 254
Stigmatization, 253–256
Stoics, 185, 186, 221
Stranger approach, 2, 27–28, 51–52, 77–78,
    127
  attachment affecting response to, 28, 75
  change over time in response to, 32
  comparison ability affecting response to,
    19, 28
  deception about fear in, 124–125
  extreme fear in, 230
  facial patterns in, 37, 39, 64, 67, 221
  in highchair restraint, 37, 77–78, 220
  individual differences in response to, 13
  interest in, 52
  movement away in, 37, 64, 77–78
  nature of unfamiliar adult in, 77
  observed behaviors in, 64
  physiological responses in, 64
  presence of mother affecting response to,
    42, 78
  social referencing in, 206, 211
  of unfamiliar child, 77, 203
  wariness in, 28, 32, 39, 52, 64, 67, 74,
    76, 77
Stress
  coping styles in, 215–216
  cortisol levels in. See Cortisol levels
  in empathy, 237
  facial expressions in, 37, 220, 221
  immune function in, 132
  influence of earlier elicitors on subsequent
    experiences, 57
  in inoculation, 37, 184–185, 186–187,
    190, 214–215, 220, 221
  reactivity to, 169, 220
  in shame and embarrassment, 132, 169,
    171–172
  soothing in, 189–192, 214–216, 314
  and temperament, 169, 182, 187,
    188–192, 220, 221
Success or failure
  and anger, 176
  attributions on, 14, 128, 159–160, 162,
    164–165, 169, 172–173, 174, 217–218,
    223
  as elicitor of action pattern, 33
  and embarrassment, 171
  evaluative self-conscious emotions
    in, 20–21, 33, 159–160, 162, 163,
    164–165
  in experimental tasks, 170–171, 175–176
  and guilt, 162, 163, 167, 171, 256–257

  and happiness, 33
  and hubris, 128, 162, 163, 167–168
  and narcissism, 259–260
  in performance and task orientation, 14,
    128, 175–176
  and pride, 33, 128, 162, 163, 168–169,
    171, 173, 217, 258
  responsibility for, 14, 128, 159, 163, 164,
    166, 223
  and shame, 128, 162, 163, 166–167, 171,
    173, 217
  socialization affecting evaluation of,
    164–165, 172–173, 217–218
  standards, rules, and goals as measure of,
    14, 159–160, 164, 165, 166, 167
  studying differences in responses to,
    169–176
  willfulness in, 188
Sucrose, calming effect of, 189–190, 215
Superego, 105, 146, 160–161, 249
Surprise, 19

Task orientation, 14, 128, 218
  compared to performance orientation,
    175–176
  guilt in, 218, 256, 257
  and willfulness, 188
Taste, and disgust action pattern, 18, 83, 84,
    125, 266
Temperament, 15, 58–59, 177–196
  and abuse, 245–246
  and action patterns, 11, 40, 56, 69–70,
    76, 195, 221–222, 230, 266, 283
  and attachment, 59, 178–179, 198
  classification of, 181–182
  and consciousness, 195–196
  definition of, 179–181
  and embarrassment, 59, 151–152, 154,
    238, 239, 269–270
  emotional tone and intensity in, 182
  and fear, 27, 76, 193, 194
  and guilt, 257
  maternal reports on, 182–183
  measures of, 182–188
  and moods, 47, 180, 192–195
  and pain reaction, 184–187, 195
  process and content approaches to,
    180–181
  and reactivity, 59, 169, 180, 182, 184–
    187
  and self-conscious emotions, 169,
    195–196
  and sociability, 183–184
  and socialization, 12, 13, 23, 188–192,
    197, 207
  and soothability, 181, 182, 188–192,
    215

Temperament (*continued*)
  stability and consistency of, 186–187
  and stress, 169, 182, 187, 188–192, 220, 221
  and willfulness, 187–188
Temporal lobe
  in autism spectrum disorders, 102, 233–234
  eating behavior after surgical removal of, 97
  in self-referential behavior, 94, 101–102, 108, 232, 233–234
Test of Self-Conscious Affect (TOSCA), 248–249
Theory of mind, 268, 269
  in autism spectrum disorders, 231
  functional imaging studies of, 291–292
  levels in development of, 118–120
Thoughts, 1
  emotions as, 1–3
  idea of "me" in. *See* Idea of "me"
Tickling, 79, 194, 195, 230
Transformational model, 271

Unconscious processes, 8, 9
  in multiple personality disorder, 252
Unity of self, 10
  in multiple personality disorder, 249–250, 253
Upset action pattern of infants, 71

Variance around mean value, 11–12
Violence in shame, 247–249
Visual cliff studies, 13, 74, 75–76
Visual cortex, 33–34
Vocalizations, emotional expression in, 36, 37

Wariness
  approach and withdrawal patterns in, 74
  facial expression of, 39, 64
  in stranger approach, 28, 32, 39, 52, 64, 67, 74, 76, 77
  in visual cliff studies, 74
Weddings, multiple emotions at, 5, 50, 51, 55
We-self cultures, 10
White lies, 138–140, 298
White matter, 101
Willfulness, 69, 187–188
Withdrawal emotions or action patterns, 22, 110, 229
  with approach pattern in fear, 22, 73–74, 76
  in blocked goal, 188, 230
  cerebral hemisphere differences in, 33
  consciousness affecting, 125–126
  in disgust, 22, 73, 83, 84, 125–126, 229
  emotional expressions in, 36, 40
  in sadness, 69, 72, 73, 81

Xenophames, 89